Transforming Government

General Editor: **R. A. W. Rhodes**, Professor of Political Science, Research School of Social Sciences, Australian National University.

The Economic and Social Research Council mounted the Whitehall Programme on 'The Changing Nature of Central Government in Britain' between 1994 and 1999. The Programme sought to repair gaps in our knowledge about the workings of British central government and to explain how and why British government changed in the post-war period. Also, because we cannot understand the effects of these changes by focusing only on Britain, the Programme analysed the experience of the advanced industrial democracies of Europe and the Commonwealth. Initially the 'Transforming Government' series reported the results of that five-year research programme, publishing ten books. Now, the series publishes any research consistent with its long-standing objectives:

• **Develop theory** – to develop new theoretical perspectives to explain why British government changed and why it differs from other countries

• **Understand change** – to describe and explain what has changed in British government since 1945

• **Compare advanced industrial democracies** – to compare change in Britain with other EU member states and other states with a 'Westminster' system of government, especially the Old Commonwealth

• **Build bridges** – to create a common understanding between academics and practitioners and to make academic research accessible to a varied audience covering 6th-formers and senior policy makers.

The series encompasses any theoretical approach to the study of government and governance. We welcome books on such notions as hollowing-out, governance, postmodernism, core executives, new institutionalism and cultural theory alongside the more traditional topics of the civil service, prime ministers and government departments. All books should meet the conventional criteria of theoretical and empirical rigour, but also seek to address topics of broad current interest that open the field of study to new ideas and areas of investigation.

Titles include:

Simon Bulmer, Martin Burch, Caitríona Carter, Patricia Hogwood and Andrew Scott
BRITISH DEVOLUTION AND EUROPEAN POLICY-MAKING
Transforming Britain to Multi-Level Governance

Nicholas Deakin and Richard Parry
THE TREASURY AND SOCIAL POLICY
The Contest for Control of Welfare Strategy

Neil C.M. Elder and Edward C. Page
ACCOUNTABILITY AND CONTROL IN NEXT STEPS AGENCIES

Oliver James
THE EXECUTIVE AGENCY REVOLUTION IN WHITEHALL
Public Interest Versus Bureau-Shaping Perspectives

David Marsh, David Richards and Martin J. Smith
CHANGING PATTERNS OF GOVERNANCE IN THE UNITED KINGDOM
Reinventing Whitehall?

Hugh Pemberton
POLICY LEARNING AND BRITISH GOVERNANCE IN THE 1960s'

B. Guy Peters, R. A. W. Rhodes and Vincent Wright (*editors*)
ADMINISTERING THE SUMMIT
Administration of the Core Executive in Developed Countries

R. A. W. Rhodes (*editor*)
TRANSFORMING BRITISH GOVERNMENT
Volume One: Changing Institutions
Volume Two: Changing Roles and Relationships

Martin J. Smith
THE CORE EXECUTIVE IN BRITAIN

Kevin Theakston
LEADERSHIP IN WHITEHALL

Kevin Theakston (*editor*)
BUREAUCRATS AND LEADERSHIP

Patrick Weller, Herman Bakvis and R. A. W. Rhodes (*editors*)
THE HOLLOW CROWN
Countervailing Trends in Core Executives

Transforming Government
Series Standing Order ISBN 0–333–71580–2
(*outside North America only*)

You can receive future titles in this series as they are published by placing a standing order. Please contact your bookseller or, in case of difficulty, write to us at the address below with your name and address, the title of the series and the ISBN quoted above.

Customer Services Department, Macmillan Distribution Ltd, Houndmills, Basingstoke, Hampshire RG21 6XS, England

Policy Learning and British Governance in the 1960s

Hugh Pemberton
British Academy Postdoctoral Research Fellow,
London School of Economics and Political Science, UK

palgrave
macmillan

First published 2004 by
PALGRAVE MACMILLAN
Houndmills, Basingstoke, Hampshire RG21 6XS and
175 Fifth Avenue, New York, N. Y. 10010
Companies and representatives throughout the world

PALGRAVE MACMILLAN is the global academic imprint of the Palgrave Macmillan division of St. Martin's Press, LLC and of Palgrave Macmillan Ltd. Macmillan® is a registered trademark in the United States, United Kingdom and other countries. Palgrave is a registered trademark in the European Union and other countries.

ISBN 1–4039–1251–3

This book is printed on paper suitable for recycling and made from fully managed and sustained forest sources.

A catalogue record for this book is available from the British Library.

Library of Congress Cataloging-in-Publication Data

Pemberton, Hugh
Policy learning and British governance in the 1960s / Hugh Pemberton.
p. cm. – (Transforming government)
Includes bibliographical references and index.
ISBN 1–4039–1251–3
1. Great Britain–Economic policy–1945–1964. 2. Great Britain–Economic policy–1964–1979. 3. Great Britain–Politics and government–1945–1964. 4. Great Britain–Politics and government–1964–1979. I. Title. II. Series.

HC256.5.P36 2004
330.941'0856–dc22

2004045423

10 9 8 7 6 5 4 3 2 1
13 12 11 10 09 08 07 06 05 04

Printed and bound in Great Britain by
Antony Rowe Ltd, Chippenham and Eastbourne

Contents

List of Tables

List of Figures

Acknowledgements

One inevitably accumulates a lot of debts in writing a monograph like this. The book has its roots in a doctoral thesis submitted to the University of Bristol and I would like first to thank my PhD advisers, Rodney Lowe and Mark Wickham-Jones, for their help and advice, for the many long and interesting conversations we had over several years, and for the hard work which I know supervising any PhD candidate demands. I am also very grateful to Rodney Lowe for persuading me to do the PhD in the first place, for his unwavering support during difficult times, and for his continuing encouragement (and hospitality). For their detailed and perceptive comments on my PhD thesis I thank Rod Rhodes and Roger Middleton. I am also indebted to Rod Rhodes for agreeing to publish this book in his Transforming Government series at Palgrave Macmillan. The book has taken a long time to write and during its gestation I have talked to many people and benefited from their insights and suggestions (though naturally any errors in the book are mine alone). In particular, I thank the following for their comments, support, and/or advice: Lawrence Black, Mark Blyth, Alan Booth, Angela Bourne, Paul Bridgen, Lord Croham, Martin Daunton, Peter Dorey, Ian Gough, Ian Greener, Peter A. Hall, Peter Jay, Paul Johnson, Harriet Jones, Margaret Jones, Walter Kickert, Desmond King, Richard Little, Robert Millward, Roger Middleton, Michael Oliver, Chris Pollitt, Astrid Ringe, Piers Robinson, Neil Rollings, and Jim Tomlinson. Nick Rennison provided very welcome hospitality on many of my trips to the PRO. I'm also grateful to Alison Howson, my editor at Palgrave Macmillan, for agreeing to publish the book and to the other staff there who have helped with its production. To those whom I have forgotten to mention I tender my sincere apologies. The comments of the anonymous referees of several journal articles published as the book developed were also invaluable in helping me to refine my arguments.

Not surprisingly, I have also built up a number of institutional debts. I thank the UK Economic and Social Research Council (awards R00429734705 and T026271086), the Institute for Historical Research at the University of London, and the British Academy for their financial support during my doctoral and postdoctoral research. I thank the Department of Politics at the University of Bristol, the Department of Historical Studies at Bristol, and the Department of Economic History at the London School of Economics and Political Science for hosting this research. I also thank the Economic History Society, Political Studies Association, Royal Society, and University of Bristol Alumni Foundation for assistance with expenses incurred both in attending and holding a number of conferences. I am also very grateful for the help of the archivists at the Public Record Office in Kew, the University of Warwick's Modern Records Centre, the Bodleian Library at Oxford, and the British Library of Political and Economic Science at the LSE.

Perhaps my greatest debt, however, is to my partner Susan Osborne for her unstinting support and for putting up for so long with so many monologues on the politics and economics of the 1960s.

1

Introduction

This book is about change, or rather it is about the politics of change, the mechanics of policy learning and the way in which learning and governance interact in the process of policy learning and policy change. Specifically, it is about how radical changes in the framework of economic policy can come about, and why such changes may not prove to be enduring. In explaining both change and continuity, the book draws on two bodies of political science theory – in the fields of social learning and governance. It argues that combining insights from both theories can simultaneously eliminate shortcomings in each approach and enrich our understanding of the policy process. To this end, a composite model is advanced which unites key insights from both literatures in a graphical schema of British economic policy making. This model is then applied in a case study of policy networks and policy learning in the field of British economic policy making in the 1960s – a time of radical change during which economic policy objectives were revised and widespread changes to policy instruments were set in train as policy makers struggled to cope with emerging problems with the existing Keynesian policy framework and emerging evidence of Britain's economic decline relative to other advanced economies.

This focus on the politics of forty years ago may seem surprising. On the one hand, what can the history of decades old developments in economic policy have to tell us about governance and policy learning in Britain at the start of the twenty first century? On the other hand, what can theories developed to explain the specific circumstances of today (or at least of the period since 1979) tell us about the nature of policy making in the 1960s? On both counts, the answer is that they can tell us quite a lot. In particular, the use of political science theory can help us to understand why policy should have changed so radically in 1961–62 and why it failed to amount to a permanent 'paradigm shift' in economic policy. Equally, this study is founded on the assumption that detailed historical analysis can illuminate both the process of policy learning and the operation and consequences of policy networks; and in doing so can allow us to refine these theories.

The truth is that both contemporary history and political science could benefit from a much closer collaboration than is presently the case (Pemberton 2003; Oliver and Pemberton 2004). The late J.C.R. Dow (2000: 5), for example, noted that a 'close confrontation with historical reality may fertilize productive theorizing' and, whilst he was thinking more in terms of economics, his remark applies equally to theorising about politics and policy. Andrew Gamble (1995: 528) has challenged political scientists 'not to provide yet more ahistorical economic models of political behaviour'. Dennis Kavanagh (1991) noted that history can enrich the study of politics by providing data to test theory, providing the means of understanding how political contexts developed, and by revealing the lessons drawn from the past by policy makers. Even amongst historical institutionalists, there is a growing awareness that the historical dimension is given too little attention (Lieberman 2001).[1]

One problem is that political scientists, including many historical institutionalists, do not always 'do' history very well, tending not to subject the past to close historical analysis. Instead of utilising primary sources, such as government files or the records of companies and trade unions, they often rely heavily on the work of earlier political scientists (and perhaps contemporary media) when outlining historical developments. If, as we are often told, journalists write the first draft of history then during the twentieth century social scientists increasingly came to write the second. It is not enough, however, for contemporary political science to rely upon these sources. Whilst the insights of both contemporary journalists and past political scientists are undoubtedly useful to current analysis, inevitably much of the policy making process was hidden from them. It is only when the records of the past become available that historians can begin to write a more definitive account of past events. In studying British government, for example, there is a strong argument to be made that access to the vast quantities of declassified material available under the government's code of practice on access to government information (Lord Chancellor's Department 2000), particularly for the post-war period up to 1971 during which time bureaucratic record keeping was particularly rigorous, makes it easier to map the 'multi-form maze of government which characterises the modern state' (Lowe and Rollings 2000: 99-100). The period covered by the case study outlined in this volume is one in which the wealth of records, and the high standard of bureaucratic record keeping, offers the potential for both widening and deepening our understanding of the core executive (Lowe 1997a). As Lowe and Rollings (2000: 100) point out, the 'mile of records accessioned by the Public Record Office every year provides the richest single source of evidence for both the core executive itself *and* the policy networks of which individual ministries are often, although not exclusively, the heart'. There are also rich non-governmental archives available that can be used to elucidate the actions of all the sets of actors and networks within the policy making ambit.

Equally, although contemporary historians tend to be loth to admit it, much contemporary history would benefit from the analytical rigour imposed by an explicit theoretical framework (Marsh and Hay 1999: 223). Recently there has been a slight shift in favour of such greater interdisciplinarity in contemporary history (see for example Lowe and Rollings 2000; Catterall 2002; Kelly 2002) but this remains the exception rather than the rule. Too often, historians are content merely to flesh out a narrative of events and avoid asking penetrating questions about why particular events occurred and why they occurred in the way that they did. Even when they do ask those questions, in answering them they too often operate within implicit rather than explicit analytical frameworks. The 'Westminster model', for example, although long recognised by political scientists to be a very incomplete description of the British polity, continues to exert a powerful hold over the imaginations of contemporary historians, implicitly informing much contemporary British political history even though the events under discussion are now well within the period when the model began to be called into question.

This book is therefore explicitly interdisciplinary and has both a political science and a contemporary history dimension. It seeks both to develop political science theory and to apply, and therefore test, this theory via a rigorous historical study involving the close analysis of contemporary records, both governmental and non-governmental. It also asks some specifically historical questions.

The 'great reappraisal' of economic policy in the early-1960s

Analyses of UK economic policy since 1945 have commonly divided it into two main periods – a Keynesian era followed by one in which a 'monetarist' or 'neoliberal' policy framework held sway – the division between the two occurring at some point in the latter half of the 1970s (Donaldson and Farquhar 1988; Hall 1992 and 1993; Feinstein 1994; Oliver 1997; Pope 1998).[2] In July 1961, however, after 10 years in which it had pursued an increasingly *laissez faire* microeconomic policy within a broadly macroeconomic Keynesian framework of short-term demand management, the Conservative government radically altered course. In a parliamentary debate on the emergency deflationary measures required to meet yet another in a succession of severe post-war sterling crises, the then chancellor, Selwyn Lloyd, suddenly announced that he intended to embrace long-term 'planning' – hitherto 'a dirty word' for the Conservatives (Cairncross 1996: 62). Pressed further, Selwyn Lloyd conceded that the new policy was going to involve five year forward planning of consumption, of government spending, and of public and private investment and would, he indicated, entail far more than just 'some planning board within the Treasury'.[3] This radical change, it will be argued, had come about through a process of learning and it will be suggested that the alteration in the framework of policy that it involved was potentially a policy shift of a similar order to that which was to occur a decade later with the 'monetarist revolution'.

During the latter half of the 1950s, emerging evidence of Britain's relatively poor performance had produced serious concerns about the direction of UK economic policy both amongst policy makers and amongst commentators and the wider public. Sufficient time had passed since the war for 'reconstruction' as an explanation for the better Continental performance to be no longer tenable. The complacency summed up by the apocryphal Conservative claim that Britain had 'never had it so good' gave way to a fear that something was seriously amiss in the British economy.[4] Consequently, Britain became gripped by concern about how its apparent relative decline could be solved (Tomlinson 1996b and 2000).[5] At the same time, as we shall see, those responsible for economic policy had begun to worry that the prevailing Keynesian framework was inadequate, and that it could not support higher growth without running into supply bottlenecks and higher inflation.

This change in the intellectual environment led in the early years of the 1960s to what Samuel Brittan (1964: Ch. 7) called 'a great reappraisal' in the Treasury in respect of British economic policy. This in turn led directly to Selwyn Lloyd's announcement in July 1961, to higher growth becoming an explicit objective of government policy in 1962, and to a wide ranging reshaping of economic policy by the government to attain a target rate of economic growth of 4 per cent per annum.[6]

Essentially, there were three dimensions to the array of new domestic economic policies that resulted from the adopting of an explicit target for higher economic growth.[7] First, changes began to be made to fiscal policy to make both the tax structure and government expenditure decisions more related to the attainment of higher growth. Second, the government began to pursue an 'incomes policy', granting unions and employers some influence over the formulation of policy in return for restraint on wages, and later on prices; the aim being to avoid higher growth triggering higher inflation, and thus avoid the pursuit of higher growth precipitating yet another sterling crisis. Third, it began to craft an innovatory set of policies on the supply-side of the economy that was intended to raise the efficiency of industrial production and remove bottlenecks. In particular, a range of new institutions was created that were intended 'indicatively' to plan the development of the economy – the National Economic Development Council (NEDC), its associated Office (NEDO), and the subordinate industry level EDCs). Other initiatives included the new structure of Industrial Training Boards set up by the Conservatives' Industrial Training Act in 1964, and Labour's later creation of the Department of Economic Affairs, Ministry of Technology, and Industrial Reorganisation Corporation.[8]

Nevertheless, the policy framework that was ushered in by the Conservatives' adoption of a specific objective for higher growth, and which was taken up by Labour in opposition and continued by it when the party entered power in October 1964, proved to be short lived. In response to a sterling crisis in July 1966, the growth objective was effectively jettisoned in favour of deflation to maintain the value of sterling (MacDougall 1987: 169). Whilst this attempt to defend the sterling parity was ultimately to prove fruitless, the government finding itself forced to devalue sterling by 14.3 per cent on 18 November 1967, the abandonment of an explicit target for annual economic growth was to prove permanent. Along with the growth target, a number of the policies that had been introduced to attain it also disappeared. Indicative planning was the most notable casualty but the attempt to build a permanent voluntary incomes policy specifically aimed specifically at enabling higher growth also came to an end. Some of the new policies continued, for example the attempt to plan public expenditure over the medium to long-term, and a number of micro-economic initiatives on the supply-side, but they did so within a policy framework that no longer had at its heart the attainment of faster growth.

Subsequently, the years after 1961 came to be labelled not as the beginning of a new era of economic policy but merely as the start of 'Keynesian-plus' (Gamble and Walkland 1984: 80-5).[9] What had seemed at the time to be a major shift in the framework of economic policy had come to naught, or at least to very little. In this sense, July 1966 was far more important than the devaluation of sterling from $2.80 to $2.40 on 18 September 1967. It marked, as George Brown noted, the 'complete abandonment' of an economic philosophy founded on faster growth and the idea that this would allow Britain to break out of the constraint posed by sterling and the balance of payments and, through better planning, create an efficient and modern industry able to support greater social justice and improved social welfare.[10]

Historical dimensions of the study

As noted above, the analysis set out in this volume includes three detailed case studies of economic policy during the 1960s. For reasons of space, it is assumed that the reader is familiar with the broad outline of economic policy during the 1950s and 1960s. In analysing the advent and development of the growth-oriented policies that flowed from the Treasury's 'great reappraisal' in 1960–61 the book will address two specific historical questions. First, did the revision of the economic policy framework in the early-1960s represent a significant innovation in economic policy? Second, did this innovation amount to a 'paradigm shift' and if it did not, why not?

For each of the three central growth policy elements, the study will ask several questions. In what sense did the political system 'learn' and how did this learning affect the underlying rationale and objectives of policy? Who was involved in this process? How did such learning translate into policy change? Who was involved in the change of policy framework and how successfully was it institutionalised? Did partisan politics shape the implementation of the new policies or, the way they were administered?

By examining in detail a period in which determined efforts were made to improve British economic growth the study adds to the growing body of literature concerned with Britain's relative economic decline. Its concern with the relationship between internal and external macroeconomic objectives, and between these and the government's microeconomic objectives, goes to the heart of much of the debate over this 'decline'. More particularly, the study examines a period the significance of which has been vigorously debated by later commentators. Eric Hobsbawn (1994: 258), for example, identified the 1960s as the mid-point of a 25 year boom in which 'the gold glowed more brightly against the dull or dark background of the subsequent decades of crisis'. Less optimistically, Bob Rowthorne and John Wells (1995) identified 1966 as the year in which the UK economy reached the high point of its industrial maturity, after which manufacturing employment inevitably declined. Others have seen the decade as just another stage in Britain's relentless relative economic decline (Matthews, Feinstein and Odling-Smee 1982; Elbaum and Lazonick 1984). More accusatory are those who have identified the 1960s as a period in which the seeds were sown for an acceleration in that decline (Bacon and Eltis 1976; Congdon 1978; Broadberry and Crafts 1996) or as a period in which the potential to arrest that decline was squandered (Dow 1964; Einzig 1969; Beckerman 1972; Leruez 1975; Coates 1983; Eichengreen 1996). Alternatively, the 1950s and 1960s have lately come to be seen as the period in which a baseless concern about economic decline came to dominate policy (Tomlinson 1996b and 2000).

The study also considers the roles played by a range of actors who have been variously seen as the 'problem' in analyses of the post-war relative decline of the UK economy: the City (Longstreth 1979; Elbaum and Lazonick 1984), industrial management (Gospel 1992), the unions (Hayek 1980; Barnett 1986), the civil service and the Treasury (Ham 1981; Pollard 1982), and politicians (Hall 1986b). In particular, it will scrutinise a persistent assumption in the literature on post-war economic policy making that, as Leruez (1975: 104) put it, the Treasury was 'a stronghold of conservatism and caution which was happier as watchdog of the public purse at home and guardian of the pound abroad than acting as the spearhead of modernisation', that any redirection of policy towards growth which took place had to be forced upon it (see also Heclo and Wildavsky 1981: 48-9; Pollard 1982; Middleton 1996: 38; Thain and Wright 1995: 5), and that it was only too happy to bring the policy down in 1966 (Opie 1972; Shanks 1977: 89-91; Alford 1996: 260-1; Graham 1996: 153-4).

Theoretical dimensions of the study: governance and policy learning

We have already remarked that the traditional Westminster model – with its conception of a powerful political centre exercising power through established hierarchies – remains popular with contemporary historians. It can be argued, however, that the concept of policy networks provides a much more realistic portrayal of the British polity (Marsh and Rhodes 1992; Rhodes 1995 and 1997; Marsh 1998; Smith 1999a). Guy Peters (1998: 26) has noted, that 'there can be little doubt that policy making systems are segmented and that the specialized relationships that exist between the actors within individual segments are important for understanding the decisions made'. However, as examined in more detail in Chapter 2, the model has critics who argue that it is inadequately theorised and, most importantly, lacks explanatory power (Atkinson and Coleman 1992, 156-63; Blom-Hansen 1997; Bogason and Toonen 1998, 225; Daugbjerg and Marsh 1998; Dowding 1995 and 2001; Hay and Richards 2000: 25; Evans 2001). As Jeremy Richardson (2000) notes, policy network theory has tended to view networks as stable and David Marsh (1998: 11-12) has acknowledged that an important feature of the model is that change, both in terms of networks and policy outcomes, is brought about exogenously.

To deal with this lack of dynamism, several authors have suggested that we need to look not just at the policy network but at the broader context within which it is embedded (Hay 1998; Marsh and Smith 2000; Pemberton 2000). In Colin Hay's (1998: 44) view, networks may be 'conceived of as strategic alliances recursively reconstituted through the process and practice of networking'. In this process, Hay has argued that policy outcomes affect the context within which actors in policy networks make strategic calculations. Subsequent calculations and actions by these policy actors take place within this changed context. These changed actions in turn feed into policy outcomes and so have the potential to create further environmental change. Thus, argued Hay, there is a two-way relationship between strategic learning by policy actors and network change. Moreover, those taking strategic action are not necessarily passive recipients of context; they may actively seek to change the environment within which they operate (Pemberton 2000).

This two-way relationship between policy outcomes and networks has also been acknowledged by David Marsh and Martin Smith (2000: 10) in their 'dialectical approach' to policy networks. Marsh and Smith are almost certainly unrealistic in treating context and learning as discrete. Keith Dowding (2001) also notes that, because virtually all the relationships in their model are 'dialectical', it tells us very little about the process it seeks to analyse. Nevertheless, although Marsh and Smith's approach is problematic and adds little that is substantive to Hay's analysis, the insight that outcomes and structure are related via a two-way relationship in which learning by actors operating in policy networks may play a core role remains an important one. By including policy learning within the policy network model its lack of dynamism can be addressed.

A key theme in the recent public policy literature is a recognition that 'learning' is an important driver of policy change and identifying a link between learning, environmental change and networks. But this is not as novel as either Hay or Marsh and Smith assume. It had, for example, been noted a decade ago by Peter Hall (1993: 289) in his analysis of 'social learning' in British economic policy during the 1970s and 1980s. Hall outlined a typology of learning with three degrees or 'orders' of change (he made no distinction between learning and change, a potential problem to which we shall return). In 'first order change' the settings of a policy instrument are altered. 'Second order change' sees changes in the actual policy instruments used. Both first and second order policy change occur within an unchanged overarching set of policy goals. However, occasionally the goals themselves may change. Such an alteration is so fundamental that Hall argued that it amounts to a 'paradigm shift' on Kuhnian lines (Kuhn 1996 [1962]). Hall cited as an example of such a shift the transition from a 'Keynesian' to a 'monetarist' paradigm in UK economic policy making during the 1970s.[11] This 'third order' of change involved an ideational transformation in the very framework of policy. In this process, Hall observed that something like a 'policy network' or 'issue network' sprang up in response to a decline in the authority of government economic policy makers – a decline resulting from the manifest failure of decisions taken within the existing Keynesian framework to solve the problem of simultaneous high unemployment and high inflation. The network which resulted, Hall (1993: 288) noted, 'spilled well beyond the boundaries of the state to involve the media, outside interests, and contending political parties' in a debate over the remedies that the UK economy required and it 'provided outsiders with influence over a formerly closed policy process'.

Hall's suggestion of a link between networks and 'third order learning' is the starting point for this book and for its detailed historical analysis of a period of radical economic policy change in the UK during the 1960s. I make no apology for undertaking such a detailed case study, though such studies are often criticised. Susan Barrett and Colin Fudge (1981: 250), for example, note that their narrow focus is often seen as a major problem. Certainly, case studies can sometimes be criticised for being discrete and/or poorly related to any theoretical literature (Heclo 1972: 89). There is also the potential problem of 'identification' (Amenta 1991: 173). Yet, as Charles Ragin (1992: 224-5) put it, case studies can be a powerful tool: enabling us to link 'the equivocal nature of the theoretical realm and the complexity of the empirical realm'. Moreover, Ragin noted that it can enable us both to formulate and to test theory since it can 'use theory to make sense of evidence and ... use evidence to sharpen and refine theory'. A theoretically grounded case study, with clearly formulated questions, is therefore a particularly powerful research tool if we want to know how and why policy is made and who it is made by – questions at the core of this book (Yin 1993: 3-27 and 1994: 117). Detailed qualitative case studies also give us access to large amounts of information (thus allowing more hypotheses to be tested) and allow us to go into more depth than quantitative analysis can achieve, albeit on a smaller range of cases (Eckstein 1975; King et al 1994: 12; Neuman 1994: 321).

The core hypothesis of this book is that policy learning can both bring into being policy networks and affect the configuration of existing networks, but that policy networks also play an important role both in the process of learning and in the translation of lessons learnt into effective policies. I will argue that mounting problems with the Keynesian policy paradigm in the 1950s and emerging evidence of Britain's relative economic decline led to the creation of a new network advocating radical change in the objectives and instruments of economic policy. Thus, environmental change (in this case policy failure) is shown to have the potential to bring into being a new policy network. However, this relationship between environmental change and network change was two-way. The new advocacy network, which had its roots in academia, was also important in changing the ideational environment and was the means by which policy learning occurred in the core executive. The network developed new policy ideas on how to achieve higher growth, and it actively (and successfully) promoted them to the core executive, not least by recruiting key policy makers into the network, to the media and to the wider electorate. In doing so, it was able both directly to influence members of the core executive and indirectly to change the environment within which its policy decisions were taken.

This environmental change played an important part in the decision to change the framework of policy in 1961–62. Nevertheless, despite the fact that the core executive 'learned' through the actions of this network of growth policy advocates that radical changes to its economic policy objectives were required, translating these new ideas about how to increase growth into effective policies to achieve it proved far more problematic. Later in the book I outline detailed case studies of policy making in each of the main elements of the new economic policy framework implemented after 1961. I argue that, whilst extensive changes were made to that framework, it proved impossible to craft, implement and sustain a coherent and enduring set of new policy instruments that would enable the changed objectives to be attained. The case studies find that the cause of this failure lay in the ability of powerful competing networks (some long standing, some brought into being as a result of the environmental change produced by the 'growth' advocacy network) to resist central control. This leads to two important conclusions. First, that, whilst networks may play an important role in policy learning, the translation of that learning into effective and enduring policy change may be impeded by competing policy networks. Second, that learning does not lead ineluctably to change of an equivalent order, as Hall (1993) assumed. In the case studies outlined here, 'third order learning' is show to have occurred, but 'third order change' was not achieved.

By focusing on economic policy developments in the 1960s, the book also brings into question a prevailing assumption that Britain has been transformed during the post-war period, but particularly since 1979, from a powerful unitary state with a strong executive able to exert control through established hierarchies, to a 'differentiated polity' typified by 'self-organising, inter-organisational networks characterised by interdependency, resource exchange, rules of the game and significant autonomy from the state' (Rhodes 1994: 138-9 and 1997: 15-16, 24, 45,

199; Smith 1999a, 204-9; Richards and Smith 2002). This phenomenon is termed 'governance' by Rod Rhodes (1997), and he has argued that its emergence explains why government now seeks to 'steer rather than 'row' (Osborne and Gaebler 1992).

This assumption that 'governance' is largely a phenomenon of the last two and a half decades was questioned by contemporary historians working in the ESRC's recent 'Whitehall Programme' – the project being an excellent (if relatively rare) example of the benefits of collaboration between political scientists and contemporary historians (for example Lowe 1997a; Bridgen 2000a; Lowe and Rollings 2000; Ringe and Rollings 2000a; for a summary of publications generated by the Whitehall Programme see Rhodes 2000c). The study conducted here provides considerable support for Lowe and Rollings' (2000: 115) assertion that, even in the 1950s and 1960s, the 'fragmentation and differentiation' of British institutions 'sapped the ability of the core executive to co-ordinate a strong central policy'. The case studies described here indicate that third order policy learning was not translated into enduring policy change of a similar order because the British core executive was already operating within a polity characterised by fragmentation, interdependency and self organising policy networks. In this sense, the book provides considerable support to those who have argued that policy networks, and the concomitant need for 'joined up government' are not the novel phenomenon they are claimed to be (Peters 1998; Pollitt 2001, 2003). Rather, policy networks have simply been awaiting the development of the concepts needed to describe them.

However, it is important that this relatively recent emergence of policy networks into the consciousness of modern political scientists be borne in mind when looking back at the 1960s. Although this study shows that the 'Westminster model' was already an inadequate description of public policy making in the United Kingdom, policy makers in the core executive, as well as many other actors such as MPs, journalists, academics, pressure groups, think tanks and voters themselves, continued fundamentally to operate within a mindset conditioned by that model.

In some ways, this might seem a surprising assertion. The 'Westminster model' embodies an essentially zero sum view of power, with power seen as 'an object which belongs to the prime minister, cabinet or civil service' (Rhodes 1997: 6). Yet, core elements of the growth policy package in the 1960s, not least 'indicative planning' in the new National Economic Development Council (NEDC) and the attempt to bring employers and unions into a voluntary incomes policy, recognised the dependence of the core executive on others if it was to achieve its objectives. This was a classic 'positive sum' approach and the book traces the flowering of a new preparedness in Whitehall in the early-1960s to see an active state working with extra governmental actors to correct market failure, and a preparedness to craft innovatory answers to the question how to raise Britain's rate of growth. Yet Britain's core executive failed effectively to build the institutions that would underpin the new policy framework.

I argue, however, that this failure was not the result of a failure of government to create a developmental state in Britain, as has often been alleged by both political scientists and economic historians (Hall 1986a and 1986b; Middlemas 1986; Garside 1998; Marquand 1988; Kirby 1992; Eichengreen 1996; Hutton 1996). In large part, the problem lay – as indicated above – in problems of 'governance' which were simultaneously a key factor in Britain's decision to adopt a relatively weak form of neocorporatism and in the failure of this solution to attain its intended results.

At a deeper level, however, the pervasive assumption in both Whitehall and in industry of a 'Westminster model' of central government was a significant problem. It meant that actors consistently overestimated the power of the core executive to carry through its radical reform of policy and underestimated the scale of the shift from government to governance that the new policy framework demanded. Whilst the more thoughtful members of the core executive (and of the peak associations on both sides of industry) recognised the dependence of the core executive on other institutions to attain its revised goals, this deep-seated assumption of a 'Westminster model' world restricted their ability to achieve their objectives as the core executive attempted to 'steer' rather than 'row'.

Outline of the following chapters

The next chapter considers in more detail how policy change occurs, discussing Heclo and Hall's theories of learning in the policy process and outlines several criticisms of learning theory – particularly the opacity of the process. It then introduces policy network theory and the concept of 'governance', and discusses their problems – particularly the inability of network theory to explain change. The chapter then describes a hybrid model of learning and policy change which combines these two bodies of theory, using important insights of each to deal with the shortcomings of the other. To illustrate its operation, and to model an example of successful paradigmatic change with which to compare the unsuccessful attempt to alter the framework of policy in the 1960s, this schema is then briefly applied to Hall's (1993) case study of economic policy in the 1970s and early-1980s.

The model embodied in the schema is then used to structure the four chapters that follow. Chapter 3 considers the process of learning that led up to the government's reappraisal of policy during 1960–61. It discusses the major problems encountered by economic policy makers in the 1950s: a 'stop-go' economic cycle, supply-side bottlenecks, inflation, and emerging evidence of relative decline. It traces the development of an extensive advocacy network promoting radical new policies to raise economic growth; explains how this network succeeded in penetrating central government, particularly the Treasury, and both major parties; and outlines how the network was able to alter the more general policy environment. It then describes how this precipitated a major policy reappraisal, the consequent adoption of an explicit objective for higher growth and the widespread policy changes implemented to attain that objective. It concludes that the policy shift *was* a significant redirection of policy; one that had all the makings of a paradigm shift or 'third order change'.

The following three chapters go on to consider why this paradigm shift did not come about. They do so via the use of detailed case studies that cover each of the three elements of the growth policy package. Chapter 4 looks at the use of taxation policy to promote the growth of the economy and improve stabilisation policy. It begins by examining how new ideas on tax developed. It argues that the Treasury, newly committed to raising growth, became convinced in 1960–61 that Britain's tax system needed reform, and that this amounted to third order learning. It goes on to examine the translation of this learning into policy change, analysing the development of tax policy between 1961 and 1966. It concludes that, under both Labour and Conservative governments, reformers faced considerable opposition from vested interests operating within self organising networks spanning both state and civil society; networks that proved able to prevent the construction of a strategic programme for reform and to challenge and channel the policy changes that did occur.

In Chapter 5, we examine the construction of an incomes policy after 1961. The chapter argues that the attempt to build a workable voluntary incomes policy was a consequence of the changed intellectual climate produced by the 'growth' advocacy network and involved a recognition of the interdependent nature of power in this field of policy. Using incomes policy to attain higher growth without inflation, it is argued, again amounted to third order learning, particularly amongst Treasury officials. Nevertheless, the chapter concludes that the translation of this learning into third order change was unsuccessful; with incomes policy undermined by the failure to build strong institutions able to overcome the resistance of organised networks of vested interests operating in the British labour market, or to co-opt or isolate these opponents.

Chapter 6 then examines a specific and unresearched instance of the new supply-side policies of the 1960s – government intervention to raise both the quality and quantity of industrial training and help raise growth. It argues that, as with taxation and incomes policy, the shift to interventionism was an example of third order learning, but that it was poorly institutionalised; with producer networks able to stymie the Ministry of Labour's attempts to overhaul Britain's training system. The result was that an apparently radical reform masked underlying continuities which prevented the achievement of either more or better training as had been intended.

Finally, Chapter 7 provides some conclusions. The principal finding is that the policy shift in the 1960s amounted to third order learning but that, unlike the 1970s, this did not produce third order change. Learning, therefore, does not necessarily lead to change of a similar order as assumed by Hall (1993). In addition, whilst Hall argued that the key to successful third order learning in the 1970s was a political battle over ideas, Chapter 7 notes that this did not occur in the 1960s because of the high degree of consensus on the need for higher growth. This should have made radical reform more easy. It did not do so. The problem was that Britain proved unable to translate this consensus on the ends of economic policy into agreement on the means to achieve them. I conclude that an adversarial political culture coupled with a profoundly fragmented polity existing side by side with a widespread 'Westminster model' mindset weakened the centre and allowed resistance from self organising policy networks to flourish. Problems of 'governance' were, therefore, already well entrenched in the 1960s. The alternative to imposing policy change from the centre, it is suggested, was to unite these fragmented institutions (or at least unite enough of them to defeat the remainder). Unfortunately, Britain lacked the institutional structure that would allow the creation of such an 'active consensus' (Shonfield 1965: 199-200). The economic policy makers at the core of the core executive found it difficult to transcend a tradition of secrecy and executive prerogative and embrace the active involvement of other actors – both governmental and non-governmental – in the formulation of policy. The NEDC had the potential to provide the missing institutional framework but proved virtually useless because other institutions remained both unreconstructed and highly fragmented.

This failure both to acknowledge the degree of fragmentation and to devise workable strategies to address it has, of course, a clear contemporary resonance. The lessons of the 1960s, it is suggested, can provide some important pointers for contemporary policy makers. Most importantly, it suggests that 'joined up government' on the lines proposed by the Cabinet Office (2000) requires more than just an overlay of coordinating bodies such as a beefed up Cabinet Office or a new 'Prime Minister's Department' (see Pollitt 2003 for a recent survey of the literature on joined up government). Rather, it demands a wide ranging overhaul of Britain's electoral system, to promote coalition building, as well as far reaching changes to its system of policy making to allow the construction of broad based support for policy change, thus reducing the power of vested interests to impede change.

2

Governance and Policy Learning

Introduction

There is a continuing fascination with changes in public policy, changing ideas and the relationship between them (see for example Supple and Furner 1990; Blyth 1997; Berman 1998; Hall 1989, 1993, 1997; King and Wickham-Jones 1999; Richardson 2000; Hay 2001; Blyth 2002; Oliver and Pemberton 2004). Clearly, there is a complex interrelationship between ideas, interests and institutions (Hall 1997; Walsh 2000). It is also clear that ideas are not in themselves a causal variable (Goldstein and Keohane 1993: 11). As Sheri Berman (1998: 22) puts it, 'ideas do not have any impact by themselves ... [but] influence politics only by acting through or on a particular political actor'. However, whilst consideration of how political systems learn has led us to open the 'black box' of policy making (Hall 1993), its interior is still pretty murky (Oliver and Pemberton 2004). In particular, the mechanism by which ideas insinuate themselves into policy making is still surprisingly opaque (Blyth 1997; Gorges 2001). The relationship between new ideas and policy change, the means by which ideas become translated into policy, and the conditions for successful ideational and policy change all remain unclear.

This chapter examines the current state of learning theory and considers how effective it is at explaining the process of policy learning. It argues that institutional structure needs to be given a greater role in such theories if we are to understand how learning is translated into policy change. Using Peter Hall's insight that something akin to a 'policy network' played an important role in Britain's replacement of its post-war Keynesian economic policy paradigm with a 'monetarist' (or more correctly, a 'neoliberal') policy framework during the 1970s, giving outsiders considerable influence over the government's economic policy, the chapter goes on to explore recent theories of 'governance' and policy networks. Whilst policy network theory embodies important insights into the UK policy process, however, the chapter finds that it too has significant shortcomings – particularly its reliance on exogenous variables in explaining change in both networks and policy outcomes. I then argue that combining these two bodies of theory can yield significant benefits: governance theory providing learning theory with an institutional mechanism for idea transmission, policy creation and policy implementation; and learning theory providing the internal dynamic missing from governance theory. A hybrid graphical model that contains key insights from both bodies of theory is presented and its mechanics are outlined. To demonstrate its workings, and to provide a modelled example of paradigm change against which to compare the 1960s policy shift, this model is then applied in a brief case study of economic policy learning based on Hall's (1993) analysis of the 'social learning' that took place in British economic policy during the 1970s and early-1980s.

Policy learning

Berman (1998: 14-15) points out that ideas tend to be neglected by political scientists partly because there are definitional problems, partly because there has been no agreement about how they influence political outcomes and partly because of the difficulty of devising empirical tests of the power and impact of ideas. She argues, however, that such problems can be overcome by asking if real differences between the ideas of different groups or individuals imply different policy choices, if a plausible connection can be made to political decisions, if the idea/s predate the decision, and if the content of an idea can be deduced from some other variable.

Ideas, of course, are closely bound up with learning, or at least they must inevitably be so if they are to have any impact. Current theories of learning in the policy process are essentially rooted in Easton's (1965: 17-18) description of political life as 'a system of behaviour embedded in an environment to the influences of which the political system itself is exposed and in turn reacts'. This concept of policy feedback, for example, implicitly informed Heclo's concept of 'political learning'. Heclo (1974: 304-15) asserted that, although policy making is always a political process in the sense that decisions are taken by the few for the many, much of the time policy making is not about power. He argued that more often it is a process of 'collective puzzlement' in which political parties, interest groups and the state bureaucracy (particularly actors at the interfaces between these groups) are involved in continual analysis and deliberation in an attempt to build consensual solutions to policy problems. Heclo found this process of 'political learning' to be largely confined to relatively autonomous experts, particularly administrators – with political power only resorted to when the consensual process of analysis and deliberation failed. The consequence, in Heclo's opinion, was that across much of the policy spectrum parties entering government tended to make changes at the margin and so, perhaps unwittingly, a policy consensus was moved forward. Thus old policies almost always condition new policies and political learning is at once an explanation for change and continuity.

Mark Blyth (1997), Desmond King and Victoria Nash (2001) all find the fact that ideas can simultaneously be seen as promoting continuity *and* change as particularly contradictory. In Blyth's view this highlights the need for a better understanding of the role of ideas in politics. Yet, far from being contradictory, Heclo's insight (as Blyth 2002 implicitly acknowledges) contains an important truth both about the conditions that sustain continuity and about those that precipitate change after a period of continuity; and it was essentially the starting point for Peter Hall's (1993) theory of 'social learning' in the policy process. Hall sought precisely to clarify the impact of ideas on politics but gave a much greater role to politicians and to the influence of external agents than did Heclo. This widening of the personnel involved explained Hall's use of the term 'social learning', which he defined as 'a deliberate attempt to adjust the goals or techniques of policy in response to past experience and new information' (Hall 1993: 278).

For Hall, the problem with Heclo's concept of political learning, and with the state theorists such as Skocpol (1985) who had developed his ideas, was that they viewed the state as a black box which had policy inputs and outputs but within which the actual process of learning was unclear. In disaggregating the process, Hall argued that 'policymakers customarily work within a framework of ideas and standards that specifies not only the goals of policy and the kind of instruments that can be used to attain them, but also the very nature of the problems they are meant to be addressing' (Hall 1993: 279). Within this ideological framework Hall proposed that change occurred through a process of 'social learning' (encompassing administrative learning and political learning) which had three degrees or orders, with learning confirmed when a policy change was made.

In Hall's typology, *first order change* occurs when the setting of a policy instrument used to attain a set of given goals, for example the rate of interest, is amended. *Second order change* occurs when, again within unchanged goals, the policy instruments used to attain them are altered; for example the transfer to a new Monetary Policy Committee by the incoming Labour government in 1997 of responsibility for setting UK interest rates according to a new symmetrical inflation target. Hall argued that these first and second order changes corresponded well to the concept of 'political learning' advanced by Heclo. However he maintained that, whilst policy within any particular field is made within an overarching set of goals, occasionally the goals themselves will be changed. Hall cited the transition from a Keynesian to a 'monetarist' paradigm in UK economic policy making during the 1970s; a transition resulting from the failure to stabilise the Keynesian paradigm in the face of mounting problems with its operation, not least the stagflation that set in after the first OPEC oil shock. This *third order change* involved an ideational transformation produced by a process that 'spilled well beyond the boundaries of the state to involve the media, outside interests, and contending political parties' in a debate over the remedies that the UK economy required (Hall 1993: 288). The result was a marked shift in the intellectual framework within which policy was made – a framework that was akin to a *gestalt,* embedded in the minds of policy makers, governing not only the goals of policy and the choice of instruments and settings to achieve these goals, but also policy makers' perception of the very problems they were meant to be addressing (Hall 1993: 279). This transformation, Hall argued, amounted to a change in the 'policy paradigm' – a deliberate evocation of Thomas Kuhn's (1996 [1962]: 23) arguments regarding scientific revolutions (see also Salant 1989).[1]

In Hall's typology, therefore, first and second order change are essentially the equivalent of Kuhn's 'normal science'. Third order change, however, amounts to a revolution in ideas and practice in economic policy that occurs after successive attempts to stabilise the prevailing paradigm via first and second order changes have failed, and this failure has led to a breakdown in the authority of policy makers at the centre of government, to the development of a 'market place for ideas' and then to a political contest in which rival parties expounding different paradigmatic solutions fight for control of policy (Hall 1993: 289).[2] Hall concluded that such third order change fitted poorly with Heclo's concept of political learning and represented an extra dimension to Heclo's analysis, running contrary to Heclo's assumption that policy makers within the state act relatively autonomously – especially in fields such as economic policy that require a high degree of technical understanding. Not only was a change in ideas pivotal in this paradigm shift but Hall argued that the politicisation of the debate was fundamental to the institutionalisation of the new paradigm (see also Hall 1989 and 1992).

Obviously, ideas are important to Hall. As Hall points out, however, they are not sufficient in themselves to explain either of the British economic policy revolutions of the twentieth century – the initial replacement of the neoclassical economic policy framework by a Keynesian framework in the 1940s, or its subsequent downfall and replacement by a 'monetarist' or 'neoliberal' framework in the 1970s (Hall 1989: 7-14,

Ch. 14; see also Oliver and Pemberton 2004). In explaining how changing ideas should have precipitated such revolutions in British economic policy making Hall concedes that that other factors interacted with these new ideas to determine policy.

Hall (1989: 371-82) noted that, in Britain's initial adoption of Keynesianism, the new Keynesian ideas had to be viable not just economically but politically and administratively. The impact of the new economic ideas propounded by Keynes was therefore influenced not just by the economic policy legacy but by the orientation of the governing party, the structure of political discourse, and the institutional structure of the state and of relations between the state and civil society (see also Weir 1989). Thus the openness of the state to the ideas of academic economists, the relative concentration of power over economic decision making, and the distribution of power between the key actors were all important. For example, it could be argued that after the second world war, the introduction of Keynesian economic policies in Britain owed much to the wartime disruption of Treasury dominance, the impact of the war in converting the Treasury to Keynesian ideas (through the adoption of national income accounting and the use of aggregate demand reduction to control wartime inflation), and the post-war restoration of the Treasury's pre-eminent role in UK economic policy making (Roseveare 1969: 278-82; Feinstein 1983: 12-13; Milward 1987: 101-7; Booth 1989: 68-9; Weir 1989). At the same time, however, Hall (1989: Ch. 1) has argued that politicians also played a role in the adoption of Keynesianism demand management in Britain (see also Pekkarinen 1989). Thus, for Hall, the significance of Keynesian ideas is that they could be attractive to economists, to administrators and to politicians. The important lesson that Hall draws from this is that ideas do have real power in politics but that their significance is bound up with both institutions and interests (see also Hall 1986, 1992 and 1997; Walsh 2000).

This complex interrelationship between ideas, institutions and interests is also identified by Hall as governing the shift in the UK during the late-1970s from a Keynesian to a monetarist policy making paradigm. The roots of this change are located by Hall (1992) not just in the growth of monetarism as an alternative idea but in Treasury disillusion with the failure of Keynesian economic policies, a two party system which encouraged a search for a political alternative, the growth of a 'market place for ideas' as policy makers failed to stabilise the prevailing Keynesian paradigm, and the changing balance of power between government, trade unions and financial capital.

Hall's point is that a recognition of the importance of ideas in social learning (in terms of both administrative and political learning) produces three observations. The first is that a politically rational course of action can be determined by the organisational structure within which the actor operates – because this structure determines their relationship to other actors. The second is that an individual's perception of their interests can be changed by ideas. The third is that the power of an idea is directly related to the strength of the organisation through which it is disseminated (Hall 1986: Ch. 10). These are all powerful insights.

Proposing a process of learning as the motor for policy change, by including the Easton policy feedback loop and, in Hall's analysis, by disaggregating the process and identifying different orders of change, therefore gives an important additional dimension to the analysis of policy making. However, the approach is not without problems. One is a tendency to regard learning as part of a constant improvement in policy. Heclo's (1974: 219-40) analysis of investigatory commissions in Sweden is a case in point here. Hall (1986: 16) dealt with this by conceding that learning may not all be positive, since policy makers may learn different, or even wrong, lessons from previous policy failures or successes. This seems reasonable since, even if this learning is wrong, the resulting policies will simply feedback into the policy process, and this will then lead to further learning and policy adjustment.

More seriously, we might also question Hall's analysis of the role politicians play in learning. On the one hand, he may underestimate the extent to which politicians can sometimes become involved in first and second order change. For example Kenneth Clarke played a decisive role in first order interest rate adjustments whilst Chancellor of the Exchequer during the Major government.[3] Or one could point to Nigel Lawson's role in initiating a policy of sterling shadowing the deutschmark in the late-1980s, a second order change since it effectively introduced a new instrument of policy (Keegan 1989; D. Smith 1992: 99-139; Lawson 1992). On the other hand, the degree of politicisation involved in third order change is also open to debate. When Hall cited the move from a Keynesian to a monetarist policy making paradigm in the late-1970s he identified the defining break as the election of the Conservative government in 1979. Hall therefore emphasised the shift in the policy framework as the outcome of a party political battle of ideas. In doing so, however, he glossed over the argument that can be made for this break occurring under Labour with Callaghan's apparent conversion to monetarist economics in 1976 (Keegan and Pennant-Rea 1979: 101; Stewart 1993: 5). Whatever the truth of this, the key point here is that learning theory might need to take a more flexible approach to the role of politicians in the learning process.

Hall's concept of 'social learning' has also been criticised for failing to provide a detailed explanation of how policy makers learn and how the ideas underlying a policy are changed (Oliver 1997: 11-17). Others have also complained that the appeal to changing ideas provides no explanation of how these operate or where they come from (Gorges 2001). Nor is there any clear agreement on what constitutes 'learning' (Bennett and Howlett 1992: 276). Furthermore, some have commented that it is difficult, indeed often impossible, to observe and record learning; and even if ideas are important, this importance is difficult to quantify (Pierson 1993: 610-7; Knoepfel and Kissling-Näf 1998). Although Blyth (2002: 264) has argued that ideas can be an independent variable in their own right, idea oriented approaches to the analysis of policy making, whilst they have the great advantage of capturing a dimension which other approaches tend to lack, are problematic because of the difficulty in disentangling them from other variables (as noted by Hall 1997: 183-6). Berman has suggested that for ideas to influence political behaviour two conditions must be fulfilled: there should be 'carriers' (individuals or groups) who will promote the idea and build coalitions of support; and the ideas need to become embedded in institutions. In order to clarify this, however, we need better to integrate institutions into learning theory and build a model that is better able to represent the interaction of ideas and institutions.

Hall's (1993) definition of third order change also presents us with a problem. The idea of a 'paradigm shift' is meaningful at the general level but surprisingly difficult to define in the particular and it is not clear how far goals have to be changed for Hall to deem the alteration a 'paradigm shift'. Is, for example, the present political debate over the advantages and disadvantages of Britain adopting the Euro a debate about policy instruments, or a debate about the overarching goals of economic policy itself? Or, a more pertinent example in respect of this book, was the adoption of an explicit growth target in the early-1960s and the slew of new policy instruments implemented to try to attain it an example of third order change, a potential third order change which failed (for whatever reasons) to fulfil its promise, or instead a particularly extreme example of second order change? Again, this is a key point. Hall's three part division of change was an important insight into the nature of learning and policy change, but we might now need to push the analysis forward and obtain a more nuanced account of change; one that recognises, for example, that degrees of learning cannot simply be mapped onto corresponding degrees of change, and that a process of policy evolution might result in major alterations to the policy framework over time without the wholesale replacement of one paradigm by another implied by a 'paradigm shift' (Oliver and Pemberton 2004).

The fact that learning is a continuous process, however, also presents us with problems. Hall presupposed a policy feedback loop in which an independent (or causal) variable, social learning, gives rise to a complex dependent (or outcome) variable in which policy change in turn triggers policy change though further learning. King et al (1994: 191) summed this 'endogeneity' problem up well when they wrote that: '... ideas can be mere consequences rather causes of policy ... they may appear to explain actors' strategies, but in fact they result from these strategies'. In examining a solution to the problem, they went on: 'To show that ideas are causally important, it must be demonstrated that a given set of ideas held by policy makers, or some aspect of them, affect policies pursued and do not simply reflect those policies or their prior material interests'.[4] However, disentangling the independent from the dependent variable in what is essentially an unending and circular process is virtually impossible. Inevitably, the point at which one chooses to break into the circle will be arbitrary. To the political scientist, this appears to bring into question the possibility of distinguishing cause from effect. To the historian, however, it is an accepted problem and if we are to address the issue we must borrow from historians the concept of 'periodisation'. This can be controversial. A period is not a 'fact'; it is 'a necessary hypothesis or tool of thought, valid in so far as it is illuminating, and dependent for its validity on interpretation' (Carr 1964: 60). The task, therefore, becomes one of making a valid selection.

> Just as from the infinite ocean of facts the historian selects those which are significant for his purpose, so from the multiplicity of sequences of cause and effect he [sic] extracts those, and only those, which are historically significant; and the standard of historical significance is his ability to fit them into his pattern of rational explanation and interpretation (Carr 1964: 105).

Thus the 'set of methodological difficulties associated with the complexity of the subjects, objects and effects of learning' can be addressed via detailed studies of particular cases (Bennett and Howlett 1992: 290), with these studies periodised on the basis of their historical significance. This is the approach adopted here.

Finally, although the importance of institutional structure to policy change is a theme which consistently runs throughout Hall's work, rather surprisingly Hall fails fully to connect ideas and institutions (Hall 1982, 1986, 1989, 1992, 1993, 1997). This suggests a need to marry learning theory to an analysis of the structure of policy making. Hall (1993: 289) himself pointed the way to a possible way of making progress on this when he wrote of the Keynesian to monetarist paradigm shift that: 'something similar to a "policy network" or "issue network" sprang up to provide outsiders with influence over a formerly closed policy process'. This points us towards recent theories of British governance that emphasise the importance of policy networks.

Governance and policy networks

There is a widespread assumption amongst political scientists that since 1979 Britain has experienced a marked change in the environment within which its politics is conducted and that the traditional 'Westminster model', with its emphasis on the sovereignty of Parliament, has become an inadequate description of the British polity (Gamble 1990a and 1990b; Rhodes 1994: 138-9, 1995, 1997 and 2000a/b; Weller et al 1997; Smith 1999a: 11-15; Milward and Provan 2000; Richards and Smith 2002). Since the 1970s, it is argued, an era of top down government characterised by the exercise of power through established hierarchies has given way to an era of 'governance, in which governing has become a shared process of exchange and negotiation involving a range of actors' (Richards and Smith 2002: 2). Britain, once characterised by its powerful unitary state, has become a 'differentiated polity' in which power has continually to be negotiated (Rhodes 1997).

In truth, there never was one definitive version of the Westminster model (Birch 1964; Rhodes 1997, Smith 1999a; Marsh et al 2001). However, one can identify several key characteristics of the model. It emphasised the unique character of the British political tradition and the unitary nature of the British state. In highlighting the dominance of central government it concentrated on the role of the central institutions of the British state in policy making: parliament, the prime minister and the cabinet (Judge 1993; Mackintosh 1977b; Gamble 1990b: 340). In the model, these institutions, and their institutional processes, are underpinned by the notion of parliamentary sovereignty based on a first past the post electoral system which both holds the executive periodically to account and delivers one party an overall electoral majority.

The Westminster model became subject to increasing criticism on the grounds that it was 'not an accurate description of how government actually works in Britain' and exaggerated the importance of Parliament (Gamble 1990b: 341). Beginning in the 1960s, the model began to be subjected to critiques from both left and right that questioned some of its key underlying assumptions: the concept of parliamentary sovereignty; the idea that the prime minister is simply *primus inter pares* in the cabinet; and the neutrality of the civil service (see, for example, Miliband

1969; Nairn 1977; Ashford: 1984; Hall 1986: 48-66; Davies 1995). Variants of the model began to emerge that variously emphasised the power of particular actors in central government: the prime minister (Crossman 1981; Young 1989: Ch. 11; Kavanagh and Seldon 2000: 251-96); an inner cabinet of trusted prime ministerial aides (Hennessy 1986: 80; MacIntyre 1999); the cabinet (Gordon Walker 1972; Jones 1975 and 1995; Mackintosh 1977a and 1982: 37); cabinet ministers as heads of departmental fiefdoms (Jones 1975); and civil servants in the departments themselves (Chapman 1979; Benn 1980; Kellner and Crowther-Hunt 1980: 284-5; Crossman 1981; Dunleavy 1989a, 1989b and 1991; Smith 1995: 123). Nevertheless, although each variant questioned the location of power within the Westminster model, none questioned its implicit assumption that power lay within the parliamentary (or at least Westminster) arena and was essentially zero sum in nature, residing with one of the several actors in the model at any one time (Rhodes 1997: 6; Smith 1999a: 11-13; Richards and Smith 2002: 4; Bevir and Rhodes 2003: 28). The Westminster model was therefore weakened but not destroyed.

A more fundamental attack on the model came with growing criticisms of its underlying assumptions about the state. Neo-pluralists, along with elitist and corporatist theorists, argued that the model neglected the role of non-parliamentary institutions in the policy process (see Hall 1986: 48-66 for a discussion of this). The neutrality of the state came to be questioned both by Marxists and neo-Marxists (Miliband 1969; Longstreth 1979; Nairn 1977) and by the 'new right' (Ashford 1984; King 1987; Eatwell 1989; Gamble 1990a: 413; Davies 1995). Finally, it was argued that the model's view of the United Kingdom as a unitary nation state had begun to look outdated as the state was 'hollowed out' during the 1980s and 1990s as a consequence of privatisation, the 'new public management', devolution, a loss of sovereignty to the European Union and to other supranational institutions such as the International Monetary Fund and World Trade Organisation, and the reduction in Whitehall power resulting from the globalisation of markets (Rhodes 1994: 138-9, 1995 and 1997; Weller et al 1997; Milward and Provan 2000).[5]

A common factor in many of these challenges was the criticism that our view of the British policy making process needed to be widened to include a range of actors and institutions which were absent from the model, and that the concept of power relations in the model needed to be made more sophisticated. This is an approach epitomised by theories of policy making which embrace notions of policy communities and networks, both formal and informal, and which see policy as emerging from a process of negotiation between important groups (Gamble 1990a: 411-14).

The origins of the policy network approach lie in analyses of central government relations and of the relationship between central and local government. An early example was the concept of 'iron triangles' in American policy making (Heclo 1978: 87-124; Jordan 1981). In terms of Britain, perhaps the most important early contribution to policy network theory was Heclo and Wildavsky's seminal book *The Private Government of Public Money* (originally published in 1974). This portrayed British government as a community characterised by 'personal relationships between major political and administrative actors – sometimes in conflict, often in agreement, but always in touch and operating within a shared framework' (Heclo and Wildavsky 1981: xv). A government department seemed to Heclo and Wildavsky (1981: 37-128) to be like a 'nuclear family' operating within the 'village life' of the civil service as a whole. The Treasury was seen as a collegial institution of tightly bound officials but one with extensive relations with other departments. These relations seemed to Heclo and Wildavsky to be fundamental to successful expenditure control, which they portrayed as a process of constant bargaining, mainly between officials.

More recently, Rod Rhodes (1995, 1997) has attempted to disaggregate the analysis of policy making and to develop what he terms a 'meso level' theory, lying between macro theories of the state and micro level rational choice theory. Rhodes' theoretical contribution has had two dimensions. Firstly, there has been an attempt to widen the analysis of the UK polity by recognising the complexity of the 'core executive'. Rhodes defines the 'core executive' as:

> all those organisations and procedures which coordinate central government policies, and act as final arbiters of conflict between different parts of the government machine. In brief the 'core executive' is the heart of the machine covering the complex web of institutions, networks and practices surrounding the prime minister, cabinet, cabinet committees and their official counterparts, less formalised ministerial 'clubs' or meetings, bilateral negotiations and interdepartmental committees. (Rhodes 1995: 12)

In this analysis, central government is seen as 'fragmented, differentiated and fissiparous' and the emphasis is on 'issues of coordination and fragmentation' (Wright 1988: 599; Rhodes 1995: 12).

In a survey of the several variants of the Westminster model, Rhodes proposed that their common denominator was that all pointed to 'a view of the executive in which there are multiple actors whose relative power shifts over time and between policy areas' (Rhodes 1995: 26). For Rhodes, the central point is that there is not one executive but multiple executives. The principal actors in the making of policy vary according to the policy area (Rhodes 1995: 12 and 22-4). Rhodes was thus able to recognise the complexity of the 'core executive' although its effective redefinition whenever the policy area is changed means that it remains a rather slippery concept.

In the second dimension of Rhodes' work, he attempted to integrate the idea of a 'core executive' with the broader concept of policy networks which emerged from the Economic and Social Research Council's project on central-local government relations and the development, as part of this project, of a power dependency model of organisational relationships (see Rhodes 1981 and his restatement of the framework in 1997: 36-9). In the power dependency framework, organisations are seen as interdependent. An organisation is always dependent on other organisations for resources and forced to exchange resources to attain its goals. Power resources are determined in part by structures but may also derive from personality and an actor's success in achieving his/her goals will depend on strategy and tactics. Thus resource deployment is an important aspect of power (Smith 1999a: 31 and 88). In this process, a dominant coalition regulates the process of exchange using known 'rules of the game'. The 'appreciative system' of this dominant coalition will influence which relationships are perceived as important and which resources will be sought and traded. The dominant coalition will retain some discretion, despite the constraint placed upon policy making by other organisations, but its discretion will vary according to its goals and differences in relative power potential between organisations. Thus relative power is seen as a product of resources, rules of the game and the process of exchange between organisations.

Rhodes describes the sets of interacting and interdependent organisations operating within the power dependency framework as 'policy networks'. He identifies five types of network. These form a continuum from highly integrated 'policy communities' through professional, intergovernmental and producer networks to loosely integrated 'issue networks' (Marsh and Rhodes 1992: 1-26; Rhodes 1988: 48-77, 1995: 29, 1997: 38). Four dimensions to the typology are postulated: membership; level of integration; resources; and power (see Table 2.1). The analysis stresses the varying relationships between policy areas and, at the same time, the limited number of groups operating within any one policy area.[6]

For Rhodes, policy networks and the structural relationships that characterise them are important because they limit participation, define the roles of actors within the network and help, via internal rules to shape the behaviour of these actors. They also determine what is or is not on the policy agenda, privilege some interests over others and tend to substitute private government for public accountability. Perhaps the most important contribution that Rhodes' model makes, however, is the recognition that policy networks can include a large range of actors and will vary both in the field of policy with which they are concerned and in their structure.

Table 2.1 Dimensions of policy networks

Dimension	Policy Community	Issue Network
1. Membership:		
Number of participants	Limited with some groups excluded	Large
Type of interest	Economic and professional interests are dominant	All affected
2. Integration:		
Frequency	Frequent, encompassing and high quality	Fluctuating frequency and intensity
Continuity	Continuity of membership, values and outcomes	Fluctuating access
Consensus	Shared basic values, legitimacy of outcome accepted	Some agreement but conflict is ubiquitous
3. Resources:		
Distribution within network	All have resources, basic relationship one of exchange	Some have limited resources. Basic relationship is consultative
Distribution within organisations	Hierarchical	Varied and variable ability to deliver membership
4. Power	Balanced. One group may dominate but in a positive sum game	Unequal (reflecting unequal resources and access). Zero sum game.

Source: Marsh and Rhodes (1992: 251).

The strength of the Rhodes approach is that, by breaking open the Westminster model, it is able to acknowledge and reveal the complexities of policy making. Rhodes (1995 and 1997) has argued that a post-war transformation of British government has seen a shift from a centralised unitary state able to exercise power via established hierarchies to a world in which policy networks have become *the* defining attribute of the British political process. This, however, has been a particular feature of the past 25 years, with the process accelerating rapidly after 1979 (Rhodes 1979, 2000a and 2000b; Rhodes and Dunleavy 1995; Richards and Smith 2002). The consequence, Rhodes argues, is that Britain is now a 'differentiated polity' characterised by 'self-organising, inter-organisational networks' – a phenomenon which Rhodes describes as one of 'governance' and which poses a problem for central government, since these networks tend to develop autonomy and begin to resist central direction. 'A "differentiated polity" is exemplified by functional and institutional specialization, the fragmentation of policies and politics', and the replacement of a strong central executive by a segmented executive, characterised by bargaining within and between networks (Rhodes 1997: 4-7). 'Governance' has replaced 'government', with the core executive now forced into 'steering rather than rowing' (Osborne and Gaebler 1992: 34). Recent attempts to promote 'joined up government' mark a further stage in this development (Richards and Smith 2002). But power dependency and the need for governments to 'work with and through complex networks' creates real problems for governments, and for joining up, and they often explain the failure of government to achieve its objectives (Bevir and Rhodes 2003: 60).

This claim that Britain has seen its polity transformed since 1979 is a significant one. It has not gone unquestioned by contemporary historians (see, for example, Bridgen 2000b; Lowe 1997a; Ringe and Rollings 2000a; Lowe and Rollings 2000). The debate, however, centres on the degree to which policy networks were already operating pre-1979 rather than whether a shift in their importance has taken place.

A more significant assault has come from political scientists who have criticised the Rhodes model on grounds of theoretical weakness. The first point of attack has been the model's typology, which a number of critics have criticised for being incomplete (see, for example, Marin and Mayntz 1991: 16-17; Bogason and Toonen 1998: 220). Certainly, it must be acknowledged that, despite the large body of theoretical work in recent years, we are still left with the question 'what is a policy network?'. Yet the Marsh and Rhodes typology is already relatively complex: varying in four non-binary dimensions it can produce an extensive variety of networks (Smith 1993: 222-6). The greater problem is that the typology is rarely discussed in terms of anything but the two ends of its spectrum – policy communities and issue networks. This is a fundamental, if implicit, criticism since it calls the usefulness of the typology into question. Indeed, if network types exist on a continuum, one might argue that the construction of a typology risks the loss of one of the major strengths of

Rhodes' analysis – his recognition of the diversity, complexity and fluidity of policy networks. Of course, not all relationships constitute a network and the analysis needs to be restricted to relationships where there is some form of interdependency (Toonen 1998). Though it is worth noting that this interdependency may not be immediately obvious and that sometimes information discrepancies may produce such inter-dependencies for, as Keegan and Pennant-Rea (1979: 91) put it, 'information is power'. We must also beware diluting policy network theory to the extent that we 'empty the concept of all analytical content' (Hay 1998: 37). Nevertheless, liberation from the constraint of Rhodes' typology might allow us to recognise that policy networks can be extraordinarily diverse and complex.

Further criticisms concern the role of network structure in conditioning policy outcomes and the distinction between structure and agency. Although Marsh (1998: 11-12) has noted that the typology is essentially structural and that network structure affects policy outcomes, the Marsh and Rhodes typology has surprisingly little to say about the impact of a given network on policy making. It has also been criticised for under-playing the role of agency and saying little about the way in which agents are constrained by structures and institutional processes (Smith 1998: 80-5). Although network theorists accept that actors or organisations can be members of more than one network (Marsh and Rhodes 1992: Ch. 11) and that networks are institutions that structure the behaviour of individual actors (Blom-Hansen 1997), network analysis tends to lose sight of the important role that individuals can play in the policy process (Dowding 1995). Thus, a model which seeks to emphasise the role of deep-seated structures in the policy process needs to make more clear the role of structure and context in conditioning policy outcomes, and needs also to take more account of the role of actors.

The role of change in policy network theory is particularly problematic. The inability of the policy network model to explain change has been trenchantly criticised by Keith Dowding (1995) and others have also raised the question of what drives the system and the actors within it (Atkinson and Coleman 1992: 162-3; Blom-Hansen 1997; Peters 1998: 25). As Dowding (1995: 136-7) and Mark Evans (2001) point out, as it stands the model is essentially metaphorical; it is not able to explain outcomes. In fact, from the outset Marsh and Rhodes (1992) conceded that policy network theory did not provide an adequate explanation for change, with policy networks tending to be associated with continuity and stability rather than change. As Marsh (1998: 11-12) has noted, an important feature of the theory is that change in both networks and policy outcomes is brought about exogenously.

Thus the fundamental criticisms of policy network theory are that it lacks both explanatory power and an internal dynamic. These are potentially devastating charges. It has been variously suggested that they might be addressed by more explicitly integrating policy network theory with other theoretical models such as rational choice theory (Blom-Hansen 1997; Dowding 1995); resource dependency and discourse theory (Bogason and Toonen 1998: 225); macro theories such as Marxism, elitism or pluralism (Daugbjerg and Marsh 1998: 61; Smith 1993); Sabatier's advocacy coalition model, epistemological communities or theories of agenda setting and 'punctuated equilibria' (Peters 1998: 29-31); or analyses of Britain's 'adversary polity' (Atkinson and Coleman 1992: 164-5).

Another angle suggestion is that the solution to both the problem of structure and agency in policy network theory and its lack of dynamism may lie in understanding the role of learning in the policy process. Hay (1998: 44) argues that networks are best 'conceived of as strategic alliances recursively reconstituted through the process and practice of networking'. A link can be made here to Blom-Hansen's (1997) argument that actors bring about change in network configuration through changes in relative bargaining power. Hay (1998) argues that this process is characterised by 'strategic learning' within networks, and that such strategic action gives rise to two effects: firstly strategic learning by actors; and secondly a partial transformation of the context within which policy actors make their future strategic calculations (see also Hay and Wincott 1998).

This two-way relationship between policy outcomes and networks is also found in Marsh and Smith's (2000: 10) 'dialectical approach' to policy networks (see Figure 2.1). This is far from unproblematic. One might, for example, question Marsh and Smith's treatment of context and learning as discrete. The approach has also been criticised, with some justification, by Dowding (2001) on the grounds that, because virtually all the relationships in their model are 'dialectical', it actually tells us very little about the process it seeks to analyse.[7] Raab (2001) has also complained that Marsh and Smith's two-way relationships fail to recognise that some relationships are more important than others, that some relationships are obviously missing, that their feedback arrow is too generalised, and that they pay too little attention to the time dimension. Nevertheless, although Marsh and Smith's diagram is problematic and adds little that is substantive to Hay's analysis, the insight that outcomes and structure are related via a two-way relationship in which learning by actors operating in policy networks may play a core role remains an important one. Moreover, Hay's injection of learning and contextual change into the policy network model could be extended further, by examining in more detail the role of ideas in policy change.[8] As Bleich (2002) points out, systematically integrating ideas into policy making analysis can greatly enhance our understanding of policy outcomes. Integrating learning theory into policy network theory could enable us not just to solve the policy network structure / agency dichotomy, as Hay suggests, but also to deal more explicitly with the model's lack of an internal dynamic (Pemberton 2000).

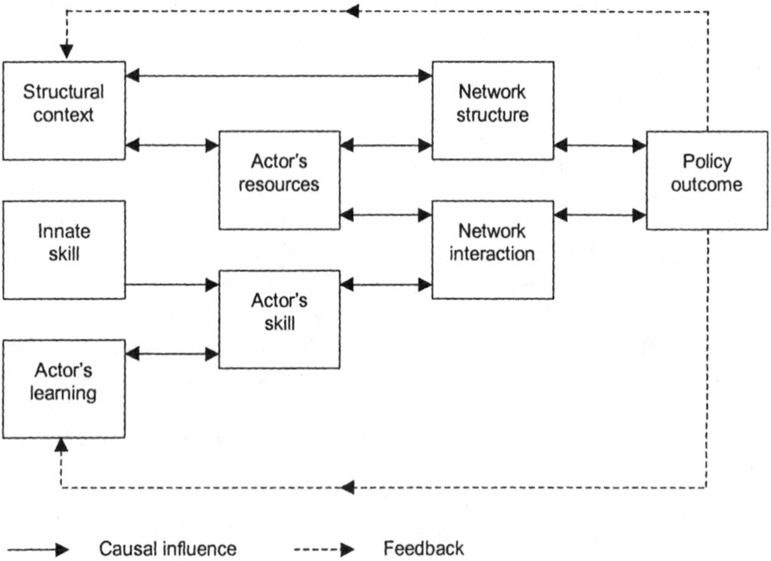

Figure 2.1 A 'dialectical approach' to policy networks and policy outcomes
Source: Marsh and Smith (2001: 10)

A policy network schema

Thus, whilst both the policy network model and the concept of social learning embody important insights into the mechanics of policy making, both have significant weaknesses. This section proposes that the strengths of each approach can be retained, and their respective drawbacks eliminated (or at least minimised), by combining the two theories in the graphical model of British policy making shown in Figure 2.2. The model takes as its starting point Hall's call for a link to be made between social

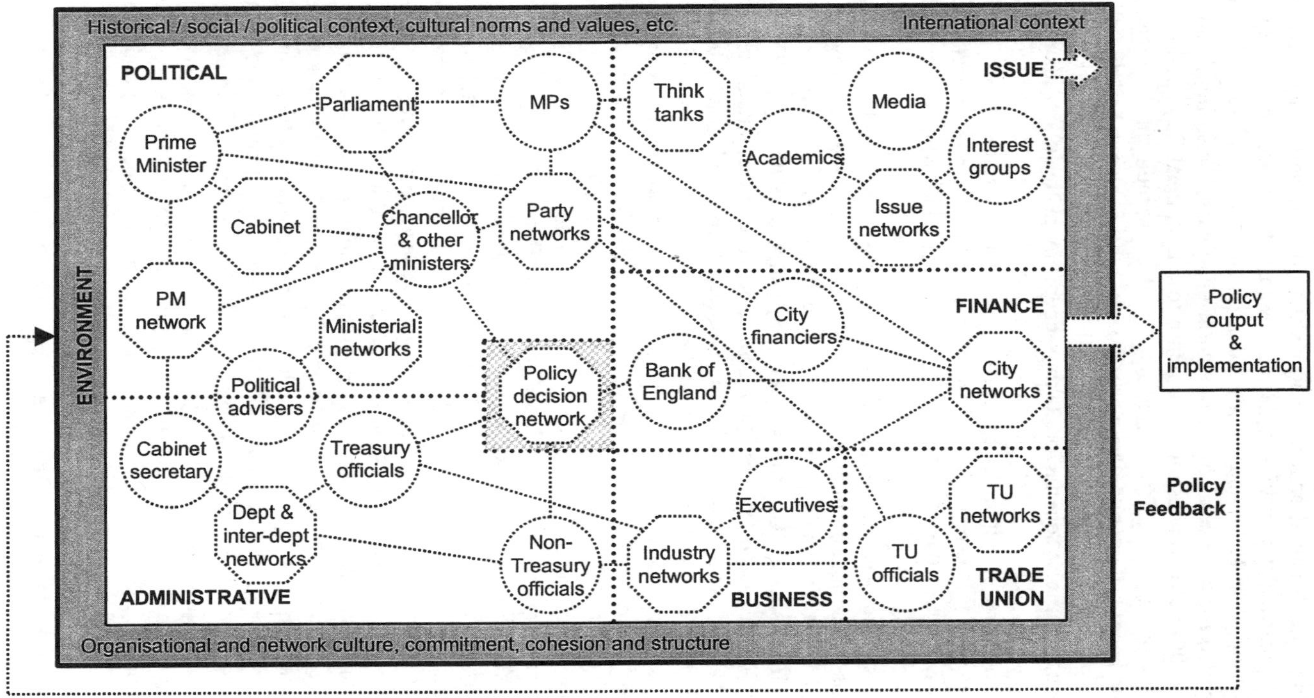

Figure 2.2 An economic policy network schema for the United Kingdom

learning and structural analysis, and his detection of policy networks in learning, particularly in third order change (a link explored by Knoepfel and Kissling-Näf 1998; and also by Atkinson and Coleman 1992: 152-63, who called for more empirical research in this field). It also builds upon Hay's (1998: 38) conclusion that a return to a traditional 'lay' definition of 'network' (as sets of interrelated actors with a common purpose) would greatly benefit the policy network model. I have also taken literally Marsh's (1998: 13-16) comment that in classifying networks any approach requires a schema (but taking schema to mean a plan rather than a typology). In support of this approach I note that graphical representations of networks are recommended by Brandes et al (1999) because they enable us to display, in a compact way, the relevant actors in a network, how they are related to each other and what the overall structure looks like.

The schema has been designed as an 'organising perspective' for the analysis of economic policy making in the United Kingdom – providing 'a framework for analysis, a map of how things relate, [and] a set of research questions' (Greenleaf 1983: 3-8; Gamble 1990a: 405; Rhodes 1997: 5-7; Bevir and Rhodes 2003: 26). At its core is the general acceptance that post-war British economic policy has emerged from a tightly bound decision making network at the heart of the core executive; a network consisting of Treasury ministers, officials from the Treasury and revenue departments, and the Bank of England (Keegan and Pennant-Rea 1979; Longstreth 1979; Hall 1982; Ingham 1984). However, this core economic decision making network does not operate in a vacuum. Firstly, the actors and institutions involved are themselves embedded in other networks. Secondly, like all networks this one is characterised 'by specific configurations of perceptions which are related to [its] history and nature' (Klijn et al 1995: 440). The proposed schema is an attempt to recognise this. It operates at the most general level, providing a map of how institutions and actors within the policy making process, in its broadest sense, interrelate and thus provides a framework for analysis.

The schema has a number of basic elements: the two large boxes, the feedback loop, and a means by which actors may inject new ideas into the policy environment. The inner of the two large boxes represents what might be termed the domestic economic policy 'terrain'. This encompasses a range of possible policy actors (represented by circles) which extends from the Prime Minister to more peripheral actors such as academics. It thus spans the traditional divide between the state and civil society. Each actor is linked to one or more 'networks' (represented by octagons). The linkages are dynamic and those shown are not exhaustive. The networks to which actors are linked can be formal or informal, or often a mixture of the two. The cabinet, for example, is a formal institution that is a 'network' in the sense that it brings together actors to discuss and decide policy. Parliament consists of the formal sittings of Parliament and parliamentary committees but also encompasses other groupings of MPs, both formal and informal. In a similar way, a civil service interdepartmental network of, for example, Permanent Secretaries would include informal contacts as well as more formal meetings with an agreed agenda and at which minutes would be taken. Within this policy terrain interested actors and networks coalesce around a given policy issue and produce a particular network, perhaps even a network of networks, or what might be termed a 'meta network'.

For analytical convenience the actors and networks in the policy terrain are divided into five groups. The political, finance, business and trade union groups are self explanatory and should be uncontentious. The presence of advisers (an increasing feature of government with a large expansion of their number beginning in the early-1960s) straddling the border between the political and administrative grouping reflects their ambiguous status in government. The administrative grouping equates to the Whitehall based civil service and it does not, for reasons of simplicity, include civil servants outside Whitehall, local government structures or government agencies staffed by non-civil service employees. The Treasury is separately modelled by virtue of its superior access to information and links to the core executive's economic policy decision making network (Heclo and Wildavsky 1974; Keegan and Pennant-Rea 1979; Longstreth 1979: 187; Cronin 1991: 11; Smith et al 1995; Tomlinson 1996c). The Bank of England is modelled not as part of the core executive but as part of civil society; reflecting an independent scope of operation and strong links with City institutions that predate its official independence since 1997. The 'issue' grouping, however, is less easily defined. It represents an extremely loosely articulated body of actors who can shape economic policy indirectly, through the generation and transmission of ideas that change the context within which policy decisions are made and directly by advising policy makers in the core executive. It may be located around institutions such as pressure groups. It may, however, may be so loosely articulated as to lack any real institutional structure, in which case it would equate to Haas' notion of a 'network of the like minded', united by a shared idea and by a commitment to translate that idea into public policy (Haas 1990: 41-2).

The second element of the schema is the outer shaded box within which the policy terrain is embedded. This represents the environment, or context, within which policy makers act. This environment operates at three levels. At the highest level is the broad historical, sociological and political context that shapes and constrains individual policy makers and the institutions and networks within which they operate. Included in this level is the environmental change produced by general elections. The second level is the international context. Strictly speaking, much of this consists of external policy actors and institutions, such as the IMF, US government or European Central Bank, to which actors and networks within our schema will be linked either formally or informally. For simplicity, and because links between UK actors in economic policy and external institutions were both less extensive and less institutionalised in the 1960s than they have subsequently become, these are treated as exogenous. Analysis of contemporary economic policy would require them to be included as a sixth set of actors within the policy terrain. Finally, at the lowest level lies the organisational culture of the institutions and networks within the policy terrain.

The schema's third element is the incorporation of Easton's 'policy feedback loop' – a recognition that the implementation of policy can change the environment and that this changed environment will, in turn, affect the subsequent actions of actors in any policy network within the policy terrain, and perhaps also the structure of the policy network itself.[9] Actors and networks within the policy terrain 'learn' from, or at least react to, policy failures and successes as suggested by Heclo and Hall. Of course, exogenous factors may also produce environmental change, change that will itself feedback into learning within the policy terrain. Thus what I have termed the policy terrain is an open system that responds to changes in its environment.

Finally, the small arrow flowing from the top right of the policy terrain into the environmental box represents the way in which actors and networks within the terrain can change the policy environment through the medium of ideas. New ideas may be developed, perhaps by academics or think tanks, and may be promoted by interest groups via issue networks. Often the impact of such ideas on the core executive decision making network will be indirect; actors in the core executive responding to a change in the overall policy environment produced by the issue network. It is this process that the 'ideas' arrow is modelling. In theory any of the actors within the policy terrain might be capable of influencing the intellectual environment in this way. In practice, however, this influence is almost invariably exercised indirectly through the 'issue' grouping, and most often through the media.[10] To a great degree, the media is the means by which ideas are communicated to society as a whole and it is an important influence on voters (Parsons 1989). Links between the media and other actors and networks within the policy terrain are so multitudinous that no attempt has been made to illustrate them. Of course, ideas may also impact on the core executive decision making network directly, via links between this network and the issue network promoting the idea. The degree to which a new idea affects the external environment, and/or is disseminated within the policy terrain, will depend on the extent of the network that builds up around it, on the strategic decisions taken by actors within the network, and also on the degree (if any) to which this network is linked to the core executive decision making network.

The schema therefore builds on the strengths of policy network theory and of theories of social and political learning. By using the network approach it widens the analysis from the limited focus of the Westminster model, acknowledges the complexity, fluidity and fragmentary nature of policy making, and recognises the existence of power dependencies. It emphasises the importance of institutional relations and of the impact of context and structure on policy making but also reintroduces actors into the analysis and thus allows networks to overlap. The ability to construct 'meta networks' within the schema allows the insight of the segmented decision making model to be incorporated and recognises that the actors and networks that will be involved in different orders of change will vary. Mapping networks in this way allows the analysis to dispense with a typology of networks and recognise that policy networks will be many and varied in form, with different degrees of commitment, integration, resources, and power. Finally, the inclusion of the policy feedback loop and of environmental change via the construction and promotion of new ideas introduces a dynamic into the analysis of the policy making process that is missing from unmodified policy network theory and, by providing a structural explanation of idea transmission, provides an important component missing from learning theories.

Hall's three orders of change considered in terms of the schema

In this section, to illustrate the operation of the schema and to provide a model of paradigm change against which to compare the policy shift that occurred in the 1960s, the schema is used to examine the particular instances of first, second and third order change outlined by Hall (1993) in his analysis of social learning in UK economic policy during the 1970s and early-1980s. Figure 2.3 shows, in bold, the policy network and learning process that can be detected in Hall's analysis of first order change in this period. The bold dashed lines indicate peripheral parts of the network.

Hall found that first order policy change took place with specific reference to the lessons of past policy and was largely driven by officials who controlled both the process of economic forecasting and the advice

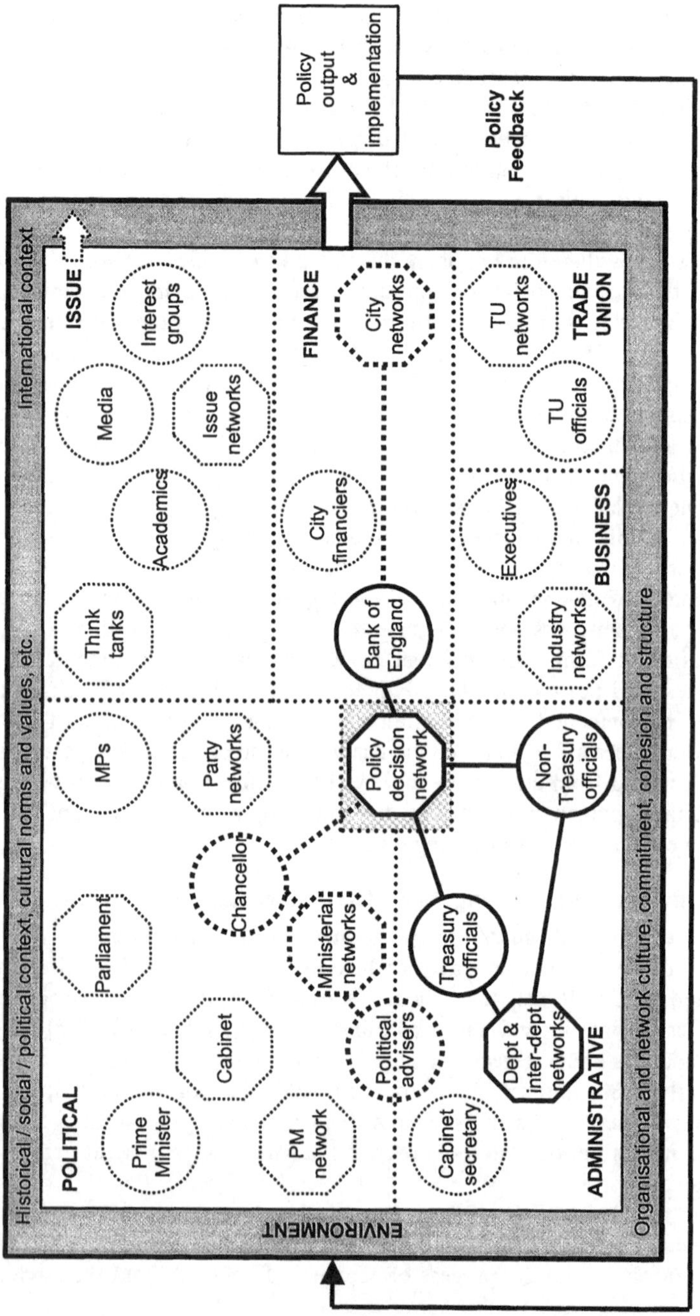

Figure 2.3 1st order change in UK economic policy in the 1970s

going to the chancellor. Treasury ministers could influence the direction of policy to a certain extent (Callaghan, for example, managing to insist on a lower rate tax band in 1978) but in general lacked the economic expertise to gainsay official advice (see also Theakston 1995: 17). Senior officials at the Treasury had a great deal of influence because they set the framework within which policy questions were considered (see also Hall 1982: 655). In addition, officials were relatively insulated from industrial, trade union and interest group networks that might have been expected to exert pressure on policy. In Hall's view, therefore, first order change was a response to policy feedback and, whilst politicians (and their advisers) were present in the core decision making network, it was officials who dominated the process. Thus, in Hall's description of first order change, a policy network emerges that is close to the traditional view of a closely bounded British economic policy making community but which gives rather more prominence to the importance of officials in the initiation of policy.

Hall (1993) also examined three instances of second order economic policy change during this period. Figure 2.4 shows, in bold, the policy network and process of learning that can be found in these. First, was the alterations to credit control mechanisms inaugurated by the Bank of England's 1971 consultative document on Competition and Credit Control (CCC). Both Hall and Middleton (1996: 550-1) emphasise the roots of CCC in growing dissatisfaction in the City with the existing system of credit ceilings and direct controls (see also Dimsdale 1991: 117-25). The CCC system reflected the then Conservative government's preference for indirect rather than direct government control, its belief in market forces and its attempts to redefine the economic role of government. Nevertheless, CCC (initiated by the Bank before the Conservatives were elected and then simply adjusted by officials to fit the Conservative agenda) was implemented within a set of overall economic goals that remained broadly unchanged, thus amounting to only a second order change (see also Oliver and Pemberton 2004).

Second, was the introduction of 'cash limits' in the mid-1970s. Hall concluded that Treasury officials, dissatisfied with the existing system of planning public expenditure in terms of volume rather than price, initiated the policy in an attempt to improve their control over public expenditure at a time of rising inflation. Again, Hall emphasised the 'technocratic' nature of the policy change; the Treasury having devised the system before Labour took office in 1974 and then presented it to the new Chancellor when appropriate circumstances arose.

Finally, post-1979, Hall emphasises the role played by Treasury and Bank of England officials during the early-1980s in persuading ministers

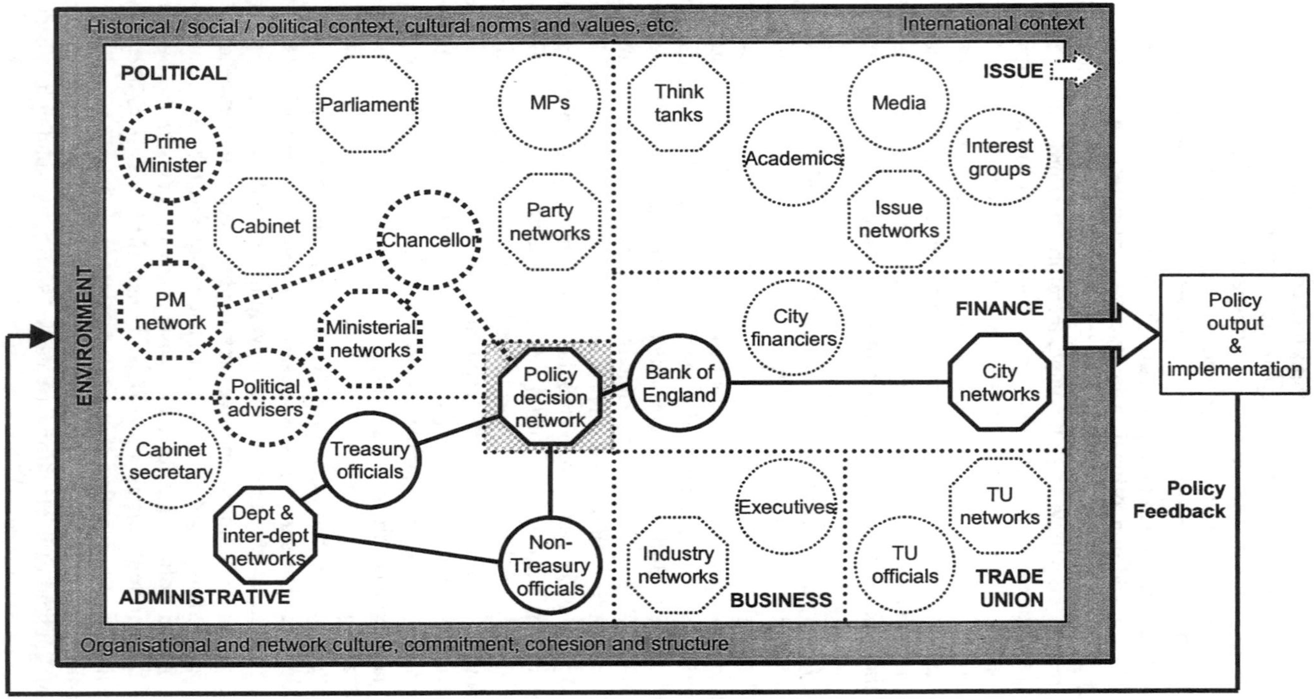

Figure 2.4 2nd order change in UK economic policy in the 1970s and early-1980s

to drop the rigid target for money supply growth (M3), as a consequence of the persistent failures to attain it, and to introduce new monetary aggregates.

In all three cases of second order change, therefore, policy feedback changed the environment and this led actors to learn from past mistakes. As with first order change, although the evidence is less clear cut, the key players in the core decision making network tended to be officials, not politicians. Thus, in Hall's descriptions of second order change, a policy network emerges that is again very close to the traditional view of a closely bounded British economic policy making community centred on Whitehall – albeit with links to financial networks in the City via the Bank of England.

A very different, and much more extensive, network emerges from Hall's analysis of third order change in the 1970s. Figure 2.5 illustrates the extensive meta network detected in Hall's (1993) description of the replacement of the Keynesian economic policy making paradigm by a monetarist paradigm. Briefly, in Hall's view the process was begun by the appearance of stagflation (rising inflation coupled with lacklustre growth in output and employment) that the Keynesian paradigm 'could neither fully anticipate nor explain' (Hall 1993: 285). In their attempts to cope with stagflation, officials tried a series of policy experiments such as the incomes policies of 1972–74 and 1975–77. In Hall's view these amounted to little more than the adjustment of traditional Keynesian (or more correctly Keynesian-plus) policy instruments. Hall argued that, because the problem lay outside the prevailing paradigm, the succession of first and second order changes was doomed to fail. The solution lay, instead, in changing the very framework within which economic policy was formed. In Hall's view the Labour government's experiment with monetary targets in 1976 did not mark a fundamental policy shift . Instead, it served only to erode further the efficacy of Keynesian policy instruments, by increasing the power of financial markets over the government at a time when rising unemployment was raising its borrowing requirement. In Hall's opinion the definitive adoption of 'monetarism' did not occur until the election of the Conservatives in 1979. This is a contentious analysis. Others have placed the turning point earlier, under the 1974–79 Labour government (for example Smith 1987: 65; Artis et al 1992). There is, however, a significant literature which supports Hall's view (see for example Cairncross 1995: 226; Morgan 1998: 507; Hay 2001: 209).

One should note, however, that Hall may overemphasise the coherence of monetarist policy in the late-1970s and 1980s and thus see the paradigm shift as more simple than it was. Whilst the 1979 election was

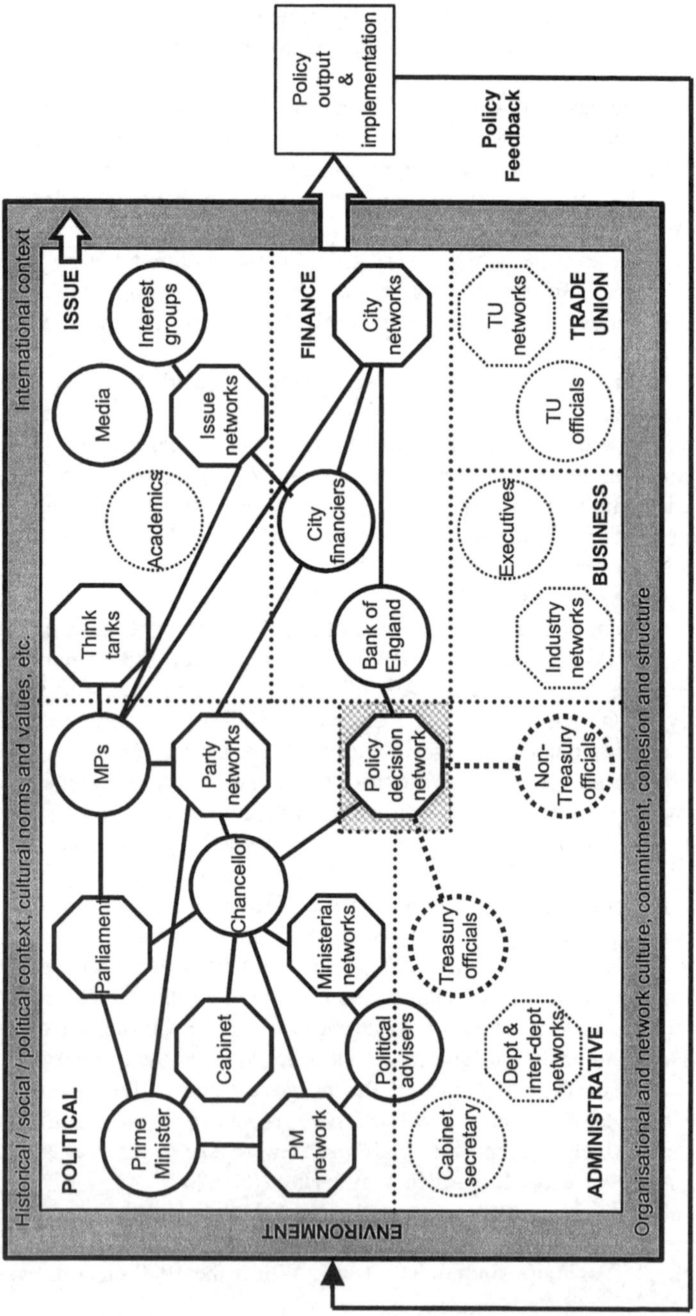

Figure 2.5 3rd order change in UK economic policy in the 1970s and early-1980s

indeed a decisive event the neo-liberal paradigm that came to characterise the last two decades of the twentieth century did not leap fully- fledged onto the stage. Instead, an initial shift to 'monetarism' was followed by a succession of first and second order changes during the 1980s during which the framework evolved into a more generalised neoliberal policy framework (Oliver 1997: 11-17 and 141-2; Oliver and Pemberton 2004). Nevertheless, Hall's description of the fraying of government authority in economic policy, the development of a 'market place for ideas', and the political salience of the 1979 election stands; and the policy network at work in the initial paradigm shift, as outlined in Figure 2.5, also holds true.

Hall's point is that the failure of the Treasury to develop an effective policy solution produced a shift of authority during the mid- to late-seventies. As the inability of the traditional government decision making network to solve the problem of stagflation became manifest, alternative ideas began to be explored in other quarters. Hall highlights the significant growth in the 'marketplace in economic ideas' as a key element in the subsequent third order change. He cites the plethora of new research institutes that sprang up to investigate economic policy options, the expansion of economic research by financial institutions, and the development of a sophisticated debate in the financial press over the direction of economic policy (see also Keegan and Pennant-Rea 1979: 131-40; Parsons 1989: 172-81; Middleton 1996: 546; Pepper 1999). Hall identifies the promotion of monetarist ideas by journalists, particularly the ideas of American academics, as central to the Conservative's developing ideological attack on Labour. British academics remained overwhelmingly Keynesian (Wickham-Jones 1992) – but those who were not were mobilised to maximum effect by 'think tanks' (such as the Institute for Economic Affairs, Centre for Policy Studies and, after 1978, Adam Smith Institute) which became the principal agents of change of the Conservative Party (Cockett 1995: 243-80).

In Hall's view, therefore, the construction and dissemination of new ideas, a process triggered by negative policy feedback, drove change. These ideas gained power through the network links that developed between those demanding new ideas and those supplying them and through the environmental change that these ideas produced (as explored by the 'ideas' arrow at the top right of Figure 2.5). The Conservative victory in 1979, Hall argued, then institutionalised the new policy paradigm. As Hall (1993: 287) puts it: the 'struggle to replace one policy paradigm with another was a societywide affair, mediated by the press, deeply imbricated with electoral competition, and fought in the public arena'. In terms of our schema, the traditional economic policy decision making network was overwhelmed by the extensive policy meta network which formed during this process and which grew out from the 'issue' sector of the schema to eventually penetrate this network at the core of the core executive. In this case it was not government officials who dominated; it was politicians and the media, with the support of the financial institutions. Figure 2.5 shows the end product of the process of policy network creation and growth.

Conclusions

This chapter has proposed a schema which combines elements of the policy network and social learning approaches, and which can be used to map the actors and networks at work in the making of economic policy. The elements of the two approaches which have been used are those which have been identified as particularly powerful, and complementary, components in the analyses. Using the insights of the policy network approach allows the analysis include a range of actors and networks from both state and civil society that are excluded from the Westminster model. The schema acknowledges the complexity, fluidity and fragmentary nature of economic policy making and recognises the existence and influence of power dependencies within policy networks. It emphasises the importance of institutional relations and the impact of context and structure on policy making. It builds on the insights of the segmented decision making model and allow the actors and networks involved in different areas of policy and orders of change to vary.

At the same time, the schema has been constructed to minimise the drawbacks which this chapter has identified in the policy network and social learning approaches. The schema reintroduces actors into policy network analysis and recognises that networks can overlap. The concept of 'meta networks' and allowing dynamic network configurations dispenses with an unnecessarily restrictive network typology. The schema recognises the fluidity and variegated nature of policy networks and also acknowledges that commitment, integration, resources, and power can vary both between networks and within networks over time.

Finally, the inclusion of learning via the policy feedback loop, of environmental change via the construction and promotion of new ideas by policy networks (via the 'ideas arrow'), and of idea transmission across networks both opens the analysis of policy networks to forces which dynamise the policy making process and recognises that both actors and networks are conditioned and constrained by the environment within which they operate.

Used in this way the policy network and social learning approaches complement each other. The policy network model benefits from the dynamism of policy learning and changing ideas. The social learning model benefits from an emphasis on the role of structure in conditioning policy making.

We will now employ the schema in the four subsequent chapters, using it to structure the analysis first of the policy shift that occurred in the early-1960s and then of the subsequent failure to institutionalise the new framework for the long-term.

3

The 'Great Reappraisal'

In the summer of 1961 the British government executed an economic policy summersault. On the 25th of July the chancellor, then Selwyn Lloyd, during a Commons debate on the emergency deflationary measures required to meet a severe sterling crisis, suddenly announced that, after ten years of 'Conservative Freedom Works' and 'Setting the People Free' the Conservatives proposed to embrace 'planning'.[1] He announced a compulsory 'pay pause' for public sector workers (intended to be the first step on the road to a full incomes policy), the first use of a new fiscal regulator to manipulate demand between budgets, and his intention to embrace five-year forward planning of consumption, investment and government spending in a new tripartite institution to be set up outside the Treasury.[2] Within eighteen months this new body had been created, in the form of the National Economic Development Council, the government had enshrined a 4 per cent growth target as its principal economic objective and, to attain this, had begun to implement new interventionary policy instruments in virtually all areas of economic policy.

However, whilst it appeared to be a 'dramatic and almost overnight conversion' (T. Smith 1975: 53) the policy shift had, not surprisingly, been some time in the making. As we shall see, it was principally the result of a 'great reappraisal' of economic policy by the Treasury during 1960–61 (Brittan 1964: Ch. 7). In turn, however, this reappraisal (or policy learning) was the product of a complex process that had unfolded over several years. This process had two dimensions; firstly, the impact of negative policy feedback from the economic policies of the 1950s and of consequent environmental change leading to learning within the core executive; secondly the growth, initiated by this environmental change, of a diffuse network of advocates of radical new economic policies, a network which was able both to promote further changes in the policy environment that favoured radical policy change and to influence members of the core executive more directly. This chapter reviews developments in each of these dimensions before going on to examine the learning that they gave rise to in Britain's core executive.

Environmental change

We begin with the environmental change that resulted from negative feedback from the economic policies of the 1950s. However, to suggest that lessons needed to be learned regarding the failure of economic policy in the 1950s appears at first sight to be rather odd. 'Measured by almost any of the available indicators, the fifties was a decade of economic progress for the British economy' (Worswick and Ady 1962: 68). By 1950, a vigorous post-war recovery had restored consumption to pre-war levels and the ensuing decade saw Britain, like other advanced economies, benefit from the high level of world demand. By historical standards, Britain's economic performance was exceptionally good during a decade in which it became a recognisably modern, affluent and consumer society' (Oppenheimer 1970; Hilton 2004; Pemberton 2004a). Macmillan's claim in 1957 that Britons had 'never had it so good' did not, on the face of it, seem unreasonable. Nevertheless, even as Macmillan spoke, there were already worries both about Britain's postwar economic performance and about its future prospects. By the end of the decade these had become widespread. Two interlinked factors worked to make the policy environment surprisingly pessimistic: emerging evidence of Britain's relative economic decline; and worries that the prevailing Keynesian policy framework contained within it the seeds of its own destruction.

Firstly, although Britain's rate of economic growth was historically impressive during the 1950s, particularly when compared with the inter-war period, the decade saw new comparative data emerge from post-war institutions such as the United Nations, GATT, IMF and OEEC that seemed to cast Britain's post-war performance in a much less positive light (Tomlinson 2000: 12-21). For example, new comparative national income statistics were published during the 1940s and 1950s by the UN and the OEEC/OECD. They showed Britain was slipping down the league table (Tomlinson 2000: 14 identifies the UN *Economic Survey of Europe* as particularly influential in promoting concerns in Britain at its relatively poor performance; see also Arndt 1978: 51; Pemberton 2004a). By 1961, both France and Germany had overtaken Britain in income per head for the first time since the industrial revolution (Cairncross 1996: 6). Similar data (see, for example, OEEC 1959) showed a relative decline in UK industrial production – seen at the time as fundamental to the health of any economy. This relatively poor growth of industrial production was reflected in comparative figures for industrial productivity growth; with Britain shown to have had the lowest productivity growth during the 1950s in a review of nine major industrialised countries by the *National Institute Economic Review* in July 1961. There was also the fear, stimulated by cold war tensions, that Britain (like the USA) was being badly outperformed by the USSR – fears fed by the launch of *Sputnik* by the latter in 1957.

Britain's relatively poor levels of growth in industrial production and industrial productivity compared to other OECD countries made themselves felt in two-ways. Firstly, they translated into a decline in the relative superiority of British living standards. Secondly, they had implications for international competitiveness; a fact made clear by OEEC *Statistical Bulletins* (Tomlinson 2000: 20). Indeed, Britain's export performance epitomized the paradox of absolute growth in conjunction with relative decline. Whilst British exports grew strongly in the 1950s in absolute terms, a reflection of the rapid expansion of world trade, contemporary data showed a marked decline in Britain's share of world trade (see Figure 3.1).

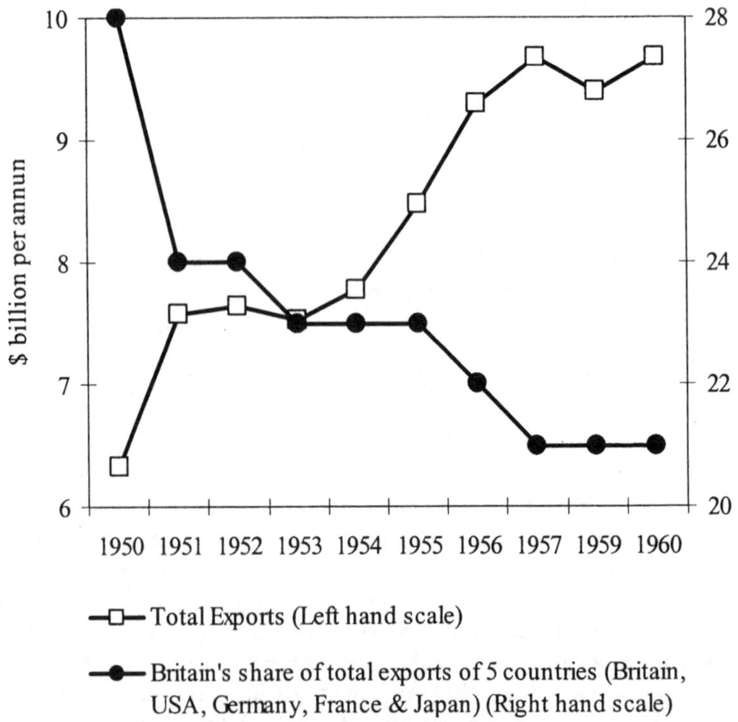

Figure 3.1 Britain's export performance in the 1950s
Source: Worswick and Ady 1962: 117.

the end of the Second World War, artificially bolstered as it was by the virtual economic destruction of significant competitors such as Germany. Economic 'decline' in this context was inevitable. It was not, however, without repercussions. Whilst relative economic decline had important psychological consequences (Hall 1986: 623; Tomlinson 1994, 2000; English and Kenny 1999b, 2001), and whilst the psychology of 'declinism' is now in vogue, relative economic decline can also be seen as an objective economic problem rather than just a subjective issue of perceptions (Pemberton 2004a). As Alec Cairncross (1995: 297) noted: 'The fundamental change was a loss of economic power: commercial power, bargaining power, financial power'. In short, Britain was becoming a much less significant actor in the world economy, with much less influence on its behaviour. Most notably, Britain continued to see itself as a world power with worldwide strategic commitments. Increasingly, Britain found that it was having to 'punch above its weight'. This had environmental implications that were both economic and political. Economically, it became increasingly difficult to sustain Britain's military, intelligence, and diplomatic expenditure commitments (Shonfield 1958; Middleton 2002a). Politically, it required a painful series of strategic adjustments as Britain was forced gradually to accept the consequences of its reduced power – for example the 1956 Suez debacle; the decision in 1960 to request the USA to supply Skybolt missiles (and thus the acceptance that Britain could no longer sustain a fully independent nuclear deterrent); the attempt to join the EEC in 1961 and the even more humiliating rejection by De Gaulle of this application; and the 1968 withdrawal from east of Suez.[3]

What cannot be denied is the power that the perception of relative decline (what Tomlinson 1996b termed the 'new declinism') exercised over the minds of policy makers, of commentators, and of the wider public at the start of the 1960s. It seemed clear to contemporaries that Britain was not just being caught up by its competitors, it was being overtaken. With her competitors amongst the advanced industrial economies achieving higher rates of growth, Britain's situation could be expected to continue to worsen. There was also a pervasive sense that this relative decline was the product of problems with the framework within which economic policy had been conducted during the 1950s (Leruez 1975: 82-3).

By the beginning of the 1960s there was a widespread sense that significant problems with the prevailing Keynesian policy framework were beginning to emerge.[4] Firstly, as can be seen in Table 3.1, whilst

Table 3.1 Performance of the British economy, 1948–1959

Year	1948	1949	1950	1951	1952	1953	1954	1955	1956	1957	1958	1959
GDP (% change)	3.5	4.5	3.5	3.5	-	4	4	3	2.0	1.5	-	4.0
Industrial production (% change)	8	6.5	6.5	3.5	-3	6	7	5	0.5	1.7	-1.1	6.0
Unemployment (%)	1.5	1.5	1.5	1.2	2.0	1.6	1.3	1.1	1.2	1.4	2.1	2.2
Retail price inflation (%)	5.9	3.3	3.0	11.8	6.7	1.4	3.4	5.9	3.3	4.4	1.5	-
Wage rate growth (%)	4.2	1.9	3.4	10.7	6.7	3.2	4.7	7.0	7.6	5.7	3.6	1.2
Balance of payments (current account, £m)	-	50	300	-425	150	125	150	-175	200	200	300	50

Note s: 1) The presence of '-' indicates nil or less than half the unit stated. 2) The figures for GDP and industrial production are the change of that year's average over the previous year.

Source: Dow 1964: 39, 75, 93.

average annual growth was impressive during the 1950s, Keynesian demand management had not abolished the business cycle; nor did it seem to have attenuated either its amplitude or its frequency. (Original data is used here because, whilst revisions to these figures over the succeeding decades have tended to indicate a slightly flatter cycle and to bring into question the relationship between economic growth and economic cycles (Middleton 2002a), it is important to view the data through the eyes of contemporaries if we are to understand the impact of the environmental change that occurred). In fact, by the beginning of the 1960s there seemed good reason to believe that Keynesian demand management was actually destabilising the economy – tending to exaggerate rather than smooth the economic cycle, with interventions to manipulate the level of demand in the economy tending to be both too late and too great as a consequence of problems with timely data collection and accurate forecasting (Dow 1964).[5]

Essentially, as Brittan (1964: 288) put it, the Treasury behaved during the 1950s and early-1960s 'like a simple Pavlovian dog responding to two main stimuli: One "a run on the reserves" and the other "500,000 unemployed"'. Sterling crises arose in 1951, 1955 and 1961. Each followed a period of rapid growth in domestic demand in which imports grew more rapidly than exports – a situation aggravated by the shift against Britain in the terms of trade after 1952, a change which made it more difficult for British industry to compete in international markets (Dow 1964: 385-92; Cairncross 1995: 114-26, 138-9; Foreman-Peck 1991: 167-9). Each such crisis produced a 'Pavlovian' reaction because, with a fixed exchange rate, a balance of payments deficit inevitably reduced (or a prospective deficit could be expected to reduce) Britain's finite reserves of gold and foreign currencies and required measures to be taken to reduce domestic demand – the more so since Britain's reserves were woefully inadequate for a reserve currency (Cooper 1968; Strange 1971), the commitment to which came to be criticised as anachronistic and symptomatic of an outdated view at the Bank of England and the Treasury of Britain's place in the world (Shonfield 1958). With the option of devaluation having been effectively removed by the collapse in 1952 of the 'Robot' proposals to float sterling and block 80 per cent of sterling balances held by members of the sterling area, this became an even more pressing issue with the advent of full convertibility in 1958 (Bulpitt and Burnham 1999; Peden 2000: 458-66).

Unemployment was a stimulus for government action because, despite the historically low levels of unemployment in the 1950s, and despite full employment being a core objective of the Keynesian policy framework, the level of unemployment was still politically very sensitive (Cairncross

1996: 22-4).[6] Although the average rate of unemployment in the 1950s now looks astonishingly benign, at the time two factors contributed to political concern. Firstly, the 'searing experience' of the mass unemployment in the 1930s continued to dominate the minds of those old enough to remember it – in other words virtually everyone over forty (Budd 1981). The commitment made in the 1944 *Employment Policy* White Paper (Cmd. 6527: para. 1) to maintain 'a high and stable level of employment', a commitment endorsed by the Conservatives in their 1947 *Industrial Charter*, made any deviation from full employment very contentious. Secondly, although the average rate of unemployment was generally very low, pockets of relatively high structural unemployment persisted in regions such as the North East and Northern Ireland, with this becoming a more pressing political issue after the 1958 recession (Cairncross 1996: 22-4; Lowe 1996).

Brittan's 'Pavlovian' cycle was exacerbated by problems encountered in executing Keynesian style demand management: difficulties in economic forecasting, particularly predicting the speed at which a given fiscal instrument would act upon demand; and the fact that demand management also seemed incapable of solving problems with the balance of payments and sterling (Dow 1964; Cohen 1971: 1-3, 29-34, 174-7; Hopkin 1981; Hatton and Crystal 1991: 68-9). The result was a series of economic upswings sharply cut off by sterling crises, credit squeezes and international borrowing – a cycle that came to be known as 'stop and go' or 'stop-go'.[7]

'Stop-go' seemed at the time to have had two unfortunate consequences. Firstly, it could be argued that each bout of deflation imposed a set of costs that was not recouped in the next upswing (Artis 1972: 265). Secondly, the unfortunate result of a poorly executed stabilisation policy which seemed in fact to *de*stabilise the economy, it could be argued, was to reduce investment – by reducing the confidence of firms that their investment would be recouped (Cohen 1971: 68; Dow 1964: 391:392; Musgrave and Musgrave 1968: 42-4; Worswick 1971; Nordhaus 1975; Budd 1978: 81). Thus stop-go seemed to be crippling both long and short-term expansion and by the early-1960s it was being identified as a significant constraint on economic growth and thus as a major failure of post-war Keynesian demand management (Worswick and Ady 1962: 273-4; Brittan 1964: 135-6; Leruez 1975: 84).[8] What was really needed, it was argued, were policies to strengthen the UK economy and build international confidence, and a preparedness to pursue steady growth and 'drive straight through fluctuations in the balance of payments' (Dow 1964: 399-403) – a point consistently made by the economist Sir Roy Harrod, practically the founding father of growth economics, to the prime minister.[9] The answer to many seemed to be some form of 'planning' and, as we shall see, calls for the injection of more 'planning' into British economic policy were legion by 1961 (Shonfield 1958; FBI 1960; PEP 1961a; Labour Party 1961; Shanks 1961).

This desire for radical change in the framework of British economic policy to address 'stop-go' and break out of the constraint posed by recurrent sterling crises was closely allied with a growing perception that achieving the objective of full employment via the maintenance of high demand might, paradoxically, be detrimental to economic growth. One fear was that full employment encouraged labour hoarding, demarcation disputes and poor industrial relations (PEP 1960: 48-50). The economist Joan Robinson well summed up such fears when she remarked in the mid-1950s that full employment was 'not so much a bottleneck as a powder barrel' (quoted by Leeson 1999: 506).[10] This, it was argued, had the effect of limiting the efficiency of industry and meant that the economy ran into capacity constraints during economic upturns more quickly than was desirable (Shonfield 1958; Dow 1964: 384). Another fear was that, in a high demand environment, firms had little incentive to innovate and compete for business (Paish 1962: 309-32).[11] The combined effect, it was argued, was to limit the efficiency of industry. This meant that the economy ran into capacity constraints during economic upturns more quickly than would have been wished, and this in turn had the potential to precipitate balance of payments problems, or at least to trigger fears of such problems that might themselves cause a run on the pound (Shonfield 1958; Dow 1964: 384).

Ironically, the competitive weaknesses in labour, technology and human capital formation which had been evident in the British economy before 1939 became more significant in the post-war period of higher demand (Middleton 1996: 466-7). This created new challenges for government in terms of intervention to correct market failure and improve efficiency. A number of significant 1950s supply-side initiatives attempted to remedy these problems, each of which might be seen as a second order change made in an attempt to stabilise the Keynesian paradigm – for example, the introduction of investment allowances, government support for research and development and the establishment of the Restrictive Practices Court in 1956. In practice, however, government attempts to dynamise the supply-side of the economy were diverted by continuing problems in declining industries and the tendency to use industrial policy for short-term stabilisation rather than encouraging long-term investment (Kirby 1991: 241-2). Towards the end of the decade, as the lessons of this failure sank in, attention began to turn, particularly within the Treasury, to how the framework of economic policy might be changed to improve the operation of Britain's supply-side.

Finally, but perhaps more important for the long-term stability of the Keynesian policy framework, was the fact that the 1950s saw a continuous rise in both prices and wages (see Table 3.1 above), and that after 1952 wages began to rise faster than the increase in productivity (Worswick and Ady 1962: 51-3). The 1956 white paper on *The economic implications of full employment* (Cmd. 9725) had highlighted the link between the 'social evil' of inflation and full employment, a link also emphasised by the 1944 White Paper on *Employment Policy* (Cmd. 6527: para. 49) and apparently confirmed by Phillips (1958) demonstration of an inverse relationship between the percentage rate of unemployment and the rate of change of average wage rates. Phillips' analysis emphasised the role of demand in causing inflation. It was highly influential but produced competing solutions. On the one hand there were calls for a reduction in the rate of demand (and thus an increase in the rate of unemployment) which would move the British economy down the Phillips curve and thus reduce inflation (Paish 1958, 1962). On the other hand were calls for action, via some sort of agreement with the unions, to ensure that wages did not rise faster than productivity and thus degrade competitiveness, the intended effect being to shift the negatively sloped Phillips curve to the left and thus allow a higher rate of growth for a given rate of inflation (a solution hinted at by the 1956 white paper on *The Economic Implications of Full Employment*).

The first option implicitly informed government policy during the 1950s (Macmillan's failed attempt in 1956 to achieve a 'price plateau' via restraint on the part of employers and unions excepted) but fell out of favour for two reasons. Firstly, it came to be seen as a significant contributor to 'stop-go'. Secondly, the government was simply not prepared to deflate the economy to the extent that proponents of this option argued was necessary if inflation was to be squeezed out of the system. In a political environment conditioned by the unemployment of the 1930s, such a course appeared to be an act of political suicide; hence the advice to ministers by the Conservative Research Department (CRD) in 1960 that Paish's proposal that the range of acceptable unemployment be raised from 2 to 4 per cent was 'politically out of the question'.[12] By the beginning of the 1960s an agreement on wage restraint, the second option, was beginning to look much more congenial; not least because it was consistent with a number of studies pointing to the role of 'cost push' in the production of inflation (Lipsey 1958, 1960; Dicks-Mireaux and Dow 1959); but also because it was consistent with growing concerns that the rate of economic growth needed to be accelerated, and with the view that this precluded a reduction in the level of demand.

By the start of the 1960s, therefore, there was considerable negative feedback from the economic policies of the 1950s. Keynesian demand management had created a pattern of 'stop-go' that seemed detrimental to growth. There were fears that the pursuit of full employment as a high priority policy objective, rather than full employment being a byproduct of policies designed to stimulate growth, was actually holding growth back. The existing Keynesian framework also seemed inherently inflationary. This was coupled with the 'new declinism' generated by emerging evidence of Britain's relative economic decline; sufficient time having passed since the war that the 'reconstruction' of the continental economies as an explanation for their better economic performance was seen to be no longer sufficient. The cumulative effect of this negative feedback was rising concern that Britain's economic policy framework was not producing adequate economic growth and the creation by the beginning of the 1960s of a policy environment that favoured radical change.

Network emergence and growth

Policy makers did not face a changed policy environment purely as a consequence of environmental feedback effects. They also faced pressure for change from a policy network that formed in response to, and fed, this negative feedback. Concern about Britain's 'growth problem' first became evident amongst academics in the middle of the 1950s. From there, a network began to form in which the problem of Britain's apparently lacklustre growth was discussed, and policy prescriptions proposed. This policy network became both complex and extensive and its final extent can be seen in Figure 3.2

Academics

Academic interest in growth was not restricted to Britain, it was an international phenomenon during the 1950s. It was driven by the experience of high levels of post-war growth; by a belief that (as Domar 1957: 18 put it) 'the preservation of full employment in a capitalist economy requires a growing income'; by the growing influence of growth theory (Harrod 1939, 1948 and 1951); by a growing acceptance that governments could play an important role in sustaining high and steady levels of demand and investment; by improvements in the data available to economists; and by a desire to understand the reason why growth rates should differ between countries, a phenomenon revealed by this new data

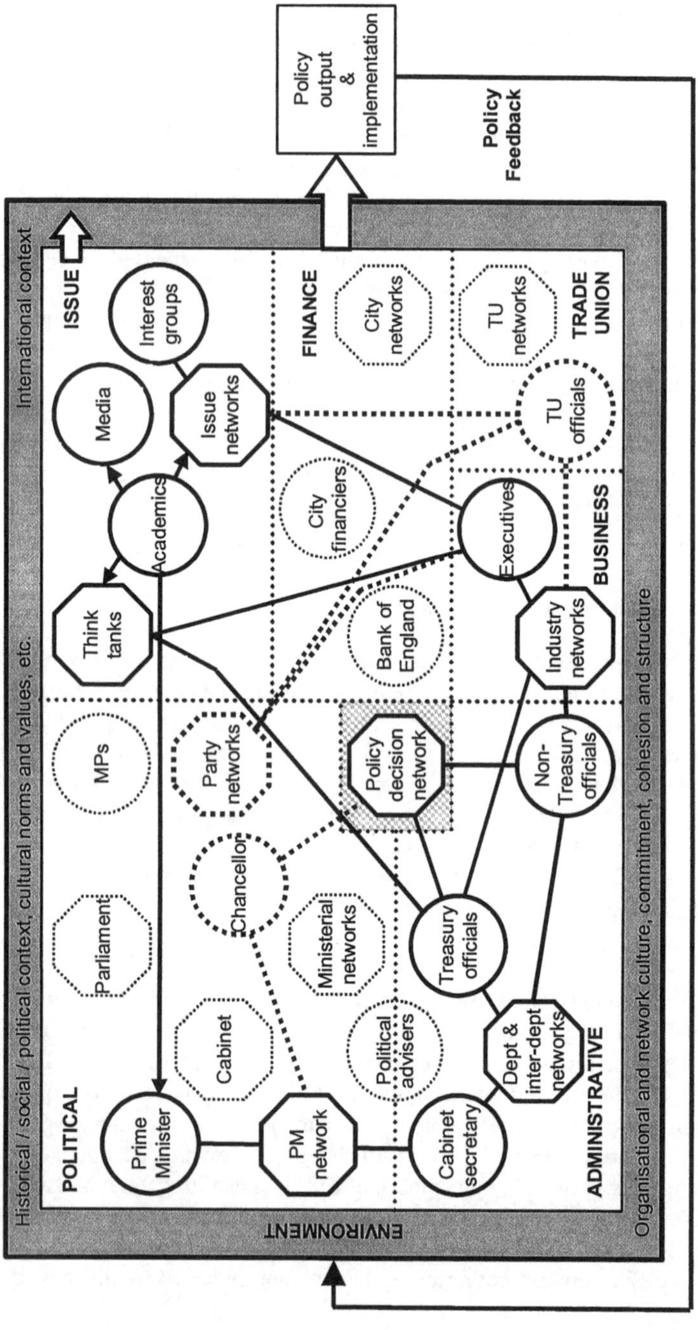

Figure 3.2 The growth advocacy network, 1955-1961

(Maddison 1964; Henderson 1966; Arndt 1978).[13] There were notable increases in academic output in the middle of the decade and at its end, as can be clearly seen in Figure 3.3 – an analysis of the most detailed available index of articles published in English language economic journals. It was associated with the parallel emergence of the new subdiscipline of development economics (Arndt 1978), the key work in this field being Rostow's (1960) stage theory of economic development. The result was a

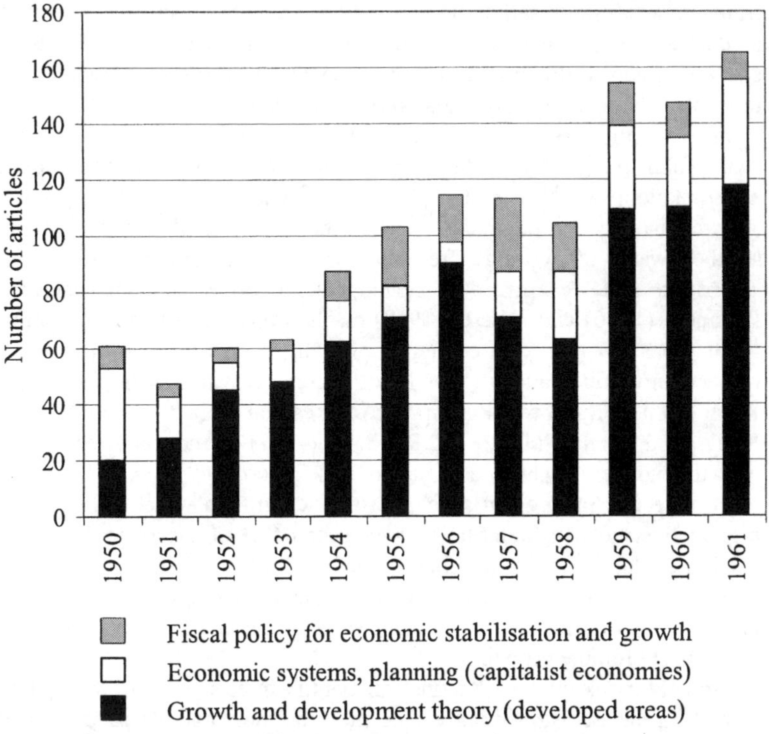

Figure 3.3 Economic journal articles (selected headings related to growth)[14]
Source: Index of Economic Journals, Vols. IV, V and VI

marked increase in economists' interest in, but not in retrospect necessarily an equivalent understanding of, the mechanics of growth. In the early-1950s it was possible for Moses Abramovitz (1952: 132), originator of the idea that catch up and convergence could explain why growth rates differ between countries, to comment that 'the problem of economic growth lacks any organized and generally known body of doctrine'. By the 1960s, it seemed that such was the analytical progress that there was a danger of diminishing returns setting in (Hahn and Matthews 1964: 890).[15]

In a specifically British context, academic interest in theories of growth became bound up with the impact of economic fluctuations on the rate of growth and with explaining why Britain's growth rate was apparently so low relative to many of its competitors (Arndt 1978). This was the product on the one hand of Britain's explicitly Keynesian framework of stabilisation policy and on the other hand of emerging evidence of its relative economic decline. One can identify two bursts of analysis, each following a recession. After, the 1955 recession, for example, there were important articles written by Harrod (1956) on cyclical fluctuations; by Kaldor (1957) on economic growth models; by Joan Robinson (1957) on the relationship between growth and capital accumulation; and by Streeten (1955) and Henderson (1955) on growth and the balance of payments.[16] After the 1958 'stop' one then finds another wave of writings from authors such as Harrod (1960) on stagnation and dynamism in developed economies; Streeten (1959), Passinetti (1960) and Neisser (1960) on the impact of short-term output fluctuations on long-term economic growth; Cairncross (1962) on long run economic fluctuations in the British economy; Cairncross (1959) and Kahn (1959) on the relationship between capital formation and growth; Kaldor and Mirrlees (1962) and Robinson (1961) on models of economic growth; and Denison (1962) on how to raise growth.

Despite this upsurge in academic production – in which 'the growth rate of the "growth literature" far exceeded that of the phenomenon it tried to explain' (Dennis Mueller, quoted by Middleton 2004: 134) – it is important to note that there was little theoretical agreement on why growth rates differed between countries or on the policy framework that might best promote growth.

Broadly speaking, by 1960 one can identify three schools of thought on growth in the British economy. The first, the most notable proponent of which was Professor Frank Paish, involved running the economy with a lower pressure of demand; thus allowing unemployment to rise above 2 per cent, the level then regarded as the trigger for reflation, shaking out inefficiently used labour, improving industrial efficiency and increasing international competitiveness.[17] A second prescription, the most notable advocate of which was Sir Robert Hall, the government's chief economic adviser and head of the Treasury's Economic Section, was to maintain fairly high demand to avoid the wasteful effects of unproductive capacity and unemployment, but address 'stop-go' by improving the government's stabilisation policy instruments, and institute an incomes policy to control inflation.[18] Thirdly, there was the more radical 'dash for growth' advocated by Sir Roy Harrod. Harrod argued that exporters needed a buoyant home market and that this required a high pressure of demand and a preparedness to 'drive through' any fluctuations in the balance of payments and, if necessary, introduce import controls or devalue.[19] Behind this idea were two assumptions. First, that higher growth would deliver lower unit costs, which would then feedback into more growth. Second that the size of the public sector would be held steady as the economy grew to allow a gradual reduction of taxes as a proportion of GDP; thus encouraging more consumption, investment and growth.

Ideas have no impact by themselves but they can play an important role in policy change when they are consumed by policy actors and a significant indirect role through their impact on public opinion (Berman 1998: 22). As Middleton (2004) points out, because academics were divided formal economic theory could contribute little to the practical formulation of policy. The importance of academic economists did not lie, therefore, in specific theoretical advances. Instead, it lay in the way in which the heated academic debate about the economics of growth, and the feeling that UK growth might be higher than it was, 'radiated' into the consciousness of others (Cairncross 1970: 14; Coats 1971: 28-44). As Arndt (1978: 35) put it:

> In a general way, academic growth theory accustomed economists, and throught them newspapers and politicians, to thinking about the economy in terms of rates of 'economic growth'. This mental revolution ... coloured policy attitudes.

Wayne Parsons (1989: 84-5, 98-109) is clearly wrong to argue that academic economists had little influence over economic policy at this time simply because they tended not to write regularly in the press. Actors in the core executive were plainly aware of academic thought if they happened to be an economist or the recipient of academic advice. Hall, for example, as an economist, took his prescription directly into the heart of the core executive of which he was a member. As an adviser to the Prime Minister, Harrod was also able to inject his ideas directly into the core executive.[20] For those not receiving such advice academic economists could seem rather distant (Graham 1996); but one should not underestimate the indirect influence on the policy environment of economists who were media friendly. The Paish approach, for example, had supporters within the Treasury (Graham 1996) who followed his developing thesis via articles in the press, though by 1962 the Treasury had rejected its fundamental assumptions.[21] In particular, one should not underestimate the role played in changing the broader climate of opinion by Roy Harrod's campaign to promote his ideas through 356 items contributed to 99 media between 1951–59 (Phelps Brown 1980: 30). Mark Blaug (1985: 84) noted that Harrod's 'journalistic output, quite apart from his more serious publications ... was so prodigious as to defy belief'. Harrod also carefully targeted business leaders through business journals and meetings.[22] Thus academic concerns about growth, and their ideas about how it might be raised, also indirectly entered the consciousness of both actors in the core executive and the wider public (Cairncross 1970: 14; Coates 1971: 28-44).

Journalists

An important factor in the 'radiation' of academic ideas on growth was the interest in them shown by financial journalists. Interest in growth by journalists lagged behind that of academic economists but also reached a crescendo in 1960–61. Their importance was that they were much more able than academics to communicate to the public the new ideas about how to raise growth.

Such journalists included Andew Shonfield (economics editor at the *Observer*), Michael Shanks (industrial editor of the *Financial Times*), Eric Wigham (the *Observer*'s labour correspondent), Norman Macrae (journalist and leader writer at *The Economist*), Samuel Brittan (economics correspondent on the *Financial Times*), Robert Collin (a journalist on the *Financial Times* and author of the *New Statesman*'s 'City Lights' column) and Nicholas Davenport (financial correspondent on *The Spectator*). Through their columns and through the publication of popular books (such as Shonfield 1958; Shanks 1961; Wigham 1961; and Macrae 1963), financial journalists publicised the concept of relative economic decline and the idea that new policies to promote higher growth could solve Britain's economic growth 'problem'. Thereby, they were a significant force in radically altering the policy environment in favour of change.

All these authors were important contributors to the 'state of the nation' literature that emerged in the closing years of the 1950s and the start of the 1960s, a literature typified by Penguin's 'What's wrong with Britain' series (Grant 2003). Shanks, for example, was the Will Hutton of his day, selling over 60,000 copies of his 1961 Penguin Special *The stagnant society*, a book that, like Hutton's (1996) *The state we're in* was rather muddled in its analysis and simplistic in its policy prescriptions but brilliantly crystallised a widespread discontent with contemporary economic policy and fed a popular desire for change.

This 'reformist literature' reached a crescendo in the lead up to Selwyn Lloyd's announcement of a policy shift in July 1961. It played an important part in the creation of an intellectual climate that favoured radical new policies and upon which the Conservatives were able to draw in crafting a new policy framework after 1961 (T. Smith 1975: 61; Keegan and Pennant-Rea 1979: 139). The importance of the financial press in transmitting economic ideas and changing 'informed opinion' is emphasised by Middleton (1998: 74) and Parson (1989), and the late-1950s and 1960s really marked the beginning of such influence. Financial journalists were then writing for a much bigger audience than hitherto as a consequence of the rise in the number of people with economics training and the number with sufficient education, as a consequence of the 1944 Education Act, to be interested in economics (Parsons 1989: 100-2).

Inevitably, financial journalists did not entirely agree on the nature of the economic problem, but there were two common elements to their analysis. The first was a view of contemporary Britain as moribund, commercially inefficient, dominated by an amateurish and complacent 'establishment', and unable to come to terms with its diminished importance in the wake of the Second World War (Shonfield 1958; Shanks 1961; Sampson 1962).[23] As Brittan (1997) remarked, 'if there is one word [sic] which summarises everything that the reformers of the 1960s were opposing it is "fuddy duddyism"'. The second common element was an agreement that economic growth had been erratic because the government's management of demand had been both badly timed and disrupted by recurrent sterling crises. As a consequence, it was suggested, industrial confidence was being undermined, investment reduced and the country's economic growth potential was being damaged. The government was also criticised for neglecting the improvement of industrial efficiency.

Nevertheless, whilst there was a striking unanimity that current economic policy was inadequate and needed to change, there was initially less agreement over *how* it should change. By mid-1961, however, opinion had coalesced around the idea that more 'planning' might be the solution. The *New Statesman*'s 'City Lights' column, for example, persistently called for policy to take a longer term view and for a policy of 'planning for expansion'. By mid-1961 it was calling for 'drastic change'.[24] Such criticism of the government's economic policy from a journal sympathetic to Labour might be expected. During 1960 and early-1961, however, there were also leading articles in the *Financial Times* calling for 'new methods of control' in order to obtain more steady growth, and in *The Times* asking if perhaps a five year plan was not required in order to steady the economy.[25] *The Economist*, in its review of economic prospects at the end of 1960, looked forward rather glumly to the prospect of another 'prolonged and wasteful, slowdown in production' and in March 1961 despairingly cried: 'We *have* to get out of this stop-go cycle'.[26] Noting that growth had 'become the favourite (and most welcome) economic fashion for the Spring of 1961', the journal initially opposed to calls for more government planning.[27] By June 1961, however it was arguing in a leading article that 'the present administrative and executive and [*sic*] attitude creating mechanism in Whitehall for providing Britain with a long-term economic policy has failed' and that it was now imperative that the Conservatives consider policy changes, particularly in the area of 'planning'.[28] Even the normally pro Conservative *Spectator* was persuaded. Its financial columnist, Nicholas Davenport, was highly critical of government policy. He strongly favoured the Harrod thesis and throughout 1960 and 1961 his weekly economics column placed the blame for stop-go on the destabilising effects of the government's so called 'stabilisation' policies.[29]

Parsons (1989: 84-5) noted that Davenport epitomised the intellectual dominance of interventionary ideas about economic policy and by 1961 he was regularly advocating tripartite planning, a four year plan and a wages policy.[30] Davenport's advocacy in early-1961 of radical change in the framework of economic policy was symptomatic of many newspapers and periodicals. Increasingly, the involvement of industry in planning economic policy was seen by financial journalists as essential if the level of investment was to be raised, thus allowing output to be increased without the need for a greater supply of by now scarce labour. A growing acceptance in the press that full employment carried a cost in the shape of labour shortages and inflation also led journalists to the conclusion that the trade unions must be involved in planning – since organised labour seemed to hold the key to both problems.[31] By the end of June 1961 there was general support for the concept of 'indicative planning'. Its definition remained somewhat vague but most commentators hoped it would improve growth via improved expectations, better knowledge, coordinated output decisions, the removal of obstacles to growth (Sandford 1976: 55). Indeed, such was the unanimity that radical change on these lines was required to end stop-go and stimulate UK economic growth that it is difficult to find any dissenting voices in the British press by mid-1961.

As Parsons (1989: 109) noted:

> That such ideas were being voiced in the leading organs of the financial press could only have served to enhance its political acceptability … what was most significant about the contribution of economic journalists was they had a capacity to aggregate and disseminate ideas by applying them to events: they caught the mood.

They did more than this, however, for by disseminating both the idea that radical policy change was required and by increasingly pressing upon the government a common policy solution, financial journalists helped to create a policy environment that favoured such change.

Moreover, the *zeitgeist* had come to favour change in a more general sense. The success of the satirical *Beyond the Fringe* (which opened in May 1961), John Osborne's 'Damn you England' letter in 1960, the Lady Chatterley trial in October 1960, and the beginnings of a popular 'new wave' of British cinema with *Room at the Top* (1959) and *Saturday Night and Sunday Morning* (1960) were evidence of a major cultural shift and of the coming of a new generation that excoriated the 'establishment' and repudiated the policies of the 1950s.[32] As Blake (1985: 295-6) noted, this rise in 'anti-establishment' sentiment created strong pressures on the Conservatives to adopt new policies.

Think tanks and pressure groups

By 1961, financial journalists, and the academics from which their ideas flowed, might be said to have formed an 'epistemic community' (Haas 1990: 40-6) sharing a common assumption that policy needed to change and increasingly a common model of how it should change, if not a common set of political values. As Haas acknowledged, however, the success of such a community depends not just on the persuasiveness of the ideas it advances but on its ability to construct links with the dominant political coalition. In the process of constructing such links this 'network of the like minded', or what one might term the 'growth advocacy network' increasingly took on a physical form. We have already noted links between academic economists and the core executive but important links were also built with other opinion formers, not least with think tanks and pressure groups.

The most influential of such pressure groups was Political and Economic Planning (PEP), a non-party organisation set up in the interwar years to promote planning which was proud of its ability to 'influence affairs and secure results'.[33] Influential actors involved in PEP in the late-1950s and 1960s did not just include academics (not least Alec Cairncross, shortly to be appointed as the government's chief economic adviser) and financial journalists such as Samuel Brittan. They also included ministers such as Harold Macmillan (who had been closely involved with PEP since the 1930s), 'Rab' Butler and Edward Boyle (Financial Secretary to the Treasury, 1959–62); industrialists such as Sir Robert Shone (then director of the Iron and Steel Board but shortly to be appointed director general of the new NEDC); and senior civil servants such as Sir Noel Hall (principal of the Administrative Staff College,

Henley) and Eric Roll (shortly to be appointed deputy leader of the UK delegation negotiating entry to the EEC in 1961 and then Permanent Secretary of the new Department of Economic Affairs in 1964).[34]

PEP issued a steady stream of books and pamphlets on the subject of growth towards the end of the 1950s and in the early years of the 1960s. *The Price of Stability*, for example, reviewed UK economic policy in 1958 and concluded that an agreement with the unions was needed if further balance of payments crises were to be avoided. In 1960 it published its highly influential report *Growth in the British Economy* – the product of a research group which had been working on the question for the past three years. This concluded that 'investment in the public sector must be controlled, and in the private sector guided, according to published targets and programmes for the growth of the most important industries' (PEP 1960: vii, 236-46). It advocated that priority be given to relieving the shortage of labour that would otherwise be generated by increased growth – by encouraging labour saving capital investment and discouraging over manning. Attention should also be given to ways of improving the mobility of labour and improving the quality of the labour force via better technical education and improved general education. The taxation system, it concluded, should be designed so as to minimise the disincentives, and maximise the incentives, to investment, enterprise and efficient labour usage. A long-term attempt should be made to find a cure for inflation in order to allow high demand to be sustained. The strain on the balance of payments should be relieved by abandoning overseas expenditures which 'appear to have survived out of regard for tradition, or for the sake of pure prestige' and by joining the EEC in order to encourage UK businesses to become more competitive.

The publication of *Growth in the British Economy* was immensely significant. The inclusion amongst its authors of industrialists and others close to industry meant that its findings and recommendations were read with great interest in industry (Blank 1973: 147, 164).[35] Its findings informed much of the subsequent analysis in the press. It was read with particular interest in the Conservative Party's research department and was fed by it into the deliberations of the party's policy committee on growth when it was set up in December 1960 (see discussion below).[36] It was also the trigger for the Treasury's own enquiries during 1960–61 into how to raise growth (also discussed in more detail below).[37]

Another very significant role played by PEP was physically to gather together the members of the growth advocacy network that emerged between 1955 and 1961. In conjunction with the think tank The National Institute for Economic and Social Research (NIESR), for example, it organised an influential two day conference on French planning in April

1961 which brought academic and business economists, financial journalists, ministers (not least Edward Boyle, Financial Secretary to the Treasury), government officials, industrialists connected with the Federation of British Industries, British Employers' Confederation and British Chambers of Commerce, trade unionists (including George Woodcock, General Secretary of the TUC), and representatives from think tanks, pressure groups and political parties together with representatives of the French Commissariat Général du Plan and related French institutions (PEP 1961b). Significant non-governmental members of the growth advocacy network that were present included economists and economic advisers such as W. Beckerman (principal researcher on the NIESR growth project, and from 1964 economic consultant at the Department of Economic Affairs), J.C.R. Dow (then at the NIESR but formerly a member of the Treasury Economic Section, and shortly to return there), I.M.D. Little (Nuffield College, Oxford but until 1955 deputy director of the Treasury's Economic Section), R. Neild (deputy director of the NIESR, later adviser to James Callaghan when shadow chancellor and, from 1964 his economic adviser in the Treasury), E.H. Phelps-Brown (LSE and from 1962 a member of the NEDC), C.T. Saunders (director of the NIESR, but an official at the Central Statistical Office until 1957), and G.D.N Worswick (Oxford Institute of Statistics); industrialists such as Sir Robert Shone (Iron and Steel Board, but from 1962 director general of the NEDC); the journalists Andrew Shonfield Michael Shanks and Samuel Brittan; Shirley Williams from the Fabian Society; and M. Brazil from the Conservative Bow Group.[38] The role of this conference in radically altering official attitudes was shortly to be acknowledged by the Treasury in its July 1961 submission to the cabinet on economic growth – a key moment in the development of a new policy framework.[39]

The link between PEP and the NIESR was significant. The 1961 conference was organised as part of a major NIESR project investigating the long-term prospects for the British economy that had began work in 1960.[40] The NIESR was itself a meeting point for economists and economic policy actors from academia, government, industry, trade unions and the media (K. Jones 1988: 39-40). The NIESR's director, Paul Chambers (managing director of ICI), also played an important role in the Conservative Party's policy committee on economic growth, which began work in 1961. The Institute was funded by industry and drew economists from industry on temporary secondments as well as employing its own staff. It also benefited from the presence of Treasury officials from the Economic Section on temporary postings. Indeed, the NIESR served as almost a semi official annex to the Treasury's Economic Section. J.C.R.

Dow, for example, whilst on secondment from the Section as the Institute's Deputy Director, was instrumental in setting up the April 1961 conference and in publishing its results. In this way, and via its bi-monthly *Economic Review*, R.A.B. Butler which began publication in 1959, the NIESR played an important part in changing the policy environment as well as proving to be an important conduit to the Treasury for new ideas about growth promoting economic policies.[41]

Industry and the trade unions

It was not just think tanks and pressure groups that were incorporated within the developing growth advocacy network. Industrialists were also profoundly affected by the changing intellectual environment and by their links to those within the growth advocacy network. During 1960, industrialists on the tripartite Economic Planning Board, sought to redefine the framework of policy towards a 'negotiated economy'.[42] By the end of 1960 a consensus had emerged within industry that economic policy was too dominated by the short-term and would benefit from more government involvement (Dow 1964: 398-9; Boswell and Peters 1997).

The Federation of British Industries (one of several employers' associations which were later merged into the Confederation of British Industry) played a central role in the development of this consensus and it had been seen by both Meadows (1978: 402) and Ringe and Rollings (2000a: 336) as the 'key force' in turning concerns about growth into changed government policy. Historically, the Federation had opposed government intervention in industry (Blank 1973: 119-39). By 1960, however, the FBI had undergone a remarkable change of heart. Its reappraisal of policy came as a consequence of growing disenchantment with 'stop-go', the rapid growth of the European economies and the changing intellectual environment produced by actors in the growth advocacy network (Blank 1973: 139-42). In response, Hugh Weeks, chairman of the FBI's Economic Policy Committee, in February 1960 set up a study group of industrialists and economists to consider ways to improve economic growth (Leruez 1975: 85-6; Ringe and Rollings 2000a). In November 1960, 'Group 3' of the federation's annual conference, which included academic and business economists from the growth advocacy network, considered the question of 'economic growth in Britain'.[43] The group concluded that relative decline had 'deep rooted and long-term' causes the removal of which required government and industry to work together to raise productivity by assessing policies and expectations, looking up to five years ahead.[44] One should not infer from the FBI's 'Brighton revolution' (Brittan 1964: 216) that British industry as a whole had committed itself to the idea of economic planning, but it did indicate a major shift in the thinking of a number of key senior industrial leaders and their incorporation into the growth advocacy network. As Blank (1973: 153) noted, economic events were increasingly seen in industry as amenable to planning. The question was the form which this planning should take.

The Conservative and Labour Parties

This shift towards radical change in the framework of economic policy produced by the growth advocacy network was also evident in both the major parties. Although there were marked divisions within the Conservative Party over economic policy at end of the 1950s it was clear that 'modernists' such as Iain Macleod and Edward Heath were gaining the upper hand. These 'reluctant collectivists' (George and Wilding 1985: 62) saw a positive role for government in areas of market failure, and they had begun to agitate for change in the party's Bow Group and the One Nation Group (Critchley 1961; Rose 1961; Gamble 1974; Campbell 1994; Shepherd 1995; Ramsden 1998; Walsha 2000; Barr 2001).

The appointment of Macmillan as Prime Minister in 1957 had shifted power in the party towards this modernising tendency (Lowe 1997c). Macmillan, who as MP for Stockton had been appalled by the unemployment and poverty that he saw there during the Great Depression, and who once went so far as to say to Sir Robert Hall that he 'hate[d] the capitalist system', was by 1960–61 very open to new policies on growth; his priority being to avoid unemployment as much as he possible could' and to run the economy 'at full steam' (Horne 1989: 235-72).[45] In Macmillan's view, outlined before the war in *The Middle Way* (1938), the state had a duty to ensure a consistent and satisfactory minimum standard of living for all its citizens. Rather than an actual transfer of wealth from rich to poor, however, this would be paid for out of economic growth that the state would promote through its creation of the social and economic organisations necessary to deliver it (Turner 1994: 33-7).[46] In this respect, the willingness of Macmillan to accept the resignation of his entire Treasury team in 1958 was a pivotal moment: marking the symbolic acceptance of full employment and price stability over the value of the pound (Lowe 1989; Gamble 1974: 130).

Macmillan's hand was strengthened by his close relations with the Conservative Research Department. Chaired by Butler, Macmillan's leadership marked its heyday: 'a time when it was closer to the centre of Party communications than ever and perhaps the time when it contributed most to the Party's success' (Ramsden 1980: 190-2, 209-11; Barnes and Cockett 1994). By 1960, it was clear to the CRD's director, Michael Fraser, that the intellectual climate created by the growth advocacy network meant that the time had come 'to draw upon the body of expansionist opinion within the party'.[47] To this end, the CRD began to explore and advocate new policies that would help to achieve higher growth. Thus by 1961, as a consequence of the actions of the growth advocacy network, the Conservatives were moving towards the adoption of growth as a specific economic objective.

An added factor in this transition was the fact that Labour had already made this shift and was developing a coherent and electorally appealing economic policy aimed at growth through modernisation just when the Conservatives had concluded that they had 'virtually exhausted the neo-liberal seam in economic policy' and must seek a new direction.[48] The awareness that there were serious problems with British economic performance had been reflected in Labour thinking from the mid-1950s onwards.[49] Nevertheless, how this increase should be achieved had been the subject of profound disagreement. During the 1950s, discussion within the party about planning became deeply embedded in the debate over nationalisation. The left argued that public ownership should be at the core of Labour policy. This presupposed physical planning, seen by many on the left as a prerequisite for raising investment (Balogh 1954, 1955). Revisionists such as Crosland, however, argued that the old arguments for detailed planning and public ownership had gone and that, within a mixed economy, planning could be restricted to the overall management of the economy. Revisionism, which fired its first salvo with *New Fabian essays* in 1952, received a fillip when Gaitskell was elected leader in 1955 (Hasseler 1969) but the full statement of the revisionist credo came with Crosland's *The Future of Socialism* in 1956. The party's 1958 *Plan for Progress* attempted to bridge the gap between the two camps but broadly reflected the revisionist reaction to stop-go; suggesting that Labour should seek not to transform the mixed economy but to run it more efficiently than the Conservatives. It was *Signposts for the Sixties,* however, which most skilfully bridged this gap by blaming Britain's relative decline on a combination of sluggish private enterprise and government reluctance to plan the economy properly.

In constructing this policy, the party had drawn upon the ideas developed in the growth advocacy network and it continued to do so in its subsequent development of policy after 1961. As shadow chancellor, Jim Callaghan sought the advice of member of the growth advocacy network in a series of seminars at Nuffield College (of which he was an Honorary Fellow): academics such as Balogh, Corina, Kahn, Kaldor, Mitchell and Neild; industrialists such as Fred Catherwood of British Aluminium; and serving and former member of the Treasury Economic Section such as Hall, Cairncross, and 'Kit' McMahon (Morgan 1998: 173-6).[50] Moreover, many of these advisers were later taken into government, along with others such as Wilfred Beckerman, Richard Opie and Michael Posner who were also active members of the growth advocacy network.[51] By such means the network extended its reach into the Labour Party's highest reaches.

Labour's 1964 election manifesto then committed the party to 'planning' as the solution to Britain's relative economic failure. The manifesto talked of:

> 'A new Britain: *mobilising* the resources of technology under a national plan; *harnessing* our national wealth in brains, our genius for scientific invention and medical discovery; *reversing* the decline of the thirteen wasted years; [and] *affording* a new opportunity to equal, and if possible surpass, the roaring progress of other western powers ... [under a] fresh and virile leadership' (Labour Party 1964: 1, original emphases).

Nevertheless, the slogans of planning, social justice and expansion which Wilson introduced were less revolutionary than they appeared.[52] As Crosland (1962 and 1964: 332) noted, despite the ritual of adversarial politics, there was clearly a high level of cross party consensus on 'planning'. The truth was that by 1961 negative policy feedback and the actions of the growth advocacy network had led both parties to commit themselves to raising growth, and both were prepared to implement similar radical new policies to achieve it.

Policy learning in the core executive

We have traced the effect of negative policy feedback in the 1950s, the impact made by the growth advocacy network on the policy environment and the links it was able to forge with key parts of the core executive and with both political parties. We now turn to the learning that occurred within the core executive during 1960–61, most notably in the Treasury, as a consequence of this process.

Complaints that the Treasury was concerned more with the control of public expenditure and the protection of sterling than with promoting the growth of the British economy were common currency in the early-1960s and have continued to dominate the literature (Leruez 1975: 104; Ham 1981; Pollard 1982). In fact, the release of government files shows that at the start of the 1960s negative policy feedback during the 1950s, coupled with the actions of the growth advocacy network, had produced a marked change in the Treasury's attitude to growth.

In terms of negative feedback, the apparent failure of Keynesian demand management to stabilise the economy was an important factor contributing to the Treasury's conversion to new policies on growth. This did not mean that Treasury officials necessarily agreed that growth would be improved simply by raising the level of demand. Both Frank Lee (its Permanent Secretary) and Thomas Padmore (head of its Home Finance section), for example, initially supported the Paish recipe of lower demand to make the economy more competitive. The deputy director of its Economic Section, Brian Hopkin also saw lower demand as an essential initial element in a policy for growth – to allow wages to be brought under control.[53] There was no support evident at higher levels within the Treasury in 1960 for the more radical 'dash for growth' advanced by Harrod and supported by Macmillan.[54] Nevertheless, by 1960 there was already support for the idea that improvements to the Treasury's demand management could play an important role in promoting growth – by smoothing Britain's growth path, removing the costs of fluctuations an ultimately raising the rate of growth.

Environmental change arising from negative feedback also played an important role in the Treasury's conversion during 1960–61 to new policies on growth in another sense; emerging evidence of relative decline seeming to point towards a failure of policy during the 1950s. This heightened concern about how to increase growth and strengthened the hand of those in the Treasury who desired new policies.

We have already noted the ability of the growth advocacy network further to contribute to this environment change. One example of such change– the 'Brighton revolution' was particularly important in changing minds in the Treasury (Brittan 1964: 216).[55] The FBI's endorsement of 'planning' and the high standard of debate at the conference particularly impressed the new Permanent Secretary at the Treasury, Sir Frank Lee (whose attendance was itself a mark of the changing intellectual climate that had been produced by the growth advocacy network). It helped bring about an important shift in the Treasury's attitude to industry.[56] In addition, Lee's experience at the Board of Trade and his links to industry brought a new perspective to bear on Treasury policy making. One of his first acts at the Treasury, for example, was to insist on the presence on the highly influential Budget Committee of his successor at the Board of Trade, Sir Richard Powell, in order that budgetary policy should be developed with its possible impact on industry in mind.[57]

At the Board of Trade, Lee had been a vocal critic of the Treasury and had overseen a 'revolution in industrial intervention' (Lowe 1997b; Rosevear 1997) Such action went against the grain of traditional Treasury doctrine, with its bias against intervention on the supply-side of the economy. However, Lee returned from the FBI's conference in November 1960 convinced that the changed attitude that the growth advocacy network had wrought in industry had created new possibilities. He remained concerned, however, about whether the unions would be able to engage constructively with indicative planning. In fact, a number of senior trade unionists, particularly the TUC's General Secretary, George Woodcock, had also concluded that higher growth might result from union involvement in negotiating economic policy with government and employers. During 1959–60, representatives of the General Council raised in the NPACI and EPB their desire to see tripartite debate about economic policy (Minkin 1992: 109; Taylor 2000: 156-9).[58] In September 1960, the General Council asked the chancellor if there was any reason why the UK should not follow the French example of setting targets for industrial growth.[59] Four months later, the Economic Committee of the TUC told Selwyn Lloyd that industry and the unions were looking to him for a lead on growth and in January 1961 the committee endorsed planning as the best means to reverse Britain's relative industrial decline (Middlemas 1983: 10).[60]

Thus, as a consequence of negative policy feedback and the efforts of the emerging growth advocacy network, a number of industrialists and trade unionists (at peak level) appeared by 1961 to be coming to similar conclusions about the need for government intervention to promote higher growth and the need for cooperation between both sides of industry if it was to be attained. As the Economic Secretary (Anthony Barber), noted after the May 1961 meeting of the NPACI, on growth there was now 'a surprising degree of agreement between those from whom one might otherwise have expected divergent views'.[61]

Lee's influence and links with industry were not the only factors pushing the Treasury into new thinking on growth. The influence of its Economic Section was also important. However, the extent to which the Section's analysis of the 'growth problem' was influenced by the new ideas being developed within the growth advocacy network, as a consequence of its links with its academic members, is not easy to trace. In January 1961, Robert Hall (1991: 256-7) noted that he was becoming interested in constructing 'a policy for growth' and that his interest had been kindled by the FBI conference and the agitation of 'demand expansionists' in what I have termed the growth advocacy network. It seems reasonable to assume that his links with institutions such as PEP and the NIESR had also played a part in his developing interest.

Growth, as Hall (1991: 257) put it, was 'now getting in to the air' at the Treasury. This change in the intellectual climate had been wrought by the negative feedback of the policies of the 1950s and the actions of the growth advocacy network – which now included Treasury officials such as Hall and Lee, and also a number of younger officials.[62] In January

1960 Lee, with the support of the Economic Section, set up a secret interdepartmental committee of permanent secretaries and began a reappraisal of the Treasury's policy on growth and a process of education of other government departments (Lowe and Rollings 2000: 112).[63] Sir Douglas Wass told Keegan and Pennant-Rea (1979: 16) that he could not remember the words 'economic growth' being mentioned in any official document before 1960, but growth was now high on the Treasury agenda. The creation of the committee was evidence of the change in the Treasury's attitude that had been produced by the growth advocacy network and the more general change in the intellectual climate, and the discussions on growth in the EPB and NPACI that this had provoked.[64] It was also an indication that the Treasury was now embarking on 'missionary work' within Whitehall to promote its ideas for raising growth (Ringe and Rollings 2000a: 346).

The impact of Lee's committee was soon evident. Almost immediately, a Treasury memorandum for the Economic Planning Board acknowledged Britain's poor relative growth and recognised the adverse impact on industrial confidence of the government's management of demand.[65] A policy environment sympathetic to new policies on growth was making itself felt in discussions in existing tripartite institutions such as the EPB and NPACI.[66] Emboldened by this, Lee authorised the creation of a working party of officials to report to his *ad hoc* committee of permanent secretaries and to prepare a submission for the chancellor on growth and on the measures that might be taken, such as tripartite consultations, to improve it. This would consist of an appreciation of post-war UK growth and a comparison with other countries; details of the attitudes of industry, labour and other relevant non-governmental institutions to the problem and details of any discussions that have taken place with them to date; an examination of the relationships between economic growth, competitive power and the balance of payments; and, finally, the identification of possible tripartite action to stimulate economic growth and competitiveness.[67]

The working party on growth brought together officials from the Treasury, the Board of Trade and the Ministry of Labour under the chairmanship of a Treasury under secretary and marked a further extension of the growth advocacy network into Whitehall. Nevertheless, it was soon clear that Treasury thought on growth, whilst it was following the lead given by the expanding growth advocacy network, was far ahead of other government departments.[68] The Treasury recognised that this was a 'serious weakness' for it would be highly dependent on these departments to implement any policy changes. The Treasury also realised that it faced the problem of how to encourage the active participation of the FBI and the TUC (given that many of their members were 'some way behind' Treasury thinking and in need of 'a great deal of hard education [on] the realities of alternative possibilities for the next five years'), and how to demonstrate the willingness of the Treasury to pursue new policies on growth 'while at the same time not moving in to "take charge of" the subject'.[69]

Notwithstanding such concerns, the result of the Treasury's policy reappraisal was a report to the chancellor and cabinet in July 1961 entitled 'Economic growth and national efficiency'.[70] This clearly set out the Treasury's position on growth and the economic policies that it thought might improve it. The report began by acknowledging that it was the product of mounting public concern that Britain's rate of growth was inadequate in comparison with rates of growth being achieved by its continental competitors. In this sense, the report can be seen as a product of late-1950s declinism. In other respects, however, the Treasury's analysis was acute. Firstly, it emphasised what it saw as the achievements of post-war economic policy – the elimination of unemployment and an historically impressive economic growth record – and the reasonably flexible way in which the economy seemed to be adapting to changing patterns of demand and to changing production possibilities. Secondly, whilst acknowledging that Britain's rate of growth of national income per head was lower than that of many countries, the report queried whether the country's relative position had deteriorated during the 1950s to the extent often claimed. Most significantly, it located the 'growth problem' not in fears about Britain's economic performance in the recent past, but in the future. In this sense, the Treasury was acknowledging that Britain's relative economic decline during the past decade had been an almost inevitable product of continental reconstruction, whilst expressing its concern at the effects, particularly the political effects and the repercussions for sterling, that would result if this relative decline continued. This was not 'declinism', but it did indicate concern that the British economy needed to perform better in the future.

The report's title is interesting. On the one hand, the Treasury's analysis was plainly the product of a policy environment sympathetic to radical change to achieve higher growth. On the other hand, the report's evocation of the Edwardian concept of 'national efficiency' might be interpreted as 'shiny new bottles for the good old cough mixtures'.[71] However, whilst there were certainly familiar elements amongst its policy proposals, the report proposed a radical break with past Treasury policy – for it concluded that higher growth would not be achieved without a much greater degree of government intervention in the economy to correct a wide array of market failures.

The report was highly sceptical that a breakthrough into higher growth could be achieved simply by raising the level of demand in the economy as suggested, for example, by Sir Roy Harrod in his voluminous correspondence with the Prime Minister.[72] In the view of the Treasury, raising demand alone would simply run into bottlenecks on the supply-side, increase costs and prices, suck in imports and lead to an inevitable balance of payments crisis.[73] The report therefore suggested a war on two fronts. Firstly, it proposed that the rate of growth of home demand should in the short-term be set at a level rather below that currently prevailing – the theory being that this would encourage manufacturers to seek overseas markets and thus eliminate the chronic balance of payments problems that had dogged the country since the war. Secondly, it proposed a longer term programme of concerted government action on the supply-side to promote 'national efficiency'. In effect, therefore, it was proposing short-term restrictions in the growth of consumption whilst simultaneously embarking on a radical and wide ranging overhaul of the supply-side of the economy – the theory being that in the medium to longer term supply-side reform would allow demand to rise again, and to rise more swiftly. By doing so it hoped to break out of the straitjacket posed by sterling and raise Britain's growth potential.[74] In the longer term, therefore, the Treasury hoped that its twin track approach would deliver faster economic growth.

To this end, the report suggested a thorough review of supply-side policy. It argued, for example, that the economy needed to be rebalanced via more and better microeconomic policies to encourage higher and better directed investment, whilst ensuring allocational efficiency by leaving investment decisions as far as possible to the operation of the free market. Tariff protections should be removed the better to expose British industry and commerce to international competitive forces. A more active labour market policy was required; and to this end the Treasury proposed a series of major policy reviews in the field of taxation, pensions, and conditions of work that would aim to encourage more people, particularly women, to enter the labour force. It also suggested that regional policy and housing policy should be used to encourage the mobility of labour. In addition, it proposed that the government should use education and training policy to raise the volume of trained and technically qualified workers, and that action should also be taken to increase the quality of training provided both by the government and by employers. The government should implement an incomes policy that would ensure that the growth of wages did not outstrip that of productivity – thus ensuring that higher growth did not trigger inflation and reduce Britain's international competitiveness. The government should also, suggested the

Treasury, bring an end to restrictive practices on *both* sides of industry: via action on business in respect of monopolies, the abolition of resale price maintenance, and the removal of anachronistic restrictions on shop opening hours; and by endeavouring to find a means to remove restrictive labour practices in industry and the professions, and other action to create a more flexible work force. The tax system should be reviewed and if necessary reformed to ensure that it did nothing overly to restrict, and preferably promoted, both growth and productive efficiency. Public expenditure decisions should henceforth be made in the context of improvements in growth and national efficiency.[75] Most importantly, it suggested that the government should seek to emulate French and German 'success in instilling an attitude of mind in business which has confidence in future growth and the development of the economy'.[76] The report concluded by emphasizing the need to develop a coherent policy 'mounted on a wide front', one which ministers should recognize would require the adoption of a more interventionist approach that would 'call for "difficult" battles with vested interests'.[77]

In short, the policy proposals in 'Economic growth and national efficiency' envisaged a radical change in the direction of economic policy; a change that would alter the very objectives of economic policy, with growth promoted to a key aim rather than being seen as a policy by-product, and radically alter the policy instruments used to attain these objectives. Change had come as a product of learning the lessons of the policy failures of the 1950s, as a result of the penetration of the core executive by ideas developed and promoted by the growth advocacy network, and as a consequence of the more general change in the intellectual climate wrought by this network.

A revolution in attitudes in the Treasury was meaningless, however, without the backing of the chancellor. This came suddenly, although the immediate cause of Selwyn Lloyd's sudden conversion to 'planning' was Macmillan's use of the sterling crisis as a lever to press on Selwyn Lloyd a more activist policy on growth – a course of action suggested by the deputy Cabinet Secretary, Freddie Bishop.[78] Although Ringe and Rollings (2000a) found that Bishop was acting alone, the coincidental timing of his suggestion and the Treasury's report to the chancellor suggest that the two were related.[79] Lee had already suggested to Selwyn Lloyd that there might well be significant arguments for the adoption of planning on French lines (if only for the sake of economic education and understanding).[80] In addition, Selwyn Lloyd had already been urged by Boyle to bring both sides of industry together 'on the basis of something that can not unreasonably be termed a plan'.[81]

Internal Treasury correspondence suggests that in mid-1961 its officials were eager to use the seemingly inevitable sterling crisis as a means of levering ministers into a new policy on growth.[82] Providentially, the Treasury report to the cabinet on growth was available just as the run on sterling began to take off. Bishop downplayed the novelty of the report in his minute for Macmillan but, nonetheless, it shaped the government's subsequent strategy.[83] Almost immediately Selwyn Lloyd made use of it to underpin his presentation of the measures to the public as a long-term policy for modernisation and economic growth; thus offsetting the acute short-term political embarrassment of the sterling crisis and the emergency deflation.[84] The new policy was made public in the House of Commons debate on 25 July 1961 on the sterling crisis, fleshed out in the next day's debate and further expanded in letters to the employers' organisations and the TUC on 23 September.[85]

The employers were receptive, since the proposal to instigate tripartite planning was in effect a development of ideas mooted at the 1960 FBI conference. As Budd (1978: 91-5) put it: 'The employers had nothing to lose, and might gain something from joining an experiment in planning'.[86] The TUC's position, however, was more problematic. It was not organised to play an active role in economic management, was strongly opposed to restrictions on collective bargaining and, most importantly, feared identification with the policies of a Conservative government.[87] At bottom, however, it could in principle hardly oppose planning since it had long advocated it (Leruez 1975: 93-5).

As Dow (1961: 25) commented in the *Westminster Bank Review,* the desire for faster economic growth was now widespread and was a 'new force'. That this was the case was the product of learning the lessons of negative policy feedback (stop-go and relative decline). More than this, however, the new policies that the lesson involved had been promoted by the emerging network of growth policy advocates (a network that encompassed academic economists, financial journalists, pressure groups, industrialists, and 'modernisers' in the civil service). It was from this network that the solution implemented after July 1961 was derived. As Tomlinson (1996a) points out, it was not easy for the Conservatives to change direction; since to do so was to admit to problems with their direction of economic policy since 1951. That it did so was a mark of the learning that had occurred but, although the party had already come to the conclusion that it had 'virtually exhausted the neo-liberal seam in economic policy', its conversion to 'planning' was hastened by the way in which Labour drew upon the critique being advanced in the growth advocacy network to mount an increasingly effective attack on government policies.

Conclusions

As indicated in Chapter 1, Selwyn Lloyd's announcement on 25 July 1961 marked the start of a wholesale overhaul of economic objectives and policy instruments. For the next five years, indicative planning, incomes policy and fiscal policy changes were to be at the centre of attempts by both Conservative and Labour governments in the 19660s to attain the new 4 per cent growth target.[88] This adoption of a new policy goal and the introduction of an array of new policy instruments to achieve it amounted to third order learning. This learning was in turn the product of several factors.

Firstly, it had been triggered by negative policy feedback: particularly stop-go and relative decline. Such feedback led to learning within the core executive (and outside it) that made the adoption of the new policies possible. As Middlemas (1986: 335) put it:

> ... each main participant in the history of industrial politics had by then become sufficiently disillusioned with the way that the post-war settlement operated, and in particular with the government's economic management during the 1950s, to require radical reform.

On its own, however, this negative feedback does not seem enough to explain why such a fundamental change should have occurred. At least as important in the change were the new ideas about growth and economic modernisation that were developed in, and disseminated through, an extensive policy meta network that began to emerge after 1955 – thus confirming Hall's (1989: 389) point that ideas have real power in politics but that they gain power via institutions and interests. This meta network, which had at its core financial journalists, academics and 'think tanks' but which by 1961 also encompassed industrialists and trade unionists (although mainly at an elite level), changed the policy environment within which the core executive crafted its economic policy.[89] It did so in two-ways, one direct and one indirect. It managed directly to influence policy through the network links that developed between academic and business economists and the core executive (particularly between Harrod and the Prime Minister and between members of the Treasury's Economic Section and PEP and the NIESR), and between industrial networks and the Board of Trade and Treasury. These links allowed the growth advocacy network to engage in a process of information exchange with, and direct lobbying of, the core executive.

More importantly, perhaps, the growth advocacy network exercised an important indirect influence on the core executive by making ideas respectable that had hitherto been taboo and by altering the intellectual climate. By changing wider public opinion, it put pressure on politicians radically to change their policies. The consequence was both a new economic objective and the adoption of radical new policies to achieve it.

This policy learning was such that the Treasury embraced higher economic growth as a specific policy objective. In doing so the Treasury transcended two major criticisms of it: that it elevated the interests of sterling over those of the real economy; and that it was historically more concerned with control of expenditure than investing for growth (Ham 1981; Heclo and Wildavsky 1981: 48-9; Pollard 1982). Despite Macmillan's fear that the Treasury's laissez faire tradition stood in the way of change, in 1961 the Treasury embraced the idea of intervention to promote better economic performance.[90] More than this, as Ringe and Rollings point out, it actively proselytised for it in Whitehall (Ringe and Rollings 2000a).[91] It also saw a need to discuss growth and efficiency issues with industry and labour – largely because it believed that the solution to many of the economies problems could not be resolved solely by government. Although Ringe and Rollings qualify this conclusion (suggesting that the Treasury's drive for growth and efficiency remained firmly embedded in the need to safeguard the balance of payments and that it saw little need for new institutions) this was a fundamental change in Treasury thinking.

Thus, a major policy shift occurred in response to negative feedback, the formation of an extensive meta network, and an environmental change produced by this network (see Figure 3.2 above). The extent of this meta network, and the complex interlinkages between its members, are clearly different from the networks associated with Hall's examples of first and second order change (mapped in Chapter 2). They are far more reminiscent of the network found in the adoption of 'monetarism' (see Figure 2.5); although the meta network of the early-1960s differs in important respects from that associated with the shift from monetarism to Keynesianism in the late-1970s. There are three notable differences. Firstly, the City and Bank of England were not involved. Relative decline and the need for new policies to promote long-term growth were of less concern to financiers than addressing short-term external pressures on the pound. They were, however, of profound concern to industry and it is the presence of business and trade union interests in the growth advocacy network that is the second major difference (although the involvement of the latter came late in the day). Most significantly, however, the involvement of politicians (particularly politicians in the governing party) is far less prevalent. With the notable exception of the Prime Minister, it was Treasury officials who provided the main links between the periphery of the meta network and decision makers at the core of the core executive.

Despite these differences, the policy shifts of the early-1960s and the late-1970s both involved alterations to both the goals and instruments of economic policy. Both drew on radical policy alternatives that were developed in and promoted by extensive, if slightly different, policy meta networks. Why was it then, that the changes of the early-1960s came to be categorised not as a radical policy departure into 'planning', a decisive break with the Keynesian policy making paradigm, but as an incremental development of the Keynesian policies of the 1950s ('Keynesian-plus')? It is this paradox that will be explored in the succeeding three chapters. Each will examine one of the three elements of the growth policy project and will consider why it was that the aims of its proponents remained unrealised and why the policy failed fully to be institutionalised.

4

The Supply-side: Industrial Training

Introduction

This chapter is concerned with the first element of the growth policy framework ushered in after 1961 – the adoption of an interventionist microeconomic policy on the supply-side of the economy that aimed to improve the operation of the British economy and so contribute to higher economic growth. Of course, the desire radically to improve the supply-side of the British economy was not a particular feature of the five years after 1961. It was, however, made much more urgent by the adoption of an explicit target for higher growth in 1962. This revision of economic goals produced a plethora of institutional changes such as the creation of the National Economic Development Council in 1962, the creation by Labour after its election in 1964 of a new Department of Economic Affairs tasked with drawing up a 'national plan', and the setting up by Labour of the Industrial Reorganisation Corporation in 1966. All sought to restructure and refocus industrial investment on higher growth and higher productivity.

The failure of the NEDC, its associated office and plethora of industry level EDCs to attain the growth objectives it set for itself in 1963 has been widely discussed (for overviews and history of its operation see Middlemas 1983 and, more recently, Wood 1997 and 2000). Explanations for its failure to raise growth have tended to focus on the government's failure to put its relations with industry on a more constructive footing and the consequent missed opportunity to create a 'developmental state' in Britain that would allow it to halt its relative economic decline (Leruez 1975; Shanks 1977; Budd 1978; Middlemas 1986; Tomlinson 1997). Recently, however, attention has shifted towards deeper institutional failings: particularly residual suspicions in industry peak associations of government intentions; the resistance of individual firms to revisionist vanguard elites in those peak associations that were prepared to embrace radical new policies on growth; and the constraints placed upon the development of the NEDC, and the coordination problems it encountered as a result of, the fragmentation of both British government and its industrial institutions (Boswell and Peters 1997; Lowe and Rollings 2000; Ringe and Rollings 2000a; Wood 2000). For Ringe and Rollings, the failure of the NEDC was not a failure of government, it was instead a failure produced by the phenomenon of 'governance' discussed in Chapter 2. If this was true of the NEDC, how true was it of other elements of the supply-side reforms of the 1960s?

The chapter examines another element of the new supply-side interventionism, the attempt to improve the quality and quantity of industrial training via the 1964 Industrial Training Act (ITA). This has been seen as a 'revolutionary' scheme which introduced a tripartite approach and effectively overturned a tradition of non-intervention in the labour market by introducing compulsory training cost sharing in industry (Perry 1976: 100-1; Beverstock 1969: 1).

The chapter begins by examining how new ideas on industrial training penetrated the core executive and caused it to conclude that policy had radically to be changed if the quantity and quality of British industrial training demanded by the new growth objective was to be realised. It concludes that the shift to interventionism in industrial training in 1964 was a product both of negative policy feedback from training policy in the 1950s and of the pronounced change, promoted by the growth advocacy network, that took place between 1960 and 1962 in the intellectual framework within which economic policy was made. It argues, however, that this third order learning in industrial training policy was poorly institutionalised and that, as a result, third order learning failed to produce third order change.

The process of learning

Attitudes to training in the 1950s

The 1964 Industrial Training Act has generally been seen as an important turning point which reversed many years of government inaction on industrial training (Perry 1976: xix; D. King 1995: 128; King and Wickham-Jones 1998). This, of course, ignores the important role that government played in the two world wars, but in each case this role proved short lived and was followed by a reversion to the conviction that, in the vast majority of cases, training was rightly the preserve of the individual firm (Sheldrake and Vickerstaff 1987: 7-10, 24-5). Consequently, during the 1950s government training 'receded to the margins of the labour market – the young, the disabled, the hard to place – [and] training policy fulfilled social welfare rather than economic aims or functions' (Sheldrake and Vickerstaff 1987: 28-30; Ziderman 1978: 77-

9). Writing in 1960, Sir Godfrey Ince (1960: 93-7) – a former Permanent Secretary of the Ministry of Labour, the ministry responsible for industrial training – noted that the could see no reason why this should change; but Ince was wrong.

Second order change: the 1958 Carr report

Ince's complacency undoubtedly stemmed from the fact that industrial training had recently been subject to a major policy review that had effectively preserved the status quo. The 1958 Carr report (NJAC 1958) had placed its faith in incremental improvements to further education, exhorting firms and trade unions to eschew the poaching of skilled labour, and in the creation of an Industrial Training Council (ITC) to keep apprentice training 'under review'. This second order policy change was a response to two challenges. The first, was the inability of laissez faire to produce enough skilled workers to meet the comparatively high level of demand of the 1950s. This had produced a shortage of skilled labour and increasing concerns about both the hoarding and poaching of skilled workers (Perry 1976: 56). This led to calls in the British Association of Commercial and Industrial Education (BACIE) – the principal industrial organisation concerned with training – for a new look at ways of training young people and the possible need for government intervention. However, the BACIE, was not yet interested in agitating for government intervention – and would not be until after the death of Ince, its director, in 1960. This lack of interest reflected the views of its members and showed that neither employers nor unions then had any real interest in changing the traditional system of apprentice training. From the employers' perspective, the system made for stable employment and easier relations with the unions. For small firms without the means of running apprenticeships it transferred training costs to those which did. For the craft unions, restrictions on entry to apprenticeship ensured the differential between skilled and unskilled wages was maintained (Elbaum 1989).

The government was no more keen than the BACIE that it reverse its laissez faire approach to training. Although a Conservative advisory committee on policy suggested in 1957 that action on apprenticeships was one of several possible 'themes' that offered a way of giving 'practical and concrete expression to ... the opportunity state', a government elected under the slogan 'Conservative freedom works' was inevitably opposed to intervention in industry. Action on training was therefore notably absent when the party began to think about how to turn these themes into practical policies in 1958.[1]

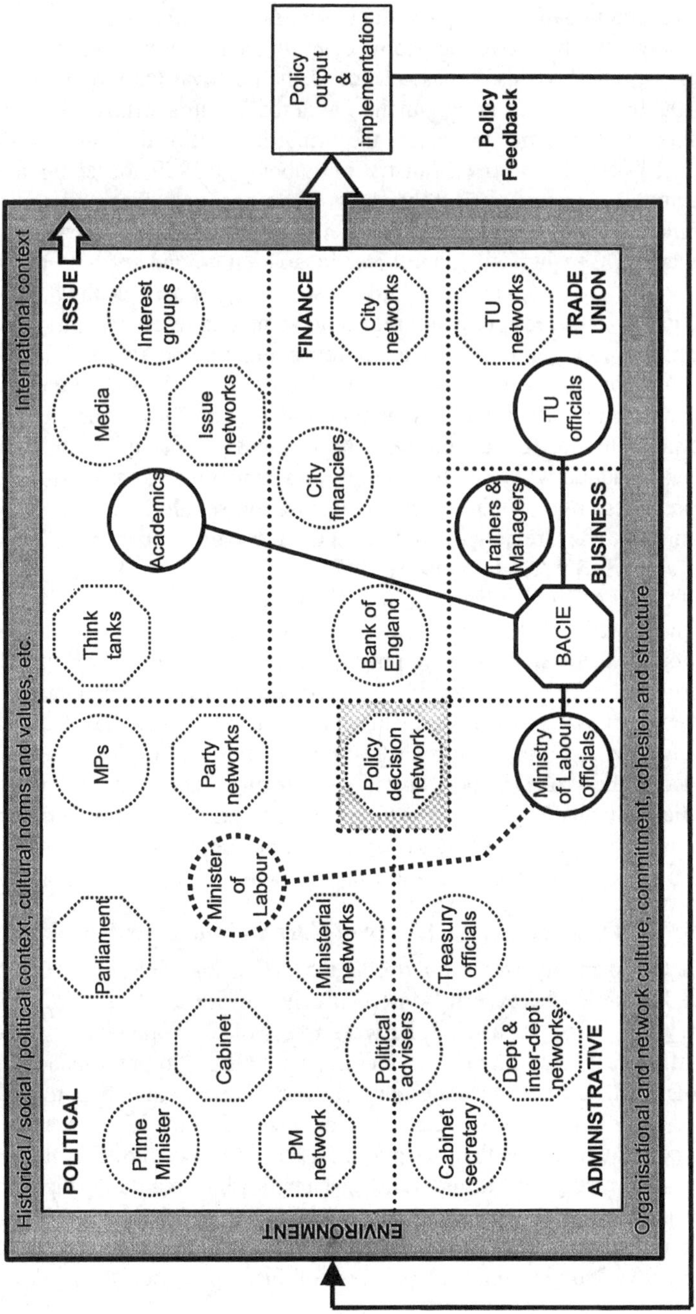

Figure 4.1 The training policy community in 1958

This second challenge to prevailing policies on training was the prospect of a large number of young people entering the labour market in the early years of the 1960s as a consequence of the post-war baby boom (known as 'the bulge'). This, in conjunction with the labour shortage issue, was a sufficient challenge to cause the tripartite National Joint Advisory Council (NJAC) of the Ministry of Labour in 1959 to set up a sub-committee, chaired by Robert Carr, to examine these two linked problems. The Carr Committee rejected government intervention – something Carr himself found objectionable on grounds of both practicability and principle (NJAC 1958).[2] Instead, it proposed dealing with the 'bulge' by concentrating additional government resources on building technical colleges rather than on reforming on the job training. The commission assumed that industry would rise to the challenge of the bulge in the interests of the nation and argued that firms needed to consider the cost of *not* training and to eschew 'poaching'. Its positive recommendations were that employers and unions should shorten apprenticeships and that a central organisation should be created to keep training 'under review'. To this end, a tripartite Industrial Training Council (ITC) was set up in July 1958.

This second order learning had taken place within a relatively tightly bound training policy community and had resulted from the negative policy feedback from training policy in the 1950s (both shown in bold in Figure 4.1). It had produced a second order institutional change that created a new policy instrument (the ITC) but which did not seek to change the wider goals of industrial training policy. In effect the 'bulge', added to the skilled labour shortage, had required action but had not been sufficiently challenging to require a solution outside the prevailing policy making paradigm. It soon became apparent, however, that this second order change had failed to resolve the problem.

Third order learning: the failure of Carr and the growth problem

The Carr strategy was a failure, as the ITC acknowledged (ITC 1965). The ITC failed because it was effectively powerless (Page 1967: 37-43; Perry 1976: 76). It 'had all the weaknesses of the voluntary approach – insufficient funds to make any real impact, no right to press its advice on firms, and no-one was under any obligation to pay attention to what it said' (Elliott 1978: 604).[3] Laissez faire persisted in the labour market and the consequence was that, despite the exhortations of the ITC, there was little real change of attitude amongst employers or unions. Lip service was paid by employers to the idea of expanding training within firms but a confidential survey by the British Employers' Confederation (BEC) in 1959 revealed that only 20 per cent of firms proposed to do anything about it.[4] A year after an appeal by the ITC for firms and unions to assess their position on recruitment, only half had done so (TUC Report 1959: 199-202). Looking back on its failure in its final report, the ITC noted that a constant theme in its publications had been the inadequate response of employers; their lack of appreciation of the economic advantages of training; their lack of understanding of the principles of sound training; their belief that the cost of training should be shared by the trainee or by other firms (sometimes entirely so); and their unwillingness to face the problems of introducing better training methods where these involved a departure from custom and practice (ITC 1965). Such failures were acknowledged by the Federation of British Industries at its 1960 conference.[5]

As Perry (1976: 71) put it, the only real benefit of the Carr Report was that its failure to solve either the problem of the bulge or that of skill shortages ultimately produced a 'total reversal of public opinion and government policy' (see also Tomlinson and Tiratsoo 1998: Ch. 8). It thereby helped create an important condition for radical change. As negative policy feedback continued, so dissatisfaction mounted within the training policy community and beyond with the failure of the existing industrial training system adequately to meet the challenge of the 'bulge'. This environmental change led to the reinvigoration of the network of professional trainers and academics in Figure 4.1, a network based largely in the membership of BACIE and in its regular conferences.

These BACIE conferences were important for two reasons. Firstly, they brought the training policy community together with journalists from the relevant technical journals and with representatives from interested pressure groups such as PEP. Secondly, they acted as a forum within which new ideas about how better to organise industrial training (such as Williams 1957 and 1959, and Croft 1960) could be discussed and helped to publicise the training problem (BACIE 1960a, 1960b, 1960c, 1961; Perry 1976: 71-87). In doing so, they played an important part in forging a growing sense within the training policy community that radical action was needed and in extending the scope of this community to become a more generalised policy network. Members of this network helped communicate this sense to industry and, in conjunction with those industrial journalists who were now incorporated within this network but particularly the journalist John Wellens, also helped disseminate to a wider public the idea that radical change was needed (Wellens 1960, 1962a-d, 1963a-b, 1964).[6]

Within two years of the creation of the ITC, and with negative feed-back continuing unabated, Ministry of Labour officials responsible for training began privately to express disquiet at its lack of progress. There was a growing feeling in the ministry that pressure would have to be applied by the ministry if the problems of British training were to be addressed.[7] At the end of 1960, John Hare, who had replaced Edward Heath as Minister of Labour in July, told the BACIE annual conference that the response of firms to the 'bulge' was unsatisfactory (BACIE 1960a: 18-22). Privately, Hare thought it was now too late to change the apprenticeship system if results were to be achieved in 1960–61 (the peak years of the 'bulge').[8] In the short-term, the problem would have to be addressed using the existing framework. An interdepartmental working party (the first of several) was created to consider how best to do this and the Ministry of Labour began a small scale project to expand first year apprentice training in government training centres (GTCs).[9] In the long run, however, Hare was convinced that if the quantity and quality of training was to be raised, the government might have to consider imposing some sort of training levy on firms to *force* them to train – a concept already floated by Williams (1959) and already under review in the BACIE.[10]

In a speech to an ITC conference in November 1960, Hare warned that if industry failed to provide the additional training required by the 'bulge' then 'the basic doctrine that the responsibility for training rests with industry [might] be subject to pressure that will be very hard to resist' (ITC 1961). He found strong support from Tom Williamson, speaking on behalf of the TUC General Council, who warned that if laissez faire meant many companies continued to take so little interest in training, and if the many firms who preferred to poach skilled labour from others rather than provide training themselves, it would 'not be long before the community will say industry has had its chance and has fallen down'. As Williamson put it, someone had to *arrange* training, and if industry could not do it then the Ministry of Labour would have to. The only alternative was cooperation and joint responsibility between employers and unions – although, as Lord Citrine commented, since none of the peak organisations had disciplinary powers over their members, achieving this would be far from easy.[11]

This new attitude on the part of the unions, and the preparedness of Hare to consider intervention, was symptomatic of the beginnings of a widespread change in the climate of opinion on training that began to gain ground from late-1959 onwards.[12] Also important, however, was the marked change in the overall policy environment produced by the actions of the growth advocacy network and the important links forged between this network and the industrial training policy network (see Figure 4.2). For example, the need to develop human as well as physical investment was highlighted by PEP's *Growth in the British economy* and we have

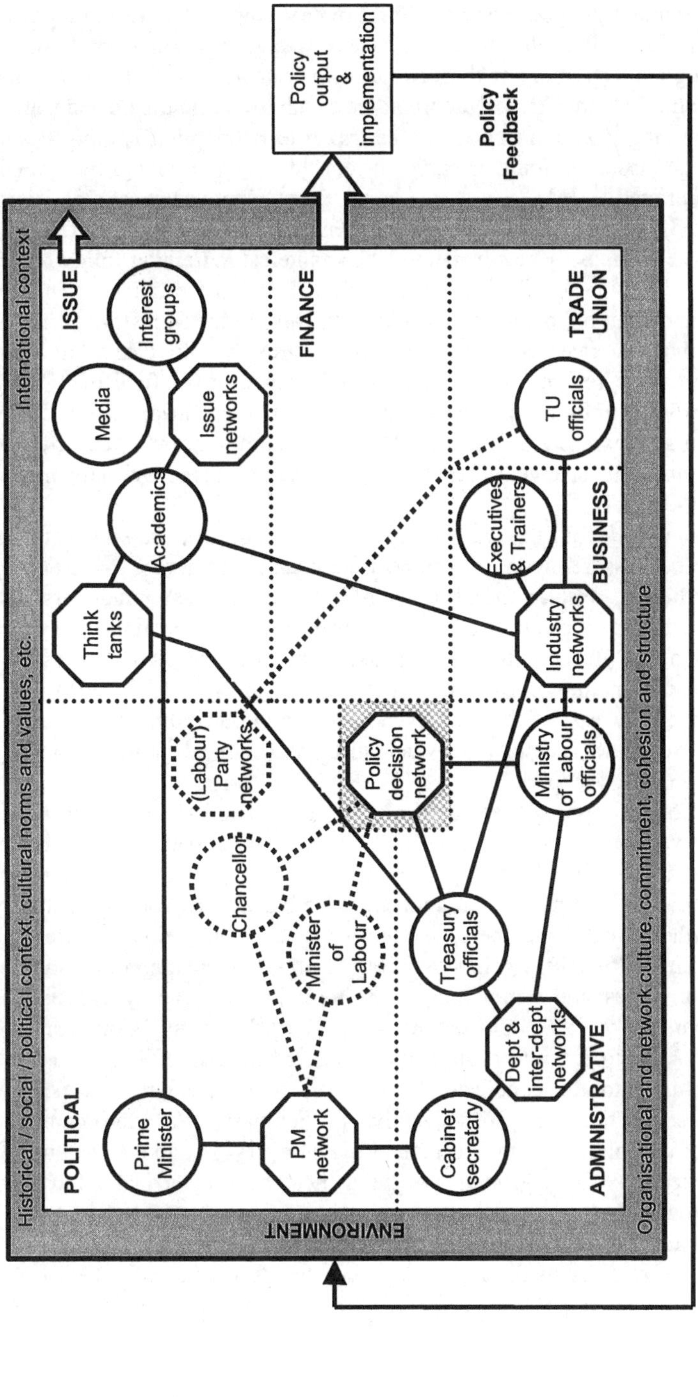

Figure 4.2 The merging of the training policy community and the growth advocacy network, 1959-1962

already noted the presence of PEP representatives at BACIE conferences after 1960 (PEP 1960: 50, 246-7). There was also a strong emphasis on training and retraining at the FBI conference in 1960 and this led to the creation of a joint FBI/BEC committee to advise on matters of education and training.[13] In January 1961, the tripartite Economic Planning Board began to discuss training as part of its consideration of how growth might be improved.[14] BACIE's 1961 conference 'Continental comparisons' explicitly acknowledged the link between growth and training (BACIE 1961). The Treasury also began to take an interest in training following its report to cabinet on 'Economic growth and national efficiency' in July 1961 and went on to conduct 'missionary work' in the Ministry of Labour regarding the need for new policies on growth.[15] In effect, the two networks had merged; the environmental change in the field of training thus being reinforced by the extensive negative feedback produced by Britain's apparently lacklustre rate of economic growth and by the environmental change created by the growth advocacy network in response to this.

The effect of all this was to galvanise the industrial training network and put pressure upon government to change its stance on training. Nevertheless, despite the upsurge of interest amongst employers and unions, the second report of the ITC revealed that it remained 'far from satisfied that all the industrial organisations are taking their responsibilities in the matter of training sufficiently seriously' (ITC 1961). This failure on the part of the employers, and the implications of this failure for growth, was emphasised not just by technical journals but by broadsheet newspapers.[16]

Although training had appeared in the manifesto of neither the Conservative nor Labour parties in 1959, the new climate on growth, the patent failure of the Carr Report, and the resultant pressure from both the industrial training network and the growth advocacy network (particularly from their media members) led both parties to examine the training question and to consider the possibility of imposing an apprentice training levy on firms and compelling firms to train and employ apprentices (Labour Party 1959; Conservative Party 1961; Young Conservatives 1961).[17] Environmental change and continued negative feedback led the government to the conclusion that it had no choice but to seek new policies on training. Consequently, in February 1961 the cabinet's Economic Policy Committee invited the Ministry of Labour to consider the extent to which growth was being held back by a lack of trained manpower.[18]

As a result of this decision, a new interdepartmental committee of officials was created. Following in the footsteps of BACIE, it immediately began to consider the practicability of a training levy / rebate system on the French model.[19] A small party of officials was despatched to France to discuss its system of a payroll tax of 0.4 per cent coupled with rebates to firms that could show that their training was related to the wider needs of their industry. It returned impressed; finding the system to be both 'remarkable' and 'admirable'.[20] Its leader, J.G. Stewart, was particularly impressed by the enthusiasm with which French trade unions embraced training. In his view, whilst the system would require amendment if it were to be implemented in Britain, 'there need not be violent opposition as long as it was made quite clear that the proposed tax was not to be linked with direct government training of apprentices' and if industry itself decided on the training standards necessary to qualify for a rebate of the levy.

Rossetti, chairman of the interdepartmental working party and Deputy Secretary at the Ministry of Labour, was equally impressed by the delegation's findings and he urged his Permanent Secretary (Sir Lawrence Helsby) to advocate the levy / rebate scheme to Hare.[21] Helsby, however, was worried about the administrative load on his ministry, the complexity of likely negotiations with industry, and the political difficulties of a national tax on companies irrespective of their need for training. His advice to Hare was therefore more circumspect.[22] Although Middlemas (1986: 306) saw Helsby as the key figure in the Ministry of Labour's conversion to intervention in industry, the files suggest otherwise – suggesting that this conversion came as a result of more junior officials learning the lessons of past policy failure and that David Price (2000: 124-6) was right to see Helsby as a profound block to a radical change in the ministry's views. Nevertheless, despite Helsby's scepticism, Hare's lack of confidence that industry would deliver on training led him to make public in March 1961 his interest in the French levy / rebate system and his preparedness to see government intervention in training.[23]

At the end of April 1961, Hare submitted a paper on training to the Economic Policy Committee (EPC) of the cabinet which established that economic growth was being impeded by the shortage of trained workers.[24] Hare told the committee that he was becoming doubtful whether the government should continue to rely solely on the policy recommended by the Carr Committee. He suggested that the government should be ready 'to consider long-term changes which might be made if the present expansion of training proves inadequate'.

Simultaneously, training was acknowledged to be a key policy area by the new Treasury inspired interdepartmental working party on economic growth and was identified as such in its report to the cabinet in July 1961.[25] This report, amongst its wide array of areas for government action, emphasised the part that investment in human capital, such as training, could play in raising growth and the role that government intervention might play in improving it. In particularly, it highlighted the levy / rebate system as worthy of further investigation..

Thus, by early-1961 officials in both the Treasury and the Ministry of Labour were expressing interest in new policies on training in general and the levy / rebate system in particular. The lesson that had been learned by officials and experts in the field of training was that if growth was to become an explicit objective of government policy then government intervention would be required in industrial training to raise both its quantity and quality: the new goal would require a radical new policy instrument to ensure an adequate supply of skilled labour to cope with the increased demand. This was third order learning, but it had now to be translated into a policy change of a similar order.

Translating learning into policy proposals

Disagreement and policy drift

The translation of third order learning into third order policy change was by no means straightforward. Infighting between ministries, a lack of political leadership and divisions within industry meant that policy drifted for over a year. Differences of opinion between ministries were immediately apparent.[26] The Ministry of Labour's levy / rebate scheme faced opposition from three quarters. Firstly, the Inland Revenue vigorously objected both to the administrative effort that would be required to collect the levy, only to return it to industry in the form of a rebate, and to the whiff of hypothecation (traditionally anathema at the Revenue). Since the ministry would depend upon it to administer the levy this was a considerable problem. Secondly, the ministry's scheme was opposed by the tightly bound economic policy community at the heart of the core executive – embodied in the Budget Committee – on which it would depend for the necessary finance. To the irritation of Ministry of Labour officials, a botched attempt to introduce a payroll regulator in April 1961 (see Chapter 6) – ironically also an attempt to intervene in the labour market to raise productivity – had now made any tax on payrolls extremely sensitive in the Treasury.[27] Finally, although Ministry of Labour officials recognised that the ministry must inevitably treat with those on whom it depended successfully to secure and implement a shift in training policy, Helsby (essentially viewing policy through the zero sum prism of the Westminster model) was loth to take on both the Inland Revenue and Treasury. Had the ministry capitalised on the opportunities afforded by the Treasury's reappraisal of policies on growth for cooperation in the development of policy, the Budget Committee and the Inland Revenue might possibly have been won over. Instead, jealously guarding its prerogative in the field of training, Helsby caused the Ministry of Labour assiduously to exclude Treasury officials from many of the relevant committees.[28] This was a considerable barrier to progress.

Consequently, instead of announcing to the House of Commons his wish to investigate the levy / rebate scheme, Hare was forced to be more circumspect. He announced in May 1961 that an adequate case had yet to be made for departing from non-intervention, but his remark that he did 'not regard the details of our present system of industrial training as sacrosanct' hinted that this might change if industry failed to deliver.[29]

In December 1961, the working party submitted its interim report to Hare. It was far from unanimous – a reflection of interdepartmental divisions. It did accept that the shortage of skilled labour was restricting growth and that this shortage was the result of inadequate training provision by many firms.[30] It was also sceptical that the existing system could be relied upon to deliver the greater amount, and higher quality, of training that was needed if growth was to be raised. There was agreement too that, despite the improvement in industrial relations brought about by full employment, the craft unions viewed apprenticeship as a barrier to entry rather than as a means of training. Most importantly, it conceded that Britain's training was inferior to that in France and Germany in both quantity and quality and that, in these countries, training was both more highly organised and characterised by cooperation between management and workers. However, whilst it was able to agree on these problems, and on the need for government action to address them, the committee remained divided on the form that this action should take.

The working party presented three different options for change: imposing a statutory requirement to train; a national system granting rebates from taxation[31]; or offering subsidies to firms doing approved training. Of these options, the working party recommended the second – the rebate – arguing that the first was 'unlikely to be workable or effective' and the third 'would involve the government in direct participation for the first time in the cost of industrial training, with all the consequent difficulties of getting out again'. As noted above, however, this recommendation was not unanimous.[32]

At the Ministry of Labour, the view of officials was that a levy / rebate was the only means by which the problems of British training could be addressed. It would, the ministry hoped, provide 'a foot in the door by which it could gradually bring more and more influence to bear on the organisation and quality of training in industry'.[33] However, although the report of the interdepartmental working party suggested that support for action might be growing within the core executive, and despite support for intervention from the Conservative Party's policy committee on economic growth, and notwithstanding his worries about the poor response of industry to the 'bulge' and the inability of the ITC to solve the problem, Hare's awareness of divisions within the core executive over how the problem should be addressed, coupled one suspects with a lingering personal antipathy to intervention in industry by a Conservative government, had led him to embark on a parallel strategy.[34]

Hare had attempted to circumvent opposition within government by approaching industry directly. Fragmentation amongst the institutions of the labour market, however, meant that this strategy met with little success. His discussions with the construction, engineering and shipbuilding industries, between February and May 1961, about the scope and quality of training, the possibility of shortening the five year apprenticeship, and making the age of entry more flexible, achieved very little (BACIE 1962: v). In July 1961, he commissioned an enquiry by the NJAC into an industry based solution.[35] This also achieved little. The problem was that the analyses of the British Employers' Confederation (the principal employers' association in the field of training) and the TUC were very different. The BEC stressed the need for flexible working and an end to demarcation.[36] The TUC emphasised the need for expanded off the job training in technical colleges and day release.[37] Such differences of opinion made it impossible for the NJAC working party to devise an industry based means of improving the quantity and quality of training and led it to call for government intervention in its final report (NJAC 1962).

In the meantime, the interdepartmental working party had continued its examination of the levy / rebate scheme. This had revealed signs of movement amongst Treasury officials, who had come to hope that the new NEDC might offer a forum for solving the training problem.[38] This, however, must necessarily be a longer term solution. Union suspicions that the NEDC was a Trojan horse for wage control had first to be overcome before a subject that touched so closely on the interests and traditions of the union movement could be addressed. This meant that a short to medium-term interventionary strategy was still required, and the committee continued on balance to favour the levy / rebate scheme for this. This, however, was at odds with the March 1962 decision of the cabinet's Economic Policy Committee that the statement promised to the House of Commons should downplay the attractiveness of the levy / rebate scheme.[39] In addition, as Hare pointed out, to make a statement on future policy required the government first to be clear about the nature of the closer partnership with industry that was proposed – and at this point it was far from clear. In an attempt to clarify matters, Hare proposed a second incarnation of the interdepartmental working party.

This second working party, however, was asked not to continue its consideration of the levy / rebate scheme but to to examine urgently the case for providing more training facilities in GTCs and technical colleges. This proposal, backing away from intervention in the labour market entirely, was a completely different approach to that considered to date. The sudden change of direction reflected an attempt by the Ministry of Education (the representative in government of a powerful education network encompassing schools, technical colleges, and academic educationalists) to seize control of training policy and craft a solution to Britain's training problem located in educational institutions rather than in on the job training in industry.[40] The result of this collision of antipathetic industrial and educational networks straddling the state / civil society divide was a stalemate reflected in both the interdepartmental committee's April 1962 report and its consideration in the EPC.[41]

The fact was that the initiative on industrial training was now utterly bogged down. Whilst the EPC was keen to take action to improve industrial training neither ministers nor officials could agree on the measures required. All the interested ministries and networks were at loggerheads and agreement between them was required if a change in policy was to proceed.

The turning point

The key factor in removing the impasse was Macmillan's decision in the summer of 1962 radically to reshape his cabinet, to construct a 'new approach' to economic and social policy, and to take personal control of the construction of the development of this policy.[42] On 26 July Macmillan, having completed the reconstruction of his cabinet after the 'night of the long knives', announced the package of measures on profits, consumer protection, training, and security of employment and status (redundancy, sick pay, pensions and contracts of service) that he hoped would tempt the unions into a bargain on incomes policy. In respect of training, he told the House of Commons that:

> Efficiency for a nation starts with the education and the training of its young people ... Accordingly, we intend, either through NEDC or through direct talks with employers and trade unions, to study urgently together how we can improve both the quality and the quantity of young people being trained for their future in industry.[43]

Government intervention in industrial training was therefore an integral element of the 'new approach' – persuasively advocated to Macmillan by Hailsham.[44] As a principal in the industrial relations department of the Ministry of Labour noted, it would require 'a more direct approach by the Ministry of Labour to the whole question of personnel practices. In future the Ministry might be expected, not only to publicise such practices, but also to tell industry that it *should* adopt them'.[45] At the same time, the tripartite approach fitted well with the government's developing strategy for the NEDC and with the recent suggestion from the Conservative Party's committee on economic growth that employers and unions be encouraged to work jointly to improve training – a point emphasised by Butler to the new chancellor.[46]

Macmillan's support for policies aimed at stimulating growth enabled those officials in the industrial training policy network seeking government intervention to defeat the Ministry of Education's counter proposals on behalf of the education network. A Treasury appraisal of the latter by Otto Clarke at the Treasury, requested by the Prime Minister's office, warned that they would be 'enormously costly' and, by regarding industrial training as a problem of education, missed the point. Clarke was emphatic; training was a problem of industry and it was in industry that it must be solved.[47] The involvement of Clarke was significant. Training was now seen in the Treasury as a question of economic policy rather than just one of industrial relations, and as a key part of its new policy on growth. Alec Cairncross, the new director of Economic Section, for example, had begun to advocate a greater emphasis on industrial training to help both labour mobility and incomes policy.[48] Industrial training was now being handled by officials involved in the Treasury's conversion to the growth objective – officials who were prepared to countenance intervention by the government to force industry to improve its training.[49] This was evidence of the merging of the growth advocacy network and the training network. The appointment of Peter Vinter (the author of the Treasury's report to the chancellor on 'Economic growth and national efficiency') as the Treasury's representative on the interdepartmental committee on the levy was symptomatic of growing Treasury interest in training as a means to faster growth.[50] With his support, the Ministry of Labour was able to isolate the Ministry of Education by making a clear distinction between education and industrial training.[51]

Another related factor that paved the way for rapid progress on industrial training was the conclusion of the EPC, under pressure from Macmillan, that the adoption of the NEDC's 4 per cent growth target presupposed making 'economic growth ... the most important desideratum in every economic and social problem which comes before the government' and ensuring that the government did everything in its power to (inter alia) improve the supply of skilled labour.[52]

By August 1962, the interdepartmental working party – now in its third incarnation at Macmillan's insistence and operating under revised terms of reference that tasked it with devising a workable levy / rebate scheme – had drawn up a plan for its implementation that envisaged its operation on an industry by industry basis. In doing so, it was drawing upon a solution that had emerged from the industrial training policy network. The turning point had come with a speech by Lady Williams to the BACIE spring conference of 10 May 1962. Williams emphasised the need to place a statutory obligation on each industry to create an apprenticeship authority to organise its training properly (BACIE 1962: 1-11). Apprentices, she suggested, should be indentured to this new institution and their wages would be paid out of a fund contributed to by all employers in the industry. Her suggestion prompted J.G. Stewart (the Ministry of Labour official in charge of training and a conference delegate) to wonder if the first interdepartmental committee on training had not dismissed too hastily the idea of an industry based levy / rebate scheme. At the time it had thought that it would be difficult to come up with a watertight legal definition of various industries. Stewart now realised that a way round this would be for the legislation not to attempt such a definition, just list the industries that would have the obligation of organising apprenticeships in its industry. Any firm that failed to declare itself a member of one of these industries, he suggested, would be required to contribute to a residual authority that would be administered by the Ministry of Labour.[53]

The government had not suddenly embraced the idea of government intervention in industrial training as a direct result of pressure from BACIE, as suggested by Page (1967) and Perry (1976). It was, however, true that BACIE had helped to create a consensus of informed opinion in favour of intervention that the government was now able to draw upon. Most of the delegates to its May conference had been in favour of more intervention by the government (Work 1964) and Hare himself later emphasised the importance of the 'changed climate of opinion' that BACIE had helped to bring about (BACIE 1963a: 5-10).

In sum, despite Hare's apparent unwillingness to abandon the Carr doctrine, the BACIE conference coincided with and helped to shape a substantial shift in government thinking that was linked to the 4 per cent growth target and to Macmillan's 'new approach'.[54] The 'new approach' rapidly reversed Hare's hitherto timid approach to the levy / rebate scheme.[55] Despite Hare's reluctance to pursue the scheme, Ministry of Labour officials had continued to examine its feasibility. They had come to the conclusion that, 'no substantial progress [was] going to be made with any scheme involving the participation of the taxation authorities', but a workable solution might be found in Lady Williams' proposals since they had 'the great merit of removing the Inland Revenue from the scene'.[56]

This scheme now formed the basis of the considerations of the third working party on the industrial training levy – the first time that the working party had been asked to consider an industry by industry scheme (and also the first time that there was any suggestion of a government grant to accompany it).[57] By 30 July, it had drawn up a plan for establishing statutory bodies in selected industries that would be charged with the duty of promoting industrial training.[58]. On 26 September, it finally managed to submit a unanimous report. This concluded that an industry by industry approach was 'distinctly more practicable than we first thought' and had a number of advantages over a universal approach.[59] Firstly, it would not require the creation of a large organisation to administer it, most of the work being undertaken by the industries themselves. Secondly, the fact that the legislation would be of an enabling character would enable progress to be made piecemeal, thus allowing the most important industries such as engineering and construction to be tackled first. Finally, it would be a much less abrupt change – although it would ultimately produce 'a significant departure from the policy of not interfering with the autonomy of industry in relation to industrial training'.

The working party was acutely aware of the sensitivity of industrial training given the way it interlocked with the question of wages. However, it detected distinct indications that fear of relative decline was changing attitudes and concluded that the chances of successfully implementing such an interventionist scheme were better than they had ever been. To this end, the working party submitted a draft bill with its report. The Treasury intimated that support would be forthcoming for the significant amount of expenditure which all this would involve.[60] Within the Treasury, Clarke minuted: 'this may be pretty expensive, but [is] a good cause'.[61]

The new focus on growth that Macmillan's cabinet changes had produced meant that approval of the plan by the reconstructed EPC was virtually a formality and by December 1962 a white paper on industrial training had been published (Cmnd. 1892). This unequivocally stated that 'There is no doubt that shortages of skilled manpower have been an important factor in holding back the rate of economic expansion' (para. 1). It bemoaned the uneven quality of British training and called for standards to be improved to meet those of Continental countries. It identified as 'a serious weakness' the fact that both 'the amount and quality of industrial training are left to the uncoordinated decisions of a large number of individual firms' and that, as a result of poaching, these firms lacked the necessary economic incentive to invest in training. It concluded that the time had come to strengthen the existing partnership between industry, government and the vocational education authorities. It outlined three objectives for the future of industrial training policy: 'to enable decisions on the scale of training to be better related to economic needs and technological developments'; to improve the overall quality of industrial training and to establish minimum standards; and to spread the cost more fairly (paras. 3-7).

The white paper proposed to meet these objectives by giving the Minister of Labour statutory powers to set up boards that would be responsible for training in individual industries. They would establish training policy for the industry; set training standards, advise and assist firms. It also proposed a review of apprenticeship lengths. Most importantly, it was proposed that the new boards would pay allowances to trainees that would be financed via the imposition of a levy on firms in the industry (paras. 9-13).

Fundamentally, the objectives and approach outlined in the white paper were a product of the learning that had taken place within the training policy network and in the Ministry of Labour – itself an important actor in this network. Nevertheless, the publication of the white paper by the government also flowed from the stimulus provided by the wider change in the climate of opinion that had been produced by the growth advocacy network, and by the intervention of a prime minister who was highly sympathetic to the ideas being promoted within this network.[62]

Implementing the new policy

From the White Paper to the 1964 Industrial Training Act

The white paper was a major achievement given the intense interdepartmental (and inter-policy network) battle that had taken place in the core executive. Now, however, the government must convert its broad proposals in a new and effective policy instrument that would achieve its objectives in industrial training and thus help raise Britain's rate of economic growth. This was a difficult process with the Ministry of Labour, which was responsible for implementing the new policy, facing dogged resistance from the fragmented institutions of the labour market.

As we have seen, the ability of such fragmentation to stymie progress had already made itself evident in Hare's attempt, via direct discussions and through the machinery of an NJAC enquiry, to get industry itself to construct a solution to the 'training problem', with BEC and TUC representatives advocating very different remedies.[63] Such differences of opinion had made it impossible for the NJAC working party to devise a way of improving training and led it to call for government intervention.[64]

Now that the government had settled on the levy / grant system it had apparently risen to the challenge. The Ministry of Labour, however, was only too aware that it could not simply force its will on industry. Looking beneath the surface of the white paper it is clear that the ministry hesitated to antagonize its 'clients' in the industrial policy networks in which it operated for, whilst the proposals introduced compulsion in the form of the levy, decisions on training would continue to be taken, and training performed, by industry.[65] This suggests a far less powerful centre than that assumed by the 'Westminster model'. Recognizing, though as we shall see underestimating, the extent of its weakness, the ministry had effectively settled on a 'non-interventionary' intervention in which it would set the policy parameters but bring both sides of industry together to decide on the detail of policy; in return for which industry would devise solutions that would enable the objectives of the white paper to be achieved. Thus the ministry hoped to achieve its aims by 'steering not rowing.' Implicitly, therefore, it recognized that it was operating in conditions of 'governance.'

The degree to which 'governance' posed a problem for the ministry's successful implementation of the new policy soon became clear as divisions emerged between the key institutions over the detail of policy that, as we shall see, were to make steering extremely difficult. From the start, in fact, there were concerns at the highest reaches about whether the strategy could succeed. Both Butler and Macmillan, for example, were worried that Hare's proposals were too timid and would not prove sufficient to obtain union cooperation on wage restraint, and thus achieve higher growth without higher inflation (the 'issue on which the election will be won or lost').[66] Officials on the economic side of the Treasury warned the chancellor that the Ministry of Labour risked being defeated by the conservatism of both sides of industry and that their restrictive practices were likely to prevail.[67] Hare himself acknowledged to the cabinet's Home Affairs Committee that the new Industrial Training Boards might be captured by such conservative interests.[68] Privately, the official in charge of training at the Ministry of Labour acknowledged that its attempt to steer employers and unions towards a radical overhaul of industrial training might fail.[69]

In turning the broad outline of the White Paper into specific proposals, Hare was careful to stress the importance of consultation to the process.

He had some reason to hope that this might succeed. In the lead up to the white paper, both the BEC Executive Council and the General Council of the TUC had indicated that they were prepared to countenance radical change.[70] This suggested a surprising degree of agreement amongst elites on both sides of industry on which the Ministry of Labour could potentially capitalize. Unfortunately for Hare, the influence of competing policy networks was to lead to marked differences emerging between the views of the employers, the unions, experts in the field, and the government (though interestingly not between the major political parties) about the details of how policy should change.[71]

The principal point of difference between the BEC and TUC initially concerned the need for a central body to coordinate the ITBs. The TUC General Council, for example, was convinced that, without some form of statutory body to oversee training, 'vested interests' would prevail in the ITBs and subvert the objectives of the white paper (BACIE 1963a: 26).[72] This was a widely held view amongst the general unions; Frank Cousins, General Secretary of the TGWU, for example, supported the intentions of the white paper but feared that it would not succeed against 'vested interests' because it was 'insufficiently compulsive' (BACIE 1963a: 26). The TUC experience of advisory bodies did not suggest that the proposed industrial training boards would be able to make a sufficient difference. To address this, the TUC called for a strong central body; one able to oversee the boards, ensure adequate representation of educational interests in industrial training, and fight for funds from government.[73]

In making such a call, however, the TUC leadership failed to recognize the diversity of opinion in the TUC and soon found itself torn between protecting the interests of craft unions that might be adversely affected by change and its desire for involvement in the planning of radical reform of training (Sheldrake and Vickerstaff 1987: 34-5). Nowhere was this split more noticeable than in the conflict between the TUC General Council and its Education Committee. The General Council, on which general unions predominated and which had hitherto been solely responsible for negotiations with the Ministry of Labour, wanted a strong central authority able to force the boards 'to set their sights high'.[74] The TUC's Education Committee, however, was dominated by craft unions that were extremely reluctant to see their powers over the existing apprenticeship system weakened.[75] Their proposed solution to the problem of training, as it had been throughout the 1950s, was to develop day release training; in other words, to address the problem through the education system rather than through reform of apprentice training – an analysis shared by other members of the education policy network of which it was a part.[76]

The General Council attempted to sideline the Education Committee by excluding it from negotiations with the Ministry of Labour. The committee bitterly resented this.[77] Ultimately its continuing trenchant objections were to lead the TUC to the view that a strong central body was undesirable and that 'on the whole training is a matter where the initiative must lie with the employer.'[78] This was a major reversal for the General Council, for the TUC staff and for the general unions. It was also clear evidence of the fragmentary nature of unionization in Britain. As the TUC Economics Committee put it, in contrast to the centralised structure of the Swedish LO, 'there was no British trade union movement – only a collection of unions'.[79] The fact was that the TUC had no power to force member unions to comply with the General Council' policy. Yet without such compliance the General Council's wish to see a strong central authority able to force through radical change was dead in the water. This interdependence in a policy area where the interests of individual unions were at stake made it extremely difficult for those trade unionists that were prepared to support radical change actually to achieve it (Finegold and Soskice 1988: 29-30; Minkin 1992: 444; Morgan 1994).[80]

Similar fragmentation and interdependence could be found amongst employers. The BEC and FBI (the two main peak organizations) and the sundry lesser groupings often disagreed and found it difficult to coordinate their response to the government's initiative.[81] More significantly, there was a notable split between what Boswell and Peters term the 'vanguard corporate elite' in employers' associations and 'backwoodsmen' amongst their memberships (Boswell and Peters 1997: 34-5). A joint BEC/FBI committee on education and training (set up after the 1960 FBI conference) accepted the proposals in the White Paper; commenting that its objectives were 'basically sound' and 'unlikely to be achieved under the existing machinery for industrial training'.[82] At executive level, both the BEC (the principal employers' association in the field of training) and the FBI were prepared to accept an active role for both government and unions in training, and to accept that training needed radically to be overhauled.[83] Nevertheless, the BEC executive feared, correctly as it turned out, that many employers (and many unions) would oppose central control. Since its structure handed more power to the membership than did that of the FBI (Boswell and Peters 1997: 34) it decided early on to oppose a strong central body and to press for the boards to have more autonomy than was proposed not less, and for each board to have a majority of employer representatives (Page 1967: 60-4).[84] There were indeed immediately strong objections from many BEC members. Many of those member firms and trade associations which objected felt the craft unions already had more than enough power over training and were very reluctant to see their power increased via the new ITB structure. The general tenor of such protests can be summed up by the China Clay Association's complaint that the BEC was 'lending itself to interference by the government in the right of industry to order its conduct according to its own precepts of sound management.'[85] At the same time, as employers' representatives on the NEDC acknowledged, many firms were very worried about radical change in the field of apprenticeships because they feared that it might worsen industrial relations.[86] The result was that a large number of members threatened to desert their respective organizations if they subscribed to the ITB structure, the levy / rebate system, and (particularly) to pressure for greater central control.[87] This threat carried considerable weight since the power of the BEC depended on the reach of its membership and it lacked the power to enforce change on resistant members. This led the leaderships of both the BEC and the FBI to the conclusion that strong central control must be vigorously resisted if other elements of the reform were to be sustained. Such resistance to change was to be expected, but the lack of power of the respective executives over member firms meant that their complaints had shaped BEC/FBI opposition to central control (Finegold and Soskice 1988: 29-30 and Morgan 1994).[88]

The BACIE was also divided over policy details. Many of its members were concerned that, unless there was a central coordinating body, organising training on an industry basis would be inefficient where skills cut across industrial classifications – a concern brushed aside by Hare (BACIE 1963a: 9). To deal with this, there were many public calls for greater central control in the writings of informed and influential members of the industrial training policy network (see for example: Boyden 1963; Wellens 1963a; Williams 1963; and Work 1964). Initially, the BACIE did indeed advocate a central body with powers over the ITBs (BACIE 1963a: Page 1967: 56-60; Perry 1976).[89] Nevertheless, despite this initial position, over time the BACIE came to insist that the powers of any central body over the ITBs be limited.[90] The reasons for this shift are not altogether clear but it not unlikely that the same forces were at work as were operating within the peak organizations.

An important ingredient in the opposition of members in both BACIE and the peak organizations on both sides of industry was the conservatism of deeply embedded self organizing networks operating at the level of individual companies and plants. At a meeting between Hare and the BEC, senior BEC executives acknowledged a strong tendency for both companies and local craft unions to combine to resist reform of craft apprenticeships.[91] Maurice Laing, for example, warned that at the level of the individual firm there was 'a deep rooted resistance to change' on both sides of industry and that in about 50 per cent of firms they would work together to oppose change to the system of craft apprenticeships even though it could 'no longer [be] justified.'[92] The alliance of individual employers and unions might have been tactical but it was no less effective for that. Of course, some low level opposition to change was to be expected, but the lack of power of the respective employers' associations over their members, the equal lack of TUC control over individual unions, and the interdependencies involved made it very difficult for the peak association elites to overcome it (also the conclusion of Finegold and Soskice 1988: 29-30 and Morgan 1994). Thus the existence of conservative, low level, self-organizing and inter-organizational policy networks was a considerable barrier to building tripartite institutions capable of reforming the apprenticeship system.

The impact of these low level policy networks in turn played an important role in undermining the Ministry of Labour's reform programme. The problem for the ministry was that it faced a classic governance conundrum; how to achieve its objectives given its inability to enforce compliance on self-organising policy networks. It struggled to find an approach that would deal with the problem. The ministry's dilemma is well illustrated by its confusion over central control. Helsby was absolutely opposed to a strong tripartite central body; finding the idea to be offensive since it would reduce his ministry's power over industrial training.[93] Helsby's opposition led the ministry initially to argue that ultimate control should remain with its minister and that to cede responsibility for the allocation of government finance to an extra-governmental authority would set a dangerous precedent.[94] The logic of Helsby's position was therefore the maintenance of a high degree of government control. This implicitly assumed a 'Westminster model' of a centralized government power. As his officials increasingly recognized, however, the ministry was operating in conditions of 'governance'. Aware of the ministry's weakness they steadily shifted towards less government intervention in an attempt to gain the support of the peak organizations and steer them to the desired outcome rather than attempt to enforce change and fail. The ministry constantly found itself pulled between these two poles of greater or lesser government control.

Pressure of time on the parliamentary timetable meant that the bill did not receive its first reading until 14 November 1963. In the second reading, on 20 November, Labour and Conservative MPs vied with each other to show the greatest enthusiasm and Ray Gunter, now shadow minister of labour promised that Labour would support the bill (Perry 1976: 123-6). The bill was passed, virtually unamended, on 21 January 1964 and came into force in March 1964. Nevertheless, the practical implementation of the ITA (the last major act of the Conservative administration) fell largely to the incoming Labour government.

Labour's learning

As with taxation and incomes policy, Labour's policy on training had undergone a marked shift during the early-1960s as a consequence of the new climate of opinion produced by the growth advocacy network and the industrial training network. An early hint of the implications of the new interest in 'planning' for the party's training policy was evident in its Youth Commission statement in 1959 that 'if the economy fails to expand at the pace required, then the government must be ready to undertake directly at least some part of industrial training' (Labour Party 1959: 29). Growing support for 'planning' led the party to consider vocational training policy during the early years of the 1960s; the first time it had done so since it entered opposition in 1951.[95] In November 1962 its Home Policy Committee noted that training and retraining had become an important gap in the party's policy programme.[96] A number of Labour research department papers subsequently analysed the problem. In December 1962, one such paper noted that both the quantity of apprenticeships and the quality of their training were worth addressing.[97] Another remarked that 'if we are to revitalise the British economy, one of the greatest needs is for an expansionist policy towards all forms of industrial training'.[98] In September 1963 Wilson, in his 'white heat' speech to the party conference, stated

> We shall need a totally new attitude to the problem of apprenticeships and training ... If there is one thing where the traditional philosophy of capitalism breaks down it is in the training for apprenticeship, because frankly it does not pay any individual firm unless it is very altruistic or quixotic or farsighted to train apprentices ... We shall have to get away from the idea of apprenticeship to a single firm. There will have to be apprenticeship to the industry as a whole. (Labour Party 1963: 140)

In considering its options in training policy, it was necessary for Labour to assess its attitude to the Conservative's Industrial Training Act. Labour's science and industry sub committee noted that the proposals in Cmnd. 1892 represented 'a radical departure from previous government policy [which] seems to accept that government intervention in industrial training is necessary'.[99] For this reason it argued that the proposals should be welcomed; although it noted the need for a central authority. In March 1963, the party's finance and economic policy sub committee also welcomed Cmnd. 1892 – although it recommended that Labour encourage the proposed ITBs to give greater emphasis to the training of young people not taking apprenticeships and to the retraining of adults.[100] It also wondered if the ITBs should not be better integrated with the NEDC and be required to meet its manpower targets.

The party's manifesto for the October 1964 election promised, as one of its many 'planning' proposals, a 'plan for training'. What it did not say was that this plan would essentially consist of implementing the Conservatives' recent Industrial Training Act. In the lead up to the election, the party's Home Policy Committee noted that Britain needed a 'training revolution' if growth were to be raised.[101] It argued that, if a Labour government was elected, the Ministry of Labour should become 'one of the key instruments of planning ... Its role [would] be comparable with the part that the Ministry played under Ernest Bevin in wartime – but without the power of conscription'. However, the changes to the Conservative's policy were almost entirely cosmetic. The new Minister of Labour, Ray Gunter, called for the definition of the industrial basis of the new ITBs to be widely defined in order to reduce demarcation, obtain economies of scale, and capitalise on the similar changes taking place in many industries. He also created an new interdepartmental committee in an attempt to ensure that the Ministry of Labour and the Ministry of Education worked together to advance the programme 'with the greatest possible speed'.[102] Fundamentally, however, Labour's programme did not differ in any important way from that of the Conservatives (a view supported by Elliott 1978: 606).

In other words, the Conservatives' analysis in 1962 that better training was needed if the new growth objective was to be attained was essentially accepted by the incoming Labour government in 1964; as was the assumption that an active labour market policy, including increased access to training, would provide the unions with an incentive to support an incomes policy and that the ITA was the means by which the training element of this package would best be delivered. George Brown noted that a 'coherent and genuine labour market policy', in which training was an important element, was 'vitally important' to Labour's strategy for achieving faster growth – giving trade unionists the greater sense of security that would secure their cooperation in a voluntary incomes policy – and this view was echoed by Gunter in his opening address to the BACIE spring conference in 1965 and by Harold Wilson in his speech to the 1964 TUC conference.[103] As an academic pointed out to the BACIE East Midlands group in 1965, the reform of training was essentially 'a technocratic response to the challenge of raising growth' that transcended ideology.[104]

Thus, both the Labour and Conservative parties had learned similar lessons from the policy failures of the 1950s and both parties attempted to construct a similar policy response, with training an important element in both their programmes. Training had a central role in Labour's 1965 *National Plan* for achieving higher economic growth and higher productivity and its 1966 manifesto repeated the pledge to modernise training (Cmnd. 2764, Ch. 1, para. 29 and Ch. 3; Labour Party 1966).[105]

Policy failure

Whilst the ITA was seen as path breaking both at the time and subsequently, it was not long before suspicions mounted that the act might not have succeeded in realising its objectives. It was, for example, immediately apparent that the ITA had failed to bridge the traditional divide between education and training – a failing acknowledged by the CTC.[106] The lack of central control was also immediately seen as a significant barrier to successful reform in the face of 'entrenched attitudes and practices (Hall 1965). A study in 1968 questioned whether there had been any real improvement in the quality of training; since firms appeared to be designing their training to ensure qualification for a grant rather than addressing their real training needs (Tavernier 1968 – a finding supported by Ziderman 1978). Sheldrake and Vickerstaff (1987: 37-8) were later more generous, finding that the ITA had been successful in industries with acute skill shortages such as engineering, though not elsewhere – particularly in trans-sectoral and semi-skilled occupations (see also Capella 1996; Prais 1981). They also concluded that overall the quality and quantity of training remained sub standard. A study by the Brookings Institution found that the ITB system actively restricted labour mobility (Denison 1968: 283). The lack of central control over the ITBs, which the BACIE had warned as early as March 1963 would likely cause problems where skills cut across industrial classifications, was decried by both the CBI and TUC (BACIE 1963a; CBI 1968; TUC 1969). A review of training by the CTC in 1968 which called for both sides of industry to end restrictive practices in training was a clear indictment of a policy that had set out to remove them (CTC 1968). In the same year, the Donovan Commission commented in respect of industrial training that 'a radical change in outlook [was] particularly urgent' – clearly implying that the ITA had failed to achieve this (Cmnd. 3623: para 330).

In 1969 the government instituted a review. Its conclusions were that the achievements of the ITA had been patchy (Department of Employment 1972). It conceded that costs had successfully been redistributed, with those firms providing little or no training now forced to contribute financially to industrial training. It also detected evidence of an improvement in the quality of training in some (though far from all) industries. Overall, however, it concluded that the ITBs were far too narrowly focused and that their structure meant that they had had done little to direct training in their industries to the economic needs either of their respective industries or of the wider economy. This was a widespread criticism. An analysis of the act in 1970 by two academics, for example, damned the ITB structure and its lack of central coordination for failing to address 'the commercial realities of a rapidly changing economy' (Lees and Chiplin 1970). Perry (1976: 311-2) noted that the ITBs were of no help in shifting labour from declining to expanding industries, 'were not well adapted to regional training needs' and tended to 'isolate training from the other vital areas which make up a national manpower policy'.[107] Moreover, initiatives on training were limited to a lowest common denominator – constrained by the conservative interests of individual firms and craft unions.

Fundamentally, the centre had failed to prevail over the fragmented institutions of industrial training. The fragmented institutional structure of the ITBs, the lack of coordination between them – and the lack of integration between the ITB and the new industry related Economic Development Councils set up under the NEDC – reflected the fragmentation of Britain's labour market and the blocking power of low level industrial networks that flowed from it. This existence of this fragmentation, and the fact that the ITA did nothing to address it, meant that, despite widespread support for a radical reshaping of industrial training, the ITBs simply consolidated the extant apprenticeship system rather than expanding the scope of training and broadening apprenticeships (D. King, 1995: 209). The key point here is that (contrary to the assertion of Richardson 1991: 128) the ITB structure did nothing to break up the existing structure of training. This is not to say that there was no progress at all. One of the objectives of the 1962 White Paper was met – the cost of training being spread more evenly (until small firms, the principal offendors, managed to have themselves excluded from the levy / grant system in 1973). However, other objectives had not been achieved. The apprenticeship system was not overhauled. The ITA involved no real compulsion and offered little incentive for developing or enforcing new approaches to training. The quantity and quality of training remained poor. More generally, despite the ITA, attempts to improve human capital to raise Britain's rate of economic growth remained 'very inadequate'. Decisions on training continued to be poorly related to economic growth and technological developments. These fundamental problems continued to preoccupy policy makers for years to come (CBI 1968; Mann 1970;

Finegold and Soskice 1988; Broadberry 1991; King 1995; Prais 1981; Bean and Crafts 1996).

Conclusions

In the field of British training those operating within the industrial training policy network had been able to secure a major shift in industrial training policy. This shift was the product of three factors. First, negative feedback from the policies of the 1950s in the field of industrial training served to make the policy environment more favourable to radical change, and to government action to achieve it. This change served to dynamise the world of industrial training and to encourage the development of an industrial training policy network that sought to change attitudes in both industry and in government through its direct links with the Ministry of Labour, with employers and with trade unions. It was also able to change the policy environment more generally via the actions of journalists linked to the network, who helped to publicise both the idea that Britain had a training problem and the industrial training policy network's ideas about how it might be solved. The actions of this network were, however, massively reinforced by the more general shift in both the climate of opinion and in the core executive produced by the growth advocacy network in the late-1950s and (particularly) in the early-1960s. Once higher grown was embraced as the primary economic objective of the government a new policy on training to raise both the quantity and quality of trained workers in Britain was its natural corollary. Thus the system 'learned' that economic objectives must be overhauled and that, to attain the new growth objective, a major overhaul of the institutions of British training was required. This revision of goals and the desire to find new policy instruments in training amounted to third order learning.

Despite this third order learning, and despite the institutional change that it gave rise to, Britain's apprentice training system remained essentially unchanged and the new ITB system proved ill suited to ensuring that decisions on training were made with a view to the wider needs of the economy and, particularly, the achievement of higher growth.[108] Third order learning was not translated into third order change.

An important factor in this failure to achieve third order change in the field of training was that Britain's apparently centralized state in the 1960s was much more fragmented and consequently a lot less powerful than has been (and was) commonly assumed. Inside Whitehall, the industrial training policy network – represented by the Ministry of Labour's training department – faced strong opposition from policy networks with different agenda. Whilst this was temporarily solved by

Macmillan's intervention in 1962, the need for him to do so indicated a serious weakness of governance. The most notable consequence was that the ITA failed to bridge the gap between industrial training and technical education (Page 1967: 69-70; Crafts 1991: 283). Similarly, the wider education reforms of the 1960s largely ignored vocational education (Finegold and Soskice 1988: 25-6).

There was also the problem that Britain's labour market was also very fragmented. Within the TUC, for example, there were institutionalised divisions between craft and general unions that the TUC General Council and its staff were unwilling, or unable, to surmount. Craft unions were able to resist reform of apprentice training and thus defend the wage premium that restricted entry into apprenticeships produced (King 1995: 207-9; Kirby 1992). This lack of power at the centre of the peak organisation of labour was also true of the employers.[109] At the peak level, both the BEC and FBI were prepared to condone an overhaul of industrial training, and to accept, albeit reluctantly, government intervention to achieve. Yet, individual firms were often guilty of retrograde attitudes.[110] At the level of the individual company or plant, unions and employers had reached a modus operandum in the area of apprenticeships which, whilst it preserved the peace between them, was profoundly antithetical to radical change. Many preferred to retain their autonomy in training (Shonfield 1965: 117-8; Finegold and Soskice 1988: 25-6; King 1995: 211). By combining together in self-organising inter-organisational networks they were able to encourage their respective peak organisations to resist important aspects of the industrial training proposals and to channel the institutional change that took place.

The Ministry of Labour was only too aware that it lacked the power to impose its will on the fragmented institutions of the labour market – an implicit recognition of the governance problem that it faced in translating third order learning in training into third order change.[111] Instead of 'rowing' it sought to 'steer' via a cooperative approach embracing both unions and employers. In theory, the fact that the ministry was already embedded within an industry based policy network embracing these groups, and the fact that elites in the several employers' associations and in the TUC were prepared to countenance radical change in return for an involvement in policy formulation, ought to have meant it was well placed to build a workable institutional solution. In practice, the ministry proved unable to mobilize this support effectively, not least because whilst it recognized the problem and implications of governance it remained imprisoned in a mindset shaped by the Westminster model. Thus, despite an apparent commitment to tripartism the ministry proved unwilling to involve non-governmental institutions in policy making, as opposed to policy implementation, for fear of losing what control it had over training; as one Ministry of Labour official put it in the lead up to the 1962 White Paper: 'if we don't want a lot of delay and confusion it would be better to consult BEC and TUC after a scheme has been worked out.'[112] This use of bilateral talks with employers and unions at once betrayed the low opinion that the ministry held for the opinions of both sides and the marked lack of trust the ministry had in its own ability to identify those trade unionists and employers who were supportive of change, mobilise them effectively and so secure wider support for its own point of view. This meant the ministry failed to capitalize on the support for change amongst 'vanguard elites' on both sides of industry.

Having devised its own approach, the Ministry of Labour then hesitated to push ahead aggressively in the face of mounting opposition from the peak organizations engendered by low level self-organizing industrial networks – for fear of spoiling its relations with industry. It backed away from setting standards for training and reforming apprenticeships. It chose not to seek representation on the new ITBs and failed to implement other means of bringing its influence to bear upon them. There was no attempt to use the government grant to exercise leadership and the setting of the levy remained a matter for industry.[113] Consequently, despite widespread concern regarding relative economic decline and the need for higher growth, and despite the extensive perception that government intervention in training to promote radical change was needed if relative decline was to be reversed and higher growth attained, there was no fundamental reform. Although there was general support amongst expert commentators and professional trainers for a radical reshaping of the apprentice system, the ITBs 'simply consolidated extant training practices, particularly in apprenticeships, rather than becoming an opportunity to expand training into new areas and to broaden the apprenticeship system'. Vested interests had prevailed.[114] Furthermore, the institutional structure created by the ITA reflected fragmentation in the labour market, indeed it was made worse by the lack of integration between the ITBs and the parallel structure of industry related EDCs established under the auspices of the NEDC.

This chapter has traced the flowering of a new preparedness in the core executive in the early-1960s (in this instance in the Ministry of Labour and in the Treasury) to see an active state working with the private sector to correct market failure, and a preparedness to craft innovatory answers to the question how to improve the quality and quantity of British industrial training and help raise Britain's rate of growth and reverse her relative decline. The failure effectively to intervene to build institutions able radically to overhaul and expand the scope of training was therefore not a failure of government will. The problem lay in the translation of this will to see radical change into successful policies to achieve it; and specifically in the barrier posed by the linked issues of fragmentation and self-organizing inter-organizational policy networks, a phenomenon which therefore clearly predates 1979. This was simultaneously a key factor in the decision to adopt a relatively weak form of neo-corporatism and in the failure of this solution to attain its intended results. Partly this reflected the lack of an institutional structure that could unite these fragmented yet interdependent institutions (Shonfield 1965: 199-200; Morgan 1994: 249-50). At a deeper level, however, the pervasive assumption in both Whitehall and in industry of a 'Westminster model' of central government was a significant problem. Whilst the more astute in the Ministry of Labour and the peak organizations realized that a solution to Britain's training 'problem' could not be devised by government alone, fundamentally they continued to be captivated by a 'Westminster model' view of policy making. This led elites both within and without the core executive vastly to underestimate the scale of the shift from government to governance that the situation demanded.

Consequently, whilst there was third order learning in the field of industrial training, this learning was not translated into third order change. There was no fundamental reform of British industrial training. The apprenticeship system remained basically unchanged. Although the cost of training was, temporarily, shared more favourably, there was little progress in solving the more fundamental problems identified by Cmnd. 1892. Despite the widespread learning of the lesson that training was central to higher growth, and that government intervention was essential if it was to be improved, the ITA was poorly related to the growth objective, involved no compulsion and offered no incentive for developing or enforcing new approaches to training. The quality of training remained inadequate and decisions on training continued to be poorly related to economic needs and technological developments. These fundamental problems continued (and continue according to Barrett and Dewson 1998) to bedevil British industrial training

5

Incomes Policy

Introduction

This chapter examines the attempt to construct a voluntary incomes policy between 1961 and 1966. It therefore deals with the second of the three elements of the growth policy package. It does not argue that incomes policy was a wholly new idea. It does, however, argue that an attempt to construct a voluntary incomes policy was an integral part of the new policies adopted in the early-1960s because, without it, the new growth objective could not be achieved without triggering higher inflation. This alteration of both the goals and instruments of economic policy, it suggests, amounted to third order learning. Nevertheless, the chapter again argues that the translation of this third order learning into third order change was unsuccessful. Neither the Conservative nor the succeeding Labour government was able to surmount the barrier posed by a profoundly fragmented institutional inheritance and successfully implement an effective and permanent voluntary policy that would tie the growth in average earnings to that of productivity and allow higher growth without inflation. The result was that the attempt to build a workable voluntary policy was abandoned in July 1966 and the emphasis shifted initially towards compulsion and then towards reform of industrial relations law. With the simultaneous abandonment of the growth objective, the idea of an incomes policy embedded within a growth policy framework also died. When governments returned to incomes policy in the 1970s, they did so as a means of avoiding sterling crises and deflation, not as a means to higher growth.

The chapter begins by briefly analysing post-war government policy towards wages and then examines the learning that took place in the years leading up to 1961. It then explores the development of policy under both Conservative and Labour governments after 1961 and considers how well learning was translated by each government into policy. The analysis focuses on six key stages in the attempt to build a voluntary policy: the introduction of a compulsory 'pay pause' for public sector workers in July 1961; the institution in 1962 of a 2-2½ per cent 'guiding light' for wage increases, administered by a new National Incomes Commission (NIC), and the failed attempt to reach agreement on voluntary restraint with unions and employers; the attempt to reach a deal in the NEDC in 1963 based around the 'dash for growth' and a guiding light of 3-3½ per cent; the continuation of this 'norm' under Labour, the December 1964 tripartite 'Joint Statement of Intent on Productivity, Prices and Incomes' and the subsequent creation of the National Board for Prices and Incomes (NPBI); the strengthening of prices and incomes policy in November 1965; and the final collapse of the attempt to craft a permanent voluntary policy in July 1966 with the introduction of a six month statutory wages 'standstill', this then followed by a further six months of 'severe restraint'.

Post-war learning up to 1961

Incomes policy was by no means a new idea in 1961. Keynes was well aware of the problem posed by the wage raising powers of trade unions and it was recognised as early as 1944 in the Treasury, that the maintenance of high demand to ensure full employment would be 'fruitless unless wages and prices [we]re kept reasonably stable' (Artis 1981: 7; Cmd. 6527: para. 49).[1] However, although the Labour government obtained TUC support for a voluntary wage freeze and FBI support for voluntary dividend restraint in 1948, this did not amount to a permanent incomes policy; being essentially a temporary product of the 1948 crisis and the 'transitional arrangements' of the immediate post-war economy. By 1950 the government had fallen back on more general pleas for restraint (Dow 1964: 35; R. Jones 1987: 39-41; Cairncross and Watts 1989: 335-7; Cairncross 1995: 65-6, 85). The likelihood of a policy for incomes then receded further with the election of the Conservatives in 1951 since – the new government being ideologically predisposed to the view that inflation was best combated by allowing a free market to bring supply and demand in the labour market into equilibrium. Attempts by Sir Robert Hall of the Treasury's Economic Section in the early-1950s to persuade ministers that some mechanism needed to be found to restrict the growth of wages if full employment was to be maintained were ignored (Booth 2001b: 303-5). Instead, the Conservatives also placed their hopes in appeals for restraint (Dow 1964: 67; Cairncross and Watts 1989: 323-42).

In 1956, however, with unemployment at a record low and an acceleration in both annual wage inflation to 9 per cent Harold Macmillan, the new chancellor and described by Hall as 'the first really strong incomes policy man in the Government', bowed to Hall's concern.[2] Following a white paper on 'The economic implications of full employment' which advocated 'self restraint in making wage claims and fixing profit margins' (Cmd. 9725: 10-12), Macmillan proposed a 'price plateau' in May 1956. This, he hoped, would break the wage / price spiral by removing the cost of living increases that were used by unions to justify wage increases.[3] However, in the absence of TUC support and with the government unwilling to take powers to compel the unions to cooperate, Macmillan's initiative again really amounted to no more than exhortation (Dorfman 1973: 94-6; Jones 1987: 53).

The next chancellor, Peter Thorneycroft, again followed Hall's advice in 1957 when he advocated a 'guiding light' for wage claims (Hall 1991: 107-9).[4] This, however, was rejected as too interventionist by the Ministry of Labour – since its officials 'hated the idea of interfering in the wage process' and its minister, Iain Macleod, successfully persuaded the cabinet that the government was at war with inflation not with the unions – and Thorneycroft was forced to fall back upon the education of public opinion via the creation of the Council on Prices, Productivity and Incomes (COPPI) (Gamble 1974: 150).[5] Then, in response to a sterling crisis in late-1957, Thorneycroft changed tack – proposing to beat inflation by lowering demand and raising unemployment.[6] This, however did not have the support of the cabinet, was publicly rebutted by Macmillan and, famously, led to the resignation of the Treasury team in January 1958 (Middlemas 1986: 293; Lowe 1989).[7]

During the 1950s, therefore, despite the advocacy of their chief economic adviser, Conservative governments had consistently shied away from a permanent incomes policy (Jones 1987: 56-8; Cairncross and Watts 1989: 348; Hall 1991). Although chancellors had from time to time been receptive, the cabinet could never be persuaded that it should risk discussions with unions that might lessen its control of economic policy. Treasury officials outside the Economic Section were generally also sceptical. Instead, there had been a succession of *ad hoc* policy initiatives as the government cast around for alternative instruments to deal with inflation. Each initiative, made within an unchanged set of policy goals, amounted to second order change.

In 1960, the Treasury became alarmed when wage increases began to accelerate and, its expectations of COPPI having by now declined almost to zero, it briefly toyed with the idea of initiating a more specific incomes policy.[8] Despite strong support from Hall, it decided against – most senior Treasury officials outside the Economic Section feeling that such a 'guiding light' had too many defects to be practicable and that the only alternative was to run the economy at a lower level of demand.[9]

Within a year, however, a consensus had emerged amongst Treasury officials that some form of restraint of free collective bargaining was essential to the achievement of higher growth (Cairncross and Watts 1989: 342). The principal reason for this change of heart lay in a network that linked key players in the core executive with the growth advocacy network in what I have termed the 'incomes policy learning network' (see Figure 5.1).

Again, the change of policy goals and instruments represented third order learning. It had two dimensions. The first, was the learning that took place within the network regarding the relationship between demand and inflation. Amongst academics, the closing years of the 1950s and the beginning of the new decade saw a vigorous debate about the causes of inflation.[10] Particularly important was Phillips' (1958) apparent demonstration of an inverse relationship between unemployment and prices, which emphasised the link between full employment and inflation. To more pessimistic economists outside the growth advocacy network, such as Frank Paish, it confirmed that the economy should be run at a lower level of demand to achieve an acceptable trade off between inflation and unemployment (Paish 1958, 1962: 327). This was not, however, a palatable solution for ministers in a climate of opinion which, as a consequence of negative policy feedback and the advocacy of the growth advocacy network, was increasingly antagonistic to 'stop-go' and critical of the government's record on managing the economy.[11]

The alternative analysis was that 'cost push' was more significant than 'demand pull'. This, for example, was the conclusion of the Council on Prices, Productivity and Incomes (COPPI 1959, 1961) and was supported by Dicks-Mireaux and Dow's (1959) finding that trade union pressure might explain a constant tendency of wage rates to rise. An OEEC report which located the source of UK wage inflation in a 'wage wage' spiral and called for the institution of a wages policy was particularly influential in the Treasury (Felner et al 1961: 46-51, 56-9; Cairncross 1995: 144).[12] As a later Treasury history of wages policy observed, the wage push analysis 'was a potent factor in bringing about the change of attitude to "wage policy" in 1961'.[13] To those economists in the core executive who tended more to the 'wage push' view, such as Robert Hall and Alec Cairncross, his successor as the government's chief economic adviser, the Phillips' curve was essentially bogus, since it was entirely dependent on the extent to which trade unions exercised their bargaining power.[14] Both advisers were convinced of the need for an incomes policy. An agreement with the unions to restrain wages, the Economic Section argued, would effectively shift the curve and allow the economy to support a higher rate of demand (and thus growth) for a given level of inflation.[15]

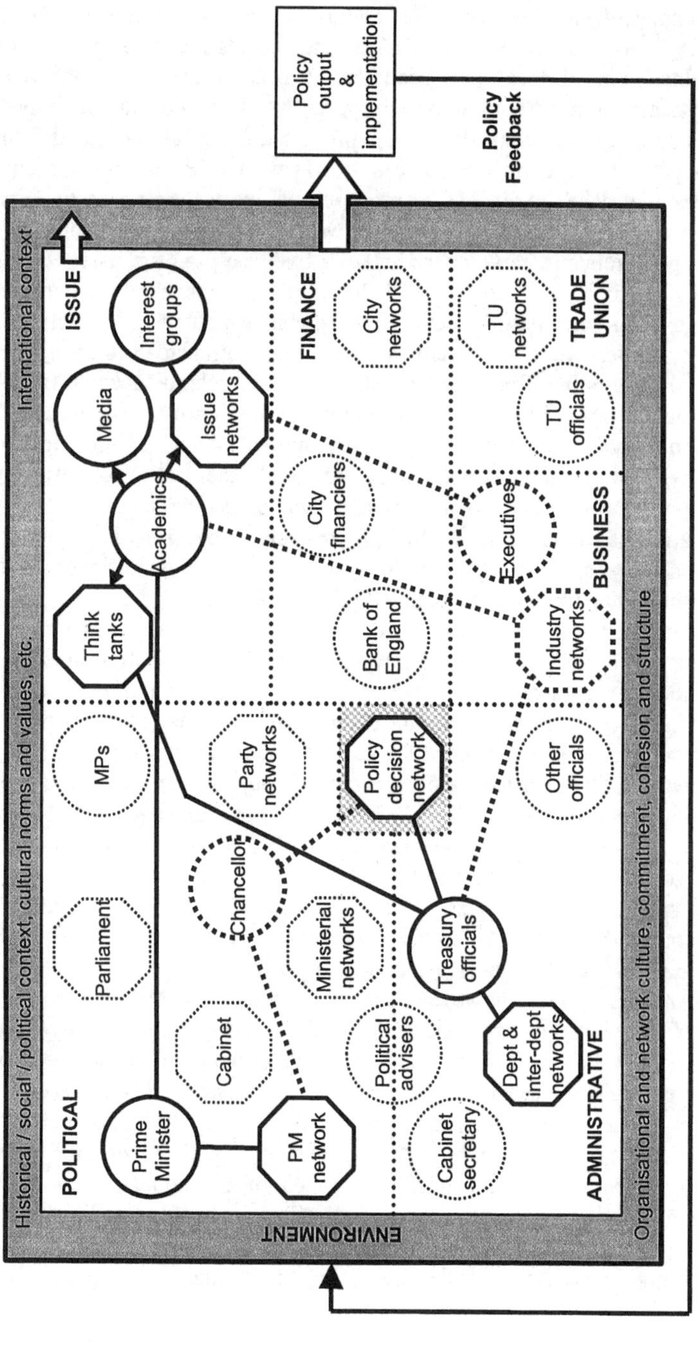

Figure 5.1 The incomes policy learning network, 1960-1961

This shift in the Economic Section towards a permanent incomes policy was the consequence of learning the lessons of negative policy feedback and of developing academic ideas about the causes of inflation. It was also intimately related to the wider intellectual change in respect of economic growth that was being promoted by academics and interest groups in the growth advocacy network, with PEP proving particularly influential. PEP (1960: 190-6) proposed linking wage rises to the growth in productivity and its impact report was evident in the advocating by the FBI conference in November 1960 of a five year plan for faster economic growth which, it noted, would help tempt the unions into a bargain on wages.[16] It can also be seen in the way in which incomes policy now began to be widely advocated by many press commentators as the means by which a policy for higher growth might be made to succeed. By 1961, the network that had built up around new growth policies in general, and incomes policy in particular, had become so extensive (see Figure 5.1 above) that an incomes policy was commonly seen as 'absolutely central ... [since] without it no long range plan for economic growth without inflation has much hope of success' (Shanks 1961: 164, 188); although, we shall see, this apparent consensus masked a significant lack of agreement on the detail of policy (Fishbein 1984: 2).

As discussed in Chapter 3, the new climate caused opinion in the Treasury to turn during 1961 towards growth and the active intervention of the government to achieve it. Its attention centred on increasing productivity, itself an important element in the containment of inflation, but the Treasury chairman of the new interdepartmental working party on growth emphasised to it the necessity of coupling 'an economic growth policy [with a] wages policy'.[17] Thus, as the growing intellectual support for a new approach to growth (support generated by the growth advocacy network) began to penetrate the Treasury both its ministers and its non-economist officials began to view the incomes policy proposals of its Economic Section in a new light and to see a permanent incomes policy as 'part and parcel of a tripartite growth plan'.[18]

At this stage, however Treasury thinking remained somewhat incoherent since its expertise in the field of wages was profoundly limited and few resources were devoted to it.[19] Proponents of an incomes policy in the Treasury also faced opposition both from detracting colleagues and from other departments. The idea was particularly unpopular at the Ministry of Labour, which feared that it would be administratively difficult, would require 'installing much of the apparatus of a 'fully planned economy', and would prejudice its traditional conciliation role.[20] The problem with this criticism, of course, was that a greater degree of 'planning' was exactly the mood of the moment and precisely the direction in which Macmillan and modernisers in the Treasury were nudging government policy.

In July 1961, the Treasury report to cabinet on 'Economic growth and national efficiency' emphasised that the disparity between the rate of growth of productivity and that of average earnings represented 'the biggest single danger to healthy growth in the future'.[21] It argued that not only was an incomes policy an essential element of increasing growth but that higher growth would make its implementation easier – by easing strife over the share of national income received by wage earners. Thus third order learning had occurred. Not only was growth now an implicit (soon to be explicit) objective of economic policy but a new instrument was to be devised that would allow growth to rise without triggering a sterling crisis in the way that had become so predictable during the 1950s.

Nevertheless, feeling amongst Treasury modernisers was that the institutions of the labour market were 'some way' behind the new Treasury thinking. Employers and unions would need 'a great deal of hard education'.[22] There would also have to be 'some drastic changes at the top of the Ministry of Labour' if the policy was to succeed, since interference in free collective bargaining remained anathema in that ministry.

The Conservatives' translation of learning into policy change

The 1961 'pay pause'

The first sign of the decision to implement an incomes policy was seen almost immediately when the chancellor's emergency measures in July 1961 imposed a 'pay pause' for public sector workers.[23] The manner of its introduction, however, betrayed the problems that advocates of an incomes policy in the core executive faced in getting it to accept the necessity for such a solution, let alone crafting a workable policy. Macmillan, had used the sterling crisis, and the desire of both the IMF and OECD to see a wages policy included in the measures used to deal with it, as a lever to force Selwyn Lloyd to act – putting forward proposals based largely on the suggestions of his informal adviser Professor Roy Harrod, a key member of the growth advocacy network.[24] Macmillan rammed home his point on 15 July with a minute to Selwyn Lloyd which firmly stated 'I do not think we ought to be afraid of a switch over towards more direction' and proposed the setting of a guiding light, fixed by an independent committee of experts acceptable to the government, employers and trade unions, to relate increases in wages, pensions and benefits to that of national productivity; with profits incorporated into the equation, perhaps via fiscal action.[25] In doing so, Macmillan was pushing open a door which had already been unlocked by Treasury modernisers. Whilst the sterling crisis provided proponents of a voluntary incomes policy with an opportunity to force through a change in policy, however, the pressure of the crisis was such that there was too little time to agree the policy with employers and unions; not least because the unions had not been part of the incomes policy learning network. Instead, the talk was of 'freeze' rather than 'guiding light' (Macmillan 1973: 35). Worries about the potential impact of this on industrial relations, however, caused the government to draw back and instead to impose the policy in the public sector alone and hope that the private sector would fall into line.[26]

Nevertheless, against the advice of the Ministry of Labour, a Conservative government had interfered in the process of free collective bargaining. This was a major break with the policies of the 1950s. Macmillan (1973: 36) himself described it as 'the first – no doubt amateurish – attempt to move towards what has afterwards become known as an "incomes policy"'. Selwyn Lloyd's statement to the House of Commons made it clear that, whilst his measures amounted to the most decisive stop since 1957, the government hoped to pluck victory from disaster through the creation of a long-term programme of growth based on consultation between government, employers and unions, and that wages policy would be an important element of this (Cairncross 1996: 92). This alteration in both the goals and instruments of economic policy amounted to third order learning – learning that had been induced by negative policy feedback and the advocacy of the growth advocacy network. In effect, the sterling crisis had been used by proponents of an incomes policy in the Treasury and by Macmillan as a means of forcing a major policy shift upon the core executive. However, whether this initial step on the translation of third order learning into third order change in the field of incomes policy could be consolidated remained to be seen.

Implementing the 'guiding light'

The 'pause' was neither a statutory wage freeze nor a voluntary incomes policy. It was a short-term expedient designed to buy time for the government to devise a more coherent, long-term and voluntary policy that would encompass the private sector as well as the government's own employees. However, lack of agreement amongst ministers and resistance from the unions meant that progress on devising its replacement was painfully slow.

Consequently, the 'pause' rapidly began to break down, undermined by union antipathy, by its incompatibility with the principle of 'fair comparison' for the setting of public sector wages, by the lack of an end date, the Treasury's shortage of personal with any real understanding of the labour market, and by the low priority accorded to incomes policy by Selwyn Lloyd (Blackaby 1978: 362, 21; Jones 1987: 49; and Cairncross 1996: 58-62).[27] Although the British Employers' Confederation was prepared to implement it in the private sector, and to restrain dividends to avoid antagonising workers, George Woodcock, bluntly warned Selwyn Lloyd that the TUC would not agree to participate in economic planning until the inequitable 'pause' was ended.[28]

Another important reason for the delay in constructing the new policy was that, since it was to be linked with solving the 'growth problem', it was inextricably bound up with the creation of the new NEDC (Rollings and Ringe 2000). Whilst the Treasury's Economic Section hoped that the NEDC would be pivotal in the construction of the new policy, by providing a means of centralising wage bargaining, agreeing the structure of the new body was a slow process.[29] This made it difficult to make progress on incomes policy. When agreement was finally achieved, the poor reception that the 'pause' had received from the TUC meant that the government then proved reluctant to introduce incomes policy into NEDC discussions for fear of provoking the unions to withdraw from the new body.[30]

Moreover, the scope of the policy was expanding rapidly – a reflection of the opportunistic nature of its implementation. Officials were grappling with the problem that, if the new policy was to be made attractive to unions, it must address workers' feelings of unfairness that wages were being restrained whilst profits and dividends were not.[31] This opened up the possibility of controls over profits and dividends and even over prices. Officials were also concerned at the lack of data and the problem posed by discrepancies between nationally negotiated wage rates and earnings at plant level ('wage drift').[32] By the end of October the Treasury acknowledged that it was 'moving fast into a large uncharted territory'.[33] Territory, moreover, whose occupation only appeared realistic with the support of the unions.[34]

That union agreement remained elusive in an atmosphere poisoned by the 'pause' created a major dilemma for the government.[35] To abandon the pause with no policy to replace it would be a 'confession of failure' but the alternative 'Paishite' solution of raising unemployment to control wages might well amount to electoral suicide. Full control of wages, profits, dividends and prices, however, was 'clearly out of the question' and 'a long way from [the] free society' to which the government remained committed. The only acceptable option seemed to be the Treasury's 'guiding light' for wage settlements of 2½ per cent per annum coupled with a commitment to keep profits in line with this figure using fiscal measures.[36] This, however, did not have the collective support of cabinet. Hare, for example, opposed it since it would require interference in the arbitration process and in wage councils that was anathema to the Ministry of Labour.[37] Erroll, the new President of the Board of Trade, and Thorneycroft both favoured lowering demand.[38] Nor was the chancellor really in favour. His arguments in support of the guiding light were essentially negative: that, having already declared that incomes should not grow faster than productivity, the next step was to define a tolerable rate of increase; that it was anyway better to give a lead which might suffer reverses than no lead at all; and that even if 2½ per cent became the minimum and 4 per cent the average this would still be an improvement on the 5 to 6 per cent experienced in recent years.[39]

Such ministerial disagreement served to shift the emphasis away from the construction of a long-term incomes policy towards immediate measures which could be taken to bring the 'pause' to an end as cleanly as possible.[40] Essentially, the cabinet now placed its hopes in its policy of cooperation on growth, hoping that a long-term policy on incomes would emerge from it.[41] The chancellor emphasised to the TUC that the guiding light was a necessary prerequisite for a viable policy on growth and that long-term economic growth coupled with short-term restraint would ultimately deliver higher real incomes. He also made it clear that profit and dividend restraint could be added to the proposals.[42]

The TUC endorsed the need for higher growth but whilst it agreed, in guarded terms, to join the NEDC it refused to cooperate on incomes (TUC Report 1962: 243).[43] In the TUC's view, an incomes policy must flow from growth, not the other way round.[44] The government preferred to make progress on both fronts simultaneously, worried that to proclaim the end of the pause without announcing the policy to succeed it might cause it to lose control of the situation. It therefore published its white paper *Incomes policy: the next step* in February (Cmnd. 1626).[45] This envisaged a 'guiding light' of 2-2½ per cent. Exceptional increases would be allowed only where 'those concerned made a direct contribution … to an increase in productivity and a reduction of costs' and where justified by labour shortages in growth industries. 'Comparability' would still be taken into account and arbitration would continue, but both must take account of 'the wider implications' of any award.

Publication of the white paper set out the aim, but did not define the mechanism by which the 'guiding light' would be administered and a workable mechanism for the new policy remained elusive. It was difficult to construct a voluntary policy without talking to the unions but the need to gain the confidence of the TUC made it impossible to do this in the new NEDC.[46] The government was therefore forced to address the problem alone but by mid-1962 consideration of incomes policy within the core executive was completely bogged down. Despite the creation of an interdepartmental group of permanent secretaries to address the incomes policy issue, officials found it increasingly difficult to make progress as the scope of the policy expanded to encompass more specific guidance on comparability, the future of arbitration and wages councils, the role of the NEDC, labour mobility, wage drift, regional differentials, the possibility of a national minimum wage, and the question of profits and prices.[47] There was also the question of profits and prices, the absence of which from incomes policy was though by some officials to be the problem in getting TUC acceptance, and which was briefly taken up by Boyle and Maudling.[48]

The cabinet was deadlocked. For many ministers, whilst they might condone new policies on growth, an incomes policy was simply too interventionist. As the scope of the policy expanded, the cabinet found itself increasingly unable to reconcile wage restraint with its commitment to a 'free society'.[49] Macmillan's patience wore thin. He bluntly told ministers and senior officials from the Treasury and Ministry of Labour that recent pay awards indicated that the 'guiding light' was not working.[50] He then outlined to a 'stunned' cabinet his ideas for a 'new approach' to economic and social policy which would convince the unions that the government was doing all it could to restrain prices, demonstrate the benefits of wage restraint in a climate of growth and assure them that everyone would get a share of the increased prosperity that it would bring (Macmillan 1973: 69-70).[51]

Macmillan proposed to gain union support by improving the status of the manual worker, action on training, improved conditions of employment, better redundancy arrangements, higher benefits and pensions to improve the lot of the poor, and action on profits. Simultaneously, the middle classes ('Orpingtonians') were to be reassured, by promises of stable prices via the abolition of retail price maintenance and more action on monopolies, lower interest rates and improved working conditions, that they were not being sacrificed to the strength of employers and organised labour.[52] A commitment to the NEDC's 4 per cent growth target was an essential part of the policy package. To ensure its attainment the level of demand would be increased via lower interest rates. The link between incomes policy and growth was explicit. It specifically reflected both the advice of Harrod of Macmillan's deputy Cabinet Secretary that 'a policy of cooperation and restraint would be much more likely to secure general acceptance if it could be based on a much higher rate of economic growth than appears to be practicable in our present circumstances'.[53] More generally, it reflected Macmillan's perception that there was now a widespread cross party consensus that an incomes policy was essential to the expansionist policy required to attain higher growth, a consensus which he felt embraced even the Trade Union leaders [and] the anarchical employers'.[54] Since the NEDC still seemed 'too delicate a plant', he proposed to create an independent standing commission to deal with the practical administration of the 'guiding light'.

Despite some concern amongst officials that the standing commission might not attract the support of the unions and that without this support it would be a 'dead letter', Macmillan placed the package before cabinet on 22 June. The meeting was inconclusive.[55] Macmillan, supported by Butler, now decided that his 'new approach' would require 'not only new measures but new men' (Macmillan 1973: 72 and 88-9).[56] He began to deal directly with officials in producing drafts for consideration by selected ministers and to prepare an extraordinarily extensive reconstruction of his cabinet. On 13 July, the multitude of ministerial sackings and appointments that this involved included the removal of Selwyn Lloyd as chancellor and his replacement by Reginald Maudling. Finally, Macmillan had the expansionist chancellor (and cabinet) that he wanted.

The reshuffle was a decisive moment in the construction of an incomes policy, not least because it marked the defeat of the Ministry of Labour. Henceforth, the ministry would be expected to put its traditional conciliation role behind it and take a more interventionist approach to the labour market.[57] Yet, even as Macmillan announced the 'new approach' to the Commons, he was aware that the TUC would not cooperate in the new commission that was to be proposed in the November white paper.[58] There was a more positive, if guarded, response from the BEC, but in the absence of TUC support, there was little that the government could do.[59] The most that ministers could hope for, it seemed, was that the TUC 'would gradually allow themselves to be brought into a more cooperative attitude'.[60] Thus the resistance of the TUC had caused Macmillan's 'new approach' to run into the sands. In effect, the guiding light and the NIC were 'quietly buried' (Cairncross 1995: 144-5).

Dashing for growth

One final attempt was made by Macmillan and Maudling to bring the unions into an agreed incomes policy when the government started its 'dash for growth' in the hope that it would create a climate of trust in the NEDC in which the unions would agree to wage restraint.[61] In preparation for this, the government arranged for a TUC delegation to visit Sweden and study the role that the LO (the TUC's Swedish equivalent) played in economic policy.[62] The delegation returned unpersuaded for, whilst it was attracted by the influence wielded by the LO through centralised bargaining, it was convinced that this was the product of the centralised structure of Swedish trade unions and could not be repeated in Britain's highly fragmented trade union structure.[63]

At the same time, Maudling tried to add profits and dividends to the scope of the NIC.[64] This was no more successful. Both the Board of Trade and the Treasury opposed the move, fearing it might jeopardise the new growth objective by removing the incentive for industry to invest – a concern already expressed by the Economic Section which in struggling to devise a workable incomes policy had started to fear that extending the policy into profits and dividends might 'seriously inhibit the forces making for growth'.[65] Nonetheless, the official cabinet committee on incomes policy began to edge towards the idea of a prices policy as a *quid pro quo* for wage restraint, although the Board of Trade remained opposed.[66]

The obvious forum for a wider bargain on incomes policy was the NEDC and discussions within it did reveal common ground. All its members agreed that an incomes policy was essential to higher growth without inflation. This was a significant breakthrough, if only at an elite level. There was also a growing recognition that to achieve a successful incomes policy it would be necessary to construct a policy on prices.[67]

During 1963, with Maudling clearly committed to the NEDC's 4 per cent growth target, the economy in an upswing, the guiding light raised to 3-3½ per cent and his relationship with the NEDC in excellent shape, there appeared to be the possibility of deal in the NEDC.[68] Maudling's strategy was clear in his statement to the House of Commons in the budget debate:

> Without expansion we cannot have an incomes policy, without an incomes policy we cannot have expansion. ... We can break out only by launching deliberately on a policy of expansion and inviting those who have responsibility in management and unions to join with us not only in the prospects, but also in the necessary conditions of a policy of expansion.[69]

It was not to be. Whilst the unions were privately supportive they remained publicly obdurate, seeing no reason to make life easy for the government in the run up to an election. On the employers' side, whilst representatives on the NEDC had struck a positive note and indicated that they were prepared to concede fiscal control of profits in return for a bargain on wages, they proved unable to carry the various employers' organisations with them.[70] The BEC was the most supportive, the FBI the most obdurate – doubting the practicality of securing the compliance of hundreds of thousands of individual firms to national agreements on prices and deeply opposed to the regulation of profits.[71]

There was a ray of hope in early-1964 when NEDC employers' representatives laid before it a draft statement proposing a 'prices discipline ... as a concomitant of a wages discipline'.[72] Nevertheless, agreement remained elusive as TUC and employers' representatives circled each other – both fearing to commit themselves without a similar degree of sacrifice from the other and both aware of the difficulties of carrying their respective organisations with them.[73] An employer representative on the NEDC summed the situation up succinctly when he wrote to the president of the BEC: 'NEDC has now reached an impasse on incomes policy and it would be idle to expect any advance until well after the General Election'.[74]

Thus despite the third order learning that had occurred – that the participation of the unions in a voluntary incomes policy was essential if the new growth objective was to be achieved without higher inflation – the Conservative government had not proved able to translate this into third order change. Whilst the government could impose a short-term pay freeze, it lacked the ability to construct a workable long-term voluntary policy. Disputes between government departments and the barrier formed by the fragmented institutions of the labour market had ultimately proved insuperable. Despite support for the principle (if not the detail) of a voluntary prices and incomes policy within the government, in the BEC, amongst many in the higher reaches of the TUC (especially in its economic committee and associated staff), in the Labour Party and in the wider growth advocacy network, it had not proved possible to translate this private consensus into public agreement. Without such an agreement, detractors within government, such as the Ministry of Labour and Board of Trade, and outside government, such as the FBI and some individual trade unions, were able to thwart Conservative attempts to construct a voluntary incomes policy. The irony was that it had required a sterling crisis for those in the core executive who had accepted the message of the growth advocacy network to force incomes policy onto the agenda yet the 'pay pause', hurriedly conceived to stem the run on sterling, implemented without consultation, and poorly received by public opinion, had helped to stymie the Conservative initiative by poisoning the atmosphere. The question now was whether a Labour government could do any better.

Labour's learning about incomes policy

When Labour entered government in October 1964 it had already experienced learning of a similar order to the Conservatives in the field of incomes policy. This section will suggest that the development and promulgation of new ideas in the growth advocacy network had led

Labour to draw a similar lesson from the failure of the Keynesian economic policies of the 1950s to achieve the stable and higher growth that was required if Britain was to avoid relative economic decline. It will argue, however, that whilst Labour ideology meant that the party was better placed than the Conservatives to broker a deal with the unions and employers on incomes it proved no more able to surmount the fragmentation and interdependence of British labour market institutions, or to overcome the resistance of low level self-organising industrial networks.

When Jim Callaghan was appointed shadow chancellor in November 1961, his knowledge of economics was not extensive and he lost no time in putting together a team of economic advisers. Incomes policy loomed large in its seminars (Morgan 1998: 173-6). To his existing counsellor, Richard Kahn (one of the authors of the OEEC report (Felner et al 1960) that had such influence on Treasury attitudes to incomes policy) were added a number of new advisers. One notes in particular the presence of Sir Robert Hall, C.R. Ross (who had worked with Hall in the Economic Section) and Robert Neild (who was then deputy director of the NIESR), all three of whom were proponents of an active incomes policy. In addition, other economists in the growth advocacy network, particularly Kaldor and Neild, also played an important role in bringing Labour's Finance and Economic Policy Committee to the conclusion that 'wage push' was a more important factor than 'demand pull' in inflation and that an incomes policy covering all forms of income was essential to the party's developing ideas on planning for growth.[75]

Thus, as a consequence of advice emanating from the growth advocacy network, Labour had come to much the same conclusion as the Conservatives. Like the Conservatives, Labour envisaged an incomes policy as an essential element of a policy for growth. It also recognised that, to achieve a bargain with organised labour, it would have to offer immediate gains as well as the prospect of a long-term rise in real incomes.[76] Consequently, in conjunction with union members of the NEDC, the Finance and Economic Policy Committee tried during 1963 to build a policy which would, as Stewart put it, 'strike a note of greater equality and fairer shares, as well as of a stable cost of living'.[77] It should not appear to be a policy of 'wage restraint' but a policy of full employment and expansion in which the government would use all its powers to stabilise prices, attack fiscal privileges, introduce a capital gains tax and improve pensions and other social security benefits.[78] In July 1963, the committee secured the support of the TUC for the principle, if not the detail, of this policy (Panitch 1976: 58).

By October 1964, clearly anticipating a Labour victory, the unions had publicly changed their attitude to an incomes policy. Congress remained rhetorically opposed to wage restraint alone, but it now accepted the place of incomes policy within economic planning as long as it was 'based on social justice, taking into account all forms of incomes' (TUC Report 1963: 446). This 'planned growth of incomes' formula, whilst largely presentational, was the key to TUC endorsement of the new policy and was fundamental to the Labour Party's (1964) election manifesto.

Thus the incomes policy learning network had expanded since 1961 (see Figure 5.2) to include the Labour Party, the unions and the Ministry of Labour – although the latter two remained somewhat weakly attached. The ideas circulating within the network had affected the thinking of each of these institutions. Most importantly it had shaped the development of Labour's economic policy framework with an incomes policy firmly embedded in the package of new policies that would, it was hoped, enable Britain to attain its objective of 4 per cent annual growth. Like the Conservatives, Labour had undergone a process of third order learning. Now, however, it must translate this order of learning into an equivalent order of policy change.

The translation of learning into change by Labour

This section will argue that Labour failed to achieve third order change in incomes policy for much the same reasons that the Conservatives had failed. Labour was no more able to impose change than the Conservatives had been and it too proved unable to prevail over vested interests and low level self-organising networks in Britain's fragmented labour market.

This failure occurred despite the Labour government having several advantages over its predecessor. Firstly, its relationship with the unions meant that it would not face union opposition on electoral grounds. Secondly, it was ideologically more disposed towards the TUC's demand that incomes policy should apply to all forms of income lest the sacrifice of wage earners accrue to profits and dividends.[79] As Brown told the TUC Economic Committee, if one accepted that profits must necessarily remain the main motivation in a mixed economy, and that with any 'direct interference with profits the system would cease to work', then the problem *had* to be approached via prices.[80] Consequently, Labour's 1964 election manifesto had publicly committed it both to higher growth and to a 'prices and incomes policy'.

In addition, whilst the Conservatives had not succeeded in constructing an agreed incomes policy, the foundations for an agreement had been laid by them in the years since 1961 and their 3-3½ per cent 'guiding light' continued whilst the new government sought to construct an agreement on incomes policy.[81] Important institutional changes within the core

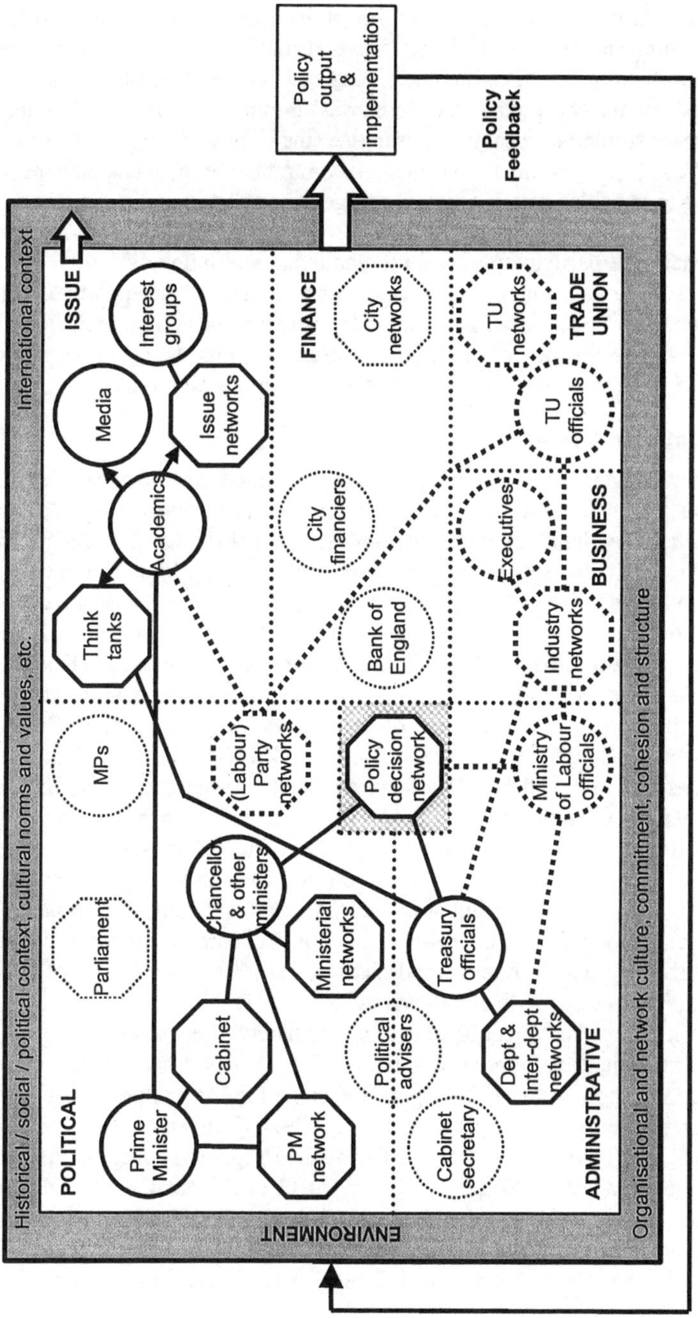

Figure 5.2 The incomes policy learning network, 1961-1964

executive had also raised the profile of incomes policy within policy formulation and improved the expertise available to policy makers: the scope of the ministerial committee on pay had been widened to include all salaries; the *ad hoc* permanent secretaries' group on incomes policy had been reconstituted as a cabinet committee (the Official Group on Incomes and Prices); a new interdepartmental committee of officials had been created to consider detailed claims and general questions of policy; and a new internal Treasury group on incomes policy had been set up. Outside Whitehall, the participation by both employers and unions in NEDC had also led to a much improved understanding of each others' position.[82] In addition, the opposition of both employers and officials to the inclusion of prices within any incomes policy had softened. Thus the stage was now set for a bargain between the government, the unions and industry.

The 'Joint Statement of Intent'

The new government made rapid progress, aided by the weakness of sterling which it used as a lever to persuade the various groups to put aside their sectional interests (Corina 1967: 301).[83] On 16 December 1964, in the august surroundings of Lancaster House, a Joint Statement of Intent on Productivity, Prices and Incomes was signed by the Secretary of State for Economic Affairs (George Brown), the Chancellor of the Exchequer (Jim Callaghan), the President of the Board of Trade (Douglas Jay) and the Minister of Labour (Ray Gunter) on behalf of the government, and by the leaders of the Trades Union Congress, British Employers' Confederation, Federation of British Industry, National Association of British Manufacturers and Association of British Chambers of Commerce. The choice of venue, with its associations with international agreements, was deliberate. The joint statement was intended to be seen as a grand treaty between these key groups. The *quid pro quo* for TUC agreement was a commitment to implement a capital gains tax, some increase in profits tax, action on business expenses and an announcement that in future fiscal measures will be used when profits or dividends move out of line with wages.

Work on this statement had begun immediately after the election in the new Department of Economic Affairs (DEA) – which had taken control of incomes policy from the Treasury as part of its responsibility for Labour's new national plan (Clifford 1997; Clifford and McMillan 1997).[84] On 9 November, George Brown had separately met the unions and employers. He told the TUC General Council that the need for an incomes policy could not be over emphasised and that 'without such a policy no effective national economic plan would be possible'.[85] Brown's proposal for a 'Joint Statement of Intent' was received sympathetically, particularly by Woodcock (identified by Fishbein 1984: 41 as an important 'agent of change' in the field of incomes policy who was convinced that the future improvement of unionists' living standards would depend more on acquiring influence over economic policy making than militant wage bargaining) but the General Council warned Brown that he would have to win over dissenting unions.[86] To achieve this, Brown recognised, one of the chief problems would be to carry union rank and file members along as well as union leaders. In this context he was keen to liaise with the Ministry of Labour in the construction of the 'vitally important' coherent and genuine labour market policy which he thought essential if unionists were to be given a greater sense of security.[87]

Using, as a Treasury history later put it, 'his vigorous persuasive powers' in a gruelling series of bilateral discussions, Brown managed to persuade both the TUC and employers' organisations publicly to endorse the Joint Statement of Intent in December.[88] The statement represented an agreement amongst the signatories on the broad objectives of economic policy (HMSO 1964). These were:

1. To promote a rapid increase in both output and real incomes whilst preserving full employment;
2. To raise productivity in order to keep the increase in money incomes and that of national output in line;
3. To ensure that the benefits of faster growth were distributed in accord with 'the claims of social need and justice'; and
4. To maintain stable prices.

To this end, the government undertook to draw up a national plan and all three signatories agreed to work together in making British industry more competitive and to cooperate in the machinery which the government would establish to keep under review the general movement in prices and incomes and to examine particular cases and advise if they were justified.

Despite this initial success, Labour failed to implement a workable and lasting voluntary policy. In retrospect, it is possible to see the seeds of this failure even at this early stage. The Joint Statement of Intent was superficially impressive but it had been obtained not as a result of consensus building negotiations but via bilateral negotiations between the government and the employers' organisations and the TUC. It therefore masked continuing divisions between the various signatories.[89] It also gave more emphasis to the need to solve the balance of payments problem than to attain the growth objective. It therefore reflected the crisis in which it had been born rather than a genuine consensus that it was in the long-term interests of all signatories. Finally, whilst it might indeed push the signatories 'beyond the point of no return'[90] it was also a short and high level statement of principles which left considerable scope for disagreement over the details of its implementation.

The Joint Statement of Intent provided the general framework for Labour's incomes and prices policy. The next task was to reach agreement on how these principles were to be applied to wage increases in particular industries and to the pricing policies of individual firms. Brown chose to proceed on two parallel tracks, negotiating with the TUC (mainly with its Economic Committee and, primarily, with George Woodcock) and with employers' organisations (primarily with Sir Norman Kipping (FBI) and Sir George Pollock (BEC)) on the machinery of prices and incomes policy whilst simultaneously discussing the criteria under which the policy would operate. This, it was agreed, would be defined by the government in consultation with management and unions in the NEDC.[91] However, although the NEDC might define the 'national interest' in respect of prices and incomes, the government, although at this stage stressing the importance of the NEDC's role, remained free to accept or ignore this advice as it saw fit (Panitch 1976: 73). Thus the 'corporatist' façade of incomes policy masked a continuing lack of trust that divisions within the labour market could be transcended.

On the question of machinery, Brown proposed the creation of a National Board for Prices and Incomes.[92] There was already a measure of agreement on how to regulate incomes. However, on the question of prices, the distinctive addition to the policies of the Conservative government, there was far less accord. The vexed question was whether or not the NBPI should rely on voluntary cooperation or should have statutory powers. Both the unions and the employers favoured a voluntary body since neither group really wanted to diminish their respective influence over incomes and prices.[93] The government, however, despite a widespread view in the Board of Trade and in sections of the Treasury that price controls would politicise the pricing process, be administratively very difficult, and represent 'a major handicap to the competitive efficiency of British industry', had come to the conclusion that the threat of statutory control was needed if the two sides of industry were to be prevented from obstructing progress.[94] Thus, whilst the February white paper on the machinery emphasised its voluntary character, it carried the warning that 'the Government would have to consider giving the Board statutory authority ... if experience showed this was necessary' (Cmnd. 2577: para. 6).

Brown faced greater difficulties in obtaining agreement on the criteria under which the policy would operate. This produced the incongruous situation in which the white paper on the criteria under which the policy would operate (Cmnd. 2639) was not published until April. On prices, he was able to obtain agreement from industry for the inclusion in the white paper of rules for firms to follow in their setting of prices. This represented a significant departure from the previous Conservative policy but still fell short of direct intervention in the pricing process, was notably weaker that the concessions being asked of the unions on wages and, in the event, led to few achievements except in the public sector (Mitchell 1972: 248). On incomes, defining the norm for 1965 was bound to be more difficult in the context of an expected increase in average earnings of over 5 per cent.[95] There was widespread agreement amongst the various groups at an elite level that the norm should be 3 per cent but might perhaps be stretched to 3.5 per cent.[96] This, however, was not going to be easy to sell to individual unions and employers and Brown recognised that much would depend on the influence which the peak organisations could exercise over their members behind the scenes.[97] George Woodcock advised Brown that the unions could best be brought round by letting the figure emerge gradually in NEDC discussions.[98] However, the interdepartmental group of permanent secretaries was concerned that negotiating in NEDC risked a loss of control by the core executive.[99] In the event, agreement was reached in NEDC on 22 March for the norm to be set in the range 3 to 3.5 per cent. This, however, marked the end of NEDC involvement. The NEDC decided that it would henceforward be better for direct discussions to be held between the First Secretary, the TUC, the CBI and the Chairman of the NBPI, the former Conservative minister John Aubrey Jones. In doing so, it thus implicitly acknowledging that 'each new advance was too heavily traded to risk reopening at the Council'.[100]

Despite this, Brown had succeeded in gaining agreement on both the machinery and the overall criteria of prices and incomes policy. The speed with which this had been achieved was impressive and a tribute to Brown's skills as a negotiator. The disadvantage of such speed was, as Brown himself acknowledged to the cabinet, that the agreement begged a number of questions not least whether the cooperation envisaged in the white paper would actually come to pass or whether it might prove necessary; how the National Board for Prices and Incomes would interact with existing machinery for negotiation, arbitration and conciliation; and how to avoid national settlements being undermined by locally negotiated agreements (the phenomenon of 'wage drift').[101]

Strengthening the prices and incomes policy

Within months it was clear that the fragmented institutions of the labour market were undermining the effective operation of the new policy. Most obviously, there was a divergence between plant level agreements and national settlements (Dorfman 1974: 134). Despite a series of addresses by ministers to individual union conferences that sought, in the absence of TUC control over them, to secure their support for the prices and incomes policy a number of unions (most notably the TGWU and public sector unions such as NALGO) remained opposed and they were pursuing (and achieving) claims above the norm (Panitch 1976: 76-85).

The consequence of these breaches was that tensions developed between the three parties over the application of the policy. On 15 June, Brown warned the cabinet that the government's prices and incomes policy was now in great danger.[102] His officials were very concerned that neither unions nor employers were making serious efforts to keep their side of the prices and incomes bargain. By the end of the month they had begun to consider seeking a voluntary wage freeze, or even the introduction of statutory controls over both incomes and prices.[103] A freeze, it was argued, would offer the opportunity of breaking out of the wage cycle and it seemed to officials that it would be easier to work backwards from a freeze to a more liberal policy than to tighten up wages and prices within the current policy.[104] The problem, as Douglas Allen (Permanent Secretary at the DEA) confided to the IMF, was that 'although such a freeze might be of considerable benefit in the very short run it would fatally damage the prospects of success in the longer term' by provoking the withdrawal of the unions.[105]

By 9 July Brown had decided against a 'crash programme'.[106] Nevertheless, he was under severe pressure to deliver something better than had been achieved to date. The creation of the DEA had increased the degree of fragmentation within the core executive and the Treasury, stripped of its responsibility for incomes policy and planning, was now pressing hard for deflation to defend sterling.[107] Consequently, the DEA began to examine ways in which the existing policy might be strengthened, in particular via a voluntary 'early warning' system for wage claims and firm undertakings from industry on prices.[108]

The shift away from a voluntary policy was given added impetus by the Americans.[109] In return for mounting an international operation to raise a $2bn reserve fund required to defend sterling they demanded a 90 day standstill on prices and incomes, an early warning mechanism for prices, powers for the government to refer to the NBPI any price or claim for higher pay, powers for the government to defer any proposed price or pay increase until the board had reported, and statutory powers for the NBPI to collect data on proposed pay and price increases.[110] Brown's response, despite his anger at having his policy dictated in this manner, was to agree to all of this, with the exception of the temporary freeze which he thought would simply dam up claims and produce a worse situation later on.[111] This was eventually accepted by the Americans.[112] On 26 August, Brown met the TUC and the employers, in the shape of the newly constituted Confederation of British Industries. During a long meeting both indicated that they were strongly opposed to any form of compulsion. Brown made it clear, however, that if voluntary agreement to the proposals was not reached then the government would impose them.[113] The fragmented nature of Britain's labour market institutions was pushing the government inexorably towards compulsion and on 1 September the cabinet approved the proposed legislation.[114]

The end of voluntarism

Despite initial hopes to the contrary, this shift away from a permanent voluntary policy continued. The key factors in this failure both related to the fragmented nature of Britain's labour market: the resistance of individual unions and employers at the national level; the ability of unions and employers to conspire together in low level self-organising networks to strike plant level bargains that subverted national agreements; and decisions by conciliators and arbitrators that broke the agreed pay norm.

TUC assent to the government's taking of reserve powers was sought by emphasising that if it failed to endorse the proposals the likely consequence would be a sterling crisis that would mean the end of the government's growth objective.[115] Very reluctantly, the General Council finally agreed, but only on condition that the TUC be given a chance to run its own early warning system effectively.[116] The CBI also agreed to the taking of reserve powers 'so that the government could not blame it for the economic situation', though it refused to administer an equivalent early warning system for prices.[117]

The beginning of 1966 brought a welcome respite on the foreign exchanges but the outlook was far from reassuring (Cairncross 1996: 141). A briefing for an official meeting with the IMF in November had conceded that, despite the positive gloss put on incomes policy by Brown when he had addressed the OECD earlier in the month, the continuing rapid rise in incomes was 'very disappointing'.[118] Pierre-Paul Schweitzer, its managing director, expressed himself 'very disappointed' with progress and suggested that 'special measures' would be required if Britain was to achieve overall balance on its external account.[119]

In January a memorandum for cabinet by Brown acknowledged that, despite the achievements since October 1964, the effect of the policy on incomes was working 'far too slowly'.[120] Fragmentation was a key factor in this lack of progress. A 'firmer line' would be required against individual unions that broke with the agreed norm. 'Prices and incomes policy must be given its full weight by the Ministry of Labour in its conciliation duties' and a way must be found to compel arbitrators to take account of the national interest.

It was rapidly becoming apparent that 'the voluntary incomes policy was not making any contribution to immediate problems' (Brittan 1969: 208).[121] Earnings had risen 9.5 per cent in the year to April and an NEDC assessment of price and income inflation during the year to March was very gloomy.[122] One problem was that, by delegating responsibility for prices and incomes policy to the Ministry of Labour and the Board of Trade, the government had lost an independent assessment, since both departments were closely linked to industrial policy networks and tended to act as their representatives in the core executive.[123] The policy was also being undermined by the recommendations of independent review bodies which, as Balogh pointed out to Wilson, were awarding professional groups pay rises which in some cases were larger than the total annual wages of some employees.[124] The award to doctors by the Kindersley Committee, for example, was described by Woodcock as 'devastating'. If there was another blow like this, he warned Brown, then TUC support for the incomes policy would be finished.[125] Furthermore, the TUC's early warning system was failing to deliver the results expected of it – querying very few of over 600 claims of which it was notified in its first nine months, even though most were above the norm (Dorfman 1973: 138: Jones 1987: 71-2).[126] In large part, this reluctance to get to grips with claims stemmed from the TUC's lack of authority over its affiliated unions and its lack of influence over local settlements (Fishbein 1984: 43).

As a consequence of such fragmentation in the labour market, the core executive was becoming disenchanted with the voluntary approach.[127] The real nail in the coffin of voluntarism, however, was the outbreak of a strike by the National Union of Seamen at the end of May 1966 over a 17 per cent pay claim – itself a perfect example of the barrier that fragmentation within the union movement posed for progress in incomes policy. The strike provoked another severe sterling crisis and on 13 June Brown was forced to acknowledge to the cabinet committee on prices and incomes policy that government must now consider the case for a standstill.[128] Nevertheless, he still hoped to avoid this and argued that other measures should be considered such as stepping up the work of the NBPI and an intensification of pressure on the TUC and the CBI to 'widen their influence and activities'.

As a consequence of Brown's determination to intensify the pressure, the cabinet rejected a wage freeze. It agreed, however, that the Prices and Incomes Bill should proceed, putting into effect the statutory backing to the early warning system.[129] This prompted the resignation of Frank Cousins from the cabinet, thus releasing the powerful head of the TGWU from collective cabinet responsibility and allowing him to campaign against the prices and incomes policy in the TUC. Moreover, the perilous position of sterling meant that the government's commitment to the growth objective was now in grave danger. In an internal DEA memorandum Brown wrote:

> We stand in constant danger of being forced into severe deflationary action.. [but this] offers no long-term solution to the structural problems of our economy which have impeded the attainment of growth and have led to recurring balance of payments crises ... [and would] mean a complete abandonment of the whole of our economic philosophy.[130]

In two meetings on meetings on 12 and 14 July the cabinet was forced to consider the Treasury's deflationary package and, as part of it, a total freeze on wages and prices.[131]

On 20 July, the Prime Minister announced the deflationary measures required to stem the flight from sterling.[132] He also announced a six months standstill on wages, salaries and other forms of income, to be followed by a further six month period of 'severe restraint'. Existing commitments on pay or hours were to be deferred for six months and exceptions would only be allowed if the grounds for exceptional treatment were 'exceptionally compelling'. At the same time, Wilson called for a twelve months standstill on prices, except where necessitated by rises in import costs, by seasonal factors or by the government action such as tax increases, and for companies to hold down their dividends. Because of the urgency, measures to combat the sterling crisis the government relied on voluntary cooperation, though in getting this Wilson made it clear that 'Where this [wa]s not forthcoming, other action must be taken.'[133]

By early August, the CBI and NEDC had agreed to support the standstill.[134] The TUC found it less easy to do so since request to companies to 'hold down' dividends for twelve months did not seem comparable to a freeze on wages. It was also only too aware that the standstill would signify the end of 'the planned growth of incomes' and reluctant to see growth not just sacrificed but sacrificed at the expense of its members. Moreover, the TUC's Economic Committee was doubtful whether it would be possible after the twelve months of freeze and 'severe restraint' to resume progress towards an agreed incomes policy.[135] On 27 July, the General Council, whilst deploring the deflation endorsed the standstill by 20 votes to 12 (TUC Report 1966: 323-5).[136] This was confirmed by the TUC conference in September 1966, but opposition, orchestrated by

Cousins, was strong and motions deploring the possibility of statutory penalties against unionists and opposing the early warning system were only narrowly defeated (TUC Report 1966: 464-5, 484).

When the white paper was published on 29 July it was firm; there would be exceptions only for genuine productivity increases (Cmnd. 3073). Incomes policy was now clearly embedded within a defensive policy for sterling rather than a policy for higher growth. Compliance remained voluntary in theory but in practice the unions' room for manoeuvre was very slight and, to all intents and purposes, both unions and employers were being compelled to participate. Brown's opposition to a standstill, his commitment to the maintenance of free collective bargaining and his national plan had all come to naught and he resigned. In October a successful legal challenge to the policy by the Association of Supervisory Staffs, Executives and Technicians caused the government to activate the statutory clauses of the Prices and Incomes Act (Blackaby 1978: 372).

Thus, ultimately the attempt by Labour to construct in conjunction with the TUC and the employers' organisations an agreed policy that would restrict the growth of prices and incomes to sustain its growth policy had failed. Superficially, the cause might seem to be the weakness of sterling. More fundamentally, however, incomes policy had been undermined by its own failure to contain inflation and thus allow growth without triggering a balance of payments and/or sterling crisis. A key factor in this failure was the resistance of key actors in the labour market to the policy: resistance by individual unions and employers at the national level, plant level bargains between individual firms and unions that subverted national agreements, and decisions by conciliators and arbitrators that broke the agreed pay norm. Despite agreement between the government and elites in the relevant peak organisations, and despite the creation of an elaborate machinery for regulating both incomes and prices, Labour's translation of third order learning on growth and incomes policy into enduring third order change, like the Conservatives', had been unsuccessful.

Conclusions

The period 1961–66 saw a concerted attempt to construct a voluntary policy for the restraint of wages (and later of prices). Despite this, both the trade unions and key ministries in the core executive had difficulty accepting that the state should be involved in the process of wage determination, even when it became clear that post-war full employment was creating inflationary pressures. Consequently, the emergence of incomes policy was gradual and marked by its reluctant adoption and incremental advance – with cumulatively stronger government intervention as the policy failed to deliver the results expected of it (Haywood 1987).

Nevertheless, 1961–66 did represent a real break with the policies of the late-1940s and 1950s. The introduction of the 'pause' in July 1961 indicated that the government was now prepared to intervene in the labour market to ensure that the 'national interest' was reflected in wage negotiations. This was not just another *ad hoc* response to a sterling crisis but was part of a conscious wish to craft a long-term incomes policy. Moreover, this policy was firmly embedded in the wider growth project. A policy that obtained the agreement of the unions and of employers to restrict the growth of wages would contain the cost push inflationary pressures that the commitment to the new 4 per cent growth objective would entail.

Thus a new policy instrument was utilised as a consequence of the revision of Britain's economic policy goals. This was a clear case of third order learning. The lesson that an incomes policy was needed had been fully learned within the core executive during the latter half of the 1950s. However, because it was restricted to the Economic Section of the Treasury, it resulted not in a significant revision of policy goals and instruments but in a succession of second order changes. By 1961, the growth advocacy network had created a widespread consensus that an incomes policy was an essential constituent of any policy to raise growth, break out of the 'stop-go' cycle and end Britain's relative economic decline (although there was less consensus on the detail of what such a policy would involve). This consensus allowed the Economic Section, in conjunction with Macmillan, to persuade the Treasury that a permanent incomes policy must be an essential element of the new policy on growth. Such was the strength of this consensus that it transcended political ideology (Kirby 1991: 247; Aubrey Jones 1973: 47). Both the Conservative, and later the Labour government, sought to obtain the agreement of employers and unions voluntary to restrict wages. Both were prepared to intervene in the labour market to compel unions and employers to restrain wage settlements if they would not do so voluntarily.[137]

Nevertheless, despite the third order learning that had occurred, the implementation and development of incomes policy between 1961 and 1966 was not a success. Firstly, although the evidence is mixed, the weight of subsequent appraisals is that it failed to attain its own objectives. Arguments in its favour are tepid at best. Tomlinson (1994: 282-3), for instance, noted that UK inflation during this period was no worse than the OECD average. Cohen (1971: 261-2) conceded that the policy had some disinflationary effects, if only for short periods.[138] The general conclusion, however, has been that incomes policy in the 1960s was a failure; marked by its on/off nature and ultimately driven by the balance of payments rather than growth (Ulman and Flanagan 1971: 42-7; Flanagan et al 1983; Haywood 1987; Jones 1987: Chs. 5-7; Kirby 1992: 640; Tomlinson 1994: 282-3; Cairncross 1996: 269-71; Middleton 1996: 595). It might also be argued that incomes policy in this period was not just unsuccessful but also counter productive: the lack of continuity reducing Britain's rate of growth and the 1966 wage freeze proving to be an important contributor to the wage explosion of the 1970s (Blackaby 1972 and 1978: 652-5; A. Jones 1973: 64; Brittan 1981: 168, 174).[139]

Secondly, incomes policy is widely judged to have failed in that it did not obtain a permanent voluntary modification of free collective bargaining. Despite the attempts of both Conservative and Labour government to create a new institutional structure for wage bargaining, no real and permanent modification of this structure evolved (Blackaby 1978: 641-2). Most notably, there was a major failure to reform plant level bargaining and thus to eliminate or at least reduce the phenomenon of 'wage drift' (Clegg 1971: 5-6). Consequently, as Cohen (1971: 262) concluded, incomes policies only really proved effective in times of emergency when the unions could be persuaded to cooperate in a wage freeze. However, as Cairncross (1996: 61) put it, a wage freeze 'was not a policy; it was an expedient'.[140] It was also a confession of failure and each time it was used it contributed to a loss of confidence in the possibility of constructing a workable and permanent voluntary policy so that by the end of the 1960s faith in incomes policy had almost disappeared (Kirby 1991: 248).

Thus, despite the third order learning that had occurred in respect of incomes policy, neither the Conservatives nor Labour were able to translate this learning into an enduring third order change. The reasons for this failure are several. Most obviously, the core executive could not simply dictate policy. In the private sector, it could not permanently dictate wage rates without repudiating the free market, which neither government was prepared to do. It even lacked control over the wages of its own employees, because of the importance of independent review bodies. Ringe and Rollings' (2000a: 349) comment on growth policy, that the Treasury 'could not simply impose its solution on Whitehall and the rest of the economy, however much it wanted and persistently it tried', was also true of incomes policy. Consequently, if an incomes policy was to be developed it must necessarily be through negotiation with the interested parties, both inside and outside government.

Negotiating an incomes policy proved extraordinarily difficult because of the interdependence of active labour market, industrial, incomes and social policies (an interdependence emphasised by Wilensky and Turner 1987: 49-51). Within the core executive, once the Treasury had become converted to the idea that an incomes policy was an essential element of a policy for growth, it could only achieve its aims if it could carry with it the Ministry of Labour and the Board of Trade. In the event, the Treasury found it extremely difficult to surmount the separate institutional legacies of each department. The Ministry of Labour proved extremely reluctant to cast off its historic conciliation role in the labour market. The Board of Trade was equally reluctant to countenance intervention in the pricing process or controls over the level of dividends.[141] This made it hard to make progress on a policy which was bound to involve intervention in both fields (a conclusion supported by Haywood 1987: 255). Thus fragmentation within government made it hard to coordinate policy making (see also Ringe 1999: 82). Substantial progress only really occurred when the Treasury could threaten departments with economic disaster unless they complied or where they were able to obtain the intervention of the prime minister.

This difficulty in reaching agreement on a voluntary policy within the core executive was also encountered in negotiations with the key players outside government. Here too there was a high degree of fragmentation. Most notably, whilst the General Secretary of the TUC was open to negotiations on incomes policy, individual unions were very reluctant to see restrictions on their historic right to bargain with employers over wages. Moreover, a deep-seated class based antagonism between the unions and the Conservative government helped to block union acquiescence in an incomes policy until the election of Labour in 1964. The *quid pro quo* for TUC cooperation on incomes policy was a clear commitment to raise the living standards of union members through higher growth and to promote social justice and the equitable distribution of wealth (Gill 1981: 180). The TUC did not believe that the Conservatives were truly committed to either. It was more cooperative with Labour because of the higher degree of trust engendered by the historic links between the party and the unions, because Labour was careful to embed incomes policy more explicitly within the rhetoric of growth ('the planned growth of incomes'), and because it was prepared to implement restraints on prices (although in practice this was always subordinate to wage restraint). Similarly, but less publicly, the employers' organisations were reluctant to accept controls over profits and appalled at the idea of any controls on their setting of prices. Fundamentally, employers' organisations and the TUC wanted restraint from each other but were reluctant to provide it themselves. Only in times of economic crisis could they be brought to put aside sectional interests and recognise common interests (Haywood 1987: 145). Yet, whilst the Conservatives in 1961 and Labour in 1966 were able to use sterling crises to implement compulsory wage restraint, in each case the crisis effectively destroyed their respective attempts to construct a viable voluntary policy by undermining the trust necessary for success.

The obvious venue for constructing an agreement between the government, the unions and the employers on such a policy was the new NEDC. It proved virtually useless. Incomes policy was too heavily traded in bilateral discussions between the government and each side of industry to risk reopening the issue in the NEDC. Significantly, the unions and the employers remained subordinate to the government in the field of incomes policy, and arguably the interests of the unions remained subordinate to those of the employers. The weakness of Britain's new corporatist structure was therefore a key contributor to its failure to construct an effective voluntary incomes policy (Katzenstein 1985; Tomlinson 1994: 272-3; Wilensky and Turner 1987).

In addition to this profound cleavage between the key players at the elite level, incomes policy was also undermined by resistance from below. The TUC lacked control over individual unions. Individual unions lacked control over their shop stewards and rank and file members. Similarly, there were significant divisions between the several employers' organisations and each organisation in turn lacked control over its member firms (Boswell and Peters 1997). Moreover, the fragmentation of negotiating bodies encouraged 'leap frogging' (Cmnd. 2583: 97-8). Even more significantly, the lack of control over plant level pay bargaining rendered wage rates agreed nationally within the prevailing pay norm largely illusory. It introduced into incomes policy Mancur Olson's (1965) collective action paradox; since those who broke with restraint would still receive its benefits and those who participated would get lower increases in real income than those who did not (see also Fishbein 1984: 2 and Boston 1985). The result was that fragmentation within labour market institutions led to wage drift. This was a significant factor in the failure of incomes policy to contain wage growth and in the final collapse of the attempt to build a voluntary policy (Clegg 1971: 79-86; Jones 1987: 82).

Finally, although incomes policy was essential to the attainment of a higher rate of economic growth, it was poorly integrated into the overall growth project. For example, cooperation on incomes policy precluded reform of industrial relations and thus inhibited improvements in productivity. Broadberry and Crafts (1992: 539 and 1996: 86) probably go too far when they accuse incomes policy of 'perverting' policies of modernisation, but they are right to argue that a cooperative incomes policy was difficult to reconcile with the quest for a more competitive, and thus productive, economy. Most importantly, unlike France, incomes policy was very poorly integrated into 'planning' (Jones 1973: 63-4; Kirby 1991: 248). The absence of incomes policy from NEDC deliberations on growth was a significant defect which continued under Labour. The 1965 Joint Statement of Intent was completely separate from the national plan and the DEA found itself devoting more and more resources to incomes policy rather than to the Plan. As George Brown (1971: 118) put it: 'This meant that the whole job was turned in on itself, as it were ... prices and incomes policy, instead of being just one of the parts of the National Plan, ... become the central core of economic policy'.

Thus, despite a high level of consensus in the early to mid-1960s amongst economic experts, the Treasury, the Conservative and Labour parties, and (at the elite level) employers and unions that a permanent and voluntary incomes policy was required, it proved impossible for either government to craft one. The existence of highly interdependent, yet at the same time highly fragmented institutions in the field of wages meant that, although an attempt to construct a more corporatist state *was* made (*pace* Eichengreen 1996) it proved to be flawed. This was not, as Broadberry and Crafts (1996) claimed, a particular failure of government. Nor was it because the Treasury was insufficiently committed to growth (Pollard 1982). Instead, in a field of policy characterised by a high level of interdependence, the fragmentation of the various actors and the weakness of Britain's quasi corporatist structures encouraged policy segmentation and policy discontinuity and led ineluctably to the failure to construct a viable and permanent incomes policy.[142]

6

Taxation Policy

Introduction

This chapter examines the third of the three inter-linked elements of the growth policy package, focusing on the array of new taxes introduced after 1960 which sought to raise growth by increasing the government's control over the economy (improving its ability to smooth the business cycle and thus raising the trend rate of economic growth), encouraging the more productive use of labour, or stimulating investment via changes to the structure of taxation. It examines in detail the introduction of six new taxes: the introduction of two 'economic regulators' in 1961 (both identified by Brittan 1964: 211 as important initial elements of the Treasury's 'great reappraisal' during 1960–61); the taxation of short-term capital gains by the Conservatives in 1962; the subsequent taxation of long-term capital gains by Labour in 1965; the introduction of Corporation Tax in the same year; and, finally the ill fated Selective Employment Tax of 1966. Changes to existing taxes and to National Insurance are ignored in part for reasons of space but also because restricting the analysis to significant *new* taxes also means that we can be sure that the policy change is the result of positive choices by policy actors – 'critical' rather than 'routine' decisions (Robinson and Sandford 1983: ix). Tax is also traditionally seen as a field of policy dominated by the Treasury; evidence of 'governance problems' here would therefore tend to indicate such problems were both widespread and deep-seated.

The chapter begins by examining how new ideas on tax developed within the core executive. It reveals that it was penetrated by ideas on tax and growth that were circulating in the extensive growth advocacy network discussed in Chapter 3. Many academic and business economists outside the Treasury, and a number of high level officials within it (particularly in its Economic Section) became convinced that Britain's tax system needed to be reformed in order to make it more related to the promotion of growth. This lesson, it is argued, was closely related to the government's new preparedness to intervene to raise growth and thus closely related to its adoption of an explicit growth objective in 1962. It thus amounted to third order learning.

The chapter goes on to examine how successfully this 'expert learning' was translated into policy change by examining in detail the implementation of the six new taxes outlined above. The chapter concludes that, under both governments, those seeking to reform taxation on the lines proposed by the growth advocacy network faced great difficulties into turning third order learning into a coherent strategic programme for reform as a consequence of the fragmentation and interdependence of policy institutions in the field of tax.

The process of learning under the Conservatives

Conservative taxation policy during the 1950s and early-1960s

In 1959 there was no sign that the Conservatives intended to revise the tax cutting objective to which they had cleaved throughout the 1950s.[1] Many in the party continued to hanker after further tax cuts (Daunton 1996; Lowe 1996), though in 1960, the party's Taxation Policy Committee could identify virtually no scope for tax reductions if the party's promises on public expenditure were to be kept, despite high marginal rates of income taxation.[2] Even the backbench Conservative Finance Committee had reluctantly to accept that taxes could not always go down.[3] The tension between the electoral attractions of higher government spending and lower taxes was palpable. As Macmillan put it:

> We have to expand without inflation. We have to meet increasing Government and local expenditure on things necessary to our economic future – roads, schools, technical colleges, health services – without (if possible) increases of taxation or even (if we can) with some reduction or at least rearrangement in order to stimulate effort.[4]

The party therefore found itself in a quandary – divided between proponents of *laissez faire* on the right who wished to reduce the scope of the state and favoured both lower government expenditure and lower taxation and 'modernists' on its left wing such as Macmillan, Macleod and Heath who saw a more positive role for government in areas of market failure and were prepared to raise taxes to pay for it (Ramsden 1980: 221; George and Wilding 1985: 62; Lowe 1997a).

This was a difficult circle to square. Bridgen and Lowe (1998: 8-11) argue that the Conservatives hoped to resolve the paradox firstly through the replacement of universal welfare benefits by benefits targeted on those most in need, and secondly through alterations to the structure of taxation in favour of middle class Conservative voters. This, however, ignores a third option available to the government: to have higher government expenditure without raising taxes by increasing the rate of expansion of the UK economy, an option clearly bound up with the proposals of the growth advocacy network.

That Conservative modernisers were prepared to countenance new approaches to tax indicates that the ideas circulating within the growth advocacy network were beginning to percolate into the party and make it more amenable to changes to the tax system that might achieve higher growth.[5] As we have seen in Chapter 3, the promotion of higher growth was under active consideration by the Conservatives in 1960 and in the summer of that year, the Conservative Taxation Policy Committee started to consider changes to the tax system that might promote higher growth and sustain the public spending on which that growth seemed to depend.[6] However, although the appointment of Selwyn Lloyd as chancellor in July 1960 coincided with the beginnings of a change in Conservative thinking on tax, he was not one of those affected by the ideas circulating in the growth advocacy network; his tax objectives remaining both orthodox and conservative (Thorpe 1989: 307, 311; Cairncross 1996: 41). He certainly had no desire to introduce new taxes. At the higher level, therefore, the party remained divided on the direction of its tax policy. Between 1961 and 1963, however, the Conservatives implemented three new taxes that were directly related to its embracing of higher growth as an explicit policy objective: two fiscal regulators and a short-term capital gains tax. What was the main source of this shift in the government's tax policy?

Learning in the Treasury

Conservative confusion over tax and its unwillingness publicly to endorse reforms that might raise taxation created a policy vacuum that was filled by Treasury officials. As already noted in Chapter 3, the need to use taxation to raise the rate of economic growth, by both smoothing the growth curve and stimulating investment, was an important lesson that Treasury officials drew from the record of the 1950s. This was the product of a process of learning and network growth that had three elements (see Figure 6.1). Firstly, the Treasury responded to the negative policy feedback produced by its stabilisation policies, particularly after 1955. Secondly, its thinking was penetrated by the ideas being promoted by the growth advocacy network as a consequence of its links with that network. Thirdly, its formulation of policy was influenced by the environmental change produced by this network.

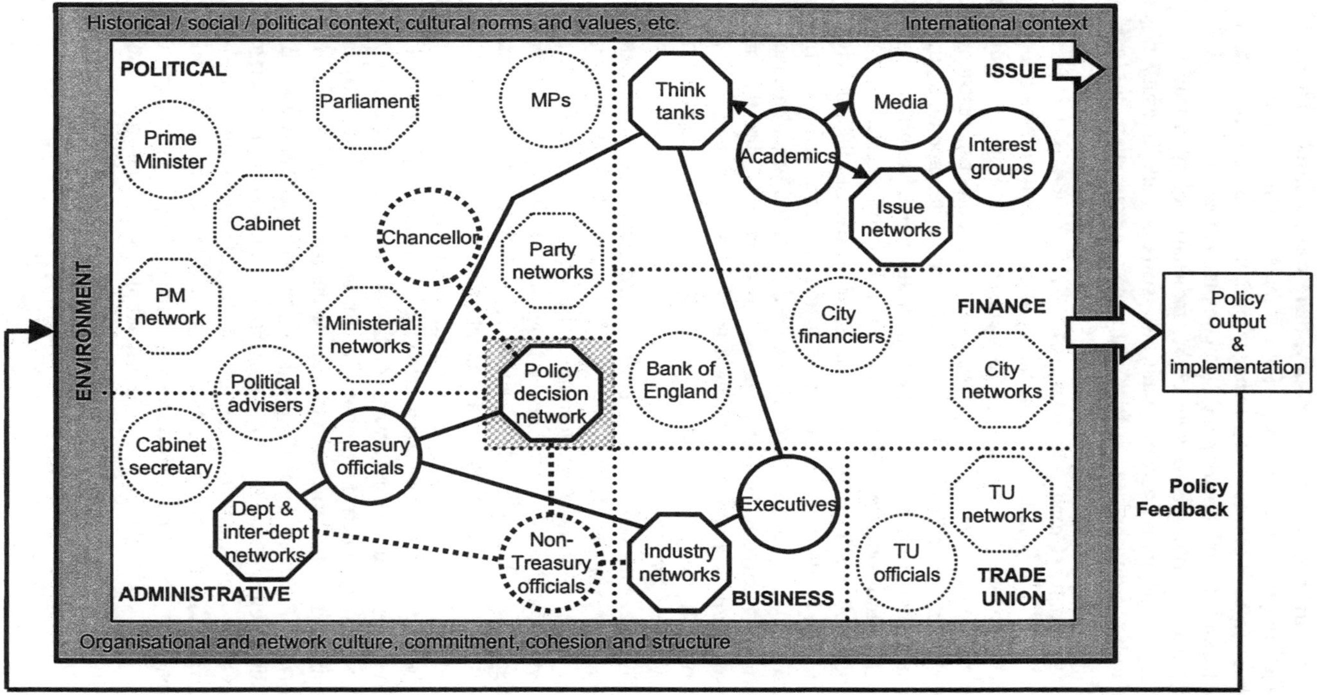

Figure 6.1 Learning in the Treasury on taxation

In the field of stabilisation policy, there was a considerable accumulation of negative feedback by 1960. Officials were acutely aware that interest rates were seen by industry and financial commentators as a 'blunt and brutal instrument' (a complaint made at the 1960 FBI conference).[7] Attempts to devise other monetary policy instruments, such as 'special deposits' had met with little success. The Treasury was also mindful too of the Radcliffe Committee's recent warning that, with sterling now fully convertible, monetary policy was ill suited to fine tuning demand (Cmnd. 827: para. 12). As Dow (1964: 407-8) later noted, none of the measures of monetary policy directly affected consumer demand, the main element of Keynesian stabilisation policy. Moreover, it was becoming ever more apparent that hire purchase restrictions and purchase tax, both favoured instruments of fiscal demand regulation, were too narrowly focused, distorted industrial output, incurred widespread criticism and were detrimental to growth. Furthermore, as the Economic Section pointed out to the new chancellor in August 1960, the rigidity of the annual budget meant that it was difficult to use taxation to 'fine tune' demand.[8] What the Treasury felt was really needed was a mechanism for altering, between budgets, taxes that would directly influence consumption – an 'economic regulator'.[9] If it could find one, it would help to eliminate 'stop-go' and, by smoothing the growth curve, raise the trend rate of growth.

The Treasury was also influenced by the growth advocacy network. In 1960, for example, PEP (1960: 12) advocated the use of taxation and allowances to stimulate investment. The use of taxation as a stimulus to growth was also advocated at the November 1960 FBI conference. This message was echoed by the financial press and in private lobbying of the Treasury by economists, industrialists and financial journalists in the growth advocacy network. By such means the idea that tax could be used to help raise growth penetrated the Treasury. By 1961, Treasury modernisers had become convinced that tax reform could be an important aid means by which the economy might be renovated and higher growth obtained. Tax was an important part of the investigations of the Treasury Working Party on Growth in early-1961 and the Treasury's Economic Section began to agitate for rethinking on the question of taxation and growth.[10] The result was that in 1961 the Treasury concluded that tax reforms should henceforth be considered primarily in terms of their impact on economic growth rather than the traditional criteria of equity and ease of collection – thus signalling the Treasury's intention to trespass in territory hitherto considered the preserve of the Inland Revenue.[11]

The support of the Economic Section is significant. Although there is no firm evidence, it seems highly likely that the section (the director of which, Sir Robert Hall, was a representative on and adviser to the influential Budget Committee and a key 'gatekeeper between ministers and professional economists' in the view of Booth 2001b: 286) formed an important conduit by which new ideas entered the Treasury – through its links with economists and other actors outside government but within the growth advocacy network, particularly economists at the National Institute for Economic and Social Research such as Brian Hopkin.

Having entered the Treasury, these ideas were given greater power as a consequence of the wider change in the intellectual climate regarding growth and economic policy that had been wrought by the growth advocacy network.[12] This made officials outside the section more open to its message. In 1960, as Hall noted, growth was 'in the air' and the Conservatives were 'less worried than they were about the word "planning"'. '[T]imes and people [were] now changing quite rapidly' (Hall 1991, diary entries for 1 and 5 January 1960) with a new generation strongly influenced by the environmental change produced by the growth advocacy network, and in some cases linked to it, rising to senior positions in the Treasury.[13] In particular, the appointment of Lee as Joint Permanent Secretary brought new thinking on growth and taxation into the Treasury.[14] Although Lee arrived at the Treasury with the belief that a lower level of demand was essential if Britain's cost inflation was to be tamed he soon changed his mind. His previous experience as Permanent Secretary at the Board of Trade, the links with industrialists which he had built up during his appointment, the advice of the Economic Section, and the changing intellectual climate all led him to the conclusion that stop-go was damaging Britain's growth. In turn, this led him to the believe that means must be found to improve the government's stabilisation policy and also to wonder if changes to the tax system might not help raise Britain's rate of economic growth. By August 1961, Lee's thinking had advanced to the extent that to help achieve higher growth he was advocating, inter alia, a tax on short-term capital gains, a payroll tax, reform of company taxation and sweeping changes to indirect taxation. [15]

As Lee later noted, the learning that had taken place in the Treasury led it to 'a turning point'.[16] By the end of 1960 – the year 'in which everything really happened but which no one really remembers (Brittan 1964: 204) – the Treasury had concluded that tax must be radically overhauled if a new growth oriented policy framework was successfully to be implemented.[17] New tax instruments must be found to achieve the increase in growth that the Treasury's July 1961 policy shift had already made an implicit objective of economic policy; an objective that would shortly become an explicit goal of government policy with the government's endorsement of the NEDC's 4 per cent growth target. This search for new instruments to support the objective of higher economic growth amounted to third order learning. Yet the learning of this lesson was only the first stage of a process of change; learning must now be turned into actual policies. In this, the Treasury was only partially successful.

What is noticeable, is that the penetration of the Treasury by the ideas of the growth advocacy network did not result in any real change to the structure of tax policy making. The tightly bound economic policy making network at the heart of the core executive (the most obvious manifestation of which was the Budget Committee) remained (see Figure 6.2). The Treasury's privileged role in this network might have been expected to make its task easier. This was not the case – because it remained dependent on the revenue departments within this network to implement any change. Conditioned by a traditional Westminster model mindset, the Treasury's initial impulse was to break the power over policy that participation in the Budget Committee conferred on these departments. However, the committee of enquiry or Royal Commission by which the Treasury proposed to do this was not set up – the Treasury fearing that it might thereby lose control over the direction of policy.[18] Instead, in September 1961, an interdepartmental steering group with representatives from the revenue departments and with a Treasury chairman, was created to review tax policy.[19] Thus, the Treasury found itself force to 'row not steer' in a field of policy traditionally seen as its fiefdom.

Although the steering group's Treasury members argued that there must be an end to the 'historical tendency of officials to consider fully questions of equity and distribution but to ignore effects on production', this message was not well received by the revenue departments, which saw economic regulation as antithetical to equity and ease of collection.[20] Under Treasury tutelage, the interdepartmental steering group did agree that long-term public expenditure commitments (many of which were important to increasing output, such as better education and improved health care) implied little prospect of reducing taxation and that changes to both the scope and structure of taxation were required to improve growth.[21] However, a number of the Treasury's proposed reforms (amongst them a permanent payroll tax, changes to the taxation of company profits, and important proposals for the taxation of consumer expenditure such as the introduction of VAT) had to be discarded because the revenue departments would not agree to the additional work involved or objected to the proposals on grounds of equity.[22] Ultimately, therefore,

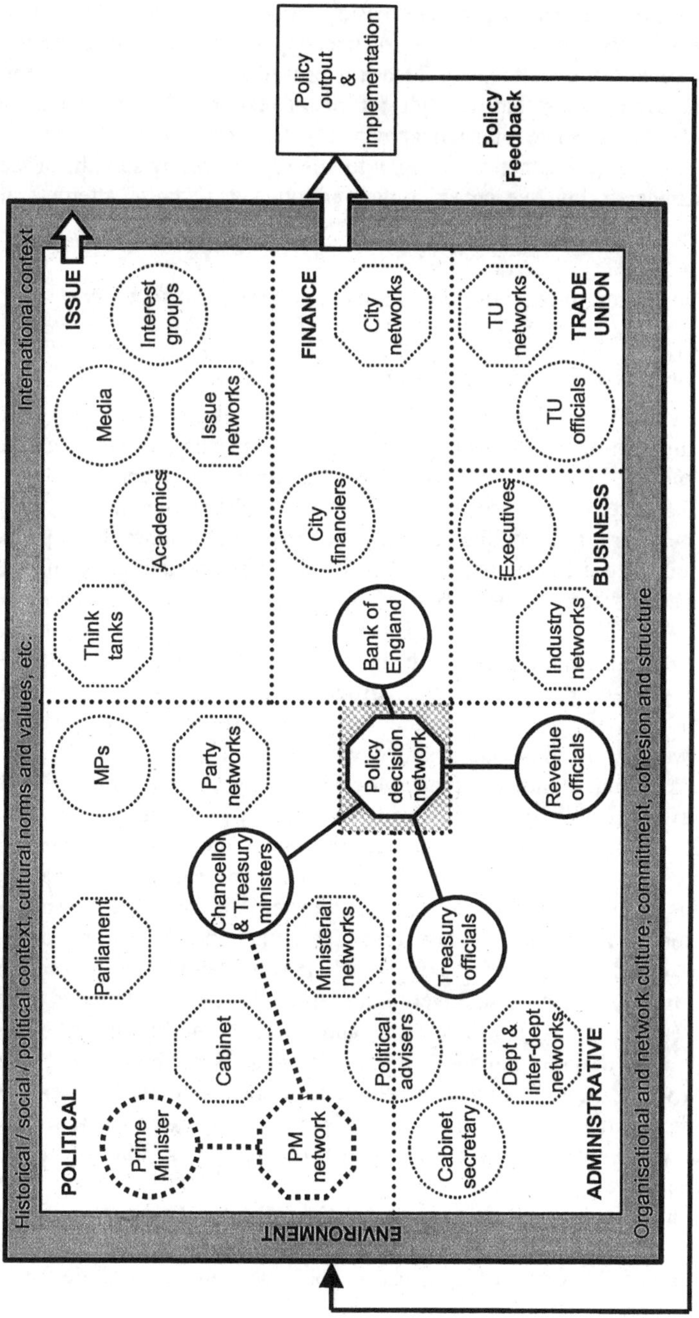

Figure 6.2 The tax policy implementation network

despite third order learning in the Treasury regarding growth and taxation, and despite its control over the membership of the interdepartmental review of taxation policy, the Treasury proved unable to persuade the revenue departments that a major reform of taxation should be undertaken. In the absence of such agreement, the Treasury was forced to sacrifice strategy for tactics. It began to attempt reform by stealth. In the sections that follow we consider how effective were these attempts at reform.

The translation of learning into change under the Conservatives

The Customs and Excise regulator

Treasury concerns about the need to improve its stabilisation policy were raised by Lee at the Budget Committee's first meeting to consider the 1961 budget.[23] On 12 September 1960, Lee made the chancellor aware that the Budget Committee was in the process of developing an improved instrument for regulating the economy. In November, it submitted a paper which outlined the basic requirements. It should be possible to amend the instrument's setting between budgets and a small change should produce a big effect. It should affect consumption rather then investment and should be quick acting. It should be widespread, in order to avoid the distorting effects produced by the narrowly based purchase taxes. Finally, it should be 'demonstrably separate' from other taxes to avoid accusations that it was simply a revenue raising device.[24]

Lee's intention was to replace purchase tax by a much wider general sales tax – thus killing two birds with one stone by providing an economic regulator whilst rebalancing taxation towards indirect taxes to maximise incentives and thus help to raise growth. Customs and Excise objected that this would be too complex to administer.[25] It made an alternative suggestion – a special surcharge on purchase tax and on customs duties which would be relatively easy to administer, would act directly on consumption, would be relatively quick to apply, be differentiated from the taxes and duties to which it was applied, and could be used both to reflate and deflate demand.[26] It would not, however, address the Treasury's desire for a wholesale reform of indirect taxation. Nor would it be widespread. However, since this was plainly as far as Customs and Excise was prepared to go, the Treasury had little choice but to accept the compromise.

At the beginning of January, the official Budget Committee recommended this regulator to Selwyn Lloyd.[27] An annually renewable power would allow the Treasury to adjust purchase tax and excise duties up or down by up to 10 per cent of the prevailing rate. The chancellor and his junior ministers were fairly receptive. Edward Boyle, for example, noted that:

> As a general proposition it seems to me clear that, the larger the number of economic regulators any government is prepared to use, the better it is placed to pursue a policy of economic expansion. Obviously, one can use the accelerator with greater confidence if one knows the brakes are in good order. … The difficulty, quite frankly, is to secure political support for the use, when necessary, of a sufficient number of these regulators.[28]

There were two main political problems. First. the possibility of parliamentary opposition to its loss of control over tax policy.[29] Second, the continuing resistance to tax increases in some sections of the Conservative Party and a reluctance deliberately to increase prices.[30] When the proposal for a Customs and Excise regulator was outlined to the Prime Minister at Chequers on 13 January, Selwyn Lloyd was still not wholly convinced by the Treasury's proposal but its officials were able to use the increasing likelihood of a summer sterling crisis to change his mind and the new tax instrument was announced in the April 1961 Budget.[31]

In its use of tax to help raise growth (by smoothing the growth curve) the 'Customs and Excise regulator' marked a significant break with the Conservative tax policies of the 1950s. It was almost immediately used to its full extent to combat the July 1961 sterling crisis and continued to be a valued instrument of economic policy until Keynesian demand management fell from favour after 1979. Its introduction had been a product of the Treasury's reappraisal of its policies on growth during 1960–61 (Brittan 1964: 204); itself the result of officials learning lessons from problems with stabilisation policy during the 1950s and of the increasing emphasis on growth both within and without the Treasury. In short, it was an example of third order learning translated into the implementation of a new policy instrument to help achieve the new growth objective, though the resistance of other government departments within the tax implementation network had caused it to be a less radical change than the Treasury had initially desired.

The payroll regulator

The Treasury had less success with its simultaneous attempt to introduce a second 'payroll regulator' to allow it to impose, between budgets, a surcharge on employers' National Insurance contributions. Its aim was again to help fine tune demand and this can be seen as a product of learning from negative feedback from 1950s stabilisation policy.

However, it also had a deeper economic purpose for its origin lay in a perception that industry needed to rationalise its use of labour if productivity was to be raised and growth increased – a perception prevalent within the growth advocacy network.[32] A payroll tax was, for example, advocated by PEP (1961a), at the FBI conference in November 1960 (FBI 1960) and by financial journalists.[33] It was also advocated directly to Hall by financial journalists, commercial interests and employer representatives on the tripartite Economic Planning Board (on which Hall sat).[34] The lobbying of Hall is significant, for he was the progenitor of the 'payroll regulator' (Price 1978b: 151). Manpower shortages continued to constrain growth and during 1960 Hall became convinced that firms were hoarding workers. He saw a permanent tax on the use of labour as a way of addressing this; as did Macmillan, who asked the Conservative Taxation Policy Committee to examine it (Brittan 1969: 155).[35]

Nevertheless, despite widespread support for a payroll tax within the growth advocacy network, and despite its success in injecting the idea into the Treasury, the fact that it might be construed as a repudiation of the government's commitment to maintain full employment was a formidable problem that effectively ruled out explicit political support. Without such support, a full blown payroll tax was obviously a non-starter. Hall was forced, therefore, to retreat. Instead, he sought to smuggle in a payroll tax by capitalising on Treasury support for new economic regulators and proposing a PAYE based payroll surcharge (an idea also floated by *The Economist*).[36]

Selwyn Lloyd disliked Hall's proposal when it was raised with him in September 1960; but was persuaded to allow its consideration to continue.[37] Much of the reason for this decision must lie in the advocacy of Lee and Hall, although a part must also have been played by the lobbying of the chancellor by the industrialists Lords Robbins and Plowden, support for the idea at the November 1960 FBI conference, and the possibility (alluded to by PEP 1960: 189-90), of defusing Labour opposition by linking the regulator to the 1944 *Employment Policy* White Paper (which had favoured variation of employer and employee National Insurance contributions to control demand).[38]

Hall's payroll regulator was an ingenious way round political reluctance to institute a payroll tax. Clever as it was, however, it introduced unfortunate contradictions between using a tax on labour to influence employment patterns and using it as an economic regulator.[39] Because an economic regulator would only be used exceptionally Hall had to accept the Inland Revenue's refusal to create a new collection structure (Daunton 2002: 263 highlights the Revenue's preference for ease of collection and profound attachment to the status quo). Instead, the surcharge was applied using the National Insurance system.[40] This had several deleterious effects. Firstly, it introduced a three month delay (to allow new National Insurance stamps to be printed) and compromised an important regulatory objective, speed of action. Secondly, National Insurance was best suited to a flat rate surcharge, but this was politically difficult since it would fall most heavily on the lowest paid. The lack of selectivity within National Insurance also meant it would not be possible to exempt areas of high unemployment or naturally labour intensive industries. In addition, a demand regulator and a payroll tax were essentially incompatible since logic dictated that to act most effectively on demand the former should be applied directly to employees whereas the latter should be applied to employers. The fact that the proposed payroll regulator would apply only to employer contributions would lessen its direct impact on consumption and thus compromise an important regulatory objective.[41] This incompatibility was to make it very hard for the FBI to endorse the new instrument when it was announced in the budget.[42] Supporters of a payroll tax amongst financial journalists also found it impossible to support a measure that that had not been properly thought out.[43] Similarly, both backbenchers and the CRD thought the aims of a regulator and a payroll tax to be incompatible and neither thought the possible impact on growth likely to outweigh the political costs of a possible increase in unemployment.[44]

Even more significant was that using National Insurance risked destroying its integrity, either by breaking the link between contributions and benefits. An 'indignant and upset' Boyd-Carpenter, the Minister of Pensions and National Insurance, threatened to resign when the idea was finally raised with his ministry by the Treasury only weeks before the budget.[45] Since the Inland Revenue wanted nothing to do with the payroll regulator, however, there was no real alternative to using National Insurance and a major cabinet level row ensued that was not resolved until a compromise was hammered out only days before the budget.[46] Under the compromise, the regulator remained in the budget but the use of National Insurance, instead of being permanent, was granted only for one financial year. Since the Treasury had already ruled out both a third increase in National Insurance during the remainder 1961 and the application of regulators in the first three months of a year, this compromise effectively strangled the payroll regulator at birth.[47] The result was that the payroll regulator, now a 'dead rat' in the eyes of the chancellor (and of the Economic Secretary), and so unpopular with both employers and unions that it risked undermining the parallel attempt to build a voluntary incomes policy, was never used (Cairncross 1996: 51; Macmillan 1972: 376).[48]

Like the consumption tax regulator, therefore, the payroll regulator was developed by Treasury officials and was a new instrument designed to attain the growth objective. It was therefore the product of third order learning. It was both a response to the negative policy feedback from the government's stabilisation policy of the 1950s and the product of an intellectual climate increasingly concerned with growth and how to raise it. It drew upon suggestions advanced by the FBI, financial journalists, PEP and Robert Hall – all key actors in the growth advocacy network. It was, however, an uneasy compromise between two incompatible objectives; a compromise forced upon the Treasury because of the lack of political support for a strategic programme of tax reform aimed at raising economic growth. The result was a measure which achieved neither of its objectives, was unpopular and lacked political champions. This, in conjunction with opposition from the administering department, meant that, whilst the Treasury was able to get the measure on to the statute book, it was unable to use it.

Taxation of short-term capital gains

Treasury officials proved more successful in their attempt to tax capital gains, although their agenda was achieved incrementally. In 1962, short-term gains, other than those relating to personal chattels, owner occupied houses and business assets, became subject to income tax and surtax. Labour then implemented a full blown capital gains tax in 1965. In both cases, the chief aim was to obtain union support for an incomes policy by showing the government's willingness to tax capital as well as income but an important subsidiary objective was to promote growth by encouraging long-term investment. Both were therefore deeply imbricated with other elements of the growth policy framework and with the third order learning from which it sprang.

The taxation of capital gains was not a new idea. It had been considered by the post-war Labour government and by the Conservatives during the 1950s. During the post-war Labour government the Inland Revenue stymied its implementation, arguing that staff shortages precluded it. Later, when Macmillan returned to the idea in 1955, it was able to cite the opposition of the majority report of the 1955 Royal Commission on the Taxation of Profits and Income.[49] The minority report of the Royal Commission (the principal authors of which, Kaldor and Woodcock, were in the growth advocacy network) had, however, argued that, for reasons of equity, the tax free status of capital gains should be ended and they should be treated as a form of income (Cmd. 9474: 79-80). From the mid-1950s, this suggestion began to gain ground in the growth advocacy network. At the same time, negative feedback, in the form of rising prices, also caused the Treasury to begin to think that the taxation of capital gains might be a necessary prerequisite for some form of compact with the trade unions on the restraint of wage inflation; although how this would be received by the Conservative Party, coupled with uncertainty about the likely economic effects, initially persuaded the Treasury that the idea was a non-starter.[50]

Once the Treasury moved towards an interventionist growth strategy in 1960, however, its officials viewed the measure far more positively. They began to think that a tax on short-term gains might encourage long-term investment as well as easing the introduction of an incomes policy.[51] In 1960, the Budget Committee, despite Inland Revenue objections to the additional administration, considered recommending such a tax to Selwyn Lloyd.[52] It concluded that the idea remained politically unacceptable. When Selwyn Lloyd announced his intention to reduce surtax, the Treasury tried to persuade him that taxing capital gains would be a suitable political '*quid pro quo*' to defuse union opposition; but the opposition of the CRD, the backbench Finance Committee, and the Inland Revenue was too much for the chancellor.[53]

Treasury officials, knowing the new tax would appeal to Macmillan, then took advantage of the July 1961 sterling crisis successfully to return to the proposal and, in his emergency budget, Selwyn Lloyd indicated his intention to tax short-term speculative gains in land and securities as part the interventionist growth strategy recommended by his officials and supported by Macmillan.[54] This, in turn, was intended to make it easier for the trade unions to cooperate in two other elements of his policy package: the new NEDC and an incomes policy. The ideological reservations of the Conservative Party were finessed by promoting the policy as a tax on speculators rather than a tax on the proceeds of legitimate investment. Despite determined resistance from the City and the Bank of England a White Paper was issued in April 1961 (Cmnd. 1710) and the 1962 Finance Act implemented the proposals.

The new tax marked a real change in Conservative policy and provoked outrage in the City.[55] Such a symbolic break with the Conservative's past tax policy in the quest of higher growth indicates a significant degree of learning. The tax on short-term gains was an important step on the road to a full blown Capital Gains Tax and reflected a widespread desire to use the tax system to encourage more long-term investment and thus raise growth. As such, its genesis lay in the environmental change arising from negative policy feedback and the efforts of the growth advocacy network. The hope that it would also help to gain union support for an incomes policy was a further, and very important, link to the new growth objective. Thus the taxation of short-term capital gains was clearly an important product of the third order learning that occurred in the early sixties although, as with the two regulators, this new tax sprang from the Treasury rather than from ministers.[56]

Conclusions

Viewed in isolation, these three new Conservative taxes might seem relatively insignificant. Nevertheless, their implementation shows that the Conservative government, largely as a consequence of pressure from the Treasury – and by extension from the growth advocacy network that had penetrated its economic side – had embraced an important new principle: that taxation should be used not just for raising revenue but for actively intervening in the economy to raise growth. This was, by any standards, a major shift in Conservative tax policy and a marked break with their strategy in the 1950s. That the measures were relatively small was a function of the distance travelled by Conservative Party ministers and officials. That they had been implemented at all was measure of the third order learning that had occurred, particularly amongst Treasury officials.

Labour's learning about taxation

For Labour, the fit between political ideology and the ideas about the need for new taxes being promoted by the growth advocacy network was less of a problem than it was for the Conservatives. Moreover, Labour had undergone a process of learning in the early-1960s about the relationship between tax and growth similar to that of the Conservative government (see also Daunton 2002: 247); although this learning occurred amongst a remarkably restricted set of actors. Detailed internal Labour Party proposals on tax and growth came from economic experts not politicians.[57] Whilst party discussions were held about the general thrust of taxation policy, there was little detailed consideration of tax by Labour politicians – a fact remarked after the 1964 election on by surprised officials.[58]

Labour's reluctance to discuss taxation policy stemmed from its defeat in the 1959 election for there was a widespread view that the loss stemmed directly from the party's pledges on income tax and purchase tax (Robinson and Sandford 1983: 59-60). Consequently Labour was loth to give hostages to fortune by making too many specific pledges for, as Rose and Karran (1987: 5) remarked, 'If keeping out of trouble is a basic law of politics, then not making decisions about taxes is one way to avoid trouble'.

Labour ideas on tax in the latter half of the 1950s and in the 1960s came from two main sources. The first was Anthony Crosland – already identified above as an important Labour member of the growth advocacy network – whose proposals on tax in *The Future of Socialism* were vetted by Robert Hall, Crosland's predecessor as lecturer in economics at Trinity College, Oxford, and by Ian Little, also in the Economic Section at the time and later one of Callaghan's Nuffield advisers (Reisman 1997: 7-9, 159; Morgan 1998: 175). An important element of Crosland's proposals was the use of taxation to encourage investment (Crosland 1956: Ch.15, 1962: Ch.9, 1964: 293). By these means, he argued, a vibrant private sector could be created which, coupled with a more competitive and efficiently managed public sector, would deliver economic growth. The increased tax revenues which would result would pay for the improvements in welfare and equality of opportunity which Crosland envisaged.

Labour's principal source of specific policy ideas on tax, however, was Nicholas Kaldor (Daunton 2002: 279) – also one of the shadow chancellor's advisory group and then, after the election, Callaghan's special adviser on the social and economic aspects of taxation policy. As we have already noted, Kaldor was deeply embedded in the growth advocacy network and had been the architect of the minority report of the 1955 Royal Commission on the Taxation of Profits and Income (Cmd. 9474: 354-470). This had recommended that the taxation of companies and individuals be separated, with company profits subject to a single tax rather than a combination of income tax and profits tax. It had also argued that the equitable treatment of different classes of taxpayer demanded that the definition of income be extended to embrace capital gains. This effectively became Labour's tax policy template as it manoeuvred in the early-1960s to capitalise on widespread disenchantment with stop-go and relative decline, and the perception that greater social justice was essential if the unions were to be persuaded to agree to the incomes policy that seemed a vital element of any policy framework on growth (Labour Party 1961: 35; Whiting 1998).[59] Tax then became an important constituent of the national plan which Labour outlined in its 1964 manifesto to build a 'new Britain', raise economic growth and arrest its relative decline; though exactly what this tax reform would consist of, beyond a promise to extend the Conservatives' taxation of capital gains, was left unclear.

Thus two lessons had been learned by Labour about taxation and growth during the late-1950s and early-1960s. The first was that reform of taxation was essential if the 4 per cent growth objective was to be achieved: new taxes could be designed that would, by promoting social justice, tempt the unions into a bargain on wages and thus pave the way to higher growth without inflation. The second was that taxation could also be used to encourage firms to increase their investment and to invest for the long-term. The principal exponent of each lesson was Kaldor.

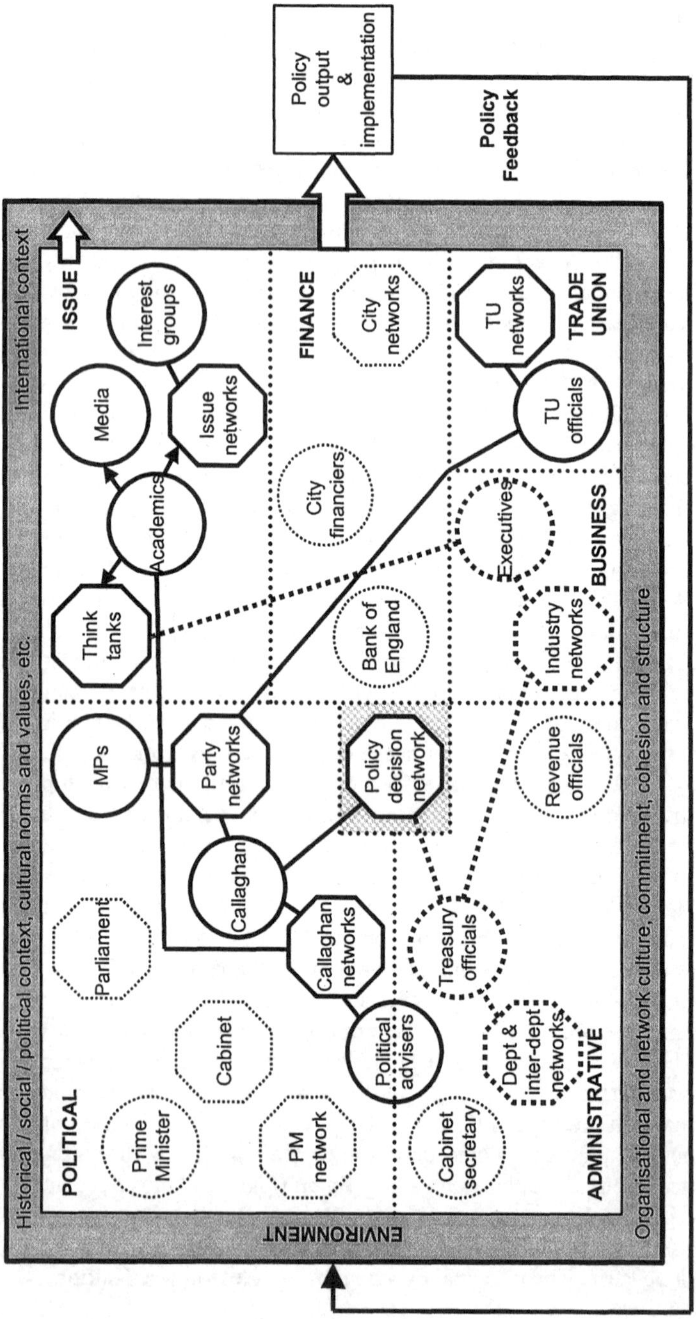

Figure 6.3 Labour's tax policy network, 1955-1964

Both lessons were a response to the negative policy feedback of the 1950s and to the change in the policy environment brought about by the growth advocacy network. Both involved changes to policy instruments to achieve the new growth objective. Thus both amounted to third order learning. Both had also been learned by the Treasury and by the Conservatives and had been translated into policy changes. In effect, therefore, the election of the Labour government brought a repenetration of the core executive, this time (with the appointment of political advisers such as Kaldor) physical as much as intellectual, by members of the growth advocacy network (see Figure 6.3).[60] However, for Labour (as for the Conservatives) it was not enough just to learn the lesson; once elected, a Labour government must translate this learning into substantive policy change.

The translation of learning into change under Labour

The Capital Gains Tax

Although the Conservatives' short-term capital gains tax had represented a marked break with its tax policy in the 1950s, its problem was that the definition of 'short-term' made the tax practically voluntary.[61] Callaghan had welcomed the tax as a step towards the full blown capital gains tax (CGT) which Labour saw as essential to union participation in an incomes policy (and thus an indispensable constituent of its policy for higher growth); and in fact Maudling had indicated to officials that the Conservatives would significantly extend the scope of capital gains taxation if they were re-elected.[62] Taxation of capital gains to increase social justice had appeared in Labour manifestos since 1955; its inclusion in Labour's 1964 manifesto was not in itself, therefore, a product of the learning that took place in the early years of the 1960s.[63] What *was* new in Labour's thinking was the idea that a full CGT was essential if the unions were to be persuaded to accept the national incomes policy that was deemed essential to achieving the 4 per cent growth objective.[64] It is clear, therefore, that third order learning had led both parties to a similar analysis of the role that capital gains taxation could play in promoting growth.

The rationale behind Labour's CGT was rooted in the minority report of the 1956 Royal Commission and in the subsequent advice from Kaldor – and thus, by extension, in the growth advocacy network – that the imposition of a corporation tax would raise a company's share price and that capital gains should therefore be taxed as if they were income (Thirlwall 1989: 129). Despite Labour's wariness about making specific tax proposals, the desire publicly to commit itself to attaining the social justice that was deemed essential for 'the planned growth of incomes' led the party to promise a full blown CGT in its 1964 manifesto and in November 1964 Callaghan indicated that he intended to include the new tax, along with a new corporation tax, in the next budget.[65] In 1965 Labour implemented a two tier tax on all capital gains – making short-term gains (those made within 12 months of acquisition of any asset) subject to full income tax and surtax and long-term gains subject to a flat rate tax of 30 per cent (a rate lower than the standard rate of income tax).

Translating the intention to tax capital gains into concrete proposals in an April 1965 white paper (Cmnd. 2645) did not prove easy. Strong resistance from the City, the institutions of which were notable by their absence from the growth advocacy network, began immediately. The simultaneous announcement of the government's intention to introduce both a Corporation Tax and a CGT, seen as essential to progress on a voluntary incomes policy, set off an exit from sterling that was only halted by a $3bn international credit. The Chairman of the Institute of Directors, somewhat hysterically, talked in terms of 'socialist revolution' (Morgan 1998: 215-22). The press clamoured for details of the proposals.[66] Callaghan, badly shaken, was forced to make a clarifying statement on 8 December in which he announced generous exemptions for gains made on property sales and at death.

The new tax also attracted strong opposition from the Inland Revenue; which argued forcefully that, since asset disposal tended to be infrequent, it would be unfair to treat it as the top slice of income. To the Inland Revenue, the lack of distinction in both Kaldor's options between assets held for only a short period and those held for some years was 'indefensible' on grounds of equity and it produced its own counter proposal – a two tier scheme with long-term gains taxed at a flat rate lower than that envisaged by Kaldor.[67] There was also considerable resistance from the Bank of England which, recognising that a CGT was politically inevitable, began to lobby for the Inland Revenue's proposal – in its view the least bad option.[68] The Governor indicated that gilts should be exempted and, with little subtlety, emphasised the government's dependence on the market for the financing of its growing borrowing needs.[69] Strong representations were also made by City institutions, which put pressure on Wilson and on Treasury ministers and officials, both directly and through a publicity campaign.[70] The new economic adviser to the Treasury, Robert Neild (a member of the growth advocacy network and one of the new chancellor's advisers in opposition), complained to Callaghan that the fuss over tax uncertainties was being turned by financial institutions 'into a major political campaign to discredit the government'.[71]

In the core executive, a compromise was hammered out which involved retaining the short-term tax (at full rates of income and surtax) for the first year of gains and a flat rate for longer term gains.[72] For companies, the level of the long-term flat rate was set at the same rate as the new Corporation Tax. For individuals, the chancellor split the difference between the rates being proposed by his political and economic advisers, and the lower rate proposed by the Inland Revenue – setting the rate at 30 per cent, less than the standard rate of income tax.[73] With this, the details of the proposed CGT scheme were now ready to be announced; but the choice of a flat rate set lower than the standard rate of income tax was a significant retreat from Kaldor's original proposal to treat gains as pure income.

A further retreat came during the passage of the Finance Bill. The City lobbied the key players, arguing that the tax would penalise risk taking, diminish saving, tend to freeze shares in the hands of investors, impede the free flow of funds in the capital market and represent be a repudiation of a moral commitment on the part of government to holders of its fixed interest securities.[74] Papers from advisers attempted to stiffen the resolve of both Wilson and Callaghan.[75] Yet turnover in gilts was depressed and Treasury Finance officials began to worry that this would force the government to renege on its promise to the IMF to reduce its bank borrowing.[76] City jobbers then staged what was effectively a 'gilts strike' on 27 May. Appalled by the implications of this for government borrowing, further retreat was now ruled out by ministers, but only after a concession exempting gains arising from price movements between the date of issue (as opposed to the date of acquisition) and that of redemption.[77]

In summary, therefore, the main aims of the new CGT were twofold. Firstly, in conjunction with the parallel introduction of CT, it aimed to encourage the retention of profits by companies and thus raise funds available for investment. Secondly, it aimed to promote the social justice that Labour thought essential if the unions were to agree to an incomes policy. Thus CGT was a major new tax instrument aimed at achieving higher growth without inflation and was an integral part of the third order learning of the early-1960s. The roots of the tax lay firmly in Kaldor's original proposals, although as implemented it represented something of a retreat from the proposals of the minority report of the 1955 Royal Commission. Kaldor's role was crucial: the policy flowed from him, not from politicians. This was therefore a profoundly technocratic new policy instrument that sprang from the ideas of the growth advocacy network.

Unlike the other five taxes in this analysis, however, it also had an explicit manifesto commitment.

Once again, the route by which the ideas of the growth advocacy network had penetrated the core executive was an 'expert' one. This time, however, it had been via a political adviser rather than via officials. That neither the Treasury nor the Inland Revenue opposed the principle of a tax they had violently objected to less than a decade before was in part a mark of the extent of the learning that had occurred in the core executive. Nevertheless, the fact that compromises were forced by opposition to the detail of policy from the Inland Revenue, from Treasury officials responsible for government borrowing, and from the Bank, indicates that the degree of learning differed between actors in the core executive and that fragmentation and interdependency within the tax implementation network was a barrier to translating third order learning into third order change. Significantly, in this field of policy, the new ideas circulating in the growth advocacy network had penetrated but had not overwhelmed the core executive. Furthermore, the fact that the Treasury found its dependence on the City for borrowing required concessions to be made indicates that resistance from competing policy networks was also a barrier to achieving matching policy change.

Corporation Tax

The second plank in Labour's 1965 Finance Act was a new system of Corporation Tax. Its chief aim was to encourage profit retention by companies and so, by increasing the funds available to them, encourage them to increase their investment and thus raise economic growth. The change reflected the new perception amongst many economic experts (a perception promoted by, and disseminated within, the growth advocacy network) that the quantity of investment was too low and that allocative efficiency might better be obtained by means other that the operation of financial markets. As with CGT, the blueprint for Labour's Corporation Tax lay in the minority report of the 1955 Royal Commission and thus Labour's policy was again driven by Kaldor and by the 'expert' third order learning promoted by the growth advocacy network.

Before the introduction of the new tax, company profits were subject to income tax at the standard rate and to an additional 'profits tax'. To avoid income tax being paid twice on distributed profits (once by the company paying the dividend and once by the recipient) the company was entitled to retain the tax it deducted from dividends at the standard rate. This meant that companies effectively paid more tax on retained profits. This was an incentive to distribute profits rather than reinvest. The introduction of the Corporation Tax replaced this structure with a single tax of 40 per cent on all profits and a separate deduction from dividends of income tax at the standard rate, thus creating an incentive to retain profits within the firm.

Like CGT, the reform of corporate taxation in the 1965 Finance Act had a long gestation. Selwyn Lloyd had begun his chancellorship with just such a reform in mind, although his motivation was the simplification of company taxation rather than the promotion of growth.[78] However, Selwyn Lloyd's proposal foundered on the rock of Inland Revenue resistance to double taxation and administrative complexity.[79] The question of company taxation was then considered by the Treasury's Reform of Taxation working party at the end of 1961. Whilst it reached no conclusions, it did acknowledge that the current structure might hamper the growth of profitable firms.[80] This was a substantial shift and thus evidence of learning in the Treasury; though not sufficient for the Treasury to consider taking on the Inland Revenue.[81] With Selwyn Lloyd's replacement by Maudling, who was unenthusiastic about the idea, the attempted reform died. By October 1962 the Inland Revenue was telling interested parties in the private sector that the whole idea of corporation tax reform had become 'moribund'.[82]

Nevertheless, there was great support for a corporation tax amongst Callaghan's pre-election economic advisers and it formed the second plank of Labour's 1965 budget. Despite this, Labour's 1964 manifesto made no reference to it. Why was this? In 1961, Wilson (then shadow chancellor) had indicated a desire to tax retained profits less heavily to encourage investment on the lines recommended by the minority report of the 1956 Royal Commission.[83] In March 1964, a party committee on taxation strongly backed a single corporation tax and the willingness to see such a reform was made public in June 1964.[84] This did not amount, however, to the firm adoption of a corporation tax as party policy; Labour proving reluctant to commit itself to CT for fear of the electoral consequences of raising the spectre of a major programme of tax reform. Shortly after the election, however, and at Kaldor's instigation, Callaghan then indicated to officials that an immediate initiative would be required on company taxation as a *quid pro quo* for union cooperation on incomes policy and as an important means by which the government's 4 per cent growth objective might be obtained.[85] So, again, we find third order 'expert' learning occurring, but learning that must now be converted into concrete policy changes.

The Inland Revenue responded to Kaldor's scheme saying that 'from a purely fiscal standpoint [it] would be an improvement', looking tidier and more modern and removing several serious anomalies.[86] However, its tone was extremely negative – describing CT as a 'revolutionary' and 'controversial' change that would damage investment by discouraging profit making. Callaghan, placing his faith in Kaldor, and recognising the conservatism of the Inland Revenue, dryly noted: 'An excellent description! I am sure it is worth doing. Of course we will get into trouble, but thanks to this paper we will at least know what is coming'.[87]

Callaghan announced his intention to introduce a Corporation Tax in the spring during his November statement; hoping thereby to encourage the unions to cooperate in Labour's attempt to craft a voluntary incomes policy. Unfortunately, the lack of detailed proposals provoked intense speculation in the press that Labour intended shifting the balance of taxation onto companies (something which in truth did attract some in the party, but not Kaldor and others in the growth advocacy network).[88] This in turn produced strong pressure from the City, the Bank of England and industry to ensure that firms were no worse off under the new regime.[89] It would, of course, have been unprecedented for the chancellor to announce the rate before details of the tax had been decided, let alone debated. Undaunted, industrial and financial interests – which had not been consulted – used the precarious state of sterling to extract a promise that the tax burden on companies would be approximately the same under the new regime.[90] This meant that the 'social justice' element of the new tax, which in fact had not been part of Kaldor's original justifications, was now much less attainable.

A further retreat, one that did mark a significant departure from Kaldor's original proposals, occurred in respect of inter-company dividends. Under the existing system of company taxation, company profits were only taxed once. Profits paid out as dividends to companies were excluded from the receiving company's calculation of taxable profit (this system, called 'franking', meant the profits of a company bore income and profits tax only once).[91] Kaldor intended that distributed profits be taxed twice, even if they were paid to a company and thus contributed to a profit which would itself be taxed by CT. By this means he aimed to discourage what he termed 'portfolio', as opposed to physical, investment by companies and so, he hoped, encourage higher growth.[92] This was opposed by the Inland Revenue and by some Treasury officials, on the grounds that such 'double taxation' was inequitable. It also produced severe pressure from the Bank of England, the City and employers' organisations (the latter concerned at the implications for cross company ownership).[93] Recognising both the blocking power of the Inland Revenue in the tax implementation network and the government's dependence on the City for its borrowing and the employers' associations for cooperation on the national plan, Kaldor compromised; excluding parent companies and investment and unit trusts.[94] This did little to stem the opposition of either the Inland Revenue or the City. The Inland Revenue warned of the risk that a 'large inter-company network [that] has been established over many years ... would suddenly be thrown into jeopardy' and asked if 'Ministers [we]re prepared to force their proposals through against industrial and commercial opposition'.[95] Balogh railed against the Inland Revenue for 'refusing to take administratively awkward or unpopular action'.[96] Nevertheless, despite a plea from Kaldor that the taxation of inter-company dividends was fundamental to the idea of CT, faced with the practicalities of managing the Finance Bill, Callaghan finally decided to exempt them.[97] Thus, despite the support of Callaghan, opposition both within and without the core executive had required a marked retreat from Kaldor's original proposal.

Another retreat was forced in respect of overseas companies. Kaldor proposed restricting their credit against UK tax for taxes paid overseas (known as 'overspill' and available up to 56¼ per cent, the combined rate of incomes and profits tax) to the lower rate of Corporation Tax.[98] This time, the Inland Revenue supported the measure on grounds of equity, arguing that overseas companies were receiving preferential treatment.[99] So too did Treasury officials in Overseas Finance and all the government advisers involved (Neild, Balogh, Cairncross and MacDougall). In the short-term, they hoped that abolishing 'overspill' would encourage companies to liquidate and repatriate some overseas investment, thus easing the severe pressure on the balance of payments. In the long-term, they hoped that it would stimulate domestic investment and thus help to raise growth.[100] However, the proposals were opposed by the DEA, Board of Trade and Bank of England, all of which were linked to industrial or financial 'clients' which argued that overseas investment was good for the balance of payments, helping to build overseas markets and encouraging UK exports.[101] Outside government, the abolition of 'overspill' was forthrightly opposed by those it would affect. BP and Shell, which would be hard hit, were especially vociferous.[102] Their cause was taken up by the FBI.[103] The fight was taken into the media.[104] Lobbying by BP, Shell and other companies with extensive overseas interests led the Board of Trade, the Ministry of Power and the Foreign Office to oppose the proposal.[105] Furthermore, there was a plethora of representations from developing nations to their sponsoring departments that any repatriation of assets would harm their interests.[106] These departments, in turn, put pressure on the Treasury to review the proposal.[107] Despite a Treasury minute noting that none of the dissenting arguments, save perhaps those of the developing countries, really stood up to examination,[108] the chorus of protest led ministers to adopt first a five year transitional period and then, after a sustained public relations and lobbying campaign by the oil companies and underdeveloped Commonwealth countries, a seven year transition.[109]

Thus Kaldor's CT proposals had been the subject of three significant concessions. Nevertheless, in its final form CT did still meet Kaldor's key objective. By instituting a differential between retained and distributed profits of 24.75 per cent it introduced a significant incentive for companies to retain profits for reinvestment (Price 1978b: 145).[110] Like CGT, CT was the product of third order learning amongst officials and advisers within the core executive's economic decision network; and like CGT, the most important factor behind its introduction was the advocacy of Kaldor. The difference between Selwyn Lloyd's unsuccessful reform and Callaghan's successful implementation of CT lay in the respective ability of their advisers to defeat the Inland Revenue by securing political support. In 1960, learning had occurred in the Treasury in respect of CT and growth but it not feel able to take on and defeat Inland Revenue objections. In 1964–65 Kaldor had two advantages. Firstly, he was working with the grain of new Treasury thinking produced by the re-appraisal of 1960–61. Secondly, Kaldor was able to link his agenda with Labour ideology and win the support of senior politicians in the battle with the Inland Revenue. The result was that third order learning had resulted in a significant, if somewhat compromised, new tax instrument designed to attain the growth objective.

The Selective Employment Tax

Another example of using the tax system to promote growth, though a much less successful one, was the 1966 Selective Employment Tax (SET). Although the payroll regulator had been stillborn in 1961, supporters of a payroll tax in the growth advocacy network continued to press their case and the idea re-emerged under Labour.[111] Again, Kaldor was the prime mover – the architect of a complex system of higher employers' National Insurance contributions and rebates to manufacturers which was conceived just after the March 1966 election and announced in the budget just four weeks later.

Kaldor's (1966) thesis was that in an advanced industrial economy the less productive service sector tended to 'soak up' labour, that this lowered the productivity of the economy as a whole, and that raising the cost of service sector labour relative to that in manufacturing would therefore increase average productivity (a recommendation also to be found in PEP 1960: 237).[112] It would also provide a covert subsidy to manufacturing exporters and, by easing the balance of payments, make it possible to run the economy at a higher level of demand and so raise growth. Kaldor had first raised the idea with the DEA in 1964, but had been rebuffed by

MacDougall who thought the scheme politically impossible, an administrative nightmare, potentially damaging internationally and perhaps illegal under the General Agreement on Trade and Tariffs.[113] In early April 1966, as worries about sterling mounted, Kaldor opportunistically pressed his proposal on Callaghan and the rest of the Treasury – offering the prospect of using the tax to help sterling as well as growth and of using it as an economic regulator, via adjustments to the difference between its revenue and subsidy elements.[114]

Official reaction was mixed. Those departments that might have to administer the tax and rebate were fiercely opposed.[115] Treasury officials supported the principle of using a payroll tax to encourage greater productivity and higher growth. They were also interested in the possibility of another economic regulator for use in stabilisation policy. However, they were not convinced that changing relative prices within the labour market was practicable, were concerned about the costs of administration and foresaw, correctly, all sorts of problems with drawing the line between services and manufacturing. There was also the question whether SET was compatible with the government's regional policy, since it would raise the cost of service sector labour even in depressed areas. With the abortive attempt to introduce the payroll regulator in mind, Treasury officials urged Callaghan to consult with employers and unions before proceeding.[116]

Despite these official misgivings, the politicians were keen. Both Wilson and Callaghan liked the idea of action to manage demand that would not raise personal taxation. In the face of such heavyweight political support, officials were forced to back down. On 19 April, only two weeks after Kaldor had revealed his proposal, the Prime Minister gave the scheme the go ahead.[117] Without exception, officials were appalled by the rushed implementation and imperfect nature of the scheme.[118]

Publication of the proposals in the selective employment tax white paper (Cmnd. 2986) in May 1966 then unleashed a storm of objection, despite the support generated by the growth advocacy network for the idea of a payroll tax. From within the government, protests came from departments such as the Board of Trade and Ministry of Labour on behalf of firms in their respective industrial policy networks.[119] The Conservatives attacked Labour's 'antipathy to the growth of services'.[120] Press reaction to the proposals was extremely negative.[121] Concern also began to grow in the NEDC and the regional division of the DEA regarding the impact of the SET on regional policy.[122] Such was the response that within days Wilson was forced to indicate to the press lobby that he expected SET to be 'further refined'.[123] By 25 May a ministerial group, an interdepartmental committee under Ministry of Labour chairmanship, and a Treasury working party were all hard at work devising concessions.[124]

Nevertheless, despite this, SET was implemented (albeit in a much revised form) and its implementation shows quite how far an expert adviser such as Kaldor, operating within the tightly bound and secretive tax policy network, could influence policy if he could secure the backing of senior politicians. The seriousness of the external situation explained how Kaldor managed to get it implemented in such short order. However, its rushed implementation led to a botched job which cut across both regional policy and the national plan (Sandford 1971: 48-52).

SET, by using the tax system to increase productivity and growth, was obviously a product of the new willingness to use taxation to intervene in the economy engendered by the growth advocacy network. However, this aim was obscured in the rush to capitalise on ministers' wish to strengthen sterling and thus obtain their support for a major innovation in taxation. As a consequence of its hasty and unplanned implementation, SET turned out to be an unhappy compromise between an attempt to manipulate labour markets to boost productivity, to improve demand management, to act upon the balance of payments and to deflate the economy in the face of a severe sterling crisis. The result was a mess and a political disaster for Labour. Subsequently, the abolition of SET became a priority for the Conservatives.

Conclusions

Between 1961 and 1966, therefore, both Conservative and Labour governments introduced new taxes which were designed specifically to improve Britain's rate of economic growth – an explicit economic objective from 1962 but already an implicit objective by 1961. Taxation of short and long-term capital gains and the new Corporation Tax were all attempts to use taxation to promote growth through structural changes in patterns of investment – encouraging higher and longer term investment. Similarly, both SET and the payroll regulator were attempts to promote long-term changes in the structure of employment and, in particular, release surplus labour to be used more productively. In addition, both regulators and, to a lesser extent, SET were attempts to raise growth by smoothing the growth curve through improved demand management. The new taxes, with the exception of SET, fell less heavily on firms and, coupled with measures such as increased investment allowances, this contributed to the rebalancing of the tax structure away from companies.[125] Again, this aim was growth related – aiming to raise corporate profits after tax, and thus increase industrial investment and innovation.

The use of tax to attain the new economic objective of higher growth was an important break with the tax policies of the past. Revenue raising and the preservation of horizontal equity were no longer the predominant criteria by which new taxes were judged. This radical change had been brought about by expert learning by Treasury officials under the Conservatives and economic advisers (particularly Kaldor) under Labour. It was a technocratic response to the negative policy feedback of the fifties, specifically stop-go, to mounting evidence of relative decline, and to the changed intellectual environment produced by the growth advocacy network.

This intellectual shift amounted to third order learning and transcended party boundaries.[126] As a consequence, both parties introduced measures that sought to attain similar ends with similar means. Of course, this congruity did not imply complete agreement between the governments, or between the technocratic members of the growth advocacy network within the core executive who were able to influence tax policy, on the policies that would best achieve the new objective. Nor was ideology altogether absent – it is clear that the policy legacy of the 1950s made it difficult for the Conservatives completely to reinvent their tax policy, whereas Labour ideology proved more congenial to technocratic reform proposals. However, both governments recognised that tax reforms could promote higher growth and introduced new taxes to do so.

Nevertheless, whilst there was continuity between governments in tax policy, viewed as a whole the new taxes did not amount to a coherent programme of reform (Pemberton 2001). At least four of the six taxes discussed here were introduced at short notice in response to economic difficulties. Technocratic reform of taxation, instead of being strategic, was largely tactical. Why was this? Most obviously, both the Conservative and Labour parties were extremely wary of specific commitments on tax. This wariness translated into a reluctance publicly to discuss extensive changes to tax and, in the case of Labour even inhibited internal discussion within the party.[127] This meant that neither party constructed a strategic programme for using taxation to attain the new growth objective. Nor, despite a good deal of degree of agreement amongst officials, advisers and ministers of both parties about the need to use taxation to promote growth, was there any attempt to build a cross party consensus on detailed proposals. In part, this failure to seek public agreement on the tax reforms was an almost inevitable result of the parties' respective unwillingness publicly to engage with taxation policy lest they invite an attack from their adversary.

The construction of a programme for strategic tax reform was made even less likely by another institutional inheritance: the reluctance of the Treasury to put taxation policy 'into commission' because for the Treasury, '"into commission" has the ring of "hung by the neck until you are dead"' (Lipsey 2000: 123). This meant the new taxes were rarely discussed outside the confines of a tightly bound budgetary policy making community until just before their announcement. The fact that policy was devised behind the veil of budget secrecy might have been expected to strengthen the hand of those within the Treasury who were promoting change. It did not. Without a publicly endorsed mandate for change, they found it extremely difficult to surmount a third adverse institutional inheritance: the fragmentation of British policy making institutions both inside and outside the core executive.

The fact was that modernisers at the centre of the core executive lacked the power to impose their solutions even in a field of policy normally seen as one dominated by the power of the Treasury. Because there was no electoral mandate for change, under both governments key elements of proposals for reform drawn from the growth advocacy network, especially those relating to the taxation of consumer expenditure, failed to attract the political backing that was necessary if the Treasury was to prevail over the conservatism of the administering departments.[128] Attempts to circumvent the revenue departments proved disastrous: consider both the payroll regulator and the SET. Furthermore, when political support was obtained it was often because of the opportunistic and hasty construction of policy by Treasury officials and advisers, and of compromises which reduced the technical efficiency of the reform.

Similar problems were encountered with vested interests outside government. Under the Conservatives, for example, although a 'vanguard elite' in the FBI supported a payroll tax as a means to faster growth, the fact that the FBI had not been involved in the construction of the payroll regulator made it easier for it to repudiate the new tax when its smaller members objected. Under Labour, the lack of a mandate to change corporate taxation made it more difficult to resist making concessions to the City of London – conspicuous by its absence from the growth advocacy network. The fact that the Conservatives had themselves actively considered implementing such a tax in the early-1960s was not acknowledged. If it had been, the City's campaign for special treatment might not have been successful.

If members of the growth advocacy network within the core executive were to triumph over their opponents, whether within or without government, they needed heavyweight political support. This was often lacking. The absence of a prior and publicly endorsed programme meant that each new tax was politically vulnerable. Ministers were acutely aware of this. Officials and advisers were forced to trim their sails accordingly. The need continually to negotiate political backing made it much more difficult to defeat the vested interests that were opposed to change, and which proved adept at organising themselves in opposition, and to construct a coherent set of reforms.[129]

The result was that, whilst there was third order learning in tax policy, the translation of this learning into policy change was poorly handled. Third order learning certainly resulted in important changes, but the incoherence of these changes, and the fact that many of the changes that were made were subsequently contested (see Daunton 2002: Chs. 8-10), suggests that the implementation of these new taxes did not amount to third order change.[130]

Thus, a major factor in the failure of the growth advocacy network's reform project in the field of taxation was the existence of a serious structural problem with British policy making – a failure to acknowledge the endemic fragmentation of its policy making institutions.[131] The failure might have been avoided if the substantial cross party consensus had been acknowledged and if an attempt had been made to widen the policy making community by involving outsiders in the development of a publicly agreed policy programme. The new NEDC, it could be argued, had the potential to provide the missing institutional framework which Britain lacked for 'an equal and open relationship between government and non-government agencies' (Lowe and Rollings 2000: 111). That the NEDC was not used to do this in respect of taxation was due to the Treasury's refusal to share the power to make tax policy and its inability to follow through the logic of its insights regarding the interdependence of economic policy institutions to their logical conclusion

7

Conclusions

Was there a significant innovation in economic policy?

The first of the two key historical questions raised at the start of this book was did the policy changes of the early-1960s represent a significant innovation in economic policy? The answer to this question must surely be yes. Economic policy goals were revised: at first implicitly, with the conversion of the Treasury in 1960/61 to the idea that growth needed to be raised and that government intervention was required to achieve this; then explicitly with the government's endorsement of the NEDC's 4 per cent growth target in 1962. As a consequence of this shift in economic priorities an array of new economic policy instruments was introduced – first by the Conservative government and then by its Labour successor after October 1964. There were changes in fiscal policy: the introduction of new demand management instruments to improve stabilisation policy and avoid the debilitating consequences of 'stops' in the 'stop-go' cycle; new taxes and alterations to the structure of taxation designed to stimulate investment and growth; and measures to ensure that government expenditure decisions were both better planned and made in the context of the new growth objective. There were innovatory changes on the supply-side of the economy such as the introduction of indicative planning and associated creation of the NEDC, the 1964 Industrial Training Act, the 1964 Resale Prices Act and the creation of the Industrial Reorganisation Corporation in 1966. Finally, to contain the inflation that higher growth might produce, and thus to maintain international competitiveness and avoid higher growth being derailed by another sterling crisis, the government tried for the first time to construct a permanent voluntary incomes policy.

In large part, this shift in both the goals and instruments of economic policy was the result of learning the lessons of the policy failures of the 1950s – particularly the tendency for Keynesian demand management to destabilise the economy, and the potential for inflation in a policy framework with full employment as a primary policy objective rather than as a byproduct of economic growth. It is doubtful, however, if this feedback would have been sufficient on its own to precipitate a major shift in economic policy priorities (a 'third order change') rather than continuing adjustments to existing instruments within unchanged policy goals ('second order change'). The study reveals that a key factor in the adoption of the new policy framework was the ability of the growth advocacy network further to change the policy environment by promoting its new ideas regarding both the need for higher growth and the means by which this might best be achieved, as well as by bringing these ideas directly into the tightly bound economic policy making community at the heart of the core executive by forging links with it.

Shonfield (1965: 103-5) was therefore right to identify the change in government thinking as the product of 'one of those sudden ideological waves which periodically seem to sweep through Whitehall'. The source of this wave, however, lay largely outside the core executive. Mapping the process of ideational change indicates that negative policy feedback during the 1950s provoked the formation of an extensive network of advocates for new policies on growth. This confirms that introducing the concepts of feedback and learning into policy network theory supplies the latter's missing internal dynamic and endogenises change within the model (Peters 1998: 25; Marsh and Smith 2000: 9; Hay and Richards 2000; Pemberton 2000; Richardson 2000: 1017-8). Policy outcomes affect, and can create, policy networks.

The new growth advocacy network originated in academia. There was a notable rise in academic interest in growth after the 1955 'stop'. The idea that Britain's growth was inadequate, a perception reinforced by new data revealing her relatively poor performance in comparison with the European economies, and the idea that new policies were required to correct this failure, then began to percolate into a wider arena towards the end of the decade. These new ideas about growth spread through the policy terrain like a virus, transmitted from person to person and institution to institution (for discussion of the virus like nature of ideas see Colander and Coates 1989; Richardson 2000; Larsen 2002).[1] The result was the creation of a growth advocacy network that began rapidly to expand after the 1958 'stop'. By 1960–61, this network had grown to encompass much of Britain's economic policy terrain. Its extent demonstrates that, contrary to the assertion of Marin and Mayntz (1991b: 17-18), policy networks can consist of more than 'a few or not too many actors' and confirms Bogason and Toonen's (1998: 220) observation that networks exist not just between organisations but within organisations and between sub groups of different organisations.

Through their links with academics, pressure groups (such as PEP) and think tanks (such as the NIESR) began to take an interest in growth and to develop and promote new policy ideas that might raise it. Both organisations were important carriers of the growth policy 'virus' to actors and organisations in other sectors of the policy terrain during 1960 and 1961. The impact on Treasury thinking of PEP's *Growth in the British economy* and the joint PEP / NIESR conference on planning in April 1961 suggest that these institutions were not just influential where their recommendations 'coincided with the calculations of decision makers' (Denham and Garnett 1999: 48) but helped to shape these calculations.[2] Through the development of direct contacts with members of the core executive, the growth advocacy network managed to penetrate the economic decision network at the heart of the core executive and to bring into it both the idea that economic policy goals needed to be changed to incorporate an explicit objective of higher growth, and the idea that radical new policies were required to achieve it. In the early years of the 1960s, the economic policy making community at the heart of the core executive effectively merged with the growth advocacy network and its thinking was fundamentally changed as a result (thus confirming that existing policy networks can change through the effects of other networks as argued by Marsh and Smith 2000: 7-8). In particular, the idea that the government should intervene in the economy – to stimulate investment, to remove supply-side bottlenecks, and to address other instances of market failure that might impede higher growth – took hold within the Treasury during 1960 and caused it successfully to advocate an interventionist growth strategy in July 1961.

The growth advocacy network did not just inject its ideas directly into the core executive. The fact that it also managed to raise public awareness of the need for both higher growth and for new policies to achieve it was also of critical importance. It helped change both the intellectual and electoral environment within which economic decision makers at the core of the core executive operated. Financial journalists were particularly significant in this process. As a consequence of their contacts with academic economists and pressure groups (such as PEP), they began to discuss ideas for higher growth in their columns and in books written for popular consumption. In doing so, and by translating academic concepts into a language that was more easily understood by the public, politicians and officials, they played an important role in transmitting these ideas to a wider audience. The importance of this role should not be underestimated for, as pointed out by (Nelson 1987: 86), in order for academic ideas on the economy to be politically influential they must first be politically intelligible. In this case, voters became infected with the idea that economic growth, despite being high in historical terms, was in fact rather lacklustre and could potentially be much higher: but only it was given a higher priority by the government and if new policies were adopted. This changed electoral and intellectual environment altered the policy calculations of the major parties and of their leaderships. This in turn helped transform the thinking of officials in the core executive. Thus the growth advocacy network was able to change the electoral and intellectual environment within which economic policy was constructed as well as succeeding in injecting its ideas directly into the core executive, by extending its tentacles into it.

The consequence of this process of policy feedback, network growth and idea transmission was a major shift in government economic strategy during 1961–62. Actors outside the core executive had therefore succeeded in changing both the objectives of, and instruments used by, the tightly bound and relatively impermeable economic policy making community at its core. This again is an important finding because it indicates that peripheral actors with little obvious power can exert great influence over policy through the medium of a policy network (see also Bleich 2002). As Smith (1999a: 33-4) points out, if actors with limited resources are to win then tactics are important. The key to the success of the growth proponents was their success in infecting others with their ideas on growth and thus drawing them into an expanding advocacy network. Power resources, are important even within advocacy networks (Rhodes 1981, 1997: 10-11; Jessop 1990; Smith 1998, 1999a: 31), the tradable resources being information and knowledge.[3] In this case, ideas about how growth might be increased gave members of the growth advocacy network a degree of power over a core executive eager to find new solutions to raising growth.

The studies undertaken here, therefore, confirm that policy networks can be a powerful lens through which to examine the actions of the core executive – although the analysis does not lay to rest Peters' (1998) worries about whether the existence of policy networks enables us to predict change. Policy networks do not explain economic policy change in the early-1960s. They were not a causal variable. It is, however, clear that they were a particularly important *intermediate* variable, for change was brought about via policy networks.

Moreover, combining policy network theory with theories of learning deepens our theoretical understanding of how policy networks grow and change configuration. Mapping the development of the growth advocacy network using has confirmed both the importance of learning in network growth and the potential fluidity of networks (Hay 1998; Pemberton 2000). If space had permitted, a sequence of 'snapshots' could have demonstrated this fluidity even more clearly. Mapping networks therefore allows the analysis to transcend criticisms of Rhodes and Marsh's typology by replacing the labelling of network types with a more general recognition that policy networks can, over time, be many and varied, with different extents and degrees of commitment, integration, resources, and power.

Second, using the schema has revealed that policy networks are themselves central to the process of learning and that different network configurations are associated with different order of policy learning. Whilst second order learning in economic policy is seen to have taken place within a relatively closed policy network embodied in the Budget Committee, third order learning (as in the 1970s) involved the breaking open of this network and growing influence of a new and widespread advocacy network. Freiberghaus' criticism (discussed in Knoepfel and Kissling-Näf 1998: 363) that the concept of learning should not be applied to networks because 'loose interest groups' lack a measurable final output proves to be unfounded. The use of historical archives has provided the necessary evidence to allow an assessment of learning to be made. Policy networks prove to be an important medium by which new ideas are translated into policy change. The schema helps to highlight both the importance of institutional relations and the importance of context and structure on policy making. Using policy network theory to frame the analysis of learning therefore provides the structural dimension that Hall (1997: 183-6, 195-8) acknowledged was lacking in his theory of social learning.

Was there a paradigm shift?

The second key historical question we set out to answer is whether the economic policy innovations of the early-1960s amounted to a 'paradigm shift' ('third order change') and if they did not, why not? Chapter 3 outlined the events leading up to the adoption of the new growth objective and the development of new growth oriented policy instruments. The development of an extensive advocacy network, the importance of alternative ideas about how the economy should be run and the significance of financial journalists and pressure groups in transmitting these ideas to a wider public are all reminiscent of the transition from Keynesianism to monetarism in the late-1970s described by Hall (1993). In contrast to Hall's theory, however, the policy change was not dominated by politicians (with the notable exception of Macmillan) but by experts. 'Administrative learning' was more significant than 'political learning'.[4]

The adoption of the growth target and the associated array of new policies were radical changes and they marked a pronounced break with the policies of Conservative governments in the 1950s. Moreover, the case studies in Chapters 4 to 6 confirm assertions that the new policy making framework ushered in by the Conservatives continued to shape policy under Labour (Brittan 1969: 190; Young and Lowe 1974; Kirby 1991: 249).

Nevertheless, there is a common thread that runs through each of our three case studies: 'third order learning' occurred but this learning was not translated into an enduring 'third order change'. The severe deflation in July 1966 marked the effective end of the growth objective, of 'planning' and of the construction of a long-term incomes policy related to growth – the reappearance of the latter in the 1970s being tied not the achievement of higher growth but to the avoidance of deflation (Fishbein 1984). A number of the new policies continued, in the field of industrial training for example, but they did so within a set of policy goals that no longer included a target for higher growth. Consequently the policy changes of the early to mid-1960s came to be seen not as a revolution in economic policy making (a paradigm shift) but as an incremental development of Keynesian demand management ('Keynesian-plus').

Industrial training

In Chapter 4 we examined a specific example of the new interventionist microeconomic policy ushered in after 1961 – the 1964 Industrial Training Act. The 1964 reform was directly related to the quest for higher growth; aiming to secure improvements in vocational training that would provide the skilled labour required to achieve higher growth. The creation of a new policy instrument to achieve the new 4 per cent growth objective suggests third order learning.

Members of the training policy network (which embraced the Ministry of Labour and professional trainers) responded to the inadequate quantity and quality of skilled labour produced by industry during the 1950s. On its own, however, this was not enough to precipitate a major reform. It was only when this negative policy feedback was coupled with the environmental impact of the growth advocacy network that third order learning occurred and a major policy shift was consequently attempted. Nevertheless, despite third order learning in training policy, and despite temporary success in spreading the cost of training more fairly, overall the achievements of the 1964 Industrial Training Act were limited. The apprenticeship system remained essentially unchanged and key objectives relating to raising the volume and quality of trainees remained unfulfilled. Third order change did not occur.

Why did it not prove possible to translate third order learning into third order change? A key factor was the fragmented yet interdependent nature of Britain's labour market institutions and of its core executive. For example, departmental infighting between rival training and education networks impeded progress and prevented the construction of a policy that embraced both further education and on the job training. Interdependencies and turf disputes between the Ministry of Labour and the Treasury also hampered the construction of new policies.

In the labour market, institutional fragmentation meant that, although the employers' organisations and the TUC were prepared to consent to government intervention and to an institutional overhaul of industrial training, they lacked the power to deliver their members. There were, for example, significant divisions between the peak organisations of employers and their member firms and trade associations. Many companies resisted change because they were reluctant to cede control of training or feared that interfering with apprenticeships would antagonise the unions and worsen industrial relations. Smaller firms were completely opposed the idea of a training levy because it would end free riding. Such opposition necessarily shaped responses of leaderships to government initiatives on training and led the peak associations to oppose the central control that was plainly necessary if vested interests were to be prevented from stymieing radical change.

The trade unions were similarly fragmented. Whilst general unions favoured radical reform and the extension of workplace training, craft unions resisted reform because they had a vested interest in restricting the number of apprentices. These divisions between craft and non-craft unions were institutionalised within the TUC and neither the General Council nor the General Secretary and his staff were willing, or able, to overcome the resistance of the craft unions to radical reform of industrial training. The result was that, despite strong initial support in the TUC for a strong central institution capable of overseeing a radical overhaul of training practices, the TUC ended up by endorsing a much more limited change than it had initially desired.

Furthermore, in individual firms and factories, employers of apprentices and the craft unions had reached a modus operandum that, whilst it preserved the peace between them, was profoundly antithetical to radical change. It encouraged them to combine together in low level self-organising inter-organisational networks which were able to channel the change that occurred and ensure that the ITB structure did not produce radical change.

The Ministry of Labour was unable to prevail over this fragmentation within and between organisations of employers and unions because it hesitated to push ahead too aggressively for fear of spoiling its relations with the industries on which it depended if it was to operate successfully in its wider functions (Brittan 1964: 328-9). Although the more astute Ministry of Labour officials recognised that they faced a considerable 'governance' problem, the 'Westminster model' mindset continued to exercise considerable sway over the minds of both senior officials and ministers. This explains the reluctance within government to involve non-governmental institutions in policy making. This, however, prevented the ministry from mobilising the considerable support that existed for a radical reshaping of apprenticeships, support that had been generated as a consequence of learning in the training policy network and the environmental change produced by the growth advocacy network.

The consequence of these various factors was that the barrier to change formed by the preference of many employers and unions to retain their autonomy proved to be insurmountable. Consequently, although the ITA caused training costs to be (temporarily) shared more favourably, there was little progress in solving the more fundamental problems inhibiting growth. The reforms simply entrenched the existing apprenticeship system rather than revolutionising it.[5] Third order learning had not been translated into third order change (Shonfield 1965: 117-8; Finegold and Soskice 1988: 25-6; King 1995: 211).

Incomes policy

The whole field of incomes policy, the subject of Chapter 5, also represented a significant break with the policies of the 1950s. Wage restraint was not a new idea, of course, but it had hitherto taken place as a temporary means of avoiding balance of payments problems. The introduction of the pay 'pause' in July 1961 was not merely another *ad hoc* response to a sterling crisis; it was part of a conscious wish to craft a long-term solution to the problem of how to raise Britain's long-term rate of economic growth. Voluntary restraint of incomes would reduce the inflationary pressure that the higher demand associated with faster growth could be expected to produce. The attempt to construct such a policy was thus a consequence of the adoption of the new economic objective of higher growth; it was a clear case of third order learning.

The lesson that an incomes policy was required had been fully learned by the Economic Section of the Treasury in the 1950s. However, it was not until the widespread intellectual change produced by the growth advocacy network during 1960–61 that the Economic Section, in conjunction with Macmillan, was able to persuade the Treasury that a permanent incomes policy must be an essential element of any new policy on growth. Such was the strength of the changed policy environment that agreement on the need for an incomes policy transcended political boundaries and both parties committed themselves to implementing one (Kirby 1991: 247).

Nevertheless, despite this widespread expert and political support, incomes policy failed to attain its own aims. It was not particularly successful in controlling the growth of wages, indeed in the longer term it was probably counter productive; it was poorly integrated into the overall growth policy package; and the link between incomes policy and growth was broken by the deflation of July 1966. Again, a key reason for failure was the inability of the centre to act alone and the barrier to change posed by the interdependent yet fragmented nature of key institutions.

Within government, the Treasury faced strong initial opposition from the Ministry of Labour, which feared that an incomes policy would prejudice its traditional conciliation role in the industrial policy network, whose representative in government it was. The Board of Trade was equally reluctant to countenance reciprocal action on prices or dividends. This made it hard to make progress on a policy which was bound to involve intervention in both fields if incomes policy was not to operate to the disadvantage of any particular interest group (Haywood 1987: 255). This fragmentation within government made it hard to coordinate policy making (see also Ringe 1999: 82).

Outside government, the TUC was reluctant to participate in incomes policy until after the 1964 election. Subsequently, the election of a Labour government made it more tractable but the price was a considerable extension of the policy into the field of prices. From the start, there was considerable resistance from industry to this. Bargaining with these two groups was long and hard. Incomes policy might have been expected to embody a positive sum approach, but fundamentally the employers' organisations and the TUC wanted restraint from each other but were reluctant to make sacrifices themselves. It might have been expected that, since incomes policy was so essential to the wider growth project, the NEDC would have helped in the construction of an agreement. It proved virtually useless. Such were the sensitivities, and such were the divisions between the various groups, that it proved impossible to break out of bilateral discussions between each and the government into a more wide ranging debate about the crucial importance of incomes policy to growth.

Moreover, labour market fragmentation went deeper than disagreement between the TUC and employers' organisations. Conciliators and arbitrators, for example, were outside the control of the government. The result was a succession of awards that broke agreed norms. Furthermore, although the peak associations of employees and employers were eventually persuaded to support the policy there proved to be too little power at the centre to make these national agreements stick at plant level, where low level self-organising networks encompassing both sides of industry conspired to undermine national agreements. This resulting 'wage drift' was a major factor in the failure of incomes policy to contain inflation. This failure, and the fact that after July 1966 incomes policy was abandoned for some years (and when it was resurrected in the 1970s was viewed as a way of controlling the balance of payments rather than as a means to attaining higher growth) suggests that, whilst there was third order learning in the field of incomes policy this learning was not properly translated into third order change.

Tax policy

In the field of taxation, examined in Chapter 6, an array of new tax instruments was introduced to help attain the new objective of higher growth. This was a marked break with past policy; for the first time, revenue raising and the preservation of horizontal equity were no longer the predominant criteria by which the acceptability of proposed new taxes was judged. This radical change was a technocratic response to negative feedback from the policies of the fifties, specifically 'stop-go' and mounting evidence of relative decline, and to the changed intellectual environment produced by the growth advocacy network. It was not brought about by politicians but by Treasury officials, particularly those in its Economic Section, and it was sustained under Labour by political advisers who were also economist members of the growth advocacy network. The study found a substantial amount of policy continuity between 1961 and 1966; an indication that both parties had learned similar lessons regarding economic policy. Paradoxically, however, it also found a lack of coherence. Third order learning occurred but, despite the alteration of economic objectives and some successes with particular taxes, the policy changes did not amount to a strategic programme of reform and thus third order change did not occur.

Why did it prove impossible to translate third order learning about tax policy into third order change? The principal cause of the failure lay in the fragmented yet interdependent nature of Britain's economic policy institutions. Politically, Britain's adversarial two party system made its politicians wary of publicly promoting tax reform for fear of the electoral consequences. Consequently, despite the existence of broad political agreement on the need to make the tax system more growth oriented, responsibility for reform devolved almost entirely to technocrats: to Treasury officials under the Conservatives and to political advisers under Labour (mainly those based in the Treasury). These technocrats, despite having the power of the Treasury behind them, could not simply dictate policy. They faced opposition from elsewhere in the core executive's tax implementation network, especially the revenue departments on which the Treasury depended to implement and administer the new taxes, and from those interests outside government (such as the City) which might be disadvantaged. If the technocrats were to defeat these opponents they needed heavyweight political support. Political reluctance publicly to commit to a programme of tax reform meant this was often lacking. As Barrett and Fudge (1981: 259) point out, without an electoral mandate for change, those at the centre of government lack the authority to interfere in existing power dependency relationships. This made it impossible for those promoting the innovative use of new taxes to help raise growth to triumph over their opponents in the fragmented yet interdependent institutions of Britain's economic policy terrain.

Without a mandate for change and without the ability to enforce change, the technocrats had only two options. One was to construct a consensus for change that would transcend the reluctance of politicians to lead the charge. This was not done. Despite a good deal of agreement amongst officials, advisers and senior politicians of both parties, there was no attempt to build a consensus on detailed proposals. For example, although the new NEDC can be seen as a product of the Treasury's frustration at the barrier to change posed by 'governance' problems (as argued by Ringe and Rollings 2000a) it was not used to construct a programme of tax reform, mainly because at bottom the Treasury continued to be captivated by a 'Westminster model' view of British politics and jealously guarded its prerogatives in the field of tax. Instead, officials and advisers attempted to implement a programme of reforms by stealth.

It might have been expected that that hand of the Treasury would have been strengthened by its power to control the agenda in the secretive Budget Committee. This was not the case. Officials could not make changes without political support to legitimise them and the absence of a prior and publicly endorsed programme of reform meant that change had continually to be negotiated. This encouraged the opportunistic and hasty construction of policy, to capitalise on favourable but short-term political conditions. It also led to compromises and proposal trimming, to minimise political risks and avoid antagonising vested interests, which reduced technical efficiency. The result was that, whilst there was third order learning in tax policy, the translation of this learning into policy change was poorly handled. Important changes to the tax system certainly occurred, but the incoherence of these changes, and the fact that many of them were subsequently rolled back, suggests that they did not amount to third order change.

Conclusion

Policy change in each of our case studies flowed from the adoption of the new growth objective; yet, in each case policy objectives were not attained and an enduring policy change that could contribute to the achievement of higher growth was not achieved. What is true of these studies was also true of the growth policies of the 1960s more generally (Shonfield 1965; Brittan 1967; Polanyi 1967; Hayward and Watson 1975; Leruez 1975; Smith 1975; Sandford 1976; Shanks 1977; Meadows 1978; Kirby 1991, 1992; Middleton 2004). Most significantly, as can be seen in Figure 7.1, fundamental targets for higher growth were not met.

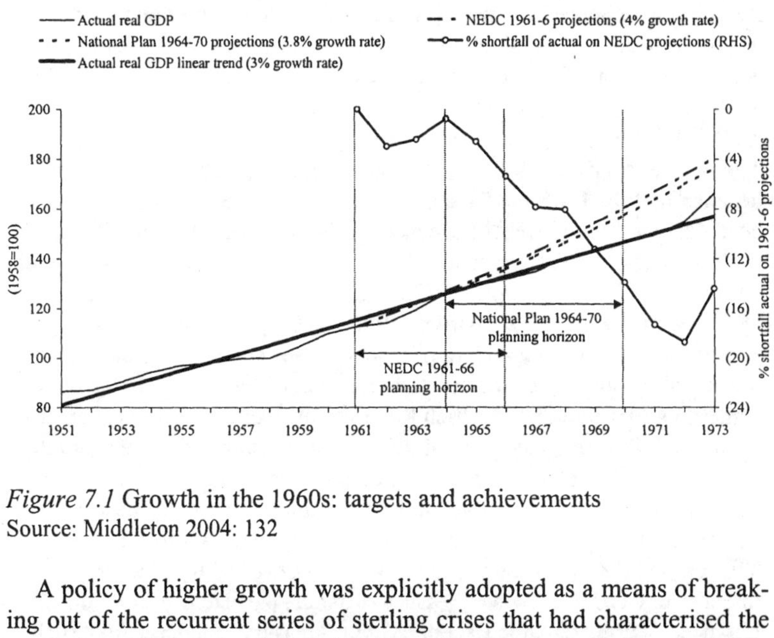

Figure 7.1 Growth in the 1960s: targets and achievements
Source: Middleton 2004: 132

A policy of higher growth was explicitly adopted as a means of breaking out of the recurrent series of sterling crises that had characterised the years since 1945 and ending Britain's relative economic decline. In Hall's (1993) typology of learning, the conjunction of changes to instrument settings, changes to the instruments used to attain economic policy objectives, and the alteration of those objectives that occurred in the early-1960s should amount to a third order change. Such a radical alteration of 'the overarching terms of policy discourse' should qualify as a 'paradigm shift'.

In the space of just a few years, however, this attempt to raise the long-term rate of British economic growth ended in ignominious defeat. In July 1966, when faced with a choice between growth and sterling, the government chose sterling. The growth objective was 'sacrificed to the balance of payments' (Crosland 1974: 18). This was more than a pragmatic adjustment of policy and a recognition that 'paradigmatic shifts ... are never so neat and clean when viewed in detail' (Barker 1996: 13; Backhouse 1983). After 1966, planning for growth become 'the love that dare not speak its name' (Smith 1975: 67). Incomes policy was abandoned and tax reforms in the field of labour usage and corporate investment became the subject of political opposition from the Conservatives.

It is clear from the case studies, therefore, that whilst 'third order learning' occurred, 'third order change' did not. This is an important point for it suggests that Hall's (1993: 278) underlying assumption that 'learning is indicated when policy changes as the result of such a process' is too restrictive. Learning does not necessarily result in change of an equivalent order. This prompts the question, why not?

Why did a paradigm shift not occur?

There is a persistent school of thought that indicative planning failed because in July 1966 the Treasury took its revenge on a policy that had been designed to reduce its influence on the economy, and that it was able to do this because there was a failure of political will to oppose financial interests over sterling (Opie 1972; Shanks 1977: 89-91; Longstreth 1979: 184; Nairn 1979: 51-2; Alford 1996: 260-1; Graham 1996: 153-4). Superficially, this argument looks persuasive, since the planning era is bracketed by sterling crises and the inception of the new policies did owe something to a *zeitgeist* in which the 'establishment' (and in particular the Treasury) was seen as part of the problem rather than the solution. However, as Chapter 3 demonstrated, the record suggests that Treasury modernisers played an active part in the adoption of the new policies. Those, such as Leruez (1975: 90-2) and Middlemas (1991: 458), who have argued that the Treasury had not been converted to 'planning' do it a disservice. Certainly, some Treasury officials, particularly in its Overseas Finance section, remained sceptical but Treasury 'modernisers' such as Lee and Hall did succeed in changing its policy in 1961. Subsequently, the Treasury, far from having a 'contempt for production' (Pollard 1982), actively sought over the next few years to promote higher output, not least because it came to see higher growth as the means by which problems with sterling and the balance of payments might be addressed. Whilst the sterling objective ultimately proved to be of a higher priority than the growth target, the Treasury did make a genuine effort to break out of the 'stop-go' cycle via a policy for growth.

An alternative thesis is that planning failed because the institutions that were built to support it proved to be inadequate. Leruez (1975: 126), for example, found that the Conservatives attempted to plan without increasing the capacity of the state to intervene. Trevor Smith (1975: 60-3) emphasised the highly fragmented institutional structure of planning and the way in which, by adding a layer between government and individual firms and unions, the NEDC helped to weaken central control. Moreover, the institutions of planning are found to have excluded important interests, not least the City, which remained antipathetic to planning and to government intervention (Kirby 1992: 653).

The case studies examined here give considerable support to this latter thesis. In each study, the fragmentation of the policy terrain, the interdependence of many of the actors and institutions within it, and the ability of competing networks to resist the reforms promoted by the growth advocacy network proved fundamental to the failure of the new policy to attain its own objectives. Thus it is a mistake to see 'governance' (in the sense of self-organising, inter-organisational policy networks spanning the divide between state and civil society and characterised by a process of exchange and negotiation between network members and between networks) as a phenomenon of the Thatcherite assault on the state post-1979 (such as it was). The studies clearly show that, far from Britain having a powerful and centralised state at this time, as asserted by Rod Rhodes (in Rhodes 1997 and 2000a, for example) and Martin Smith (1999a: 248), in the early-1960s the centre already lacked the power to impose solutions in the economic arena.

One of the important archival findings of the studies outlined here has been the scale of division within the core executive over the direction of policy. Although the Treasury was penetrated by the growth advocacy network in 1960–61 and profoundly influenced by its ideas (despite some internal resistance) this was much less true of other ministries. This was a major problem given the 'federal' nature of the core executive.[6] Having determined on the need for a new growth policy framework in 1961, the Treasury subsequently met substantial resistance from departments on which it depended for successful implementation of the new policy framework: the Inland Revenue, Customs and Excise, Board of Trade and Ministry of Labour.[7] It was therefore forced to engage in 'missionary work' in Whitehall through interdepartmental committees. This was a slow process and contributed to the policy drift between 1960 and Macmillan's intervention in the summer of 1962. The creation of the DEA by Labour then undid much of the institutional progress that had been made. By separating long-term planning from both short-term stabilisation policy and from sterling it served not only to reinvigorate but also to institutionalise the divisions that had been papered over since 1960. Fragmentation and interdependence within the core executive was therefore a considerable barrier to the entrenchment of a new policy paradigm.

Disagreement, institutionalised divisions, and interdependency between the core executive and powerful vested interests outside government were also a problem. There were some obvious problems: the City was notable by its absence from the growth advocacy network yet the government's was dependent on it for finance, and considerable power was conferred on financial interests by a fixed exchange rate; industrial interests were prepared to see a degree of government intervention in the economy to secure higher growth but proved reluctant to cede control of production and pricing decisions; the unions, whilst pressing the need for 'planning' and prepared (at an elite level) to trade restraint on incomes and cooperation on industrial reform for a degree of influence over policy, ultimately proved extremely reluctant to see intervention in the labour market without equivalent concessions from industry.

Fragmentation went deeper than this, however, for there were also significant divisions between the elites in the peak organisations and their members. As Middlemas (1986: 311) noted, the FBI's embracing of indicative planning 'represented the limited consensus of large member firms, not the sum of opinion in all trade associations and small businesses'. Resistance from below sometimes forced the FBI and the other employers' associations such as the BEC to trim their sails and often subverted agreements constructed by them in bilateral negotiations with government or in the NEDC. Similarly, the support of the TUC for involvement in indicative planning and for cooperation on incomes policy and on industrial training rested on a limited consensus amongst senior trade unionists, a consensus promoted by George Woodcock and the small TUC bureaucracy (Taylor 1999). However, there were a number of dissenting unions the opinion of which the General Council must necessarily take into account if revolt was to be avoided. Moreover, it was only too easy for individual unions and for shop stewards at plant level to collude with the employers in self-organising networks to subvert national agreements.

Thus fragmentation and interdependence in the British polity was already endemic in the early-1960s (a conclusion which confirms the findings of Bridgen 2000a; Lowe and Rollings 2000; and Ringe and Rollings 2000a). None of the actors and institutions identified by the several variants of the Westminster model as dominating policy actually did so. Parliament was virtually irrelevant; its function almost entirely restricted to the legitimation of the reforms. Both cabinet and cabinet ministers played an important part in implementing elements of the new policy package (except in tax, a field of policy in which only the PM and Treasury ministers played a significant role), but only the Prime Minister played a significant role in its initial adoption in July 1961. The prime minister was therefore a key actor, but his active involvement in economic policy was sporadic.[8] Having forced through his 'new approach' in July 1962, for example, his developing prostate problem meant that, in his own words, he began 'to get very tired ... [and] to lose [his] grip' (quoted by Horne 1989: 529), thus failing to follow his new policy through to its logical conclusion. Certainly, prime ministerial intervention, or even the threat of intervention, could 'really get things moving', as Kaufman (1997: 70-2) puts it, but the three case studies outlined here have demonstrated that, whilst the Prime Minister had power and was able to affect decisions, most decisions were made by others.[9] In a policy area of great technical complexity ministers were highly dependent on their advisers (official or political). Whilst other ministers provided an important advocacy role, they did little to make policy and this was largely a technocratic reform project. As for the Treasury, whilst it was powerful it was not all powerful. An interdependent relationship between the Treasury and other departments meant that the Treasury could not impose its solution on Whitehall any more than it could on extra-governmental actors (Heclo and Wildavsky 1981: 76-128; Chapman 1997: 103; Smith 1999a: 146-7; Theakston 1999: 25; Ringe and Rollings 2000a, 2000b). British policy making was therefore already conducted within a polity characterised by fragmentation and policy networks. This sapped the power of the centre to impose change and left it with no real option but to seek agreement to the new policies from the key actors outside the core executive (Ringe and Rollings 2000a, 2000c). Paradoxically, however, fragmentation and interdependence (coupled with a strong lingering attachment to an outdated 'Westminster model' view of British politics) was also a considerable block to reaching such agreement.

As Wilensky and Turner (1987: 49-51) pointed out, the United Kingdom was (and arguably still is) notable for the highly fragmented nature of its economic policy institutions and this was a formidable block to effective action in the linked fields of industrial, labour market, incomes and social policies. Such fragmentation meant that new taxes, incomes policy and reform of industrial training, despite their potential importance to the achievement of the new growth target, were not developed together in the new 'planning' institutions.[10] Moreover, little thought was given to how the many new agencies created after 1961 were to relate to each other (Smith 1975: 57-8). The only overlap between them was the oversight of the Treasury but this oversight was fairly haphazard since the Treasury had no system of central control.

Moreover, although Gamble and Walkland's (1984) conclusion that there was a political consensus on fundamentals at this time is fully supported by the present study, the rhetoric of adversarialism that Gamble and Walkland identified posed a significant problem for the successful implementation of the new policy framework.[11] Rhetorical adversarialism led politicians to avoid endorsing the less popular elements of the growth policy package and stifled constructive political debate about the means to faster growth, with the consequence that too little attention was paid to building a well defined and coherent policy which integrated its three main elements and provided them with a wide base of support across the full range of policy makers. Thus, instead of a coherent and widely supported policy emerging from a process of 'collective puzzlement', along the lines suggested by Heclo (1974: 304-15), policy emerged as a series of piecemeal and largely discrete measures.

The NEDC might have been expected to provide the forum in which the various policy elements could be brought together. This did not happen (Birch 1993: 203; Eichengreen 1996; Middleton 1998). In fact, this study emphasises even more than that of Stewart Wood (2000) the fragmented nature of the participants in the NEDC. Part of the reason for this was the powerful hold that the 'Westminster model' continued to exercise over economic actors. This explains the Treasury's unwillingness to share power with the institutions on which it depended for the successful implementation of the new policy framework, and it similarly explains the Ministry of Labour's reluctance actively to involve the employers and the unions in the reform of industrial training and the implementation of a voluntary incomes policy. But this worked in both directions, with important elements within the employers associations and the TUC remaining attached to the idea that fundamental change could be brought about by the government alone. This explains the unwillingness of the TUC's reluctance to become actively involved in the construction of government policy, despite Woodcock's hopes (Taylor 2000: 155); and it explains why the apparent enthusiasm of employers associations such as the FBI for new policies on growth should have produced so little in the way of really constructive engagement with their construction. Neither side of industry, therefore, was entirely committed to the new growth policy framework; nor was either side really prepared to make significant sacrifices in a higher national interest.

Moreover, the accords that were reached between the government, the TUC and employers' associations proved largely meaningless. Most importantly, important actors in the economic policy terrain, particularly the City, were absent and consequently growth policy paid too little attention to the likely reaction of overseas financial interests. Nor were the 'peak associations' of employers and trade unions able to deliver their part of any bargain on indicative targets, since they were unable to impose the required policies on their memberships. Because the planning targets were simply indicative, with no effective means of enforcement by the government (as was the case in France), they were ultimately worthless. The NEDC's lack of success was implicitly recognised by Labour in 1964, but in creating the DEA, Labour then divorced planning for growth from the balance of payments and stabilisation policy, thus further contributing to policy incoherence (Sandford 1976: 69-70; Budd 1978: 116-7).

Conclusion

Clearly, the economic policy shift that took place in the early-1960s had similarities with that which occurred in the late-1970s. Each involved a change to both the goals and instruments of economic policy. Each was a response to past policy failures. Each occurred after a process of learning that took place not just in the traditional arena of core executive economic policy making but in society as a whole. In each case we find a marked change in the policy environment arising from negative policy feedback, this in turn leading to the development of an extensive advocacy network in which new ideas about economic policy were developed, with this network actively promoting these ideas both directly to policy makers and to a wider public, thus further altering the policy environment in favour of radical change. Institutions, interests and ideas were all key elements in this dynamic. In both cases, the culmination of this process of negative policy feedback, network growth and environmental change was a revision of economic policy goals and the consequent implementation of an array of new policy instruments.

In Hall's (1993) terminology both these policy shifts amounted to 'third order change'. We need, however, to distinguish 'third order change' from 'third order learning'; for whereas the shift away from a Keynesian policy framework that occurred in the 1970s endured, the shift that took place in the early-1960s did not and what at the time seemed a revolutionary change in retrospect came to be seen merely as an incremental development of the Keynesian framework. In the 1960s, 'third order learning' did not produce 'third order change'. Learning, therefore, does not necessarily lead to change of a similar order as assumed by Hall.

That the attempt to implement a new policy framework in the 1960s should have failed whilst the implementation of a 'monetarist' (or at least 'neoliberal) framework after 1979 should have succeeded might just be due to the fact that the crisis of confidence in economic policy produced by the economic impact of the exogenous OPEC oil shocks in the 1970s was that much greater than the shock represented by emerging problems with Keynesian demand management in the 1950s and by emerging evidence of Britain's relative economic decline. Alternatively, it might be that Britain was not well suited to the construction of the 'developmental state' presupposed by the economic policy framework that Britain attempted to institutionalise in the 1960s.

One obvious difference between the policy shifts of the 1960s and the 1970s was that the Keynesian policy paradigm was fully abandoned in the 1970s only after a political battle over what should replace it. The election of the Conservatives in 1979 marked the point at which this battle was won. This is in line with Hall's (1993) model of social learning (not surprisingly, since this model was expressly designed to explain the paradigm shift in question). In Hall's view, politicians are central to third order change. A new paradigm is only installed once the political faction that supports it has triumphed over those that do not. The irony is that a political contest did not take place in the early-1960s because there was such a high degree of consensus on the need for higher growth, on the need for new policies to achieve it and (though to a lesser extent) on what those policies should consist of. This consensus transcended ideological divisions between parties and was bound up with the wider cultural changes that were at work in British society at this time.

Such a high degree of agreement over ends (if not entirely on means) should have made it *easier* to achieve an enduring policy shift in the sixties. Instead, the policy framework which was ushered in by the Conservatives' adoption of a specific objective for higher growth in 1961–62, a framework that was taken on and further developed by Labour when the party entered power in October 1964, proved to be short lived. In response to a sterling crisis in July 1966, the growth objective and indicative planning were jettisoned in favour of deflation to maintain the value of sterling, and the attempt to construct a permanent and voluntary incomes policy specifically aimed at enabling higher growth also came to an end. Subsequently, the period came to be labelled not as the beginning of a new era of economic policy but merely as the start of 'Keynesian-plus' (Gamble and Walkland 1984: 80-5). What had seemed at the time to be a major shift in the framework of economic policy had come to naught, or at least to very little.

The study conducted here provides considerable support for Lowe and Rollings' (2000: 115) assertion that, even in the 1950s and 1960s, the 'fragmentation and differentiation' of British institutions 'sapped the ability of the core executive to coordinate a strong central policy'. The case studies described here indicate that third order policy learning was not translated into enduring policy change of a similar order because the British core executive was already operating within a polity characterised by fragmentation, interdependency and self-organising policy networks. In this sense, the book provides considerable support to those who have argued that policy networks, and the concomitant need for 'joined up government' are not the novel phenomenon they are claimed to be (Peters 1998; Pollitt 2001, 2003). Rather, policy networks have simply been awaiting the development of the concepts needed to describe them.

However, although this study shows that the 'Westminster model' was already an inadequate description of public policy making in the United Kingdom by the 1960s, policy makers in the core executive, as well as many other actors such as MPs, journalists, academics, pressure groups and think tanks (and, almost certainly, most voters), continued fundamentally to operate within a mindset conditioned by that model. In some ways, this might seem a surprising assertion since core elements of the new policy framework – for example, 'indicative planning' in the new National Economic Development Council (NEDC), the attempt to bring employers and unions into a voluntary incomes policy, and the new institutions of industrial training – recognised the dependence of the core executive on others if it was to achieve its objective of raising Britain's rate of economic growth. This approach embodied a classic 'positive sum' analysis of power and the book has traced the flowering of a new preparedness in Whitehall in the early-1960s to see an active state working with extra-governmental actors to correct market failure, and a preparedness to craft innovatory answers to the question how to raise Britain's rate of growth. Yet Britain's core executive failed effectively to build the institutions presupposed by the new framework (Cawson 1978: 184).

The case studies outlined here, however, suggest that the failure to create a developmental state in Britain was not a failure of government, as has often been alleged (Hall 1986a and 1986b; Middlemas 1986; Garside 1998; Marquand 1988; Kirby 1992; Eichengreen 1996; Hutton 1996). In large part, the problem lay – as indicated above – in problems of 'governance', which were simultaneously a key factor in Britain's decision to adopt a relatively weak form of neo-corporatism and in the failure of this solution to attain its intended results.

As Bache (2000: 589) has pointed out, Rhodes' (1997: Ch. 10) characterisation of 'governance' as 'governing without government', whilst catchy, implies a separation between governance and government whereas central government is in fact a pivotal actor within the economic decision making network. The key point (as Rhodes recognises) is that governance and government are intimately connected; but governance poses considerable problems for successful government. This is highlighted by all the case studies conducted here. In each case, a modernising core executive (or at least a subset centre of this executive) encountered significant problems implementing its agenda as a result of the fragmentation and interdependence of the institutions of British economic policy – both inside and outside the core executive – and from self-organising inter-organisational networks that proved adept at resisting and channelling change to their own advantage. The fact that Britain's adversarial political culture prevented a constructive debate on the means to faster growth was also a problem, since it weakened the ability of the centre to overcome this resistance. A less adversarial polity might have been able to construct an 'active consensus' (Shonfield 1965: 199-200) capable of uniting the fragmented institutions of the economic policy terrain around a workable policy framework, or at least uniting enough of them to overcome the resistance of the remainder.

At a deeper level, however, the pervasive assumption in both Whitehall and in industry of a 'Westminster model' of central government was a significant problem. It meant that actors both inside and outside the core executive in the 1960s consistently overestimated its power to carry through a radical reform of policy goals and instruments and underestimated the scale of the shift from government to governance that the new policy framework demanded. Whilst the more thoughtful members of the core executive (and vanguard elites on both sides of industry) recognised the dependence of the core executive on other institutions to attain its revised goals, this deep-seated 'Westminster model' world view restricted the ability of the core executive to achieve its objectives as it attempted to 'steer' rather than 'row' Britain's 'differentiated polity' towards higher economic growth.

The implications of this for contemporary policy makers are not encouraging. Most importantly, it suggests that 'joined up government' on the lines proposed by the Cabinet Office (2000) requires more than just an overlay of coordinating bodies such as a beefed up Cabinet Office or a new 'Prime Minister's Department'. Rather, it demands a wide ranging overhaul of Britain's political system to promote coalition building, as well as far reaching changes to its system of policy making to allow the construction of broad based support for policy change, thus reducing the power of vested interests to impede change.

Notes

Chapter 1 – Introduction

1 There are honourable exceptions to this. One might, for example, cite Berman (1998), Hall (1986) and King (1995) as examples of political scientists using historical evidence in an exceptionally structured way to support their analysis.

2 Even those who eschew a simplistic distinction between Keynesianism and 'monetarism', not least because the era of 'pure' monetarism was so brief, have tended to see the late-1970s as a watershed in British economic policy making (for example Curwen 1992: 4-13, Booth and Glynn 1996: 304; Middleton 2000: 85-99; Oliver and Pemberton 2004).

3 *House of Commons Debates* (HoC Debs.), 25 July 1961, col. 220.

4 Though having said 'Let's be frank about it; most of our people have never had it so good', Macmillan went on to say '... what is beginning to worry some of us is "Is it too good to be true?" or perhaps I should say "Is it too good to last". For amidst all this prosperity there is one problem ... [that] of rising prices' (speech at Bedford, 20 July 1957, quoted by Horne 1989: 64-5).

5 There is, of course, a vast literature on Britain's economic 'decline', for some examples see: Aldcroft (1982); Alt (1979); Barnett (1987); Bean and Crafts (1996); Coates and Hillard (1995); Elbaum and Lazonick (1984 and 1986); English and Kenny (1999a and 1999b); Gamble (1994); Hall (1986b); Kirby (1992); Pope (1998); Supple (1994); and Weiner (1985). Useful overviews of the 'declinist' literature can be found in Middleton (1996: 28-38); Gamble (1999); Smith (1999b); and Tomlinson (2000).

6 Though, as Day (1964) pointed out, the target had little empirical justification and might perhaps be better read as a generalised desire to raise growth as much as possible. See also Middleton (2002b).

7 The significance and interdependence of these initiatives was made clear in the NEDC's (1963b) 'Orange Book'.

8 The cabinet's unanimous decision on 27 July 1961 to apply formally to join the EEC might be seen as a fourth plank in the strategy since the Treasury was convinced that it would provide both a greater stimulus to industrial and commercial efficiency and a significant new market (PRO: CAB 128/3, 27 July 1961, CC(61) 44th Cabinet Conclusions; PRO: PREM 11/3765, 3 October 1962, 'Chancellor's Mansion House speech'). The rejection of that application by De Gaulle in January 1963, however, was seen by the Cabinet's Economic Policy Committee as merely reinforcing the need for new policies on the domestic front if productivity was to be raised, resources shifted to new and developing industries, investment increased and better directed, and inno-

vation encouraged PRO: CAB 134/1698, 7 February 1963, EA(63)22, 'Economic Policy After Brussels').

9 Significantly, when Samuel Britain came to revise his book *The Treasury under the Tories* what he had termed a 'great reappraisal' in 1964 was downgraded to merely a 'reappraisal' (Brittan 1969: Ch. 6).

10 PRO: EW 28/22, 01 July 1966,

11 It might be argued that Hall's 'monetarist' policy revolution rather overstates the coherence of the framework and understates the subsequent changes made to that framework as it continued to evolve into a more general 'neo-liberal' policy consensus (Oliver and Pemberton 2004). Nonetheless, the post-1979 shift to an intermediate monetary target that was seriously intended to control nominal GDP did mark a final break with the Keynesian policy paradigm.

Chapter 2 – Governance and Policy Learning

1 Although Hall makes no reference to it, it is interesting that Kuhn (1996: 74) noted that one of the reasons that scientific paradigms change is that science is primarily about 'puzzle solving' – thus providing a link to Heclo's notion of policy making as a process of 'collective puzzlement'.

2 Hall (1993: 293, fn. 21) tentatively raised the possibility of a fourth order of change, in which policy makers 'learn how to learn' but did not explore the idea. If we assume that policy makers are constantly learning how to learn then we can relegate this to a feature of all orders of change rather than treating it discretely. In making this assumption I am dismissing Oliver's (1997: 197) contention that sometimes policy makers forget how to learn, though I concede, as does Hall (1993), that their learning may sometimes be faulty.

3 See, for example: 'Clarke surprises City with rise in bank base rate', *Financial Times,* 31 October 1996; 'Call for independent Bank', *Financial Times*, 10 June 1994.

4 Alternatively, Blyth (1997: 236) suggests a counter-factual demonstration that change would not have occurred without the idea.

5 However, whilst acknowledging that 'the hollowing-out thesis is fast becoming an academic orthodoxy in Britain', Holliday (2000: 167 and 174) has argued that the core executive has always operated within 'a complex and difficult' environment and that the idea that the centre faces problems controlling policy is merely a restatement of the 'overload' thesis of the 1970s. Hogwood (1997) suggests that the idea of 'hollowing out' confuses the loss of control and capability of the state with the loss of control and capability of officials.

6 Maurice Wright (1988) adopted a rather different terminology: a high level 'policy universe', an intermediate 'policy community' and low level 'policy networks'. But, like Rhodes, Wright viewed government as 'fragmented, differentiated and fissiparous', and he has a network structure varying in five dimensions, and network actors who operate within known 'rules of the game'.

7 It will be self-evident, however, that this author deprecates Dowding's dismissal of both policy network theory and historical institutionalism as

'pointless' and 'hopelessly vague'. See Marsh and Smith (2001) for a reply to Dowding which makes a strong case for political science models that acknowledge that social reality is often complex, involves reflexive agents, and does not necessarily provide us with data that that can be formally tested.

8 Hall and Taylor (1998: 961) emphasise that the attention paid by historical institutionalists to ideas in politics provides 'a good basis for an increasingly sophisticated understanding of the relationship between structures and agency'.

9 See Heffernan (2002) on the interrelationship between ideas, actors, institutions and environment.

10 Along the lines described by Hall (1993: 286-387) and Keegan and Pennant-Rea (1979).

Chapter 3 – The 'Great Reappraisal'

1 HoC Debs., 25 July 1961, col. 220.

2 Ibid, cols. 224-6.

3 Tomlinson (2003) identifies this 'post-Suez gloom' as a key factor in the emergence of 'declinist' fears.

4 I do not propose here to engage with the extensive debate about 'what Keynes really meant' (Blaug 1994: 1210-12) in the *General Theory* and whether post-war British economic was truly Keynesian (Tomlinson 1981, 1995; Rollings 1994) but to accept that Keynesianism, in the sense of an acceptance of the need to manage aggregate demand, entered the government's post-war economic policy and that the influence on policy during the late-1940s and 1950s of the Treasury's Economic Section played an important role in this policy shift (Feinstein 1983: 12-13; Peden 2000: 514, 2003; Booth 2000a, 2001a, 2001b, 2003).

5 One should note that Dow was not questioning the need for stabilisation but drawing attention to problems in its prosecution. Later authors reached similar conclusions regarding such shortcomings (Musgrave and Musgrave 1968; Hansen 1969; Cohen 1971; Worswick 1971; Nordhaus 1975; Budd 1978; Hopkin 1981). The thesis was attacked by Boltho (1981) on the grounds that if government investment was excluded from the equation then stabilisation policy ceased to be destabilising, although he conceded that it remained disappointing. However, the view that policy was not destabilising was not the view in the early-1960s.

6 Matthews (1968), Alford (1995) and Tomlinson (1996a) have questioned the direct causal relationship between demand management policies and low post-war unemployment – arguing that, since budgets were in surplus in the 1950s and 1960s, full employment could not be due to government contra-cyclical economic policies. This was not, however, the perception at the time and assertions that the Treasury would not have used deficits to maintain employment remain moot.

7 Although, as Dow (2000: 263) points out, it might better have been termed 'go-stop'.

8 Although one could argue that stop-go was a symptom not a cause of poor growth, the underlying cause of which was Britain's relatively poor growth of productivity and the balance of payments crises that this provoked (Feinstein 1994: 103-4). Such criticism of stop-go also assumed that the fluctuations of the 1950s and 1960s were both serious and had a permanent rather than a transitory effect on demand. With hindsight, both assumptions can be questioned (Dow 2000: 257).

9 PRO: PREM 11/2973 'Correspondence between Prime Minister and Sir Roy Harrod on economic policy and growth', 1957-1960, passim.

10 For recent discussion of this see Broadberry (1994) and Broadberry and Crafts (1996: 86). Note, however, that Tomlinson and Tiratsoo (1998) have questioned the assumption that restrictive practices in the 1950s were as widespread as anecdotal evidence suggests.

11 For later discussion of this see Aldcroft (1982); Bean and Crafts (1996: 146-7); Broadberry and Crafts (1998); Broadberry (1994: 219). Again, however, note that Tomlinson and Tiratsoo (1998) have questioned whether competition in Britain was as low as other studies have suggested.

12 CPA: CRD 2/52/11, 4 July 1960, Fraser to Butler, 'Stable economic expansion'.

13 In my discussion of the academic literature on growth I am particularly indebted to Roger Middleton's (2002b and 2004) writings and also thank him for his advice.

14 Totals derived by counting entries under the following headings in the *Index of Economic Journals*: 10.2 'Fiscal Policy for Economic Stabilisation and Growth'; 3. 'Economic Systems, Planning' including 3.0 'General' and 3.1 'Capitalist System', but not 3.2 'Socialist and Communist Systems, Soviet Economics', 3.3 'Corporative System', 3.4 'Cooperation, Cooperative Societies', or 3.5 'Solidarism'; 2.34 'Growth and development theory', but excluding 2.3405, 2.3423, 2.3441 and 2.3471 relating to 'underdeveloped areas'.

15 Hahn and Matthews' masterly survey of around 300 contributions to the literature is an excellent overview of the state of growth theory at the time.

16 Shanks (1977: 17-19) identified the 1955 'stop' as fundamental to the adoption of 'planning' in the early-1960s; the point at which 'doubts began to set in' about Britain's economic performance and the seed of the 'mood of bewilderment and apprehension' in Britain at the start of the new decade.

17 Paish (1962) outlined the approach in detail, but he had publicised his ideas some time before this. An article by him in the *Financial Times* ('Growth of the British Economy', 14 September 1960) arguing for the maintenance of a margin of unused capacity is the first item in PRO: T 230/579. Paish envisaged that unemployment would rise, but would remain below the 5 per cent which Keynes had regarded as the lowest practicable level (F. Cairncross 1981: 64) and the level of 8 per cent which Beveridge had envisaged in *Full Employment in a Free Society* (1944).

18 The view of Dow (1964).

19 See, for example articles by Harrod in the *Financial Times*: 'Still time for expansion', 24 February 1960; 'The question of imports', 20 November 1960;

'The need for a proper policy of economic growth', 2 January 1961; 'Import restrictions needed', 15 March 1961. The Harrod thesis was attacked by Colin Clarke (1961) as 'growthmanship' (a pun on the humorist Stephen Potter's satirising of 'gamesmanship'). For discussions of the thesis see Budd (1978: 84) and Dow (1964: 398).

20 Harrod's prolific correspondence with Macmillan can be found in PRO: PREM 11/2973, 3287, 3742, 4192 and 4770 passim.

21 PRO: T 230/688, 3 July 1962, 'Debate on incomes policy', notes for use by the Financial Secretary.

22 For example, in the summer of 1960 he advocated higher demand in an article in *The Director* (*The Times*, 2 June 1960) and addressed the 10th International Summer School for Savings Bankers (*The Times*, 5 July 1960).

23 'The establishment' was the subject of an excoriating attack by a number of writers in a popular paperback edited by Hugh Thomas (1962 [1959]) in which Balogh bitterly attacked the culture of amateurism and complacency of the civil service mandarinate and criticised its lack of economic experts.

24 *New Statesman*, 20 June 1961.

25 *Financial Times*, 2 November 1960; *The Times*, 5 January 1961.

26 *The Economist*, 31 December 1960 and 18 March 1961.

27 *The Economist*, 1 April 1961.

28 *The Economist*, 24 June 1961.

29 See, for example, *The Spectator*, 8 July, 29 September 1960, 8 January, and 3 February 1961.

30 *The Spectator*, 17 June and 16 December 1960, and 12 May, 21 July and 27 July 1961.

31 The subject of a leading article in *The Economist*, 29 July 1961.

32 Booker (1992 [1969]) remains the definitive guide to this cultural revolution.

33 PEPA: PEP (I) UP 10a, 27 January 1961, 'Lunch meeting, some notes by K. Lindsey'.

34 Pinder (1981); PEPA: PEP (I) UP 10/1-10, unpublished history of PEP.

35 See also PEPA: PEP (I) UP 10a 'Unpublished history of PEP, notes and correspondence, 1960–61'.

36 CPA: CRD 2/52/11, 2 December 1960, PI(60)10 'Growth', note by Brian Sewill; CPA: CRD 2/9/47, 26 October 1961.

37 A fact acknowledged later in PRO: T 171/758, 16 October 1964, GB(64)49, 'Policies for economic growth'.

38 A full list of delegates can be found at PRO: T 230/657.

39 PRO: CAB 129/105, C(61)94, July 1961, 'Economic growth and national efficiency'.

40 *NIESR 19th Annual Report*, 1961.

41 Important articles in the *National Institute Economic Review* that helped create an environment conducive to new policies on growth were 'Post-mortem on the effect of deflation' (no. 3, May 1959); 'A review of Soviet economic progress' (no. 6, Nov. 1959); Needleman (1961); and Paige, Blackaby and Freund (1961). The NIESR's influence on the Treasury can be seen in PRO: T 230/657, 5 May 1961, Lee to Hubback, 'The French system of economic planning'.

42 PRO: CAB 134/1816 and 1817, passim. The EPB had been created in 1947 as a forum in which officials could sound out industrialists and trade unionists on the government's plans. It survived the demise of physical planning and, whilst by 1960 it was largely moribund, it continued to be a useful sounding board for the Economic Section (Cairncross and Watts: 1989: 140).

43 Chaired by Beaver, with Weeks leading the discussion, the group also comprised, amongst others, Colin Clark, W. B. Reddaway, C. T. Saunders, and Robert Shone. For the full roll call see FBIA: MSS.200/F/3/S2/10/11, 24 November 1960, 'Members of group 3, Economic growth in Britain'.

44 FBIA: MSS.200/F/4/75/19, 26 November 1960, FBI Annual Conference, report of Group 3, 'Economic growth in Britain'. See also: Brittan (1964: 215-8).

45 The quotations are from BOAPAH: Interview with Lord Roberthall.

46 The emphasis on economic planning in *The Middle Way* might be said to have foreshadowed the creation of the NEDC (Horne 1989: 249), though using 'indicative' planning rather than the physical controls envisaged by Macmillan in 1938.

47 CPA: CRD 2/52/11, 4 July 1960, Fraser to Butler, 'Stable economic expansion'.

48 CPA: CRD 2/52/11, 15 May 1961, 'Labour's four year plan: further considerations', note by David Dear.

49 An article by Wilson (1955) in the *Fabian Journal* bluntly stated that: ''An increase in capital investment is the first pre-requisite of Britain's economic expansion, even of survival'.

50 The initiative for these 'Nuffield seminars' came from Crosland.

51 The enormous expansion of economic advisers that Cairncross (1999) identified as beginning in the early-1960s really began to take off after Labour's election in 1964.

52 Bogdanor (1970: 108) found Wilson's proposals to be an echo of the Fabian concept of 'national efficiency' in which economic growth could only be secured when the strategic importance of the scientific and managerial elite was recognised.

53 PRO: T 325/72, 30 May 1961, Hopkin to Clarke.

54 PRO: T 230/713.

55 PRO: CAB 129/105, C(61)94, July 1961, 'Economic growth and national efficiency' acknowledged the important role that the Brighton conference played in paving the way for its own policy reappraisal.

56 PRO: T 171/524, 28 November 1961, 'Note by the Permanent Secretary'.

57 PRO: T 171/515, 15 June 1960, 1st meeting of the Budget Committee .

58 PRO: CAB 134/1816-17, passim. The National Production Advisory Council for Industry had been set up in 1941. Like the EPB, also created during world war two, it was tripartite but by 1960 was little more than a talking shop.

59 PRO: T 230/590, 13 July 1960, 'Meeting with the TUC'.

60 PRO: T 230/590, 13 January 1961, 'Economic situation: meeting with the Economic Committee of the TUC'.

61 PRO: T 298/147, 5 May 1961, NPACI(61) 70th meeting of the National Production Advisory Council on Industry.

62 Interview with Peter Jay. The importance of the generational change at the Treasury between 1960 and 1962 (indeed more generally of the 'unprecedented number of senior civil servants [who] reached retirement age around 1961' and other changes such as the replacement of Vincent Tewson as TUC General Secretary by George Woodcock) for the adoption of new policies on growth is underlined by Middlemas (1986: 338-9).

63 PRO: T 230/579, 30 January 1961, Vinter to Hopkin; PRO: T 230/523-526 passim; PRO: T 298/334-335 passim; PRO: T 277/1073-4 passim.

64 PRO: T 230/579, 30 May 1961, Vinter to Cairncross. The opening sentence of its report on 'Economic growth and national efficiency' noted that: 'In the past year public interest in the rate of economic growth in this country has been intensified and it is necessary to consider more fully the questions to which this gives rise.' (PRO: CAB 129/105, C(61)94, July 1961).

65 PRO: CAB 134/1816, 3 January 1961, EPB(60)35, 'Economic growth: note by the Treasury'.

66 PRO: T 325/72, 14 March 1961, Hall to Lee and Padmore, 'Economic growth'; PRO: T 230/579, 27 February 1961, Vinter to Clarke, 'Elements of a policy for economic growth'.

67 PRO: T230/525, 23 March 1961, WPEG(61)1, 'Scope of the enquiry'.

68 PRO: T 325/72, 13 March 1961, Clarke to Hall, Padmore and Lee, 'Economic growth'.

69 PRO: T 325/72, 23 February 1961, Clarke to Lee; PRO: T 230/523, 7 July 1961, Vinter to Clarke.

70 PRO: CAB 129/105 C(61)94, July 1961.

71 PRO: T 325/72, 23 February 1961, Clarke to Lee.

72 PRO: PREM 11/2973, 'Correspondence between Prime Minister and Sir Roy Harrod on economic policy and growth', 1957–60, passim; and PRO: PREM 11/3287, 'Correspondence with Sir Roy Harrod on economic problems and policy', 1960–61, passim.

73 PRO: CAB 129/105, C(61)94, July 1961, 'Economic growth and national efficiency', p. 9.

74 Ibid., pp. 8-10, 40-109.

75 An approach that underpinned the Plowden Report on *Control of public expenditure* in July 1961 (Cmnd. 1432), the principal author of which was Sir Richard 'Otto' Clarke.

76 PRO: CAB 129/105, C(61)94, Op. Cit., para. 39d.

77 Ibid., para. 39e.

78 PRO: PREM 11/3841, 12 July 1961, Bishop to Macmillan (which echoed PRO: PREM 11/4209, 25 November 1960, Bishop to Macmillan); and PRO: PREM 11/3841, 15 July 1961, Macmillan to Selwyn Lloyd. The key role played by Macmillan largely undercuts Tomlinson's (1997: 12) assertion that advocates of new policies on growth 'found it hard to get a hearing'. Hennessy (2000: 262) notes the way that Macmillan converted the Cabinet Office 'into something approaching a miniature think-tank in order to help him initiate policy'.

79 Lowe and Rollings (2000: 111-2), whilst assigning immediate responsibility for Macmillan's initiative to Bishop, also emphasise the role of the Treasury in bringing about the change.

80 PRO: T 230/657, 5 May 1961 Lee to Hubback, 'The French system of economic planning'.

81 PRO: T 311/16, 17 May 1961, Boyle to Selwyn Lloyd, 'Wages policy'.

82 PRO: T 311/131, 14 June and 29 June 1961, Vinter to Clarke, 'Economic growth'; PRO: T 230/579, 3 July 1961, Hopkin to Cairncross, 'Planning for economic growth'. Middlemas (1986: 298-9), on the basis of interviews with officials, also found that the Treasury used the sterling crisis 'to put their desiderata firmly on the agenda ... the experts and officials guided Ministers to the water of necessity and this time, unlike Robot, made sure that they drank'. Note that this is at odds with Tomlinson's (1997: 33) assertion that there is 'little evidence of any ministry taking up the modernisation issue and pursuing it with wholehearted enthusiasm' and that much of the Treasury's response to the proposals of what I term the 'growth advocacy network' was sceptical if not downright cynical

83 PRO: PREM 11/3304, 12 July 1961, Bishop to Macmillan 'Economic growth and national efficiency'.

84 Budd (1978: 91) was unconvinced by the apparent suddenness of Selwyn Lloyd's conversion, commenting that 'The timing may have been tactical but the idea was not revolutionary'. However, his point could equally be used to show that Selwyn Lloyd's conversion was sudden (as suggested by T. Smith 1975: 53), but that he was drawing on a body of ideas that was by now widespread and respectable.

85 HoC Debates, 25 July 1961, col. 220 and 26 July 1961, col. 439.

86 The economic directorate of the FBI itself privately noted that 'the Chancellor's long-term proposals for economic planning were so closely in accordance with FBI thinking the Federation might not only welcome his proposals but also inform him that it would be prepared to contribute to its views' (FBIA: MSS.200/F/3/P7/3/1, 26 July 1961, 'Meeting to consider Chancellor's speech about the economic situation on 25 July').

87 Its General Secretary, George Woodcock, had recently launched an internal enquiry 'with a view to making trade unions better fitted to meet modern industrial conditions' (TUC Report, 1962: p. 244,). However, the reluctance of the TUC to be seen to endorse the policies of a Conservative government is emphasised by Ringe and Rollings (2000a).

88 It is hard to reconcile Booth's recent (2000: 847) assertion that the impact of the new growth consciousness on wider economic policy is hard to detect and Tomlinson and Tiratsoo's (1998: 28) emphasis on the rhetorical nature of growth policy with the wide array of policy changes that occurred.

89 As the FBI put it, during 1961 'a widespread opinion ha[d] crystallised that it [wa]s necessary to seek long-term solutions to the country's economic problems' (PRO: T 171/593, 14 February 1962, budget submission by the FBI).

90 PRO: PREM 11/3294, 14 August 1961, Macmillan to Selwyn Lloyd.

91 The fact that the Treasury actively promoted its ideas within government supports Supple and Furner's (1990: 20) finding that 'governments are neither purely consumers nor purely producers of economic knowledge. The relationship is essentially symbiotic' and that officials can play an active part in integrating new ideas into public policy (pp. 26-30).

Chapter 4 – Industrial Training

1 CPA: ACP 3/5, 21 January 1957, (57)52, 'Forward policy themes'; CPA: ACP 3/5, 12 February 1958, (58)61, 'Some preliminary ideas'.

2 *BACIE Journal*, vol.12, no.1, June 1958.

3 Elliott (1978) is remarkably long and detailed for an MA dissertation and includes a number of revealing interviews with actors in the training field in the lead up to the 1964 ITA.

4 CBIA: MSS.200/C/3/EDU/1/27, 16 July 1959, N.Y. Cobb (Deputy Secretary, BEC) to Lord McCorquodale.

5 FBIA: MSS.200/F/4/76/7, 26 September 1960, 'Invest in the Future', a report of a conference organised by the FBI, 26-28 September 1960'.

6 Williams and Wellens were judged by Entwistle (1965: 89-98) to have played key roles in increasing public awareness of the need for government intervention to improve training.

7 PRO: LAB 43/339, note of discussions held at Chequers on 23 and 24 January 1960.

8 PRO: LAB 19/602, 10 November 1960, 'Points to be raised by the Minister of Labour at a meeting with the Minister of Education on 10 November 1960'.

9 PRO: LAB 18/744, 'First year apprenticeship training scheme: policy and early history 1958-1962', passim.

10 PRO: LAB 19/602, 10 November 1960, note of an informal meeting between the Ministers of Education and Labour.

11 HoC Debs., 30 November 1960, cols. 1143-50.

12 The key point here is that Hare was following the change of opinion, not creating it as argued by Price (2000: 124-6).

13 FBIA: MSS.200/F/4/75/19, 26 November 1960, conference on 'The next five years. Report of group 3: Economic growth in Britain'; CBIA: MSS.200/C/3/EDU/1/35, correspondence between Sir Norman Kipping (Director General of the FBI) and Sir George Pollock (Director of the BEC).

14 PRO: CAB 134/1816, 3 January 1961, EPB(60)35, 'Economic growth: note by the Treasury'.

15 PRO: CAB 129/105, July 1961, C(61)94, 'Economic growth and national efficiency', paras. 61-70. The importance of improving training if growth was to be raised, emphasised by this report, found its way into the NEDC's *Conditions favourable to faster growth* almost unchanged; indeed the emphasis on improved training was perhaps greater in the latter (NEDC 1963a: paras. 31-8).

16 See, for example: *The Times*, 'Challenge of the bulge to industry', 21 November 1960; and the *Daily Telegraph* editorial, 'Shortage of skill', 13 February 1961.

17 A later briefing note for Macmillan emphasised the relationship between training and growth and the 'humiliating and dangerous' contrast with America and Western Europe in terms of both the quantity and quality of training (PRO: PREM 11/3873, 26 November 1962, briefing note for the Prime Minister by Michael Cary).

18 PRO: CAB 134/1689, 15 February 1961, EA(61) 2nd meeting of the Cabinet Committee on Economic Policy.

19 The BACIE West Midlands Group had visited France in May 1960 (BACIE 1960d) and published a study of the French model (BACIE 1960c).

20 PRO: LAB 18/729, 6 February 1961, Stewart to Rossetti and 5 February 1961, 'Summary of the visit to France to study their apprentice tax and training methods'.

21 PRO: LAB 18/729, 6 February 1961, Stewart to Rossetti.

22 PRO: LAB 18/729, 17 February 1961, Helsby to Hare.

23 HoC Debs., 27 March 1961, cols. 945-6.

24 PRO: CAB 134/1690, 28 April 1961, EA(61)31, 'Shortages of trained manpower, memorandum by the Minister of Labour'.

25 PRO: T 230/523, 23 March 1961, Vinter to Atkinson; PRO: CAB 129/105, July 1961, C(61)94, 'Economic growth and national efficiency'.

26 PRO: CAB 134/1689, 3 May 1961, EA(61) 10th meeting of the Cabinet Committee on Economic Policy.

27 PRO: LAB 18/729, 4 May 1961, Morgan to Stewart and 5 May 1961, Sir Alec Johnston (Inland Revenue) to Helsby; PRO: LAB 18/784, 8 September 1961, 'Joint note by the Treasury and Inland Revenue on the suggested Apprentice Training Levy' and 19 September 1961, Rossetti to Robertson (Treasury).

28 PRO: LAB 19/602, 17 November 1960, 1st meeting of the Interdepartmental Working Party on the Bulge.

29 HoC Debs., 31 May 1961, col. 287.

30 PRO: LAB 18/729, 12 December 1961, 'Interim report of the Working Party on Training Levy / Rebate Schemes'.

31 The working party assumed a national rather than industry based scheme since an improvement in the supply of skilled labour would benefit the nation as a whole.

32 PRO: LAB 18/729, 18 December 1961, Rossetti to Helsby.

33 PRO: LAB 18/729, 14 December 1961, Stewart to Rossetti.

34 CPA: ACP 3/9, 1 March 1962, ACP 3/9(62)96, 'Report of the Policy Committee on Economic Growth'.

35 PRO: LAB 10/1488, 26 July 1961, minutes of the National Joint Advisory Council.

36 As noted by Tomlinson (1997: 34) the BEC was more important in many of the key areas of change demanded by the new growth policy framework but was much less committed to economic modernisation than was the FBI.

37 PRO: LAB 10/1604, 21 September 1961, minutes of the 3rd meeting of the NJAC Working Party on the Manpower Situation.

38 A shift to be seen in PRO: T 230/586, 17 April 1962, WPEG(62)10, 'Paper for NEDC on national efficiency and obstacles to economic growth'.

[39] PRO: CAB 134/1695, 26 March 1962, EA(62)47, 'Industrial training arrangements: memorandum by the Minister of Labour'; PRO: CAB 134/1693, 28 March 1962, EA(62) 11th meeting of the Cabinet Committee on Economic Policy.

[40] An expansion in the training role of the Ministry of Education was part of the one of a long list of suggestions made by in a minute by David Eccles to Macmillan on 30 April 1962 (PRO: PREM 11/3765) and in further submissions on 3 May (PREM 11/4169, 'Education – a programme to regain the initiative') and on 5 June (PREM 11/4169, 'Programme for education').

[41] PRO: LAB 18/759, April 1962, 'Interdepartmental Working Party on Industrial Training: report to ministers on further government action on industrial training'; PRO: CAB 134/1695, 4 May 1962, EA(62)63, 'Industrial training: memorandum by the Minister of Labour' and 7 May 1962, EA(62)64, 'Industrial training: memorandum by the Minister of Education'; PRO: CAB 134/1693, 9 May 1962, EA(62) 17th meeting of the Cabinet Committee on Economic Policy.

[42] For details of the construction of the 'new approach' see PRO: CAB 130/186, GEN 766, 'Cabinet committee: incomes policy: the new approach', passim; PRO: CAB 130/187 GEN 771 'Cabinet committee: incomes policy', passim; and Macmillan (1973: Ch. 5).

[43] HoC Debs., 26 July 1962, cols. 1766-77.

[44] PRO: PREM 11/4071, 8 June 1962, Hailsham to Macmillan; PRO: CAB 130/186, 7 June 1962, 2nd (and final) meeting of GEN 766.

[45] PRO: LAB 10/1788, 10 August 1962, 'Notes on a meeting held to discuss action to be taken by IR4 concerning measures outlined in the Prime Minister's speech' [the emphasis is original].

[46] CPA: CRD 2/09/47, 20 May 1962, 'Report of the Policy Committee on Economic Growth'; PRO T 311/3, 23 July 1962, Butler to Maudling.

[47] PRO: PREM 11/4169, 9 May 1962, Bligh to Macmillan.

[48] PRO: T 311/13, 8 May 1962, Cairncross to Helsby.

[49] Clarke's attitude can be seen in a memorandum to Cairncross, written later in the year, in which he advocated government intervention to solve the problem of market failure and improve labour mobility and, by extension, raise economic growth (PRO: T 230/580, 22 October 1962, 'The means to faster growth').

[50] PRO: CAB 129/105, July 1961, C(61)94, 'Economic growth and national efficiency'.

[51] PRO: LAB 18/761, 15 May 1962, Vinter to Clarke.

[52] PRO: CAB 134/1696, 28 June 1962, EA(62)85, 'Economic growth'.

[53] PRO: LAB 18/761, 1 May 1962, Stewart to A.M. Morgan.

[54] The proposals on training were highlighted by Butler when the report was sent to Maudling on 23 July (PRO: T 311/3). The shift was reflected in the finding of the party's Policy Committee on Economic Growth that every effort must be made to improve training (CPA: CRD 2/09/47, May 1962).

[55] Entwistle (1965: 182) cited an interview with Hare's former Assistant Private Secretary who dated the change to a meeting that that Hare attended at Chequers in July 62 on the 'new approach'.

56 PRO: LAB 19/714, 18 June 1962, H.W. Evans to Stewart.

57 PRO: LAB 19/714, 'Industrial training levy, 1961–62', passim; and LAB 18/761, 'Third interdepartmental working party on training levy schemes, passim. The report provided by the Ministry of Labour to the EPC for its 7 March 1962 meeting had rejected the idea of a subsidy without examining it in any detail (PRO: CAB 134/1694, 22 February 1962, EA(62)23, 'Shortages of trained manpower: question of a levy rebate system. Memorandum by the Minister of Labour').

58 PRO: LAB 9/377, 30 July 1962, TLS(20) 'Interdepartmental Working Party on Industrial Training: Plans for training schemes'.

59 PRO: LAB 18/761, 26 September 1962, 'Interdepartmental Working Party on Industrial Training: Report on industry-by-industry levy / rebate schemes'.

60 PRO: LAB 18/761, 26 September 1962, note by Rossetti to the secretary of the Interdepartmental Working Party on Industrial Training.

61 PRO: T 224/1003, 19 October 1962, Clarke to Maude.

62 *The Times* (14 January 1963) commented that 'The technical details, the exact functions that the boards must perform, and the functions that they may at their discretion perform are likely to follow the consensus of informed opinion'.

63 PRO: LAB 10/1604, 21 September 1961, minutes of the 3rd meeting of the NJAC Working Party on the Manpower Situation.

64 *Ministry of Labour Gazette*, February 1962, 'Report of the NJAC working party on the manpower situation'.

65 As Hare acknowledged in a speech to the BACIE on 15 January 1963 (BACIE 1963a: 5-10).

66 PRO: T 311/3, 10 December 1962, Butler to Macmillan; PRO: PREM 11/4412, 26 December 1962, Macmillan to officials; PRO: PREM 11/4202, 21 February 1963, 'Meeting at Chequers between the Prime Minister and the Chancellor'.

67 PRO: T 230/582, 7 February 1963, 'Economic policy after Brussels'.

68 PRO: CAB 134/1994, 26 February 1963, HA(63)21, 'Industrial training: government proposals', memorandum by the Minister of Labour for the Cabinet's Home Affairs Committee.

69 PRO: LAB 9/377, 7 January 1963, Stewart to Clucas.

70 PRO: LAB 43/396, 21 November 1962, notes of separate meetings between Hare and representatives of the BEC and TUC.

71 See *Technical Education and Industrial Training*, vol. 6, January 1964 for a survey of the reactions to the ITA; and LPA: RD 772, May 1964, 'Home Policy Committee: Manpower policies in a changing society' for Labour's decision to endorse the Conservatives' approach.

72 TUCA: MSS.292B/132.14/1, 22 January 1963, NJAC(GC) 3/3, 'Trades Union Congress: White paper on industrial training'.

73 TUCA: MSS.292B/132.14/1, 4 February 1963, R. Boyfield (secretary of the TUC Organisation department) to Woodcock; TUCA: MSS.292B/132.14/1, 28 February 1963, Woodcock to the Minister of Education.

74 TUCA: MSS.292B/132.14/1, 4 February 1963, Boyfield to Woodcock.

75 The Education Committee, responding to criticism of craft unions in the NEDC, noted that 'some craft unions (e.g. the AUBTW) are opposed to adult training but not all craft unions are opposed' but this was hardly a repudiation of the criticisms, and the fact that the Committee went on to note that 'no union objects to the provision of training courses in other than craft skills' tended to suggest that, when it came to craft skills, a lot of craft unions *did* object (TUCA: MSS.292B/811/3, 12 February 1963, Education Committee 5/2, 'Comments on growth of the UK economy: NEDC (63)2'). D. McGarvey of the United Society of Boilermakers (which restricted the ratio of apprentices to journeymen to 1:5) told the 1963 TUC conference that it was 'very difficult to ask craft unions to take more apprentices when some of the craftsmen who have served their apprenticeship are walking the streets ... We have bitter memories of what happened when we inundated the craft with apprentices during the "hungry thirties"' (TUC Report, 1963: 438-41). Shortly afterwards, a TUC briefing note for Ray Gunter on the Industrial Training Bill conceded that craft unions did restrict the number of apprenticeships (TUCA: MSS.292B/132.14/1, 15 November 1963).

76 TUCA: MSS.292B/811/3, 12 February 1963, Education Committee 5/2, 'Comments on Growth of the UK Economy (NEDC (63)2)'.

77 TUCA: MSS.292B/132.14/1: 27 November 1962, Winnard to Woodcock, 'Industrial training: proposal for statutory boards', 7 March 1963, Winnard to Woodcock, and 23 July 1963, Winnard to Boyfield.

78 TUCA: MSS.292B/132.14/1, 15 November 1963, TUC briefing note for Ray Gunter on the industrial training bill.

79 TUCA: MSS.292B/560.1/5, 9 January 1963, minutes of the 4th meeting of the TUC Economic Committee.

80 It also indicates that whilst 'blaming the workers' for retrograde attitudes might be unfair (Tomlinson 2002: 175) one might reasonably blame some of the workers.

81 At the first meeting of the joint FBI/BEC education and training committee, for example, its members found themselves at a loss as to what the purpose of the committee really was (CBIA: MSS.200/C/3/EDU/1/35, 22 June 1961). The parallel responsibilities of the FBI and BEC was eventually addressed by their merger into the CBI in 1965 but the lack of power over member firms continued (Blank 1973: 227-36).

82 CBIA: MSS.200/C/3/EDU/1/38, 13 February 1963, FBI Grand Council minutes; CBIA: MSS.200/C/3/EDU/24/5, 'Preliminary work on the 1964 industrial training act, correspondence and related papers', passim; CBIA: MSS.200/C/3/EDU/1/35, 1 April 1963, JC 22, 'Joint BEC/FBI Education and Training Committee: white paper on industrial training – note by BEC'.

83 CBIA: MSS.200/C/3/EDU/1/38, 13 February 1963, FBI Grand Council minutes; CBIA: MSS.200/C/3/EDU/1/35, 1 April 1963, JC 22, 'White paper on industrial training – note by the BEC'.

84 CBIA: MSS.200/C/3/EDU/24/5 'Preliminary work on the 1964 industrial training act, correspondence and related papers', passim – but see particularly 14 February 1963, 'BEC note on central body under the training act' and 21 February 1963, C. Henniker-Heaton to P. J. Casey.

85 CBIA: MSS.200/C/3/EDU/24/5, 12 March 1963, China Clay Association to BEC and other correspondence passim.

86 BECA: MSS.200/B/3/3/201.5, 1 July 1964, summarised verbatim minutes of NEDC meeting.

87 CBIA: MSS.200/C/3/EDU/1/38 'Joint BEC/FBI Education and Training Committee: papers, Oct 1961 to Dec 1965', passim;

88 This pattern mirrors that which occurred in the NEDC (see Wood 2000).

89 See also BACIE: MSS.97/BACIE/1/1/4, 6 March 1963, 'Industrial training: government proposals'.

90 *BACIE Memoranda*, April 1963, reprinted BACIE memorandum to the Minister of Labour regarding Cmnd. 1892.

91 PRO: LAB 43/396, 21 November 1962, 'Note of a meeting with representatives of the BEC to discuss future industrial training arrangements'.

92 The resistance to change of many employers was also acknowledged by their representatives on the NEDC (BECA: MSS.200/B/3/3/201.5, 1 July 1964, verbatim NEDC minutes). The failure of many company managements to innovate and embrace change at this time has recently been highlighted by Bowden et al (2001), though Tomlinson (2002: 198) rightly notes that management failings never acquired the political salience of equivalent trade union failings.

93 PRO: LAB 18/835, 2 January 1963, Helsby to Hare.

94 PRO: LAB 18/835, 27 December 1962, Rossetti to Helsby; PRO: LAB 18/835, 24 January 1963, Rossetti to Maude (Treasury).

95 Wickham-Jones (2000) has argued that the lack of attention given to training in the 1950s was a function of the influence of the unions in the making of party policy, though this chapter suggests that it may have been the influence of craft unions that was most important.

96 LPA: RD 349, November 1962, 'Programme of work', p. 1.

97 LPA: RD 276, December 1962, Sub-committee on Science and Industry, 'Training skilled workers for industry'.

98 LPA: RD 432, March 1963, Finance and Economic Policy Sub-committee, 'Industrial training'.

99 LPA: RD 376, December 1962, Sub-committee on Science and Industry, 'Training skilled workers for industry'.

100 LPA: RD 432, March 1963, Finance and Economic Policy Sub-committee, 'Industrial training' (2nd revision).

101 LPA: RD 772, May 1964, Home Policy Committee, 'Manpower policies in a changing society'. Draft policy report (revised July 1964).

102 *BACIE Memoranda*, January 1965, address by Ray Gunter to the British Employers' Confederation; PRO: LAB 18/941, 13 November 1964, Gunter to Wilson, 'Interdepartmental committee on training for skill'.

103 PRO: LAB 43/424, 17 November 1964, Brown to Gunter; *BACIE Journal*, vol. 19, no. 2; TUC Report, 1964: 385.

104 *BACIE Journal*, vol. 20, no. 3, 'The rise of the technocrats' (an address by Prof. W.H.G. Armitage – Department of Education, Sheffield University – to the BACIE East Midlands group, 1965).

[105] The centrality of training to the National Plan is emphasised by Sheldrake and Vickerstaff (1987: 36).

[106] CBIA: MSS.200/C/3/EDU/1/1, 1 April 1965, Industrial Education and Training Committee, 'Central Training Council – Industrial training and further education, memorandum no. 1'.

[107] The Centre for Policy Studies called for their abolition in the early-1980s (Elliott and Mendham 1981). The Conservative government duly delivered and the levy / rebate system withered as part of the shift during the 1980s from a tripartite to a neo-liberal regime in training policy (King 1993). It has, however, survived in the construction and engineering construction industries.

[108] King (1995: 130), for example, concluded that the autonomy of the ITBs was a significant factor in the overall failure of the 1964 Act to solve the training problem.

[109] Morgan (1994: 86) noted the top-down nature of policy making in the respective peak organisations and the split between union and employer leaderships, who 'were clearly committed to the revision of industrial training arrangements' and the dogged pursuit by individual firms and unions of their own interests.

[110] BECA: MSS.200/B/3/3/201, 6 January 1965, BEC 65/27, 'Obstacles to efficiency: the joint statement of intent on productivity, prices and incomes'; FBIA: MSS.200/F/3/S2/10/12, 22 January 1965, 'Conclusions of Group 4: problems of labour'.

[111] Wilensky and Turner (1987: 49-51) noted that Britain had one of the most fragmented labour markets of all advanced economies. Finegold and Soskice (1988: 29-30), and Bean and Crafts (1996) also note the problems played by such fragmentation in Britain's poor record on training.

[112] PRO: LAB 18/729, 17 February 1961, note by Rossetti.

[113] PRO: LAB 9/378, 2 January 1963, 'Government proposals for industrial training', note of a meeting in the office of the secretary to the official committee on pay .

[114] The weakness of government in relation to vested interests on both sides of industry is also highlighted by Crafts (1991: 283). The key point here is that (contrary to the assertion of Richardson 1991: 128) the ITB structure did nothing to break up the existing cosy structure of training.

Chapter 5 – Incomes Policy

[1] Note the equality of emphasis given to wages and prices.

[2] BOAPH: Roberthall, p. 26.

[3] For a detailed discussion of the 'plateau' see PRO: T 267/24, 'Incomes policy: 1961-1964', pp. 11-12.

[4] PRO: CAB 129 C(57)103, April 1957, 'Wages, prices and the pound sterling: memorandum by the Chancellor of the Exchequer'.

[5] BOAPAH: Roberthall, p. 43.

[6] Such was the change in policies that Brittan (1964: 186-187) remarked 'it is difficult to believe they were [uttered] by the same man'.

7 PRO: PREM 11/1824, 1 September 1957, C(57)194, 'The economic situation: memorandum by the Prime Minister'; PRO: CAB 128/32, 5 and 6 January 1958 CC(58)3-4, Cabinet conclusions.

8 PRO: T 267/24, 'Incomes policy: 1961-1964', pp. 16-18. PRO: CAB 129/100, 4 February 1960, C(60)40, 'Council on Productivity, Prices and Incomes: memorandum by the Chancellor of the Exchequer'; PRO: T 311/16, 28 April 1960, Stevenson to Lee, 'Wages and prices group'.

9 PRO: T 267/10, 'The government and wages, 1945-1960', pp. 150-2; PRO: T 230/497, 4 May 1960, 'Wages and prices: meeting of permanent secretaries'; PRO: T 311/16, 12 May 1960, Hall to Lee, 'Guiding light: a draft statement' and 14 June 1960, 'Possible government statement on wages', meeting of Treasury officials.

10 A useful summary of the debate is provided by Dow (1964: 350-63).

11 CPA: CRD 2/52/11, 4 July 1960, Fraser to Butler, 'Stable economic expansion' (draft memorandum written by James Douglas).

12 PRO: T 311/21, Lee to Clarke, 16 April 1962; BOAPH: Boyle, p. 42; PRO: T 267/24, 'Incomes policy: 1961-1964', p. 19.

13 PRO: T 267/7, 'The government and wages, 1945-1960', introduction by Sir Richard Clarke.

14 BOAPAH: Roberthall, pp. 36-7; PRO: T 230/579, 26 November 1961, 'Treasury doctrine', memorandum by Cairncross.

15 See, for example: PRO: T 311/16, 12 May 1960, Hall to Lee, 'Guiding light'; PRO: T 311/16, 29 July 1960, Hall to Bell, 'Wages and policy'; PRO: T 230/579, 9 March 1961, Atkinson to Vinter; PRO: PREM 11/3287, 3 November 1961, Cairncross to the Prime Minister commenting on Sir Roy Harrod's advocacy of a wages policy.

16 FBIA: MSS.200/F/4/75/19, 26 November 1960, 'Report of Group 3. Economic growth in Britain'.

17 PRO: T 230/579, 27 February 1961, Vinter to Clarke, 'Elements of a policy for economic growth'.

18 PRO: T 311/16, 2 May 1961, Clarke to Padmore, 'Wages policy'; PRO: T 311/16, 9 May 1961, Clarke to Lee, 'EA(61)30'; PRO: T 311/16, 17 May 1961, Boyle to Selwyn Lloyd, 'Wages policy'.

19 PRO: T 267/24, 'Incomes policy: 1961-1964', pp. 19-20; PRO: T 311/16, 21 April 1961, 'Wages policy'; PRO: T 311/17, 16 June 1961, Cairncross to Hancock, 'Wages'.

20 PRO: CAB 134/1690, 28 April 1961, EA(61)30, 'Wages policy: memorandum by the Minister of Labour'.

21 PRO: CAB 129/105, C(61)94, July 1961, 'Economic growth and national efficiency', paras. 18-20, 71-4.

22 PRO: T 230/523, 7 July 1961, Vinter to Clarke.

23 HoC Debs., 25 July 1961, vol. 645, cols. 222-3.

24 PRO: T 267/24, 'Incomes policy: 1961-1964', pp. 23-4; PRO: PREM 11/3620, 4 July 1961, Macmillan to Selwyn Lloyd. Harrod's advice is at PRO: PREM 11/3287.

25 PRO: PREM 11/3841, 15 July 1961, Macmillan to Selwyn Lloyd.

26 PRO: T 311/17, 30 June 1961, Minister of Labour to Chancellor of the Exchequer.
27 See also PRO: T 267/24, 'Incomes policy: 1961-1964', p. 26.
28 BECA: MSS.200/B/3/3/201, 4 August 1961, President of the BEC to the Chancellor and 23 August 1961, 'Meeting between Economic Committee and the Chancellor'.
29 PRO: T 311/19, 7 December 1961, 'Wage policy', paper by Cairncross.
30 PRO: T 311/17, 12 August 1961, Lee to Clarke, 'Wages and prices'.
31 PRO: T 311/18, 11 October 1961, Cairncross to Stevenson, 'Wage policy and distribution of income'.
32 PRO: T 311/18, 19 October 1961, Cairncross to Hancock, 'Wages data' and 22 November 1961, Cairncross to Stevenson, 'Wage drift'.
33 PRO: T 311/18, 30 October 1961, Clarke to Padmore, 'Wage policy'.
34 PRO: PREM 11/3287, 3 November 1961, Cairncross to Macmillan regarding letters from Sir Roy Harrod.
35 PRO: PREM 11/4207, 28 November 1961, 'Planning – minutes of a meeting between the Chancellor and TUC representatives'.
36 PRO: CAB 129/107, 5 December 1961, C(61)202, 'Incomes policy: memorandum by the Chancellor of the Exchequer'.
37 PRO: CAB 134/1692, 28 December 1961, EA(61)124, 'Arbitration'.
38 PRO: T 311/19, 15 December 1961, Thorneycroft to Selwyn Lloyd.
39 It is this continuing resistance of some key ministers to the very concept of a robust incomes policy that explains the Conservatives' apparent reluctance to strike a deal with the unions on wages that is remarked on by Tomlinson (1997: 20).
40 PRO: T 267/24, 'Incomes policy: 1961-1964', p. 37.
41 PRO: CAB 129/107, 4 December 1961, C(61)205, 'Incomes policy'; PRO: CAB 128/35, 7 December 1961, CC(61)68, Cabinet conclusions. See also Macmillan (1973: 48-50).
42 PRO: CAB 128/36, 8 January 1962, CC(62)3; PRO: CAB 21/4946, 10 January 1962, Chancellor of the Exchequer to the chairman of the Economic Committee of the TUC, 'Incomes policy'.
43 TUCA: MSS.292B/560.1/3, minutes of TUC Economic Committee meetings on 10 and 17 January 1962; PRO: PREM 11/4207, 24 January 1962, TUC reply to the Chancellor's invitation to join the NEDC.
44 PRO: T 230/684, 9 January 1962, 'Note for the record'.
45 PRO: T 230/685, 25 January 1962, meeting of officials from the Treasury and Ministry of Labour.
46 PRO: CAB 134/1693, 2 May 1962, EA(62) 16th meeting of the Cabinet Committee on Economic Policy. Incomes policy was notably absent from the 'matters for further examination' in the Treasury's initial paper for NEDC (PRO: T 230/586, 17 April 1962, WPEG(62)10) – despite the fact that the paper was closely based on its July paper 'Economic growth and national efficiency'.
47 PRO: PREM 11/4066, 9 March 1962, Minister of Labour to the Prime Minister, 'Arbitration'; PRO: CAB 134/1695, 23 March 1962, EA(62)46, 'Wages councils: memorandum by the Minister of Labour'; PRO: T 230/686,

17 April 1962, 'Future incomes policy: note of a meeting in Sir Frank Lee's room'; PRO: T 230/687, 24 April 1962, Atkinson to Stewart, 'Incomes policy and the treatment of profits and prices'; PRO: CAB 21/4946, 27 April 1962, 'Incomes policy: briefing note for the Chancellor'; PRO: EW 8/192, 1 May 1962, PS(IP)(62)31 Permanent Secretaries' Group on Incomes and Prices, 'A national minimum wage: paper by the Ministry of Labour'; PRO: T 230/687, 10 May 1962, 'Incomes policy and the treatment of profits and prices: memorandum by the Economic Section, Treasury'; PRO: CAB 134/1695, 11 May 1962, EA(62)67 'Incomes policy: revaluation; note by Sir Frank Lee'; PRO: T 311/19, 17 May 1962, Boyle to Selwyn Lloyd, 'Incomes policy'.

48 PRO: T 230/687, 11 May 1962, Helsby to Cairncross.

49 PRO: CAB 128/36, CC(62)33 and CC(62)35-7, Cabinet conclusions for 15 May, 24 May and 28 May 1962.

50 PRO: PREM 11/4071, 20 May 1962, 'Note for the record – incomes policy and economic policy: meeting at Chequers'.

51 PRO: CAB 128/36, CC(62)35-37, Cabinet conclusions for 24 and 28 May 1962; PRO: PREM 11/4071, 28 May 1962, transcript of Macmillan's remarks to Cabinet.

52 Though the absence of any specific action on prices other than the abolition of resale price maintenance and greater competition is noteworthy.

53 On the lines advocated by PRO: PREM 11/3477, 29 November 1961, 'Last will and testament of Mr. Bishop'.

54 PRO: PREM 11/3930, 28 May 1962, 'Remarks made by Prime Minister at Cabinet'.

55 PRO: CAB 21/4713, 15 June 1962, Hopkin to Padmore, 'Standing commission on pay'; PRO: CAB 129/109, 19 June 1962, C(62)99, 'Incomes policy: memorandum by the Prime Minister'; PRO: CAB 128/36, CC(62)41 Cabinet conclusions, 22 June 1962.

56 PRO: CAB 21/4713, 25 June 1962, note of a meeting between the Prime Minister and senior officials; PRO: CAB 21/4714, 2 July 1962, Macmillan to Lee, 'Incomes policy'.

57 Typescript personal memoir of the Ministry of Labour by P.H. St John-Wilson.

58 Cmnd. 1844; HoC Debs., 26 July 1962, cols. 1735-1868; PRO: PREM 11/4073, 26 July 1962, 'Note for the record – meeting with the TUC'.

59 PRO: PREM 11/4073, 19 July 1962, summary record of a meeting between ministers and representatives of the BEC. The powerlessness of the government had already been emphasised by PRO: PREM 11/4073, 18 July 1962, Chancellor of the Exchequer to the Prime Minister.

60 PRO: CAB 130/187, 30 July 1962, 2nd meeting of GEN 771, 'Incomes policy: meeting of ministers and senior officials'; PRO: PREM 11/4073, 7 August 1962, 'National Incomes Commission – record of a meeting with the TUC'; TUCA: MSS.292B/560.1/4, 8 August 1962, minutes of the 12th meeting of the TUC Economic Committee.

61 Middlemas (1986: 316-7) noted the deterioration in the TUC's trust in both ministers and Treasury officials that had occurred since the 1955 stop.

62 PRO: CAB 134/1902, 3 December 1962, ES(I)(62)4, 'TUC visit to Sweden: report from the ambassador to Sweden'.

63 TUCA: MSS.292B/560.1/5, 9 January 1963, minutes of the 4th meeting of the TUC Economic Committee.

64 PRO: PREM 11/4073, 5 October 1962, Maudling to the Prime Minister.

65 PRO: T 230/687, 10 May 1962, 'Incomes policy and the treatment of profits and prices: memorandum by the Economic Section, Treasury'; PRO: T 230/692, 11 September 1962, Lee to Hubback, 'National Incomes Commission'; PRO: CAB 129/110, 12 September 1962, C(62)140, 'National Incomes Commission: memorandum by the President of the Board of Trade'; PRO: PREM 11/4073, 5 October 1962, Maudling to the Prime Minister; PRO: CAB 128/36, CC(62)59, Cabinet conclusions, 9 October 1962.

66 PRO: CAB 134/1902, 31 January 1963, ES(I)(63) 1st meeting of the Economic Steering (Incomes) Committee.

67 PRO: CAB 134/1891, 27 June 1963, ES(G)(63)56, 'Methods of achieving the price/income objective', note by the secretaries to the Economic Steering (General) Committee; BECA: MSS.200/B/3/3/201.5, 3 July 1963, E.171.63, verbatim minute of NEDC meeting; FBIA: MSS.200/F/3/E3/2/14, 29 August 1963, E.214.D.63, memorandum from the secretary of the FBI Economic Study Committee; FBIA: MSS.200/F/3/E3/2/14, 4 September 1963, 'Incomes policy', memorandum by Hugh Weeks.

68 PRO: T 311/71, 26 February 1963, ES(I)(63)3, note by Maude, 'Incomes policy: the elements of a "deal"'.

69 HoC Debs., 3 April 1963, col. 475.

70 TUCA: MSS.292B/110.44/1, 11 December 1963, minutes of the TUC Economic Committee; BECA: MSS.200/B/3/3/201.1, 11 December 1963, BEC internal note on 'Incomes policy'.

71 FBIA: MSS.200/F/3/E3/2/14, 30 October 1963, minutes of the FBI Economic Study Committee; BECA: MSS.200/B/3/3/201.5, 4 December 1963, verbatim minute of NEDC meeting; BECA: MSS.200/B/3/3/201.4, 11 December 1963, 'Minutes of a meeting between management members of the NEDC and representatives of the 4 employers' organisations to discuss incomes policy'.

72 BECA: MSS.200/B/3/3/201.5, 8 January 1964, verbatim minute of NEDC meeting.

73 FBIA: MSS.200/F/3/D3/5/20, 8 January 1964, 'Joint meeting of the FBI, BEC, NABM and ABCC with management members of the NEDC to discuss the profits / 3 year wage agreement proposal'; BECA: MSS.200/B/3/3/201.5, 5 February 1964, verbatim minutes of NEDC meeting.

74 BECA: MSS.200/B/3/3/201.5, 15 February 1964, W. Keeler to the President of the BEC.

75 LPA: RD 370, December 1962, Finance and Economic Policy Sub-committee, 'Incomes policy: an appraisal'; LPA: RD 389, January 1963, Finance and Economic Policy Sub-committee. 'Comments on sub-committee's discussion on incomes policy, by Michael Stewart'.

76 LPA: RD 333, October 1962, 'An incomes policy for the Labour Party'.

77 LPA: RD 389, January 1963, Finance and Economic Policy Sub-committee. 'Comments on sub-committee's discussion on incomes policy, by Michael Stewart'.

78 LPA: RD 433, March 1963, Finance and Economic Policy Sub-committee, 'An incomes policy, note by W. Simpson'; LPA: RD 742, April 1964, Working Party on Taxation, 'Report on taxation and incomes policy'.

79 TUCA: MSS.292B/110.44/1, 10 January 1962, Econ. Ctee 5/2, 'TUC: Wage restraint and a national incomes policy'. LPA: RD 333, 1 October 1962, 'Finance and Economic Policy Sub-committee: An incomes policy for the Labour party' by Michael Stewart.

80 TUCA: MSS.292B/110.44/2, 17 March 1965, Econ. Ctee 10/1, 'TUC: Prices and incomes policy', report of a meeting between the TUC Economic Committee and the Minister for Economic Affairs.

81 The central importance to Labour's policy of the Conservatives' initiatives in economic policy was emphasised by Howell (1976: 253-354).

82 See PRO: FG 2/41, 'Incomes policy, 1962-1967', passim and TUCA: MSS.292B/110.44/1, 'Wages and incomes policy: correspondence, 1960-1964', passim.

83 The awareness on both sides of industry of the need to secure a favourable impact abroad is palpable in the files. See, for example: FBIA: MSS.200/F/3/P8/12/1, 9 December 1964, 'President's report to FBI Grand Council'; TUCA: MSS.292B/110.44/2, 9 December 1964, 'Minutes of the TUC Economic Committee'; and FBIA: MSS.200/F/3/P8/12/3, 16 December 1964, circular to members of the ABCC, BEC, FBI and NABM by the presidents and senior officials of the organisations.

84 The separation of responsibilities was to pose significant problems of co-ordination by making explicit the tension between external balance of payments objectives and internal industrial and fiscal policy that had hitherto been contained within the Treasury.

85 TUCA: MSS.292B/110.44/2, 9 November 1964, Econ. Ctee 2/8, 'TUC: NEDC and incomes policy: report of a meeting between the Chancellor of the Exchequer and other ministers and the General Council'.

86 TUCA: MSS.292B/110.44/2, 11 November 1964, Econ. Ctee 2/5, 'TUC: The government's statement on the economic situation'.

87 PRO: LAB 43/424, 17 November 1964, Brown to Gunter. Despite some reservations in the FBI, the employers generally welcomed these proposals for an active labour market policy (FBIA: MSS.200/F/3/P8/12/1, 19 November 1964, 'Joint statement of intent on prices and incomes'; PRO: T 267/27, 'Incomes policy: 1964-1968', p. 6).

88 PRO: T 267/27, 'Incomes policy: 1964-1968', p. 6. It is interesting to note that the word 'productivity' was only incorporated into the title of the statement when the TUC objected that to concentrate on 'prices and incomes' was to 'perpetuate the fallacy' that changes in prices were caused by changes in wages (TUCA: MSS.292B/110.44/2, 20 November 1964, Econ. Ctee 3/3, 'TUC: Prices and incomes, note on the government's draft statement of intent').

89 The TUC, for example, noted that the statement had been drafted in order to be 'as inoffensive and unprovocative as possible' in order to secure agreement (TUCA: MSS.292B/110.44/2, 20 November 1964, Econ. Ctee 3/3, 'TUC: Prices and incomes, note on the government's draft statement of intent').

90 Ibid

91 PRO: EW 8/1, 23 November 1964, meeting between the First Secretary and other ministers, and officials from the DEA and the TUC; PRO: EW 8/83, 27 November 1964, OGIP(64)2, 'First Secretary's meeting with the TUC Economic Committee on 23 November'; BECA: MSS.200/B/3/3/201.5, 2 December 1964, summarised verbatim minutes of NEDC meeting.

92 For a history of the new National Board for Prices and Incomes see Fells (1972).

93 PRO: EW 8/149, 29 January 1965, meeting between representatives of employers' organisations and the First Secretary; TUCA: MSS.292B/110.44/2, 25 January 1965, Econ. Ctee 6/1, 'TUC: Prices and incomes policy, report of a meeting between the Economic Committee and the Minister for Economic Affairs'.

94 PRO: T 171/758, 16 October 1964, GB(64)50(ii), General briefing for the new Chancellor, 'A policy for prices'; PRO: EW 8/100, 2 December 1964, OGIP(64) 2nd meeting of the Official Group on Incomes and Prices.

95 PRO: EW 8/136, 22 January 1965, 'Government attitude to wage claims and settlements in 1965: memorandum by the Minister of Labour'.

96 PRO: EW 8/153, 24 February 1965, meeting between the First Secretary and DEA officials.

97 PRO: CAB 129/120, 3 February 1965, C(65)16, 'Prices and incomes: memorandum by the First Secretary of State and Secretary of State for Economic Affairs'.

98 PRO: EW 8/153, 24 February 1965, meeting between the First Secretary and DEA officials.

99 PRO: EW 8/100, 19 February 1965, OGIP(65) 2nd meeting of the Official Group on Incomes and Prices.

100 Catherwood to Roll, quoted in PRO: T 267/27, 'Incomes policy: 1964-1968', p. 85.

101 PRO: CAB 129/120, 23 March 1965, C(65)47, 'Prices and incomes'.

102 PRO: CAB 128/39, CC(65)33, Cabinet conclusions, 15 June 1965.

103 PRO: EW 8/79, 23 June 1965, WPIP(65)14, 'Making the policy more effective', note by the chairman of the Working Party on Incomes and Prices.

104 PRO: EW 8/2, 24 June 1965, WPIP(65) 8th meeting of the Working Party on Incomes and Prices.

105 PRO: EW 8/442, 7 July 1965, meeting between DEA and IMF officials.

106 TUCA: MSS.292B/110.44/2, 10 July 1965, Murray to Woodcock, 'Prices and incomes policy'.

107 PRO: EW 8/9, 'Policy for prices: papers, 5 July to 30 September 1965', passim. The Chancellor's package of deflationary measures was announced on 27 July.

108 PRO: EW 8/9: 9 July 1965, 'Prices and incomes policy'; 14 July 1965, 'Prices and incomes policy: note of a meeting between the First Secretary and the

Minister of Labour'; 22 July 1965, 'Meeting between the First Secretary and representatives of the FBI and BEC'. For the TUC's initial reaction to Brown's proposal see TUCA: MSS.292B/110.44/2, 10 July 1965, Murray to Woodcock, 'Prices and incomes policy'.

[109] PRO: T 267/27, 'Incomes policy: 1964-1968', p. 23.

[110] PRO: PREM 13/259, 19 August 1965, Wilson to Brown.

[111] PRO: PREM 13/259, 20 August 1965, 'Telephone conference between the Prime Minister, First Secretary of State, Chancellor of the Exchequer, Sir Burke Trend and Sir Eric Roll'.

[112] PRO: PREM 13/259, 24 August 1965, 'Meeting between Sir Eric Roll and Mr. Fowler [Secretary to the US Treasury]'.

[113] PRO: T 267/27, 'Incomes policy: 1964-1968', p. 23; PRO: PREM 13/259, 26 August 1965, telegram from Brown to Roll in Washington.

[114] PRO: CAB 128/39, CC(65)46, Cabinet conclusions, 1 September 1965.

[115] PRO: T 267/27, 'Incomes policy: 1964-1968', p. 24.

[116] PRO: PREM 13/259, 2 September 1965, 'Discussion with the TUC'. The system was outlined in Cmnd. 2808 in November 1965.

[117] CBIA: MSS.200/C/1/1/C/CC.1.65-38.65, minutes of CBI Council meetings on 15 September and 20 October 1965.

[118] PRO: EW 8/442, 25 November 1965, 'First Secretary's speech to the ministerial council of OECD, 25-26 November 1965' and 3 December 1965, DEA brief for Douglas Allen in consultations with the IMF.

[119] PRO: EW 8/442, 7 January 1966, memorandum from the ambassador to Washington regarding a meeting with Schweitzer.

[120] PRO: CAB 129/124, 12 January 1966, C(66)3, 'Prices and incomes policy: memorandum by the First Secretary of State and Secretary of State for Economic Affairs and the Minister of Labour'.

[121] Balogh warned Wilson that the looming wage explosion would be contained only by a miracle (PRO: CAB 147/1, 21 April 1966, Balogh to Wilson, 'The economic outlook').

[122] PRO: T 267:27, 'Incomes policy: 1964-1968', p. 34.

[123] PRO: EW 8/149, 21 April 1966, Roll to Allen, 'Prices and incomes: machinery'; PRO: CAB 147/28, 26 May 1966, Joan Mitchell to Balogh.

[124] PRO: T 267/27, 'Incomes policy: 1964-1968', p. 38.

[125] PRO: EW 8/16, 25 May 1966, 'Note of a meeting between the First Secretary of State and representatives of the CBI, TUC and NBPI'.

[126] The failure of the committee was privately acknowledged by Len Murray (PRO: EW 8/16, 7 July 1966, 'Prices and incomes policy: brief for the First Secretary's meeting with Mr. Woodcock on 8 July') and by the TUC's Economic Committee (TUCA: MSS.292B/560.1/12, 26 July 1966, minutes of the 17th meeting of the Economic Committee).

[127] CBIA: MSS.200/C/1/1/C/CC.30.66, 20 April 1966, CBI Council minutes.

[128] PRO: CAB 134/3056, 13 June 1966, PI(66) 2nd meeting of the Ministerial Committee on Prices and Incomes.

[129] PRO: CAB 128/41, CC(66)31, Cabinet conclusions, 23 June 1966.

[130] PRO: EW 28/22, undated note by Brown on 'The government's economic policy'.

[131] PRO: CAB 128/41, CC(66)35 & 36, Cabinet conclusions for 12 and 14 July 1966.

[132] They included the full use of the regulator, tighter hire purchase controls and a range of tax rises and expenditure cuts (although, to avoid antagonising the unions and Labour supporters, these cuts did not fall on the social services). The imposition of the deflation and the standstill came as a 'profound shock' to those involved in incomes policy (Mitchell 1972: 13-16).

[133] HoC Debs., 20 July 1966, cols. 1201-4.

[134] CBIA: MSS.200/C/3/ECO/10/1, 2 August 1966, minutes of NEDC Liaison Committee; CBIA: MSS.200/C/1/1/C/C.58.66, 3 August 1966, minutes of a special meeting of the CBI Council.

[135] TUCA: MSS.292B/110.44/5, 22 July 1966, Econ. Ctee 15/2, 'TUC: The government's economic measures' and 22 July 1966, Econ. Ctee 15/4, 'TUC: Report of a meeting of the Economic Committee with the First Secretary'.

[136] TUCA: MSS.292B/110.44/5, 27 July 1966, minutes of the TUC General Council.

[137] Looking back on the period in the mid-1970s, the Treasury noted that 'one of the odd things about the incomes policy' in this period was 'its continuity, its bi-partisan character and the lack of serious consideration of alternative policies ... There was an extraordinary degree of consensus ... with argument tending to concentrate on questions of tactics rather than strategy' (PRO: T 267/28, 'Special study of incomes policy', preface by A.K. Ogilvy Webb).

[138] A study by Kurosawa and Pudney (1993) was more positive, finding a significant impact effects of incomes policy on both the size and timing of negotiations, but this relates to national wage settlements not rates of pay at plant level.

[139] See also PRO: T 267/28, 'Special study of incomes policy', preface.

[140] Cairncross was referring to the 1961 pay 'pause' but his judgement might just as well apply to the 1966 wage freeze.

[141] In October 1964, its Permanent Secretary had argued that: 'It would be better to abandon all attempts to seek an agreed incomes policy than to embark on a course which might lead to controls of this kind' (PRO: T 311/188, 8 October 1964, TGIP(64) 7th meeting of the Treasury Group on Incomes Policy).

[142] Though, of course, in the sense that the pay of government employees is largely determined by government, and that this pay bill comprises more than half of all government expenditure and forms a substantial proportion of overall incomes, all governments are forced to have an 'incomes policy', or at least a 'policy for the pay of public employees'. This, however, is a much more limited concept than was embodied in the attempt in the 1960s to build a permanent voluntary incomes policy linked to the growth objective and covering both the private and public sectors.

Chapter 6 – Taxation Policy

[1] CPA: ACP 3/5, 12 February 1958, (58)6, 'Some preliminary ideas'.

2 CPA: CRD 3/7/26/1, 18 January 1960, 'Taxation policy, 1960 and after'; CPA: CRD 3/7/26/2, 30 August 1960, TPC(60)21, draft report of the Taxation Policy Committee.

3 Note that this analysis is at odds with Price's (1978b: 139) argument that tax reduction remained the dominant tax objective until Labour's election in 1964.

4 PRO: PREM 11/3225, 3 January 1961 (Macmillan's emphasis).

5 At the end of 1960, for example, the CRD had recommended that policy committees take note of PEP (1960) (CPA: CRD 2/52/11, 2 December 1960, PI(60)10 'Growth', note by Brian Sewill).

6 CPA: CRD 3/7/26/2, passim.

7 *The Times*, 26 November 1960.

8 PRO: T 230/493, 25 August 1960, 'Answers to the Chancellor's questionnaire'.

9 PRO: T 230/493, 26 November 1960, note from Lee to the new Chancellor; PRO: T 171/516, 2 November 1960, BC(M)(60)5, Lee to Selwyn Lloyd. For a more detailed analysis of the Customs and Excise and payroll regulators see Pemberton (1997).

10 PRO: T 230/579, 27 February 1961, Vinter to Clarke, 'Elements of a policy for economic growth'; and 9 March 1961, Atkinson to Vinter.

11 PRO: T 233/2330, 23 August 1961, Crombie to Lee. See PRO: T 171/515, 15 June 1960 Budget Committee minutes for an instructive discussion of the contrasting points of view of the Treasury modernisers and the revenue departments (the latter, for reasons of administrative simplicity, tending to want to cut the number of taxpayers, and thus to oppose new taxes).

12 Such was the change in the climate of opinion produced by the growth advocacy network that by 1963 even the Governor of the Bank of England, hardly a champion of radical change, was complaining about the lack of progress on reforming the structure of taxation to promote higher growth (PRO: PREM 11/4202, 18 March 1963, Cromer to Maudling).

13 See de Vries (2000) for a penetrating analysis of the role of generation change in driving policy.

14 Edward Boyle later commented that Lee's appointment made 'a big difference' to the Treasury and largely explained the apparent contradiction between Selwyn Lloyd being 'a bit of a plodder' yet 'a very fecund Chancellor of the Exchequer' (BOAPH: Boyle interview, pp. 36 and 42).

15 PRO: T 233/2330, 21 August 1961, Lee to Cairncross, 'The Budget Committee: Taxation issues'.

16 PRO: T 311/21, 16 April 1962, Lee to Clarke.

17 PRO: T 230/579, 13 March 1961, Clarke to Hall, Padmore, and Lee, 'Economic growth'.

18 PRO: T311/131, May 1961, 'Economic growth: report of a working party of officials', paras. 98-101; PRO: T 233/2330, 5 May 1961, G.R. Bell to Armstrong.

19 PRO: T 233/2330-1 passim.

20 PRO: T 233/2331, 2 October 1961, RTP(61) 1st meeting of the Review of Taxation Policy Working Party and 18 October 1961, RTP(61)2, 'Inland Revenue taxation: note by the Inland Revenue'.

21 PRO: T 233/2331, 29 November 1961, RTP(61)2nd meeting of the Review of Taxation Policy Working Party

22 PRO: T 233/2331, passim. See also Daunton (2002).

23 PRO: T 171/515, 15 June 1960 Budget Committee meeting.

24 PRO: T 171/516, 8 November 1960, 'Possible economic regulators'.

25 It would need up to 500,000 collection points instead of the 70,000 required to collect purchase tax.

26 PRO: T 171/516, BC(60)41, Customs and Excise memorandum, 'Budget ideas'.

27 PRO: T 171/527, 3 January 1961, Lee to Hubback.

28 PRO: IR 63/215, 15 November 1960, BC(M)(60)5, E. Boyle, 'Possible economic regulators'.

29 PRO: T 171/515, minutes of Budget Committee meetings on 24 February and 20 March 1961.

30 To avoid criticism from within the party, Edward Boyle recommended that the government emphasise the role that such an instrument could play in securing economic expansion (PRO: T 171/516, 16 November 1960, Boyle to Selwyn Lloyd).

31 PRO: PREM 11/3762, 13 January 1961, 'Budget discussions at Chequers'; PRO: T 171/515, Budget Committee minutes for 10 January, 20 February, 24 February 1961 and 20 March 1961; PRO: T 171/515, 14 March 1961 Lee to Hubback.

32 A paper prepared for the Royal Statistical Society by Sir Robert Shone and H.K. Fisher (1958) had drawn attention to the extent to which social services were financed on the Continent by employer taxes. It also suggested that altering industry's labour/capital cost ratio would accelerate the rate of growth of productivity.

33 For press advocates see *The Economist* 22 October 1960 and 28 January 1961; *Financial Times*, 2 November 1960; *The Times*, 11 January 1961.

34 PRO: T 230/521, 12 January 1961, record of an interview by Samuel Brittan; PRO: T 230/521, 19 January 1961, Sir Robert Hall, minute of a meeting with Oliver Franks; PRO: CAB 134/1817, 22 February 1961, EPB(61)4, 'Memorandum on economic growth by the secretaries'.

35 CPA: CRD 3/7/26/2.

36 PRO: T 171/516, BC(60)38, 20 October 1960, 'A wages or pay-roll tax: note by the Economic Section'; *The Economist*, 22 October 1960. The idea was then fleshed out in PRO: T 233/2438, 4 November 1960, Collier to Robertson, 'National Insurance contributions as a weapon to control demand'.

37 PRO: T 171/524, 23 November 1960, minutes of a discussion on 'Economic regulators'; PRO: T 171/515, Budget Committee minutes for 20 and 22 December 1960, and 10 January 1961; PRO: T 171/527, 3 January 1961, Lee to Hubback.

38 PRO: T 171/515, 5 January 1961 Lee dinner note; PRO: T 171/527/5, Collier to Robertson.

39 Clarke and Padmore, for example, supported a permanent tax on payrolls but were unconvinced by Lee's proposals for a regulator (PRO: T 171/527/5, 14 December 1960, Clarke to Padmore with marginal note by Padmore).

40 PRO: T 171/516, BC(M)(60)5, 8 November 1960. This idea had been floated at the 1960 FBI conference, which Lee had attended.

41 PRO: T 171/515, 3 February 1961 Budget Committee minutes. Consumer demand would be reduced either by firms passing on the surcharge in the form of higher prices, by a reduction in their use of labour or by the lower wage rises. This would take time and higher prices might contribute to wage pressure.

42 PRO: BT 213/128, 26 April 1961, C. E. Harrison (FBI) to the Chancellor, 'The budget: economic regulators' – the FBI representation was released to the press.

43 *The Times*, 18 April 1961; *The Economist*, 22 April 1961.

44 CPA: CRD 2/10/15, 7 June 1961.

45 PRO: T 171/516, 29 March 1961, minute by Thomas Padmore; PRO: T 171/516, 30 March 1961 meeting between Selwyn Lloyd and Boyd-Carpenter; PRO: T 171/516, 7 April 1961, Selwyn Lloyd to Macmillan; PRO: T 171/516, 6-14 April 1961, various notes.

46 PRO: IR 63/215, 23 March 1961, PS 1926/60, 'National Insurance surcharge', note by 'LJHB', Inland Revenue. No minutes survive for the ministerial meeting at which the compromise was agreed.

47 PRO: T 171/527, 10 February 1961, 'Employee surcharge', paper by Collier.

48 PRO: T 171/592, 12 June 1961, Budget Committee minutes; PRO: CAB 129/106, 21 July 1961, C(61)112.

49 PRO: IR 83/282, pp. 13-15.

50 PRO: IR 83/282, pp. 15-16.

51 PRO: T 233/2330, 3 February 1960, Vinter to Armstrong, 'Economic effects of taxation'.

52 PRO: T 171/515, 12 September 1960, Budget Committee minutes.

53 PRO: T 171/515, 22 June and 12 September 1960, Budget Committee minutes; PRO: T 230/493, 26 July 1960, Lee to Selwyn Lloyd, 'Personal note for the new Chancellor'; CPA: CRD 2/10/11, 8 August 1959 letter to Sir John Winterton. PRO: T 171/521, 6 October 1960, BC(60)43M 'Long-term programme of tax changes: memorandum by the Board of the Inland Revenue'; PRO: IR 63/215, 31 January 1961, Boyle to Selwyn Lloyd details the Conservative Finance Committee's opposition.

54 HoC Debs., 25 July 1961, col. 222; PRO: CAB 128/35, CC 43(61), 21 July 1961, 'The economic situation'; PRO: T 171/592, 8 September 1961, Budget Committee minutes; PRO: PREM 11/4769, 5 September 1961, Selwyn Lloyd to Macmillan.

55 See, for example: PRO: T 171/594, 28 November 1961, Stock Exchange memorandum to the Chancellor; and PRO: T 171/594, 4 December 1961, note of a meeting between the Stock Exchange, Treasury ministers, Sir Alec Johnston and William Armstrong; PRO: T 171/594, 19 December 1961, Governor of the Bank of England to the Chancellor; PRO: T 171/759, 17 January 1964, Budget representation by the Institute of Directors.

56 The report of the party's Policy Committee on Economic Growth (CPA: CRD 2/09/47, May 1962) did not even mention a short-term CGT.

57 Labour's dependence throughout its history on a very restricted number of individuals in the formation of its tax policy is remarked on by Whiting (2001).

58 PRO: IR 83/282, p. 24.

59 LPA: RD.139, April 1961, 'Finance and Economic Policy Sub-committee: Taxation of profits and income proposals for reform (memorandum by Douglas Houghton MP)'; LPA: RD.742, April 1964, 'Working Party on Taxation: Report on taxation and incomes policy'. Here I am taking a rather more positive view of Labour's attack on unearned income and inherited wealth than that of Daunton (2002: 284).

60 Though the impact of the political advisers was deeply resented by officials, even by those who sympathised with the policies they espoused (Cairncross 1999: 236-7).

61 *The Economist*, 14 April 1962, leading article.

62 HoC Debs., 6 July 1962, col. 856 and 15 April 1964, cols. 447-8; PRO: IR 83/282, pp. 16-17.

63 PRO: T 171/804, 29 October 1964, Kaldor to Chancellor of the Exchequer, 'First memorandum on tax reform'. See also Reddaway (1989: 148-9) and Thirlwall (1989: 132).

64 Callaghan, HoC Debs., 15 April 1964, cols. 447-8.

65 HoC Debs., 15 July 1965, col. 805.

66 The *Financial Times* 'Lex' column on 30 November 1964, for example, sought answers to an array of questions: what assets were involved; whether there was to be a distinction between short and long-term; whether it would be flat rate or marginal; what exemptions could be expected; whether gilts would be excluded ('as they ought to be'); whether pension funds and investment trusts would be excluded; what provision there would be for companies disposing of fixed assets; if balancing charges on fixed assets be eliminated; and whether reinvested gains would be exempt.

67 PRO: T 171/764, 20 October 1946, M341, 'Capital Gains Tax', submission by the Inland Revenue to the Chancellor; PRO: T 171/805, 19 November 1964, Kaldor to Chief Secretary, 'Capital Gains Tax – the rate of taxation'; PRO: IR 83/282, p. 25.

68 PRO: T 230/664, 19 November 1964, Radice to Goldman, 'Capital Gains Tax'; PRO: T 171/805, 2 December 1964, Lord Cromer to Sir William Armstrong.

69 See, for example: PRO: T 171/805, 4 February 1965, Cromer to Callaghan; PRO: PREM 13/271, 31 March 1965, Cromer to Callaghan. A concise summary of Cromer's argument can be found in IR 83/282, p. 64.

70 See, for example: PRO: T 171/805 passim; PRO: PREM 13/283, 18 December 1964, note by Mitchell for the Prime Minister regarding lobbying by Rees-Mogg; PRO: T 171/764, 18 December 1964, Kaldor to Callaghan. See also *The Times* 17 March 1965 for an influential article entitled 'Anatomy of the gilt-edged market'.

71 PRO: T 171/804, 11 December 1964, Neild to Callaghan.

72 PRO: T 171/804, 21 January 1965, NT(65) 1st meeting of the New Taxes Committee.

73 PRO: T 171/804, 31 March 1965, 'Capital gains and corporation taxes: Meeting of Treasury ministers and officials'. This meeting also set the rate for companies not subject to Corporation Tax at 35 per cent.

74 See for example PRO: PREM 13/283, 18 May 1965, note for the record by the Prime Minister.

75 PRO: PREM 13/283, 20 May 1965, M.J. Stewart to Mitchell, 'Note for the Prime Minister on Capital Gains Tax and gilt-edged securities'; PRO: T 171/805, 20 May 1965, note by Kaldor for the Chancellor on switching in the gilt-edged market.

76 PRO: T 171/805, 25 May 1965, Radice to Walker, 'Capital Gains Tax and gilt-edged'.

77 PRO: PREM 13/283, 28 May 1965, Bancroft to Mitchell.

78 HoC Debs., 17 April 1961, cols. 802-4.

79 PRO: IR 63/215, 28 February 1961, minute of a meeting held to discuss the budget.

80 PRO: T 233/2331, 18 October 1961, RTP(61)2, 'Inland Revenue taxation: note by the Inland Revenue' and RTP(61)4, 'Taxation and exports: note by the director, Economic Section'.

81 PRO: T 171/607, 27 July 1962, M307, 'A Corporation Tax', Inland Revenue.

82 PRO: IR 83/282, p. 123

83 HoC Debs., 18 April 1961, col. 988.

84 PRO: IR 83/282, p. 125.

85 PRO: T 171/761, 2 November 1964, Budget Committee with Treasury Ministers.

86 PRO: T 171/764, 6 November 1964, M342, 'A Corporation Tax', memorandum by the Inland Revenue.

87 PRO: T 171/764, 9 November 1964, Bancroft to Corlett.

88 LPA: RD.139, 1 April 1961, 'Finance and Economic Policy Sub-committee: taxation of profits and income proposals for reform (memorandum by Douglas Houghton MP)'.

89 PRO: T 171/804, NT(65)31, 18 February 1965, 'The new taxes: representations from outside bodies'; PRO: PREM 13/273, 19 November 1964, 'M.R.' to Wilson regarding a conversation with Lord Boothby; PRO: T 171/764, 19 November 1964, Bancroft to Corlett regarding a meeting between the Chancellor and City editors; PRO: T 171/764, 23 November 1964, Sir Alex Johnston to Bancroft.

90 PRO: PREM 13/273, 25 November 1964, briefing note on Corporation Tax prepared by the Treasury for the Prime Minister; Callaghan, HoC Debs., 27 November 1964, col. 234 and 8 December 1964, cols. 1322-4.

91 For a useful summary of 'franking' principles see PRO: IR 83/282, pp. 133-4.

92 Kaldor pressed the point in PRO: IR 63/230, 3 December 1964, Kaldor to Chief Secretary, 'Statement on new taxes'; and PRO: T 171/807, 9 December 1964, Kaldor to Callaghan, 'Corporation Tax: the problem of franking'.

93 PRO: IR 63/230, 1 December 1964, Sir A. Johnston to Callaghan; PRO: IR 63/231, 3 February and 10 February 1965, 3rd and 4th meetings of the New

Taxes Committee; and IR 63/231, NT(65)33, 8 February 1965, 'Corporation Tax: Inland Revenue note on non-franking of inter-company dividends'. Fundamental to this disagreement was a debate, also taking place in the DEA, NEDC and MinTech, over whether firms should be encouraged to co-operate or whether such encouragement might be monopolistic and detrimental to growth.

94 PRO: T 171/807, 9 December 1964, Kaldor to Callaghan, 'Corporation Tax: the problem of franking', reissued as NT(65)21.

95 PRO: IR 63/231, 8 February 1965, NT(65)33, Corporation Tax: Inland Revenue note on non-franking of inter-company dividends.

96 PRO: CAB 147/50, 26 February 1965, Balogh to Wilson.

97 PRO: T 171/804, 10 February 1965, 4th meeting of the New Taxes Committee; Cmnd. 2646.

98 A useful introduction to 'overspill' can be found at PRO: IR 83/282, pp. 159-61.

99 PRO: IR 63/230, 1 December 1964, Sir A. Johnston to Chancellor of the Exchequer. This view was supported by Kaldor (IR 83/282, p. 165).

100 PRO: CAB 130/203, 25 February 1965, MISC.1/5, 'Overseas investment policy and the Corporation Tax'. The view of the advisers can be seen in PRO: PREM 13/273, 21 January 1965, 'Paper for the Prime Minister on Corporation Tax', prepared by Balogh; and PRO: T 171/806, 17 February 1965, NT(65)25, memorandum by Kaldor, 'The tax system and overseas investment'.

101 PRO: IR 83/282, pp. 167-8.

102 PRO: BT 213/331, 15 February 1965, Michael Stewart to Callaghan; PRO: IR 63/232, 19 February 1965, minutes of a meeting to discuss overseas investment; PRO: T 171/801, 25 February 1965, Burke Trend, Cabinet Office note, 'Overseas investment policy and the Corporation Tax; PRO: T 171/806, 12 March 1965, PC 64/91, 'The Corporation Tax and the oil companies: note by the Ministry of Power'; PRO: T 171/806, 23 March 1965, ministerial discussion on 'Overseas investment and the Corporation Tax'; PRO: T 171/806, 25 March 1965, Minister of Power to the Chancellor of the Exchequer.

103 PRO: IR 63/232, 4 December 1964, 'FBI submission to the Chancellor: A UK Corporation Tax'; PRO: EW 27/21, 17 December 1964, 'Impact of Corporation Tax on companies with large overseas operations'.

104 PRO: BT 213/329, 20 January 1965, FBI press release, 'A UK Corporation Tax'.

105 See, for example, PRO: BT 213/331 passim for the numerous representations.

106 See PRO: BT 213/331, 22 December 1964, Malaysian Commercial Association and 1 January 1965, India, Pakistan and Burma Association to the Secretary of State for Commonwealth Relations.

107 See, for example, PRO: BT 213/331, 15 February 1965, Michael Stewart to Callaghan.

108 PRO: T 171/806, 15 March 1965, Goldman to Rickett.

109 HoC Debs., 6 April 1965, cols. 265-6; PRO: BT 213/331 passim; PRO: IR 63/232, passim; PRO: T 171/806, passim; PRO: PREM 13/828, passim.

[110] The incentive effects on investment of Corporation Tax were disputed by Merrett (1965) on the grounds that they were outweighed by the disincentive impact of the new CGT. This is part of a wider debate on the impact of the tax reforms of the 1960s on incentives (for examples, see Peston 1973 and Prest 1973).

[111] See, for example, PRO: CAB 134/1805, EP(64) , 22 July 1964 32nd meeting of the Cabinet Committee on Economic Policy; and FG 2/22, 1 August 1962, NEDO recommendation regarding 'Taxation and economic growth'.

[112] PRO: T 171/813, 6 April 1966, Kaldor to Callaghan, 'The case for a payroll tax and for a new incentive for exports' and 16 April 1966, Chancellor and officials' discussion of employers' contribution surcharge. A later Brookings Institution report (Caves *et al* 1968) disputed the link between growth and the labour supply.

[113] PRO: EW 16/2, 25 October 1964, 'A tax instrument for adjusting the balance of payments' and 5 November 1964, MacDougall to Economic Secretary.

[114] PRO: T 171/813, 6 April 1966, Kaldor to Callaghan, 'The case for a payroll tax and for a new incentive for exports'; PRO: T 171/812, 7 April 1966, CM(66) 1st Chancellor's meeting on the budget.

[115] PRO: T 171/813, 7 April 1966, 'Surcharge on National Insurance contributions: note by Ministry of Pensions and National Insurance'.

[116] PRO: T 171/813, 6 April 1966, 'Meeting between ministers and officials regarding the surcharge on National Insurance contributions'; PRO: T 171/812, 7 April 1966, CM(66) 1st Chancellor's meeting on the budget; PRO: T 171/813, 14 April 1966, official meeting to discuss employers' National Insurance contributions; PRO: T 171/813, 15 April 1966, Armstrong to Bancroft, 'Surcharge on employers' contributions and a subsidy for manufacturers'.

[117] PRO: T 171/812, 19 April 1966, minute of a prime ministerial meeting on the budget with the Chancellor of the Exchequer and President of the Board of Trade, and with Armstrong and Roll.

[118] PRO: T 171/813, 15 April 1966, Armstrong to Bancroft.

[119] For example, protests on behalf of the construction industry can be found in PRO: PREM 13/863, 28 April 1966, Prentice to the Prime Minister and 28 April 1966, Crossman to Wilson. The Minister of Labour complained about the levy being applied to apprenticeships and the disincentive which the levy would create for the employment of the disabled and the elderly (PRO: T 171/814, 28 April 1966, Pliatzky to Pettish, 'Employment levy: effect on apprenticeships').

[120] PRO: T 171/814, 6 May 1966, transcript of a television address by Iain Macleod.

[121] A review of the *Financial Times*, *The Times*, *Daily Telegraph*, *Guardian*, *Birmingham Post*, *Glasgow Herald*, *The Economist* and *The Spectator* on the days of 4 to 6 May indicates that none was impressed by the proposals.

[122] PRO: FG 2/396, 19 May 1966, Kingsley Lewis to Caplan, 'The Selective Employment Tax' and 24 May 1966, Dallas to Caplan, 'Selective Employment Tax'; EW 16/19, 25 May 1966, 'Minister of State's progress meeting'. The problem was that SET would bear down on the service sector in

all regions, including those with higher unemployment than the national average.

123 PRO: T 171/814, 18 May 1966, Brown to Callaghan.

124 PRO: LAB 43/456, 25 May 1966, Callaghan to Brown, 'Selective Employment Tax: arrangements for interdepartmental discussion'.

125 In its original form, of course, Kaldor had not envisaged that SET would contribute significant revenue.

126 For discussion of this consensus see Daunton (2002: 280-1).

127 Whiting (2001) remarks on the way in which Labour's consistent inability to construct a coherent strategic plan for tax continually allowed vested interests greater scope to pick of its attempts at reform as they emerged.

128 Daunton (2002: 232) also highlights the blocking power conferred on the Inland Revenue by its technical and administrative authority in the field of taxation.

129 The fact that the appointment of special advisers by Labour had resulted in an extraordinarily incoherent set of tax reforms was remarked on by Hallett (1967).

130 The emphasis on governance issues as the source of incoherence contrasts with Steinmo's (1989, 1993) emphasis on the role of partisan politics.

131 A point that emerges from other recent studies of the period (for example: Ringe and Rollings 2000a; and Lowe and Rollings 2000).

Chapter 7 – Conclusions

1 See also Supple and Furner (1990: 34), Middleton (1998) and Berman (1998) for discussion of how economic ideas are transmitted.

2 It is also at odds with James' (1993) assertion that think tanks have only had considerable influence on government policy since 1970.

3 Though since they are very difficult to measure it is difficult to see how Marin and Mayntz's (1991: 22) desire to see them quantified can be satisfied.

4 The distinction between the two was first made in by Hall (1982: 706), developed in Hall (1986), and is central to Hall (1993).

5 Vickerstaff (1985) noted the danger that neo-corporatist structures can entrench rather than overcome the power of vested interests.

6 'The first thing to be noted about the central government of this country is that it is a federation of departments' (Sir William Armstrong, 'The civil service and its departments', *O & M Bulletin*, vol. 25, no. 2 (May 1970), pp. 63-79, quoted by Heclo and Wildavsky 1981: lxiv-lxv). Armstrong became joint permanent secretary of the Treasury after Sir Frank Lee's resignation in 1963 and later head of the civil service

7 Thus confirming that, in an implementation network, actors depend on each other because no one actor or institution has a monopoly of resources (Smith 1999a: 1).

8 Macmillan's (1973) memoirs illustrate the heavy burden that foreign policy placed upon his time. Of the fifteen chapters that comprise the narrative ten are devoted to foreign and security policy and only three to the evolution of economic policy.

9 The lack of prime ministerial involvement in day-to-day decision making is remarked upon by Smith (1999a: 72) and Rhodes (1995: 15-17). It is a significant factor contributing to the weak political management within the core executive that is decried by Brady and Catterall (1997).

10 This goes further than Shanks' (1977: 89) complaint that there was a failure to link short-term income restraint with long-term economic growth.

11 In fact it suggests that the degree of consensus was even greater than Gamble and Walkland suspected for, behind a façade of adversarialism, even incomes policy (the only economic policy area in which they detected an adversarial cycle) was characterised by a high level of continuity between the two governments.

Bibliography

Newspapers and periodicals

BACIE Journal
BACIE Memoranda
Birmingham Post
Daily Telegraph
The Economist
Fabian Journal
Financial Times
Glasgow Herald
The Guardian
Ministry of Labour Gazette
New Statesman
The Observer
The Spectator
Technical Education and Industrial Training
Sunday Times
The Times

Personal interviews and recollections

Interview with Peter Jay, 8 Aug. 1998.
Correspondence with Lord Croham, Jul. and Aug. 1998.
Typescript personal memoir of the Ministry of Labour by P.H. St John-Wilson

Miscellaneous papers

Papers of Sir Hugh Beaver, British Library of Political and Economic Science, London
Papers of Alistair Hetherington, British Library of Political and Economic Science, London
MISC 745 Samuel Brittan, diary, British Library of Political and Economic Science, London

British Oral Archive of Political and Administrative History (BOAPH), British Library of Political and Economic Science, London

Transcript of an interview with Lord Boyle conducted by Anthony Seldon
Transcript of an interview with Lord Butler conducted by Anthony Seldon
Transcript of two interviews with Lord Roberthall conducted by Anthony Seldon

Records of Political and Economic Planning (PEPA), British Library of Political and Economic Science, London

PEP (I) M13-4	Executive Council minutes, 1958–1964
PEP (I) P13	The shape of the sixties
PEP (I) PWS 10/1-12	'Growth in the British Economy' - working papers
PEP (I) UP 10/1-10a	Unpublished history of PEP
PEP (I) UP 20	'Industrial Training' (unpublished pamphlet, 1960–61)
PEP (I) UP 23	'Incomes Policy' (unpublished pamphlet)

Conservative Party Archive (CPA), Oxford University

Advisory Committee on Policy and Political Education (ACP)

3/5-13	Advisory Committee on Policy: papers

Conservative Research Department (CRD)

2/09/47	Policy Committee on Economic Growth
2/10/11, 15	Taxation policy
2/10/17	Finance Committee: the structure of taxation, 1960–1961
2/10/19	Taxation Policy Committee, 1956–1964
3/7/06/1	Economic Policy Group papers 1-49: Oct. 1966 to Sept. 1967
3/7/06/9	Future Economic Policy Group, Jan. to Dec. 1965
3/7/06/10	Future Economic Policy Group on Taxation, Jan. to Dec. 1965
3/7/11/1	Incomes Policy, 1964–1967
3/7/26/1-3	Taxation Policy Committee: correspondence and papers, 1959–63
3/7/26/19-20	Tax reform: suggestions, Feb. 1965 to Dec. 1969

Records of the Labour Party (LPA) on microfiche

NEC	Minutes of the National Executive Committee, 1960–1964
RD	Labour Party Research Department Memoranda, 1947–1970

Records of the Confederation of British Industry and predecessors at the Modern Record Centre, University of Warwick

Records of the British Employers' Confederation (BECA)

MSS.200/B /3/3/201	Economic situation, Apr. 1958 to Apr. 1964
MSS.200/B /3/3/201.1	Incomes policy, Dec. 1957 to Apr. 1965
MSS.200/B /3/3/201.3	Council on Prices, Productivity and Incomes, 1958–1961
MSS.200/B /3/3/201.4	NEDC, 1961–1964
MSS.200/B /3/3/201.5	NEDC, 1963–1965
MSS.200/B /3/3/201.6	Statement of intent, Dec. 1964 to Jan. 1965
MSS.200/B /3/3/264.1a	'Britain's economic problems and policies: the next five years', 1964–5
MSS.200/B /3/3/610	Recruitment, education and training policy, Jun. 1958 to Apr. 1961

Records of the Confederation of British Industry (CBIA)

MSS.200/C /1	**CBI Committee Minutes**
/1/C/CC.1.64-6	CBI Council circulars, minutes and reports, 1964–66
MSS.200/C /3/ECO	**Economic Affairs Directorate**
/10/1	NEDC Liaison Committee 1966–67
/16/1	CBI Taxation Committee
MSS.200/C /3/EDU	**Education and Training Directorate**
/1/1-2	Education and Training Committee: 1964 to 1965
/1/27-8	The expansion of industrial training, 1959 to 1961
/1/35-8	Joint BEC/FBI Education and Training Committee: 1960 to 1966
/1/97	General policy on training, 1958 to 1964
/24/1	Industrial Training Council, 1958 to 1964
/24/5	1964 Industrial Training Act

Records of the Federation of British Industry (FBIA)

MSS.200/F /3/D3	**Records of the third Director General of the FBI, D.G. Kipping**
/5/20	Incomes policy, 1957–1966
MSS.200/F /3/E	**FBI Economic Directorate**
3/2/14	Economic Study Committee, 1962–64
MSS.200/F /3/P	**FBI Presidential Papers**
7/17/4	Anglo-French conference on economic planning, 27-29 Apr. 1962
7/19/1	Political and Economic Planning: attitudes in British industry, 1962
7/3/1	Material related to the FBI Economic Directorate in 1961
8/12/1-3	Price and incomes policy
8/9/1-10	FBI Grand Council
MSS.200/F /3/S	**Secretaries' papers**
2/10/11	FBI conference, Brighton, 1960: conference papers and publications
2/10/12	'Britain's economic problems and policies: the next five years', 1965
MSS.200/F /4	**FBI Publications**
/75/19	Report to delegates on the Next Five Years' conference, Nov. 1960
/76/3	'The Next Five Years', 24-26 Nov. 1960 – conference report
/76/7	'Invest in the Future', 26-28 Sept. 1960 – conference report

Records of the TUC, 1960–1970 at the Modern Records Centre, University of Warwick (TUCA)

MSS.292B/110.44/1	Wages and incomes policy : correspondence, 1960–1964
MSS.292B /110.44/2	Incomes and prices policy: correspondence, 1964–1965
MSS.292B /110.44/3-4	Productivity, prices and incomes: wages policy, 1965–66
MSS.292B /110.44/5	Wages. government income policy. Wage Freeze, 1966

MSS.292B /110.44/6	Wages. prices and incomes legislation, Sept. to Dec. 1966
MSS.292B /132.14/1	Youth - industrial training: statutory training boards, 1962–4
MSS.292B /132/1	Young persons: employment and training for employment
MSS.292B /132/3-4	Young persons: recruitment and training
MSS.292B /132/5-6	Apprenticeships
MSS.292B /560.1/1-14	Minutes of the TUC Economic Committee, 1960–67
MSS.292B /560/1	Economics: correspondence and papers re academic research
MSS.292B /811/1-4	Education Committee minutes, 1960–64
MSS.292B /815.7/3	Education: BACIE, 1962–1966

British Association for Commercial and Industrial Education at the Modern Records Centre, Warwick University (BACIE)

MSS.97/BACIE /1/1/3-5	Executive Council minutes, 1952–1970
MSS.97/BACIE /1/2/6-7	General Council minutes, 1952–1970

The National Archive, Public Record Office (PRO), Kew

Board of Trade (BT)

BT 213	**Board of Trade: Commodity and General Division**
BT 213/128	Payroll tax, 1961–1962
BT 213/309	Corporation and capital gains taxes, 1964–1965
BT 213/329	Corporation tax, 1964–1965
BT 213/331	Corporation tax: taxation of overseas dividends, 1964–1965

Cabinet Office (CAB)

CAB 21/4710	General economic situation: wages and prices, 1959–1960
CAB 21/4711	COPPI, 1957–1961
CAB 21/4713-4	Incomes policy: general correspondence, May to Jul. 1962
CAB 21/4946	Economic situation in the UK: wages and prices, 1962–1963
CAB 128/34-46	Cabinet conclusions [i.e. Cabinet minutes] 1960 to 1967
CAB 129/93-127	Cabinet memoranda 1958 to 1966
CAB 130/186	GEN 766 Cabinet committee. The new approach (1962)
CAB 130/187	GEN 771 Cabinet committee. Incomes policy (1962)
CAB 130/202-59	MISC 1 Cabinet committee. Economic affairs, 1964–1966
CAB 134/1685-1810	Cabinet committee on economic policy, 1960 to 1964
CAB 134/1815-17	Economic Planning Board 1960 to 1962
CAB 134/1891-7	Economic steering committee (general), 1963 to 1964
CAB 134/1902-3	Economic steering (incomes) committee, 1962–1964
CAB 134/1989-94	Home affairs committee, 1962 to 1964
CAB 134/2407-9	Official committee on prices and incomes, 1964 to 1965
CAB 134/2562-3	Wages committee, 1964
CAB 134/2572-3	Committee on wages policy, 1958 to 1959
CAB 134/2714-15	Economic development (official) committee, 1966
CAB 134/3056	Ministerial committee on prices and incomes, 1966 to 1970
CAB 147/1	Personal files of Dr Thomas Balogh
CAB 147/9	Dr Thomas Balogh, 'Usefulness of the Treasury in the Economic field'
CAB 147/28	Dr Thomas Balogh, 'Prices and Incomes Policy, 1964–67'
CAB 147/50	Dr Thomas Balogh, 'Corporation Tax, 1964–65'

Customs and Excise (CUST)

CUST 118/597-8	1961 Budget Committee

Records of the Department of Economic Affairs (EW)

EW 8/1	Papers leading up to 'Joint statement of intent', 1964 to 1965
EW 8/2	Working party on incomes and prices, 1964–66
EW 8/9-10	Policy for prices, 1965
EW 8/16	Meetings with TUC, CBI and NBPI, 1966–1968
EW 8/79	Working party on incomes and prices, 1964–1965
EW 8/83-4	Official Group on incomes and prices: circulated papers, 1964–1966
EW 8/100	Official Group on incomes and prices: minutes, 1964–1966
EW 8/136	Ministerial committee on economic development: sub-committee on prices and incomes 1964–1965
EW 8/149	Prices and incomes policy: proposed machinery, 1965–1966
EW 8/153	Prices and incomes policy: determination of an incomes norm, 1965–66
EW 8/192	Concept of a national minimum wage: notes and papers, 1962–1967
EW 8/215	Incomes policy: functions and powers of wages councils, 1964–67
EW 8/442	IMF: consultations on the British economy; 1965
EW 16/2	'Tax instruments for adjusting balance of payments', N. Kaldor
EW 16/19	SET: machinery for consultation
EW 27/21	Capital gains and corporation tax
EW 28/22	Note by G. Brown on the government's economic policy

Records of the NEDC (FG)

FG 2/22	Taxation policy, 1962
FG 2/41	Incomes policy, 1962–1967
FG 2/92	French economic planning
FG 2/396	Selective employment tax

Inland Revenue (IR)

IR 63/215-51	Finance bills, 1961 to 1967
IR 83/282	History of the Finance Act, 1965

Ministry of Labour (LAB)

LAB 9/377	Working party on industrial training levy schemes, 1962–1964
LAB 9/378	Industrial training: draft bill, 1963
LAB 10/1488	NJAC: minutes and agenda, 1954–1967
LAB 10/1604	BEC paper on the manpower situation, 1961
LAB 10/1757	Permanent secretaries' group on planning: setting up of the NEDC, 1961–1962
LAB 10/1788	Prime Minister's speech on status and security at work, action arising
LAB 18/729	Consideration of an industrial training levy, 1961–1962

LAB 18/744	Apprenticeship training scheme: policy and early history 1958–62
LAB 18/759	Second inter-departmental working party on training levy schemes
LAB 18/760	Attitude of industry to training levy schemes, 1962–1964
LAB 18/761	Third inter-departmental working party on training levy schemes
LAB 18/784	Inter-departmental working party on training levy, 1961–1964
LAB 18/835	Industrial training: correspondence with the TUC General Secretary
LAB 18/940-41	Inter-departmental committee on industrial training, 1964
LAB 19/602	Inter-departmental working party on the 'bulge' problem
LAB 19/714	Industrial training levy, 1961–62
LAB 43/339	Ministers meeting with senior officials, Chequers, 23-24 Jan. 1960
LAB 43/396	Industrial training: government proposals
LAB 43/424	Correspondence with George Brown
LAB 43/456	SET: effects on the employment of part-timers

Prime Minister's Office, Papers 1951 to 1964 (PREM 11)

PREM 11/1824	Financial Policy, 1957
PREM 11/3287	Correspondence with Sir Roy Harrod, 1960–1961
PREM 11/3294	French economic planning: correspondence with the chancellor, 1961
PREM 11/3304	'Economic growth and national efficiency': report by Treasury officials to the chancellor
PREM 11/3477	F Bishop's personal views on current home and world problems
PREM 11/3619-20	Wages, 1961
PREM 11/3742	Correspondence with Sir Roy Harrod, 1961–1962
PREM 11/3762-5	Financial policy, 1961–62
PREM 11/3841	Industrial relations, 1961–62
PREM 11/3873	Scheme for apprenticeship levy, 1961–1962
PREM 11/3930	Remarks made by prime minister at cabinet on 28 May 1962
PREM 11/4064-73	Wages policy, 1961–1962
PREM 11/4169	Education, 1960–1963
PREM 11/4192	Correspondence with Sir Roy Harrod, part 4 - Jan. to June1963
PREM 11/4202	1963 Budget - discussions with the chancellor
PREM 11/4207	Economic planning - setting up of the NEDC
PREM 11/4412	PM to private secretary and ministers: summary of tasks ahead
PREM 11/4769	Discussions on taxation of short-term capital gains
PREM 11/4770	Correspondence with Sir Roy Harrod: part 5, Oct. 1963 to Jan. 1964

Prime Minister's Office, Papers 1964–1970 (PREM 13)

PREM 13/28	PM wished to see all cabinet committee papers and minutes
PREM 13/259	Formulation of prices and incomes policy: parts 1 and 2
PREM 13/271	Apr. 1965 budget: part 2
PREM 13/273	Proposals for capital gains and corporation taxes, to Apr. 1965
PREM 13/283	Capital gains tax: application to gilt-edged securities, 1964–1965
PREM 13/360	Economic planning in government: views of Dr. Balogh
PREM 13/828	Proposals for capital gains and corporation taxes, 1965–1966
PREM 13/858-9	Policy on prices and incomes, 1966
PREM 13/862-3	1966 budget

PREM 13/1242 — Trade unions and prices and incomes policy, Aug. to Sept. 1966

The Treasury (T)

T 171 — **Budget**
T 171/515-828 — The budget, 1961 to 1967

T 224 — **Agriculture, Transport and Trade Division**
T 224/1003 — Apprenticeship and craft training by industry, 1960–1963

T 230 — **Economic Section**
T 230/493 — Notes for the incoming chancellor
T 230/497 — Official committee on wages and prices: minutes and meetings, 1960
T 230/521 — Economic situation and UK economic policy, 1961
T 230/523-6 — Working party on economic growth, 1961/2
T 230/579 — Policy for economic growth, 1960–61
T 230/580 — Policy for economic growth, 1962–64
T 230/581-3 — Economic situation and UK economic policy, 1962–1964
T 230/584-7 — Working party on economic growth, 1962
T 230/590 — Attitudes of TUC to the government's economic policies, 1960–62
T 230/657 — French economic planning, 1960–61
T 230/664 — Long term taxation policy, 1963–64
T 230/684-9 — Incomes policy, 1962–1964
T 230/691 — The new approach: setting up of a price investigation authority
T 230/692 — National Incomes Commission: policy
T 230/706-9 — Economic Section discussion papers, 1961–64

T 233 — **Home Finance division**
T 233/2330-31 — Review of taxation policy, 1960–1961

T 267 — **Treasury Historical Memoranda**
T 267/7 — THM No. 4 The government and wages, 1945–1960 [Jul. 1962]
T 267/8-10 — THM No. 5 The government and wages, Vol. 1 1945–1951; Vol. 2 1952–1956,;Vol. 3 1956–1960
T 267/20 — THM No. 18 The Control of Demand: 1958–1964
T 267/24 — THM No. 24 Incomes policy: 1961–1964
T 267/27 — THM No. 28 Incomes policy: 1964–1968
T 267/28 — THM No. 29 Special study of incomes policy [Feb. 1976]

T 277 — **Treasury: Committee Section: Minutes and Papers**
T 277/1073-4 — Permanent secretaries' group on planning, 1961

T 298 — **National Resources Divisions (2NR)**
T 298/147 — National Production Advisory Council on Industry, 1961
T 298/334-5 — NEDC: preparation of a report on national efficiency and obstacles to economic growth, 1961 to 1962
T 298/346 — Second phase of incomes policy: period of restraint, 1962
T 298/347 — 'Incomes policy: the next step', 1961–1962

T 311 — **National Economy Group (NE1 and NE2)**
T 311/1-2 — Promotion of UK economic growth policy, 1960–1962
T 311/3 — CRD: Policy committee on economic growth, 1962; comments
T 311/16-18 — Incomes policy, 1960–1961

T 311/21	Preparation and issue of Historical Memorandum No.5, 1961–1962
T 311/71	Incomes policy: general papers, 1963
T 311/131	Promotion of UK economic growth: 1961–1964
T 311/188	Treasury group on incomes policy: minutes of meetings
T 320	**Public Income and Outlay Division**
T 320/51-2	Review of taxation policy, 1962
T 320/73-4	PM's steering committee on modernising Great Britain, 1962
T 325	**Papers of Sir R. W. B. Clarke**
T 325/72	Economic growth, 1961/1962 and NEDC, 1962
T 325/95	Taxation and the economy

Official publications

Cabinet Office, Performance and Innovation Unit (2000) *Wiring it up,* (http://www.strategy.gov.uk/files/pdf/coiwire.pdf).

Cmd. 6527 (1944) *Employment Policy White Paper*, London: HMSO.

Cmd. 9474 (1955) *Royal commission on the taxation of profits and income (final report),* London: HMSO.

Cmd. 9725 (March 1956) *The economic implications of full employment*, London: HMSO.

Cmnd. 827 (1959) *Report of the Committee on the Workings of the Monetary System (The Radcliffe Committee)*, London: HMSO.

Cmnd. 1432 (July 1961) *Control of public expenditure (Plowden committee report)*, London: HMSO.

Cmnd. 1626 (February 1962) *Incomes policy: the next step*, London: HMSO.

Cmnd. 1710 (April 1961) *Taxation of Short-term Gains*, London: HMSO.

Cmnd. 1844 (November 1962) *National Incomes Commission*, London: HMSO.

Cmnd. 1892 (December 1962) *Industrial training: Government proposals*, London: HMSO.

Cmnd. 2577 (February 1965) *Machinery of prices and incomes policy,* London: HMSO.

Cmnd. 2583 (February 1965) *National Incomes Commission Report No. 4 (Final): Agreements of November – December 1963 in the engineering and shipbuilding industries*, London: HMSO.

Cmnd. 2639 (April 1965) *Prices and incomes policy*, London: HMSO.

Cmnd. 2645 (April 1965) *Taxation of capital gains*, London: HMSO.

Cmnd. 2646 (April 1965) *The Corporation Tax*, London: HMSO.

Cmnd. 2764 (Sept. 1965) Department of Economic Affairs, *The National Plan*, London: HMSO.

Cmnd. 2808 (Nov. 1965) *Prices and incomes policy: an 'early warning system'*, London: HMSO.

Cmnd. 2986 (May 1966) *Selective Employment Tax*, London: HMSO.

Cmnd. 3073 (July 1966) *Prices and incomes standstill*, London: HMSO.

Cmnd. 3623 (June 1968) *Royal Commission on Trade Unions and Employers Associations, 1965–1968 (The Donovan Report)*, London: HMSO.

Cm. 4310 (March 1999) *Modernising government*, London: HMSO.

COPPI (1959) *Third report of the Council on Prices, Productivity and Incomes,* London: HMSO.

COPPI (1961) *Fourth report of the Council on Prices, Productivity and Incomes,* London: HMSO.

CTC (1968) *Training for skill: the time for change*, London: Central Training Council.

Department of Employment, (1972) *Training for the future: a plan for discussion*, London: Department of Employment.

HMSO (1964) *Joint statement of intent on productivity, prices and incomes, 16 December 1964*, London: HMSO.
ITC (1960) *Industrial Training Council: First Report, July 1958 to December 1959*, London: Industrial Training Council.
ITC (1961) *Industrial Training Council: Second Report, January 1960 to March 1961*, London: Industrial Training Council.
ITC (1965) *Industrial Training Council: Final Report, January 1963 to November 1964*, London: Industrial Training Council.
NJAC (1958) *Training for skill: recruitment and training of young workers in industry (the Carr Report)*, London: HMSO.
NJAC (1962) 'Report of the NJAC working party on the manpower situation', *Ministry of Labour Gazette*, February 1962.
NEDC (1963a) *Conditions favourable to faster growth*, London: HMSO.
NEDC (1963b) *Growth of the United Kingdom economy to 1966*, London: HMSO.
NEDC (1964) *The growth of the economy*, London: HMSO.
OEEC (1959) *General statistics, 1959*, Paris: OEEC.

Books and articles

Abramovitz, Moses (1952) 'Economics of Growth', in B. F. Haley (ed.) *A Survey of Contemporary Economics, Vol. II*, Homewood IL: R. D. Irwin.
Aldcroft, Derek H. (1982) 'Britain's economic decline, 1870–1980' in G. Roderick and M. D. Stevens *The British malaise: industrial performance, education and training in Britain today*, Lewes: The Falmer Press.
Alford, B. W. E. (1995) *British economic performance, 1945–75*, Cambridge: Cambridge University Press.
Alford, B. W. E. (1996) *Britain in the world economy since 1880*, Harlow: Longman.
Alt, James E. (1979) *The politics of economic decline*, Cambridge: Cambridge University Press.
Amenta, Edwin (1991) 'Making the most of a case study: theories of the welfare state and the American experience' in C. C. Ragin, *Issues and alternatives in comparative social research*, New York: E. J. Brill.
Arndt, H. W. (1978) *Economic development: the history of an idea*, Chicago, IL: University of Chicago Press.
Artis, Michael (1972) 'Fiscal policy for stabilization' in W. Beckerman, *The Labour government's economic record: 1964–1970*, London: Duckworth.
Artis, Michael (1981) 'Incomes policies: some rationales' in J. L. Fallick and R. F. Elliott, *Incomes policies, inflation and relative pay*, London: George Allen and Unwin.
Artis, Michael, Cobham, D. and Wickham-Jones, Mark (1992) 'Social democracy in hard times: the economic record of the Labour government 1974–1979', *Twentieth Century British History*, vol. 3, no. 1 (1992), pp. 32-58.
Artis, Michael, Fleming, John and Weale, Robin (2000) 'Christopher Dow on major recessions', *National Institute Economic Review*, no. 173, pp. 89-105.
Ashford, Nigel (1984) 'The political and moral bankruptcy of collectivism' in A. Seldon, *The 'New Right' enlightenment*, London: Economic and Literary Books.
Atkinson, Michael M. and Coleman, William D. (1992) 'Policy networks, policy communities and the problems of governance', *Governance*, vol. 5, no. 2 (April 1992), pp. 154-80.
Bache, Ian (2000), 'Government within governance: network steering in Yorkshire and the Humber', *Public Administration*, vol. 78, no. 3, pp. 575-92.

BACIE (1960a) *Policy in perspective: Report of the BACIE annual conference, 22-24 September 1960*, London: British Association for Commercial and Industrial Education.

BACIE (1960b) *Education for survival (Report on the ninth annual conference of the BACIE, March 1960)*, London: British Association for Commercial and Industrial Education.

BACIE (1960c) *Education and training in France*, London: British Association for Commercial and Industrial Education.

BACIE (1960d) 'Education and training in France', *BACIE Journal*, June 1960.

BACIE (1961) *Continental comparisons (papers presented at the BACIE annual conference, August 1961)*, London: British Association for Commercial and Industrial Education.

BACIE (1962) *Industrial training – whose responsibility? Papers presented at the BACIE Spring Conference, 10 May 1962*, London: British Association for Commercial and Industrial Education.

BACIE (1963a) *Cmnd. 1892: the next step (report of the BACIE conference, London, 15 Jan. 1963)*, London: British Association for Commercial and Industrial Education.

Backhouse, Roger (1983) *Macroeconomics and the British economy*, Oxford: Martin Robertson.

Bacon, Robert and Eltis, Walter (1976) *Britain's economic problem: too few producers*, London: Macmillan.

Balogh, Thomas (1954) 'Austerity and progress', *Fabian Journal*, October 1954, pp. 13-18.

Balogh, Thomas (1955) 'A socialist economic policy?: the problem for the Labour Party', *Fabian Journal*, October 1955, pp. 22-8.

Balogh, Thomas (1959) 'The apotheosis of the dilettante: the establishment of mandarins' in H. Thomas (ed.) *The establishment*, London: Anthony Blond.

Barker, Rodney (1996) 'Political ideas since 1945, or how long was the twentieth century?', *Contemporary British History*, vol. 10, no. 1 (Spring 1996), pp. 2-19.

Barnes, John (1994) 'Ideology and factions' in A. Seldon and S. Ball, *Conservative century*, Oxford: Oxford University Press.

Barnes, John and Cockett, Richard (1994) 'The making of party policy' in A. Seldon and S. Ball, *Conservative century*, Oxford: Oxford University Press.

Barnett, Corelli (1987) *The audit of war: the illusion and reality of Britain as a great nation*, London: Macmillan.

Barr, James (2001) *The Bow Group*, London: Politicos.

Barrett, George and Dewson, Sarah (1998), *Sectoral support for training: a review of international practice [A report by Ecotec Research and Consulting Ltd.)*, London: Department for Education and Employment.

Barrett, Susan and Fudge, Colin (1981) (eds.) *Policy and action: essays on the implementation of policy*, London: Macmillan.

Bean, Charles and Crafts, N. F. R. (1996) 'British economic growth since 1945: relative economic decline . . . and renaissance?' in N. F. R. Crafts and G. Toniolo, *Economic Growth in Europe since 1945*, Cambridge: Cambridge University Press.

Beckerman, Wilfred (1972) (ed.) *The Labour government's economic record: 1964–1970*, London: Duckworth.

Benn, Tony (1980) *Arguments for socialism*, Harmondsworth: Penguin.

Bennett, Colin J. and Howlett, Michael (1992) 'The lessons of learning: reconciling theories of policy learning and policy change', *Political Sciences*, vol. 25, pp. 275-94.

Berman, Sheri (1998) *The social democratic moment*, Cambridge, MA: Harvard University Press.

Beveridge, William (1944) *Full employment in a free society*, London: Allen & Unwin.

Beverstock, A. G. (1969) *Industrial training practices*, London: Classic Publications.

Bevir, Mark and Rhodes, R. A. W. *Interpreting British governance*, London: Routledge.

Birch, Anthony H. (1964) *Representative and responsible government*, London: Allen & Unwin.
Birch, Anthony H. (1993) *The concepts and theories of modern democracy*, London: Routledge.
Blackaby, Frank (1972) *An incomes policy for Britain: policy proposals and research needs*, London: Heinemann.
Blackaby, Frank (1978) 'Incomes policy' in F. Blackaby, *British economic policy, 1960–74*, Cambridge: Cambridge University Press.
Blake, Robert (1985) *The Conservative Party from Peel to Thatcher*, London: Methuen.
Blank, Stephen (1973) *Industry and government in Britain: the Federation of British Industries, 1945–1965*, Farnborough: Saxon House.
Blaug, Mark (1985) *Great economists since Keynes*, Brighton: Wheatsheaf.
Blaug, Mark (1994) 'Recent biographies of Keynes' *Journal of Economic Literature*, vol. 32, no. 3, pp. 1204-15.
Bleich, Erik (2002) 'Integrating ideas into policy-making analysis: frames and race policies in Britain and France', *Comparative Political Studies*, vol. 35, no. 9, pp. 1054-76.
Blom-Hansen, Jens (1997) 'A "New Institutional" perspective on policy networks', *Public Administration*, vol. 75, Winter 1997, pp. 669-93.
Blyth, Mark (1997) '"Any more bright ideas?" The ideational turn of comparative political economy', *Comparative Politics*, Jan 1997, vol. 29, no. 2, pp. 229-50.
Blyth, Mark (2002) *Great transformations: economic ideas and institutional change in the twentieth century*, Cambridge: Cambridge University Press.
Bogason, Peter and Toonen, Theo A. J. (1998) 'Networks in public administration' (introduction to a special issue on policy networks) *Public Administration*, vol. 76, no. 2 (Summer 1998), pp. 205-28.
Bogdanor, Vernon (1970) 'The Labour Party in opposition, 1951–1964' in V. Bogdanor and R. Skidelsky, *The age of affluence*, London: Macmillan.
Bogdanor, Vernon and Skidelsky, Robert (1970) (eds.) *The age of affluence*, London: Macmillan.
Boltho, A. (1981) 'British fiscal policy, 1955–71 – stabilizing or destabilizing?', *Oxford Bulletin of Economics and Statistics*, 1981, vol. 43, no. 4, pp. 357-62.
Booker, Christopher (1992) *The neophiliacs*, London: Pimlico.
Booth, Alan (1989) *British economic policy: was there a Keynesian revolution?*, Hemel Hempstead: Harvester Wheatsheaf.
Booth, Alan (2000), *The British economy in the twentieth century*, London: Palgrave.
Booth, Alan (2001a), 'Britain in the 1950s: a "Keynesian" managed economy?', *History of Political Economy*, vol. 33, no. 2, pp. 283-313.
Booth, Alan (2001b), 'New revisionists and the Keynesian era in British economic policy', *Economic History Review*, vol. LIV, no. 2 (2001), pp. 346-66.
Booth, Alan (2003), 'New revisionists and the Keynesian era: an expanding consensus?', *Economic History Review*, vol. LVI, no. 1 (February 2003), pp. 125-30.
Booth, A. and Glynn, Sean. (1979) 'The public records and recent British historiography', *Economic History Review*, vol. 32, no. 3, pp. 303-15.
Boston, Jonathan (1985) 'Corporatist incomes policies, the free-rider problem and the British Labour government's social contract' in A. Cawson, *Organised interests and the state*, London: Sage.
Boswell, Jonathan and Peters, James (1997) *Capitalism in contention: business leaders and political economy in modern Britain*, Cambridge: Cambridge University Press.
Bowden, Sue *et al* (2001) 'The post-war productivity failure: insights from Oxford (Cowley)', *Business History*, vol. 43, no. 3 (July 2001), pp. 54-78.
Boyden, J. (1963) 'Industrial training: an over-all planning board?', *Technical Education and Industrial Training*, vol. 5, no. 3 (March 1963), pp. 126-27.

Brady, Christopher and Catterall, Peter (1997) 'Managing the core executive', *Public Administration*, vol. 75 (Autumn 1997), pp. 509-29.

Brandes, Ulrik *et al* (1999) 'Explorations in the visualization of policy networks', *Journal of Theoretical Politics*, vol. 11, no. 1 (January 1999), pp. 75-106.

Bridgen, Paul (2000a) 'The state, redundancy pay and economic policy-making in the early-1960s', *Twentieth Century British History*, vol. 11, no. 3, pp. 233-58.

Bridgen, Paul (2000b) 'The Conservatives and pensions in the 1950s', *Contemporary British History*, vol. 14, no. 3 (Autumn 2000), pp. 83-104.

Bridgen, Paul and Lowe, Rodney (1998) *Welfare policy under the Conservatives, 1951–1964*, Kew: Public Record Office.

Brittan, Samuel (1964) *The Treasury under the Tories*, Harmondsworth: Penguin.

Brittan, Samuel (1969) *Steering the economy: the role of the Treasury*, London: Secker & Warburg.

Brittan, Samuel (1981) 'Why British incomes policies have failed' in R. E. J. Chater *et al, Incomes policy*, Oxford: Oxford University Press.

Brittan, Samuel (1997) *A backward glance: the reappraisal of the 1960s: lecture given at the ICBH, April 1997* (http://www. samuelbrittan. co. uk/spee4_p. html).

Broadberry, S. N. (1991) 'Unemployment' in N. F. R. Crafts and N. Woodward, *The British economy since 1945*, Oxford: Oxford University Press.

Broadberry, S. N. (1994) 'Employment and unemployment' in R. Floud and D. McCloskey, *The economic history of Britain since 1700, Vol. 3*, Cambridge: Cambridge University Press.

Broadberry, S. N. and Crafts, N. F. R. (1992) 'Britain's productivity gap in the 1930s: some neglected factors', *The Journal of Economic History*, vol. 52, no. 3 (September 1992), pp. 531-58.

Broadberry, S. N. and Crafts, N. F. R. (1996) 'British economic policy and industrial performance in the early post-war period', *Business History*, vol. 39, no. 4, pp. 65-91.

Broadberry, S. N. and Crafts, N. F. R. (1998) 'The post-war settlement: not such a good bargain after all', *Business History*, vol. 40, no. 2 (April 1998), pp. 73-9.

Brown, George (1971) *In my way*, London: Gollancz.

Budd, Alan (1978) *The politics of economic planning*, Glasgow: Fontana.

Budd, Alan (1981) 'Comment on "The development of demand management"' in F. Cairncross, *Changing perceptions of economic policy*, London: Methuen.

Bulpitt, Jim and Burnham, Peter (1999) 'Operation Robot and the British political economy of the early-1950s', *Contemporary British History*, vol. 13, no. 1 (Spring 1999), pp. 1-31.

Cabinet Office (2000) *Wiring it up: Whitehall's management of cross-cutting policies and services* (a report by the Performance and Innovation Unit, January 2000), London: TSO.

Cairncross, A. K. (1959) 'Reflections on the growth of capital and income', Scottish Journal of Political Economy, vol. 6 (June 1959), pp. 98-115.

Cairncross, A. K. (1962) 'The British economy, 1850–1960', Business History, vol. 5 (December 1962), pp. 54-6.

Cairncross, Alec (1970) 'Economists in government', *Lloyds Bank Review,* 95 (Jan. 1970), pp. 1-18.

Cairncross, Alec (1981) 'The legacy of the golden age: the 1960s and their economic consequences' in F. Cairncross, *Changing perceptions of economic policy*, London: Methuen.

Cairncross, Alec (1995) *The British economy since 1945*, Oxford: Blackwell.

Cairncross, Alec (1996) *Managing the British economy in the 1960s*, London: Macmillan.

Cairncross, Alec (1998) *Living with the century*, Countess of Moray's, Fife: Lynx.

Cairncross, Alec (1999) 'Economic Advisers in the United Kingdom', *Contemporary British History*, vol. 13, no. 2 (Summer 1999), pp. 232-41.

Cairncross, Alec and Watts, Nina (1989) *The Economic Section, 1939–1961*, London: Routledge.

Cairncross, Frances (1981) (ed.) *Changing perceptions of economic policy*, London: Methuen.

Campbell, John (1994) *Edward Heath*, London: Pimlico.

Capella, Peter (1996), 'Youth apprenticeships in Britain: lessons for the United States', *Industrial Relations*, vol. 35, no. 1 (Jan. 1996), pp. 1-31.

Carr, E. H. (1964) *What is history?*, Harmondsworth: Penguin.

Catterall, Peter (2002) 'Contemporary British history: a personal view', *Contemporary British History*, vol. 16, no. 1 (Spring 2002), pp. 1-10.

Caves, Richard. E. *et al* (1968) (eds.) *Britain's economic prospects*, Washington, DC: The Brookings Institution.

Cawson, Alan (1978) 'Pluralism, corporatism and the role of the state', *Government and Opposition*, vol. 13 no. 2, pp. 178-98.

CBI (1968) 'The operation of the Industrial Training Act', *CBI Education and Training Bulletin*, September 1968.

Chapman, L. (1979) *Your disobedient servant*, Harmondsworth: Penguin.

Chapman, Richard A. (1997) *The Treasury in public policy-making*, London: Routledge.

Clarke, Colin (1961) *Growthmanship: a study in the mythology of investment,* London: Institute of Economic Affairs (Hobart Paper no. 10, March 1961).

Clegg, Hugh (1971) *How to run an incomes policy: and why we made such a mess of running the last one*, London: Heinemann.

Clifford, Christopher (1997) 'The rise and fall of the Department of Economic Affairs, 1964–69: British government and indicative planning', *Contemporary British History*, vol. 11, no. 2 (Summer 1997), pp. 94-116.

Clifford, Christopher and McMillan, Alistair (1997) 'The Department of Economic Affairs', *Contemporary British History*, vol. 11, no. 2 (Summer 1997), pp. 117-42.

Coates, A. W. (1971) 'The role of scholarly journals in the history of economics: an essay', *Journal of Economic Literature*, vol. 9, no. 1 (1971), pp. 28-44.

Coates, David (1983) 'The character and origin of Britain's economic decline' in D. Coates and G. Johnston (1983) *Socialist strategies*, Oxford: Robertson.

Coates, David and Hillard, John (1995) *UK economic decline*, Hemel Hempstead: Harvester Wheatsheaf.

Cockett, Richard (1995) *Thinking the unthinkable: think-tanks and the economic counter-revolution, 1931–1983*, London: Fontana.

Cohen, C. D. (1971) *British economic policy, 1960–1969*, London: Butterworth.

Colander, D. C. and Coates, David (1989) *The spread of economic ideas*, Cambridge: Cambridge University Press.

Congdon, Tim (1978) *Monetarism: an essay in definition*, London: Centre for Policy Studies.

Conservative Party (1959) *Conservative Party manifesto – 'The next five years'*, London: Conservative Party.

Conservative Party (1961) *The young idea: a report by the Young Conservatives on youth in the 1960s*, London: Conservative Political Centre.

Conservative Party (1964) *1964 Conservative Party manifesto*, London: Conservative Party.

Cooper, Richard N. (1968) 'The balance of payments' in R. E. Caves *et al*, *Britain's economic prospects*, Washington, DC: The Brookings Institution.

Corina, John (1967) 'Can an incomes policy be administered', *British Journal of Industrial Relations*, vol. V, no. 3, pp. 287-310.

Crafts, N . F. R. (1991) 'Economic growth' in N. F. R. Crafts and N. Woodward, *The British economy since 1945*, Oxford: Oxford University Press.

Critchley, Julian (1961) 'The intellectuals', *Political Quarterly*, vol. 32 (1961), pp. 267-74.

Croft, Margaret (1960) *Apprenticeship and the 'bulge'*, London: Fabian Society (Research Series, no. 216).
Cronin, James E. (1991) *The politics of state expansion: war state and society in twentieth-century Britain*, London: Macmillan.
Crosland, Anthony (1956) *The future of socialism*, London: Jonathan Cape.
Crosland, Anthony (1962) *The Conservative enemy: a programme of radical reform for the 1960s*, London: Jonathan Cape.
Crosland, Anthony (1964) *The future of socialism* [2nd edition], London: Jonathan Cape.
Crosland, Anthony (1974) *Socialism Now*, London: Jonathan Cape
Crossman, R. H. S. (1981) *The backbench diaries of Richard Crossman* (edited by Janet Morgan), London: Jonathan Cape.
Curwen, Peter (1992) *Understanding the UK economy*, London: Macmillan.
Daugbjerg, Carsten and Marsh, David (1998) 'Explaining policy outcomes: integrating the policy network approach with macro-level and micro-level analysis' in D. Marsh, *Comparing policy networks*, Buckingham: Open University Press.
Daunton, Martin (1996) '"A kind of tax prison": rethinking Conservative taxation policy, 1960–1970' in M. Francis and I. Zweiner-Bargielowska, *The Conservatives and British society, 1880–1990*, Cardiff: University of Wales Press.
Daunton, Martin (2002), *Just taxes: the politics of taxation in Britain, 1914–1979*, Cambridge: Cambridge University Press.
Davies, A. J. (1995) *We the nation: the Conservative Party and the pursuit of power*, London: Little Brown.
Day, A. (1964) 'The myth of four per cent', *Westminster Bank Review*, November 1964.
De Vries, Michiel S. (1999), 'Developments in Europe: the idea of policy generations', *International Review of Administrative Science*, vol. 65, pp. 491-510.
Denham, Andrew and Garnett, Mark (1999) 'Influence without responsibility: think-tanks in Britain', *Parliamentary Affairs*, vol. 52, no. 1 (January 1999), pp. 46-57.
Denison, E. F. (1962) 'How to raise the high employment growth rate by one percentage point', *American Economic Review*, vol. 52 (May 1962), pp. 67-75.
Denison, Edward F. (1968) 'Economic growth' in R. E. Caves *et al*, *Britain's economic prospects*, Washington, DC: The Brookings Institution.
Dicks-Mireaux, L. A. and Dow, J. C. R. (1959) 'The determinants of wage inflation', *Journal of the Royal Statistical Society*, vol. 122 (1959).
Dimsdale, Nicholas H. (1991) 'British Monetary Policy Since 1945' in N. F. R. Crafts and N. W. C. Woodward *The British Economy Since 1945*, Oxford: Oxford University Press.
Domar, E. D. (1957) *Essays in the theory of economic growth*, Oxford: Oxford University Press.
Donaldson, Peter and Farquhar, John (1988) *Understanding the British economy*, Harmondsworth: Penguin.
Dorfman, Gerald A. (1974) *Wage politics in Britain, 1945–1967*, London: Charles Knight.
Dow, J. C. R. (1961) 'Problems of economic planning', *Westminster Bank Review*, November 1961, pp. 14-25.
Dow, J. C. R. (1964) *The management of the British economy, 1945–1960*, Cambridge: Cambridge University Press.
Dow, J. C. R. (2000) *Major recessions: Britain and the world, 1920–1995*, Oxford: Oxford University Press.
Dowding, Keith (1995) 'Model or metaphor? A critical review of the policy network approach', *Political Studies* (1995), XLIII, pp. 136-58.
Dowding, Keith (2001), 'There must be an end to confusion: policy networks, intellectual fatigue, and the need for political science methods courses in British universities', *Political Studies*, vol. 49, no. 1 (March 2001), pp. 89-105.

Dunleavy, Patrick (1989a) 'The architecture of the British central state. Part 1 – Framework for analysis', *Public Administration*, vol. 67 (1989), pp. 249-75.

Dunleavy, Patrick (1989b) 'The architecture of the British central state. Part 2 – Empirical findings', *Public Administration*, vol. 67 (1989), pp. 391-417.

Dunleavy, Patrick (1991) *Democracy, bureaucracy and public choice: economic explanations in political science*, Hemel Hempstead: Harvester Wheatsheaf.

Easton, David (1965) *A systems analysis of political life*, New York: John Wiley.

Eatwell, Roger (1989) 'Right or Rights? The rise of the "New Right"' in R. Eatwell and N. O'Sullivan, *The nature of the new Right: European and American politics and political thought since 1789*, London: Pinter Publishers.

Eckstein, H. (1975) 'Case study and theory in political science' in F. I. Greenstein and N. Polsby, *Handbook of political science. Vol. 7, Strategies of enquiry*, Reading MA, Addison Wesley.

Eichengreen, Barry (1996) 'Institutions and economic growth: Europe after World War II' in N. F. R. Crafts and G. Toniolo, *Economic Growth in Europe since 1945*, Cambridge: Cambridge University Press.

Einzig, P. (1969) *Decline and fall: Britain's crisis in the 1960s*, London: Macmillan.

Elbaum, Bernard (1989) 'Why apprenticeship persisted in Britain but not in the United States', *Journal of Economic History*, vol. XLIX, no. 2, pp. 337-49.

Elbaum, Bernard and Lazonick, W. (1984) 'The decline of the British economy: an institutional perspective', *Journal of Economic History*, vol. 44, pp. 567-83.

Elbaum, Bernard and Lazonick, W. (1986) (eds.) *The decline of the British economy*, Oxford: Oxford University Press.

Elliott, Clive and Mendham, Stanley (1981) *Industrial Training Boards: why they should be dismantled*, London: Centre for Policy Studies.

Elliott, R. (1978) 'Industrial relations and manpower policy' in F. Blackaby, *British economic policy, 1960–74*, Cambridge: Cambridge University Press.

English, Richard and Kenny, Michael (1999a) (eds.) *Rethinking British decline*, London: Macmillan.

English, Richard and Kenny, Michael (1999b) 'British decline or the politics of declinism', *British Journal of Politics and International Relations*, vol. 1, no. 2 (June 1999), pp. 252-66.

English, Richard and Kenny, Michael (2001), 'Public intellectuals and the question of British decline', *British Journal of Politics and International Relations*, vol. 3, no. 3 (Oct. 2001), pp. 259-83.

Entwistle, R. (1965) *Industrial training policy: a study of influences on government intervention, 1958–1962*, University of Manchester: unpublished MA thesis.

Evans, Mark (2001) 'Understanding dialectics in policy network analysis', *Political Studies*, vol. 49, no. 3 (August 2001), pp. 542-50.

Fabian Society (1952) *New Fabian essays*, London: J. M. Dent.

Federation of British Industries (1960) *The next five years*, London: Federation of British Industries.

Feinstein, C. H. (1983) *The managed economy: essays in British economic policy and performance since 1929*, Oxford: Oxford University Press.

Feinstein, C. H. (1994) 'Success and failure: British economic growth since 1948' in R. Floud and D. McCloskey, *The economic history of Britain since 1700, Vol. 3*, Cambridge: Cambridge University Press.

Fellner, William *et al* (1960) *The problem of rising prices*, Paris: OEEC.

Fells, Allan (1972) *The British Prices and Incomes Board*, Cambridge: Cambridge University Press.

Finegold, David and Soskice, David W. (1988) 'The failure of training in Britain: analysis and prescription', *Oxford Review of Economic Policy*, vol. 4, no. 3, pp. 21-53.

Fishbein, Warren P. (1984) *Wage restraint by consensus*, London: Routledge and Keegan Paul.

Flanagan, Robert J. *et al* (1983) *Unionism, economic stabilization, and incomes policies*, Washington, DC: The Brookings Institution.

Foreman-Peck, J. (1991) 'Trade and the balance of payments' in N. F. R. Crafts and N. Woodward, *The British economy since 1945*, Oxford: Oxford University Press.

Gamble, Andrew (1974) *The Conservative nation*, London: Routledge & Kegan Paul.

Gamble, Andrew (1990a) 'Theories of British politics', *Political Studies*, vol. 38, pp. 404-20.

Gamble, Andrew (1990b) 'The Thatcher decade in perspective' in P. Dunleavy *et al*, *Developments in British politics, 3*; London: Macmillan.

Gamble, Andrew (1994) *Britain in decline*, London: Macmillan.

Gamble, Andrew (1995) 'The new political economy', *Political Studies*, vol. 43, pp. 516-30.

Gamble, Andrew (1999) 'Theories and explanations of British decline' in R. English and M. Kenny, *Rethinking British decline*, London: Macmillan.

Gamble, Andrew and Walkland, S. E. (1984) *The British party system and economic policy, 1945–1983: studies in adversary politics*, Oxford: Clarendon Press.

Garside, W. R. (1988) 'Industrial policy and the developmental state: British responses to the competitive environment before and after the 1970s', *Business and Economic History*, vol. 27, no. 1, pp. 47-65.

George, V. and Wilding, P. (1984) *Ideology and social welfare*, London: Routledge and Keegan Paul.

Gill, Ken (1981) 'Incomes policy: the trade union view' in R. E. J. Chater *et al*, *Incomes policy*, Oxford: Oxford University Press.

Glynn, S. and Booth, A. (1996) *Modern Britain: an economic and social history*, London: Routledge.

Goldstein, J. and Keohane, R. O. (eds.) (1993), *Ideas and foreign policy: an analytical framework*, Ithaca NY: Cornell University Press.

Gordon Walker, Patrick (1972) *The cabinet*, London: Fontana.

Gorges, Michael J. (2001) 'New institutionalist explanations for institutional change: a note of caution', *Politics*, vol. 21, no. 2 (2001), pp. 137-45.

Gospel, Howard F. (1992) *Markets, firms, and the management of labour in modern Britain*, Cambridge: Cambridge University Press.

Graham, Andrew (1996) 'The influences on economic policy: Andrew Graham interviewed by Anthony Seldon', *Contemporary British History*, vol. 10, no. 1 (Spring 1996), pp. 152-67.

Grant, Matthew (2003) '"What sort of island?" Historians, the Penguin Specials and the state-of-the-nation literature, 1958–64', *Contemporary British History*, vol. 17, no. 3.

Grant, Wyn (1985) *The political economy of corporatism*, London: Macmillan.

Grant, Wyn (2002), *Economic policy in Britain*, London: Palgrave Macmillan.

Greenleaf, W. H. (1983) *The British political tradition. Vol. 1, The rise of collectivism*, London: Methuen.

Hahn, F. H. and Matthews, R. C. O. (1964), 'The theory of economic growth', *Economic Journal*, vol. 74, no. 296, pp. 779-902.

Haas, Ernst B. (1990) *When knowledge is power: three models of international organizations*, Berkeley, CA: University of California Press.

Hall, Peter A. (1982) *The political dimensions of economic management: a study of the formulation and implementation of macroeconomic policy in Great Britain from 1970–1979*, Harvard University: unpublished PhD thesis.

Hall, Peter A. (1986a) *Governing the economy: the politics of state intervention in Britain and France*, Cambridge: Polity Press.

Hall, Peter A. (1986b) 'The state and economic decline' in B. Elbaum and W. Lazonick, *The decline of the British economy*, Oxford: Oxford University Press.

Hall, Peter A. (1989) *The political power of economic ideas*, Princeton, NJ: Princeton University Press.

Hall, Peter A. (1992) 'From Keynesianism to monetarism' in S. Steinmo *et al*, *Structuring politics: historical institutionalism in comparative analysis*, Cambridge: Cambridge University Press.

Hall, Peter A. (1993) 'Policy paradigms, social learning and the state: the case of economic policy making in Britain', *Comparative Politics*, vol. 25, pp. 275-96.

Hall, Peter A. (1997) 'The role of interests, institutions and ideas in the comparative political economy of the industrialized nations' in M. I. Lichbach and A. S. Zuckerman, *Comparative politics: rationality, culture and structure*, Cambridge: Cambridge University Press.

Hall, Peter A. and Taylor, R. C. R. (1998) 'The potential of historical institutionalism: a response to Hay and Wincott', *Political Studies*, vol. 46, no. 5 (1998), pp. 958-62.

Hall, Robert (1991) *The Robert Hall diaries, 1954–1961* (edited by A. Cairncross), London: Unwin Hyman.

Hall, Robert T. (1965) *The Industrial Training Act, 1964*, Paris: OEEC.

Hallett, Graham (1967) 'The role of economists as government advisers', *Westminster Bank Review* (May 1967), pp. 2-20.

Ham, A. (1981) *Treasury rules: recurrent themes in British economic policy*, London: Quartet.

Hansen, Bent (1969) *Fiscal policy in seven countries, 1955–1965*, Paris: OECD.

Harrod, R. F. (1948) *Towards a dynamic economics: recent developments in theory and their application to policy*, London: Macmillan.

Harrod, R. F. (1952) *Economic essays*, London: Macmillan.

Harrod, R. F. (1939) 'An essay in dynamic theory', *Economic Journal*, vol. 49, no. 1, pp. 14-33.

Harrod, R. F. (1948) *Towards a dynamic economics: recent developments in theory and their application to policy*, London: Macmillan.

Harrod, R. F. (1951) 'Notes on trade cycle theory', *Economic Journal*, vol. 61, no. 2, pp. 261-75.

Harrod, R. F. (1952) *Economic essays*, London: Macmillan.

Harrod, R. F. (1956) 'The British boom, 1954–55', *Economic Journal*, vol. 66 (March 1956), pp. 1-16.

Harrod, R. F. (1957) 'A model of economic growth', *Economic Journal*, vol. 67 (December 1957), pp. 591-624.

Harrod, R. F. (1960) 'Second essay in dynamic theory' *Economic Journal*, vol. 70 (June 1960), pp. 277-93.

Haseler, Alan (1969) *The Gaitskellites: revisionism in the British Labour Party, 1951–64*, London: Macmillan.

Hatton, T. J. and Chrystal, K. (1991) 'The budget and fiscal policy' in N. F. R. Crafts and N. Woodward, *The British economy since 1945*, Oxford: Oxford University Press.

Hay, Colin (1998) 'The tangled webs we weave: the discourse, strategy and practice of networking' in D. Marsh, *Comparing policy networks*, Buckingham: Open University Press.

Hay, Colin (2001) 'The "crisis" of Keynesianism and the rise of neo-liberalism in Britain: an ideational institutionalist approach' in J. L. Campbell and O. K. Pedersen *The rise of neoliberalism and institutional analysis*, Princeton NJ: Princeton University Press.

Hay, Colin and Richards, D. (2000) 'The tangled webs of Westminster and Whitehall: the discourse, strategy and practice of networking within the British core executive', *Public Administration*, vol. 78, no. 1 (2000), pp. 1-28.

Hay, Colin and Wincott, Daniel (1998) 'Structure, agency and historical institutionalism', *Political Studies*, vol. 46, no. 5 (1998), pp. 951-7.

Hayek, F. A. von (1980) *1980s unemployment and the unions: the distortion of relative prices by monopoly in the labour market*, London: Institute of Economic Affairs (Hobart Paper no. 87).

Hayward, Jack and Watson, Michael (1975) (eds.) *Planning, politics and public policy*, Cambridge: Cambridge University Press.

Haywood, P. A. (1987) *The political development of incomes policy in Britain from 1945–75, with special reference to relations between government and the trade union movement*, Oxford: unpublished DPhil thesis.

Heclo, Hugh (1972) 'Policy analysis', *British Journal of Political Science*, vol. 2, no. 1, pp. 83-108.

Heclo, Hugh (1974) *Modern social politics in Britain and Sweden*, London: Yale University Press.

Heclo, Hugh (1978) 'Issue networks and the executive establishment' in A. King, *The new American political system*, Washington, DC: American Enterprise Institute for Public Policy Research.

Heclo, Hugh and Wildavsky, Aaron (1981) *The private government of public money: community and policy inside British politics*, London: Macmillan.

Heffernan, Richard (2002), '"The possible as the art of politics": understanding consensus politics', *Political Studies*, vol. 50, no. 4, pp. 742-60.

Henderson, P. D. (1955) 'Some comments' [on growth and the balance of payments], *Bulletin of the Oxford Institute of Statistics*, vol. 17 (February 1955), pp. 70-88.

Henderson, P. D. (1966) *Economic growth in Britain*, London: Weidenfeld and Nicolson.

Hennessy, Peter (1986) *Cabinet*, Oxford: Blackwell.

Hennessy, Peter (1989) *Whitehall*, London: Secker & Warburg.

Hennessy, Peter (2000) *The prime minister*, London: Allen Lane.

Hilton, Matthew (2004) 'The polyester-flannelled philanthropists: the Birmingham Consumers' Group and affluent Britain' in L. Black and H. Pemberton, *An affluent society? Britain's post-war 'golden age' revisited*, Aldershot: Ashgate.

Hobsbawm, Eric (1994) *Age of extremes: the short twentieth century, 1914–1992*, London: Michael Joseph.

Hogwood, Brian W. (1997) 'The machinery of government, 1979–97', *Political Studies*, XLV, pp. 704-15.

Holliday, Ian (2000) 'Is the British state hollowing out?', *Political Quarterly*, vol. 71, no. 2, pp. 167-76.

Hopkin, Sir Bryan (1981) 'The development of demand management' in F. Cairncross, *Changing perceptions of economic policy*, London: Methuen.

Horne, Alistair (1989) *Macmillan, 1957–1986*, London: Macmillan.

Howell, David (1976) *British social democracy: a study in development and decay*, London: Croom Helm.

Hutton, Will (1996) *The state we're in*, London: Vintage.

Ince, Sir Godfrey (1960) *The Ministry of Labour and National Service*, London: Allen and Unwin.

Ingham, Geoffrey (1984) *Capitalism divided: the City and industry in British social development*, London: Macmillan.

James, Simon (1993) 'The idea brokers: the impact of think-tanks on British government', *Public Administration*, vol. 71 (Winter 1993), pp. 491-506.

Jessop, B. (1990) *State theory*, Oxford: Blackwell.

Jones, Aubrey (1973) *The new inflation: the politics of prices and incomes*, London: Andre Deutsch.

Jones, G. W. (1975) 'Development of the cabinet' in W. Thornhill, *The modernisation of British government*, London: Pitman.

Jones, G. W. (1995) 'The downfall of Margaret Thatcher' in R. A. W. Rhodes and P. Dunleavy, *Prime minister, cabinet and core executive*, London: Macmillan.
Jones, Kit (1988) 'Fifty years of economic research: a brief history of the National Institution of Economic and Social Research, 1938–88' in *National Institute Economic Review*, May 1988, pp. 36-59.
Jones, R. (1987) *Wages and employment policy*, London: Allen and Unwin.
Jordan, A. Grant (1981) 'Iron triangles, woolly corporatism or elastic nets: images of the policy process', *Journal of Public Policy*, vol. 1, no. 1 (1981), pp. 95-124.
Judge, D. (1993) *The parliamentary state*, London: Sage.
Kahn, R. F. (1959) 'Exercises in the analysis of growth', *Oxford Economic Papers*, vol. 11 (1959), pp. 143-56.
Kaldor, Nicholas (1957), 'A model of economic growth', *The Economic Journal*, vol. 67, no. 268. (Dec. 1957), pp. 591-624.
Kaldor, Nicholas (1966) *Causes of the slow rate of economic growth of the United Kingdom*, Cambridge: Cambridge University Press.
Kaldor, N. and Mirrlees, J. A. (1962) 'A new model of economic growth', *Review of Economic Studies*, vol. 29 (June 1962), pp. 28-33.
Katzenstein, Peter J. (1985) *Small states in world markets: industrial policy in Europe*, Ithaca, NY: Cornell University Press.
Kaufman, Gerald (1997) *How to be a minister*, London: Faber and Faber.
Kavanagh, Dennis (1991) 'Why political science needs history', *Political Studies*, vol. 39 (1991), pp. 479-95.
Kavanagh, Dennis and Seldon, Anthony (2000) *The powers behind the Prime Minister: the hidden influence of Number 10*, London: Harper Collins.
Keegan, William (1989) *The battle of Downing Street*, London: Hodder and Staughton.
Keegan, William and Pennant-Rea, Rupert (1979) *Who runs the economy?*, London: Maurice Temple Smith.
Kellner, Peter and Crowther-Hunt, Lord (1980) *The civil servants: an enquiry into Britain's ruling class*, London: Macdonald.
Kelly, Scott (2002) *The myth of Mr Butskell*, Aldershot: Ashgate.
Keynes, J. M. (1973) *The general theory of employment, interest and money*, London: Macmillan.
King, Anthony et al (1994) *Designing social enquiry*, Princeton, NJ: Princeton University Press.
King, Desmond (1987) *The New Right: politics, markets and citizenship*, London: Macmillan.
King, Desmond (1993) 'The Conservatives and training policy, 1979–1992: from a tripartite to a neo-liberal regime', *Political Studies*, vol. 41, no. 2, pp. 214-35.
King, Desmond (1995) *Actively seeking work? The politics of unemployment and welfare policy in the United States and Great Britain*, Chicago, IL: University of Chicago Press.
King, Desmond and Nash, Victoria (2001) 'Continuity of ideas and the politics of higher education expansion in Britain from Robbins to Dearing', *Twentieth Century British History*, vol. 12, no. 2, pp. 185-207.
King, Desmond and Wickham-Jones, Mark (1998) 'Training without the state? New Labour and labour markets', *Policy and Politics*, vol. 26, no. 4, pp. 439-55.
King, Desmond and Wickham-Jones, Mark (1999) 'Social capital, British social democracy and New Labour', *Democratization*, vol. 6, no. 4, pp 181-213.
Kirby, M. W. (1991) 'Supply-side management' in N. F. R. Crafts and N. Woodward, *The British economy since 1945*, Oxford: Oxford University Press.
Kirby, M. W. (1992) 'Institutional rigidities and economic decline: reflections on the British experience', *Economic History Review*, vol. XLV (1992), no. 4, pp. 637-60.

Klijn, Erik-Hans *et al* (1995) 'Managing networks in the public sector: a theoretical study of management strategies in policy networks', *Public Administration*, vol. 73, no. 3 (Autumn 1995), pp. 437-54.

Knoepfel, P. and Kissling-Näf, I. (1998) 'Social learning in policy networks', *Policy and Politics*, vol. 26, no. 3, pp. 343-67.

Kuhn, Thomas S. (1996, first edition 1962) *The structure of scientific revolutions*, Chicago: University of Chicago Press.

Kurosawa, M. and Pudney, S. (1993) 'A method for the analysis of the timing and magnitude of events in a continuous time panel – the effects of British incomes policy, 1950–1973', *Journal of Econometrics*, vol. 59, no. 1-2, pp. 161-85.

Labour Party (1957) *Industry and society*, London: Labour Party.

Labour Party (1958) *Plan for progress*, London: Labour Party.

Labour Party (1959) *The younger generation*, London: Labour Party.

Labour Party (1960) *Labour in the sixties*, London: Labour Party.

Labour Party (1961) *Signposts for the sixties*, London: Labour Party.

Labour Party (1963) *Labour Party Annual Conference Report*, London: Labour Party.

Labour Party (1964) *1964 Labour Manifesto: 'Let's GO with Labour for the NEW Britain'*, London: Labour Party.

Labour Party (1966) *Labour 1966 election manifesto: 'Time for decision'*, London: Labour Party.

Lamb, Richard (1995) *The Macmillan years: the emerging truth*, London: John Murray.

Larsen, Christian Albrekt (2002), 'Policy paradigms and cross national policy mis(learning) from the Danish employment miracle', *Journal of European Public Policy*, vol. 9, no. 5 (October 2002), pp. 715-35.

Lawson, Nigel (1992) *The view from no. 11*, London: Bantam Press.

Lees, D. and Chiplin, B. (1970) 'The economics of industrial training', *Lloyds Bank Review*, no. 96 (April 1970), pp. 29-41.

Leeson, Robert (1999) 'Keynes and the "Keynesian" Phillips curve', *History of Political Economy*, vol. 31, no. 3, pp. 493-509.

Leruez, Jacques (1975) *Economic planning and politics in Britain*, London: Martin Robertson.

Lieberman, Evan S. (2001), 'Causal inference in historical institutional analysis: a specification of periodization strategies', *Comparative Political Studies*, vol. 34, no. 9 (November 2001), pp. 1011-35.

Lipsey, David (2000) *The secret Treasury*, London: Viking.

Lipsey, Richard G. (1958) 'The relationship between unemployment and the rate of change of money wage rates in the United Kingdom, 1861–1957', *Economica*, vol. 25 (1958), pp. 283-99.

Lipsey, Richard G. (1960) 'The relationship between unemployment and the rate of change of money wage rates in the United Kingdom, 1862–1957: a further analysis', *Economica*, vol. 27 (1960), pp. 1-31.

Longstreth, Frank (1979) 'The City, industry and the state' in C. Crouch, *State and economy in contemporary capitalism*, London: Croom Helm.

Lord Chancellor's Department (2000) *Code of Practice on Access to Government Information* (http://www. lcd. gov. uk/foi/ogcode982. htm).

Lowe, Rodney (1989) 'Resignation at the Treasury: the Social Services Committee and the failure to reform the welfare state, 1955–57', *Journal of Social Policy*, vol. 18 (1989), pp. 505-26.

Lowe, Rodney (1996) 'The replanning of the welfare state, 1957–64' in M. Francis and I. Zweiner-Bargielowska, *The Conservatives and British society, 1880–1990*, Cardiff: University of Wales Press.

Lowe, Rodney (1997a) 'The core executive, modernization and the creation of PESC, 1960–64', *Public Administration*, vol. 75 (Winter 1997), pp. 601-15.

Lowe, Rodney (1997b) 'Milestone or millstone? The 1959–1961 Plowden Committee and its impact on British welfare policy', *The Historical Journal*, vol. 40, no. 2 (1997), pp. 463-91.

Lowe, Rodney (1997c) 'Plumbing new depths? Contemporary historians and the public record office', *Twentieth Century British History*, vol. 8, pp. 463-91.

Lowe, Rodney and Rollings, Neil (2000) 'Modernising Britain, 1957–1964; a classic case of centralisation and fragmentation?' in R. A. W. Rhodes, *Transforming British government, Vol. 1*, London: Palgrave Macmillan.

MacDougall, Donald (1987) *Don and mandarin*, London: John Murray.

MacIntyre, Donald (1999) *Mandleson and the making of New Labour*, London: Harper Collins.

Mackintosh, John P. (1977a) *The British cabinet*, London: Stevens & Sons.

Mackintosh, John P. (1977b) *The politics and government of Britain*, London: Hutchinson.

Mackintosh, John P. (1982) *The government and politics of Britain*, London: Hutchinson.

Macmillan, Harold (1938) *The middle way*, London: Macmillan.

Macmillan, Harold (1972) *Pointing the way: 1959–1961*, London: Macmillan.

Macmillan, Harold (1973) *At the end of the day, 1961–1963*, London: Macmillan.

Macrae, Norman (1963) *Sunshades in October*, London: Allen & Unwin.

Maddison, Angus (1964) *Economic growth in the West*, London: George Allen and Unwin.

Malik, Rex (1964) *What's wrong with British industry?*, London: Penguin.

Mann, D. J. (1970) 'Working with the Act', *BACIE Journal*, vol. 24, no. 1 (Mar. 1970), pp. 27-31.

Marin, Bernd and Mayntz, Renata (1991) 'Introduction: studying policy networks' in B. Marin and R. Mayntz, *Policy networks: empirical evidence and theoretical considerations*, Frankfurt am Main: Campus.

Marquand, D. (1988) *The unprincipled society*, London: Fontana.

Marsh, David (1998) 'Introduction: the development of the policy network approach' in D. Marsh *Comparing policy networks*, Buckingham: Open University Press.

Marsh, David and Hay, Colin (1999) 'Conclusion: analysing and explaining postwar British political development' in D. Marsh et al, *Postwar British politics in perspective*, Cambridge: Polity Press.

Marsh, David and Rhodes, R. A. W. (1992) *Policy networks in British government*, Oxford: Clarendon Press.

Marsh, David and Smith, Martin. J. (2000) 'Understanding policy networks: towards a dialectical approach', *Political Studies*, vol. 48, pp. 4-21.

Marsh, David and Smith, Martin. J. (2001) 'There is more than one way to do political science: on different ways to study policy networks', *Political Studies*, vol. 49, no. 3, pp. 528-41.

Marsh, David, Smith, Martin. J. and Richards, D. (2001) *Changing patterns of governance: reinventing Whitehall*, London: Palgrave.

Matthews, R. C. O. (1968) 'Why has Britain had full employment since the war?', *Economic Journal*, vol. 78 (1968), pp. 555-69.

Matthews, R. C. O. *et al* (1982) *British economic growth, 1856–1973*, Stanford, CA: Stanford University Press.

Maudling, Reginald (1978) *Memoirs*, London: Sidgwick & Jackson.

Meadows, P. (1978) 'Planning' in F. Blackaby, *British economic policy, 1960–74*, Cambridge: Cambridge University Press.

Merrett, A. J. (1965) 'Will the new taxes spur investment?', *The Banker*, vol. 115, no. 469 (March 1965), pp. 149-55.

Middlemas, Keith (1983) *Industry, unions and government: twenty one years of NEDC*, London: Macmillan.

Middlemas, Keith (1986) *Power, competition and the state, Vol. 1: Britain in search of balance, 1940–1961*, London: Macmillan.

Middlemas, Keith (1990) *Power, competition and the state, Vol. 2. Threats to the post-war settlement: Britain, 1961–74*, Basingstoke: Macmillan.

Middlemas, Keith (1991) *Power, competition and the state, Vol. 3: The end of the postwar era: Britain since 1974*, Basingstoke: Macmillan.

Middleton, Roger (1996) *Government versus the market: the growth of the public sector, economic management and British economic performance, c. 1890–1979*, Cheltenham: Edward Elgar.

Middleton, Roger (1998) *Charlatans or saviours? Economists and the British economy from Marshall to Meade*, Cheltenham: Edward Elgar.

Middleton, Roger (2000) *The British economy since 1945*, London: Macmillan.

Middleton, Roger (2002a) 'Struggling with the impossible: sterling, the balance of payments and British economic policy, 1949–72' in W. L. Young and A. Arnon, *The open economy macro model: past present and future*, Amsterdam: Kluwer.

Middleton, Roger (2002b) 'Economists and economic growth in Britain, c. 1955–65: a triumph of ersatz over academic economists?' a paper presented to the 'Affluent Britain?' conference at the University of Bristol, 24-5 May 2002.

Middleton, Roger (2004) 'Economists and economic growth in Britain, c. 1955–65' in L. Black and H. Pemberton, *An affluent society? Britain's post-war 'golden age' revisited*, Aldershot: Ashgate.

Miliband, R. (1969) *The state in capitalist society*, London: Quartet.

Milward, A. S. (1987) *War, economy and society: 1939–1945*, Harmondsworth: Penguin.

Milward, H. B. and Provan, K. G. (2000) 'Governing the hollow state' in *Journal of Public Administration Research and Theory*, vol. 10, no. 2 (April 2000) pp. 256-8.

Minkin, Lewis (1992) *The contentious alliance: trade unions and the Labour Party*, Edinburgh: Edinburgh University Press.

Mitchell, Joan (1972) *The National Board for Prices and Incomes*, London: Secker and Warburg.

Morgan, John F. (1994) *The politics of industrial training in Britain, 1960–1990*, Leeds: unpublished PhD thesis.

Morgan, Kenneth O. (1998) *Callaghan: a life*, Oxford: Oxford University Press.

Musgrave, R. A. and Musgrave, P. B. (1968) 'Fiscal policy' in R. E. Caves *et al*, *Britain's economic prospects*, Washington, DC: The Brookings Institution.

Nairn, Tom (1977) 'The twilight of the British state', *New Left Review*, 101-2 (Feb–April 1977).

Nairn, Tom (1979), 'The future of Britain's crisis', *New Left Review*, 113-14 (Jan–April 1979).

Needleman, L. (1961) 'The burden of taxation: an international comparison', *National Institute Economic Review*, no. 14, March 1961, pp. 55-61.

Neisser, H. (1960) 'Cyclical fluctuations and economic growth', *Oxford Economic Papers*, vol. 13 (1960), pp. 221-24.

Nelson, Robert H. (1987) 'The economics profession and the making of public policy', *The Journal of Economic Literature*, vol. 25, no. 1 (March 1987), pp. 49-91.

Neuman, Lawrence (1994) *Social research methods: qualitative and quantitative approaches*, Boston, MA: Allyn and Bacon.

Nordhaus, W. D. (1975) 'The political business cycle', *Review of Economic Studies*, vol. 42 (1975), pp. 169-90.

Oliver, Michael J. (1997) *Whatever happened to monetarism?*, Aldershot: Ashgate.

Oliver, Michael J. and Pemberton, Hugh (2004) 'Learning and change in 20th century British economic policy', *Governance*, vol. 17, no. 3 (July 2004).

Olson, Mancur (1965) *The logic of collective action*, Cambridge, MA: Harvard University Press.

Opie, Roger (1972) 'Economic planning and growth' in W. Beckerman, *The Labour government's economic record: 1964–1970*, London: Duckworth.

Oppenheimer, Peter (1970) 'Muddling through: the economy, 1951–1964' in V. Bogdanor and R. Skidelsky, *The age of affluence*, London: Macmillan

Osborne, D. and Gaebler, T. (1992) *Reinventing government*, Reading: Addison-Wesley.

Page, G. Terry (1967) *The Industrial Training Act and after*, London: Andre Deutsch.

Paige, D. C. , Blackaby, F. T. , and Freund, S. (1961) 'Economic growth: the last hundred years', *National Institute Economic Review*, no. 16 (July 1961), pp. 24-49.

Paish, Frank (1958) 'Inflation in the United Kingdom, 1948–1957', *Economica*, vol. 25 (May 1958), pp. 94-105.

Paish, Frank (1962) *Studies in an inflationary economy: the United Kingdom 1948–1961*, London: Macmillan.

Panitch, Leo (1976) *Social democracy and industrial militancy: the Labour Party, the trade unions and incomes policy, 1945–1974*, Cambridge: Cambridge University Press.

Parsons, Wayne (1989) *The power of the financial press: journalism and economic opinion in Britain and America*, Aldershot: Edward Elgar.

Passinetti, Luigi (1960) 'Cyclical fluctuations and economic growth', *Oxford Economic Papers*, vol. 12 (1960), pp. 215-42.

Paterson, Peter (1993) *Tired and emotional: the life of Lord George Brown*, London: Chatto and Windus.

Peden, G. C. (2000) *The Treasury and British public policy, 1906–1959*, Oxford: Oxford University Press.

Peden, G. C. (2003) 'New revisionists and the Keynesian era in British economic policy: a comment' in *Economic History Review*, vol. LVI, no. 1, pp. 118-24.

Pekkarinen, Jukka (1989) 'Keynesianism and the Scandinavian models of economic policy' in P. A. Hall, *The political power of economic ideas*, Princeton: Princeton University Press.

Pemberton, Hugh (1997) *The 1961 budget*, Bristol University: unpublished MA dissertation.

Pemberton, Hugh (2000) 'Policy networks and policy learning: UK economic policy in the 1960s and 1970s', *Public Administration*, vol. 78, no. 4 (2000), pp. 771-92.

Pemberton, Hugh (2001) 'A taxing task: combating Britain's relative decline in the 1960s', *Twentieth Century British History*, vol. 12, no. 3 (2001), pp. 354-75.

Pemberton, Hugh (2003) 'Learning, governance and economic policy', *British Journal of Politics and International Relations*, vol. 5, no. 4 (November 2003), pp. 500-24.

Pemberton, Hugh (2004a) 'Affluence, Relative Decline and the Treasury' in L. Black and H. Pemberton, *An affluent society? Britain's post-war 'golden age' revisited*, Aldershot: Ashgate.

Pemberton, Hugh (2004b) 'The transformation of the economy, 1939–2000' in P. Addison and H. Jones, *Companion to contemporary Britain, 1939–2000*, Oxford: Blackwell.

PEP (1960) *Growth in the British economy*, London: Political and Economic Planning.

PEP (1961a) 'The promotion of economic growth', *Planning*, vol. XXVII, no. 450, 20 March 1961.

PEP (1961b), 'Economic planning in France', *Planning*, vol. XXVII, no. 454, 14 August 1961.

PEP (1963) 'The shape of the sixties', *Planning*, vol. XXIX, no. 471, 29 March 1963.

PEP (1963b) 'French planning: some lessons for Britain', *Planning*, vol. XXIX, no. 474, 9 September 1963.

Pepper, Gordon (1999) *Inside Thatcher's monetarist revolution*, London: Macmillan.

Perry, P. J. C. (1976) *The evolution of British manpower policy: from the Statute of Artificers 1563 to the Industrial Training Act 1964*, London: British Association for Commercial and Industrial Education.

Peston, Maurice (1973) 'Incentives, distortion and the system of taxation' in B. Crick and W. A. Robson, *Taxation* policy, Harmondsworth: Penguin.

Peters, Guy (1998) 'Policy networks: myth, metaphor and reality' in D. Marsh, *Comparing policy networks*, Buckingham: Open University Press.

Pettman, B. O. (1971) *The Industrial Training Act and the work of the Industrial Training Boards: a selected and annotated bibliography*, London: Institute of Scientific Business.

Phelps Brown, Henry (1980) 'Sir Roy Harrod: a memoir', *Economic Journal*, vol. 90, no. 357 (March 1980), pp. 1-33.

Phillips, A. W. (1958) 'The relation between unemployment and the rate of change of money wages in the United Kingdom, 1861–1957', *Economica*, vol. 25, November 1958, pp. 283-99.

Pierson, Paul (1993) 'When effect becomes cause: policy feedback and political change', *World Politics*, vol. 45, no. 4, pp. 595-628.

Pimlott, Ben (1992) *Harold Wilson*, London: Harper Collins.

Pinder, John (1981) (ed.) *Fifty years of Political and Economic Planning: looking forward, 1931–1981*, London: Political and Economic Planning.

Polanyi, George (1967) *Planning in Britain: the experience of the 1960s*, London: Institute of Economic Affairs.

Pollard, S. (1982) *The wasting of the British economy: British economic policy 1945 to the present*, London: Croom Helm.

Pollitt, Christopher (2001), 'Big concepts, small payoffs? A skeptical critique of network theory in public administration'. A paper presented to the European Group on Public Administration, Vaasa, Finland, 5-8 September 2001.

Pollitt, Christopher (2003), 'Joined-up government: a survey', *Political Studies Review*, vol. 1, no. 1 (January 2003), pp. 34-49.

Pope, Rex (1998) *The British economy since 1914: a study in decline*, Harlow: Addison Wesley.

Prais, S. J. (1981), 'Vocational qualifications of the labour force in Britain and Germany', *National Institute Economic Review*, (Nov. 1981), pp. 47-51.

Prais, S. J. (1995) *Productivity, education and training: an international perspective*, Cambridge: Cambridge University Press.

Prest, Alan R. (1973) 'Taxation and growth' in B. Crick and W. A. Robson, *Taxation policy*, Harmondsworth: Penguin.

Price, David (2000) *Office of hope: the history of the employment service*, London: Policy Studies Institute.

Price, R. W. R. (1978a) 'Public expenditure' in F. Blackaby, *British economic policy, 1960–74*, Cambridge: Cambridge University Press.

Price, R. W. R. (1978b) 'Budgetary policy' in F. Blackaby, *British economic policy, 1960–74*, Cambridge: Cambridge University Press.

Raab, Charles C. (2001), 'Understanding policy networks: a comment on Marsh and Smith', *Political Studies*, vol. 49, no. 3 (August 2001), pp. 551-6.

Ragin, Charles C. (1992) '"Casing" and the process of social enquiry' in C. C. Ragin and H. S. Becker, *What is a case?*, Cambridge: Cambridge University Press.

Ramsden, John (1980) *The making of Conservative Party policy: the Conservative Research Department since 1929*, London: Longman.

Ramsden, John (1998) *An appetite for power: a history of the Conservative Party since 1830*, London: Harper Collins.

Reddaway, W. B. (1989) 'Tax reform in the United Kingdom' in T. Lawson. *et al*, *Kaldor's political economy*, London: Academic Press.

Reisman, David (1997) *Anthony Crosland: the mixed economy*, London: Macmillan.

Rhodes, R. A. W. (1981) *Control and power in central-local government relations*, Farnborough: Gower.

Rhodes, R. A. W. (1988) *Beyond Westminster and Whitehall: sub-central governments in Britain*, London: Allen and Unwin.

Rhodes, R. A. W. (1994) 'The hollowing out of the state', *The Political Quarterly*, vol. 15, no. 2, pp. 138-51.

Rhodes, R. A. W. (1995) 'From prime minister to core executive' in R. A. W. Rhodes and P. Dunleavy, *Prime minister, cabinet and core executive*, London: Macmillan.

Rhodes, R. A. W. (1997) *Understanding governance: policy networks, governance, reflexivity and accountability*, Buckingham: Open University Press.

Rhodes, R. A. W. (2000a) (ed.) *Transforming British government, Vol. 1*, London: Palgrave Macmillan.

Rhodes, R. A. W. (2000b) (ed.) *Transforming British Government, Vol. 2*, London: Palgrave Macmillan.

Rhodes, R. A. W. (2000c) 'A guide to the ESRC's Whitehall Programme, 1994–1999', *Public Administration*, vol. 78, no. 2, pp. 251-82.

Rhodes, R. A. W. and Dunleavy, Patrick (1995) (eds.) *Prime minister, cabinet and core executive*, London: Macmillan.

Richards, David and Smith, Martin J. (2002) *Governance and public policy in the UK*, Oxford: Oxford University Press.

Richardson, Jeremy (2000) 'Government, interest groups and policy change', *Political Studies*, vol. 48, no. 5, pp. 1006-25.

Richardson, P. (1991) 'Trade unions and industrial relations' in N. F. R. Crafts and N. Woodward, *The British economy since 1945*, Oxford: Oxford University Press.

Ringe, Astrid (1999) *Incomes policy: a case of intransigence and inconsequential initiatives*, University of Bristol, Department of Historical Studies: unpublished research paper.

Ringe, Astrid and Rollings, Neil (2000a) 'Responding to relative decline: the creation of the National Economic Development Corporation', *Economic History Review*, vol. LIII, no. 2 (May 2000), pp. 331-53.

Ringe, Astrid and Rollings, Neil (2000b) 'Domesticating the "market animal"?: the Treasury and the Bank of England, 1955–1960' in R. A. W. Rhodes, *Transforming British government, Vol. 1*, London: Palgrave Macmillan

Ringe, Astrid and Rollings, Neil (2000c) *Modernisation by consensus* (paper presented at the annual conference of the Economic History Society, Bristol, April 2000).

Robinson, Anne and Sandford, C. T. (1983) *Tax policy-making in the United Kingdom: a study of rationality, ideology and politics*, London: Heinemann.

Robinson, J. (1957) 'Economic growth and capital accumulation: a comment', *Economic Record*, vol. 33 (April 1957), pp. 103-8.

Robinson, J. (1961) 'Equilibrium growth models', American Economic Review, vol. 51 (June 1961), pp. 360-69.

Rollings, Neil (1985) 'The "Keynesian revolution" and economic policy making: a comment' *Economic History Review*, vol. 38, pp. 95-100.

Rollings, Neil (1994) 'Poor Mr. Butskell: a short-life wrecked by schixophrenia?', *Twentieth Century British History*, vol. 5 (1994), pp. 183-208. .

Rose, Richard (1961) 'The Bow Group's role in British politics', *The Western Political Quarterly*, vol. 14 (1961), December, pp. 845-78.

Rose, Richard and Karran, Terence (1987) *Taxation by political inertia*, London: Allen & Unwin.

Roseveare, H. (1969) *The Treasury*, London: Allen Lane.

Rostow, Walt (1960) *The stages of economic growth: a non-communist manifesto*, Cambridge: Cambridge University Press.

Rowthorne, R. and Wells, J. 'De-industrialisation in the UK: three theses' in D. Coates and J. Hillard, *UK economic decline*, Hemel Hempstead: Harvester Wheatsheaf.

Salant, Walter S. (1989) 'The spread of Keynesian doctrines and practices in the United States' in P. A. Hall, *The political power of economic ideas*, Princeton, NJ, Princeton University Press.

Sampson, Anthony (1962) *Anatomy of Britain*, London: Hodder and Staughton.

Sandford, C. T. (1976) *National economic planning*, London: Heinemann.

Shanks, Michael (1961) *The stagnant society*, Harmondsworth: Penguin.

Shanks, Michael (1977) *Planning and politics: the British experience, 1960–1976*, London: George Allen and Unwin (for PEP).

Sheldrake, John and Vickerstaff, Sarah (1987) *The history of industrial training in Britain*, Aldershot: Gower Publishing.

Shepherd, Robert (1995) *Iain Macleod: a biography*, London: Pimlico.

Shone, Robert and Fisher, N. K. (1958) *Industrial Production and Steel Consumption: An expanding economy*, London: Royal Statistical Society.

Shonfield, Andrew (1958) *British economic policy since the war*, Harmondsworth: Penguin.

Shonfield, Andrew (1965) *Modern capitalism*, Oxford: Oxford University Press.

Skocpol, Theda (1985) 'Bringing the state back in: strategies for analysis in current research' in P. B. Evans *et al*, *Bringing the state back in*, Cambridge: Cambridge University Press.

Smith, David (1987) *The rise and fall of monetarism*, Harmondsworth: Penguin.

Smith, David (1992) *From boom to bust: trial and error in British economic policy*, Harmondsworth: Penguin.

Smith, Martin. J. (1993) *Pressure, power and policy: state autonomy and policy networks in Britain and the United States*, London: Harvester Wheatsheaf.

Smith, Martin. J. (1995) 'Interpreting the rise and fall of Margaret Thatcher: power dependence and the core executive' in R. A. W. Rhodes and P. Dunleavy, *Prime minister, cabinet and core executive*, London: Macmillan.

Smith, Martin. J. (1998) 'Reconceptualizing the British state: theoretical and empirical challenges to central government', *Public Administration*, vol. 76, no. 1 (Spring 1998), pp. 45-72.

Smith, Martin. J. (1999a) *The core executive in Britain*, London: Macmillan.

Smith, Martin. J. (1999b) 'Institutional approaches to Britain's relative economic decline' in R. English and M. Kenny, *Rethinking British decline*, London: Macmillan.

Smith, Martin. J. *et al* (1995) 'Central government departments and the policy process' in R. A. W. Rhodes and P. Dunleavy, *Prime minister, cabinet and core executive*, London: Macmillan.

Smith, Trevor (1975) 'Britain' in J. Hayward and M. Watson, *Planning, politics and public policy*, Cambridge: Cambridge University Press.

Steinmo, Sven (1989) 'Political institutions and tax policy in the United States, Sweden and Britain', *World Politics*, vol. 41 (1988–1989), pp. 500-35.

Steinmo, Sven (1993) *Taxation and democracy: Swedish, British and American approaches to financing the modern state*, New Haven, Connecticut: Yale University Press.

Stewart, Michael (1993) *Keynes in the 1990s: a return to economic sanity*, Harmondsworth: Penguin.

Strange, Susan (1971) *Sterling and British policy*, Oxford: Oxford University Press.

Streeten, Paul 'Productivity, growth and the balance of trade', *Bulletin of the Oxford Institute of Statistics*, vol. 17 (February 1955), pp. 11-17

Streeten, Paul (1959) 'Unbalanced growth', *Oxford Economic Papers*, vol 11, no. 2 (1959), pp. 167-90.

Supple, Barry (1994) 'Fear of failing: economic history and the decline of Britain', *Economic History Review*, vol. 47 (1994), pp. 441-58.

Supple, Barry and Furner, Mary O. (1990) (eds.) *The state and economic knowledge*, Cambridge: Cambridge University Press.

Tavernier, G. (1968) 'The economics of training', *Personnel and Training Management*, Aug. 1968, pp. 8-16.

Taylor, Andrew (1999), 'The Conservative Party and the trade unions' in J. Mcilroy, *British Trade Unions and industrial politics: the high tide of trade unionism, 1964–79*, Aldershot: Ashgate.

Taylor, Robert (2000) *The TUC: from the general strike to the new unionism*, Basingstoke: Palgrave.

Thain, Colin and Wright, Maurice (1995) *The Treasury and Whitehall*, Oxford: Clarendon Press.

Theakston, Kevin (1995) *The civil service since 1945*, Oxford: Blackwell.

Theakston, Kevin (1999) *Leadership in Whitehall*, London: Macmillan.

Thirlwall, A. P. (1989) 'Kaldor as a policy adviser' in T. Lawson. *et al*, *Kaldor's political economy*, London: Academic Press.

Thomas, H. (1962) (ed.) *The establishment*, London: Ace Books.

Thorpe, D. R. (1989) *Selwyn Lloyd*, London: Cape.

Tiratsoo, Nick and Tomlinson, Jim (1998) *The Conservatives and industrial efficiency: 1951–1964: thirteen wasted years?*, London: Routledge

Tomlinson, Jim (1981) 'Why was there never a "Keynesian revolution" in economic policy?', *Economy and Society*, vol. 10, pp. 72-87.

Tomlinson, Jim (1985) *British macro-economic policy since 1945*, London: Croom Helm.

Tomlinson, Jim (1994) 'British economic policy since 1945' in R. Floud and D. McCloskey, *The economic history of Britain since 1700, Vol. 3*, Cambridge: Cambridge University Press.

Tomlinson, Jim (1995) 'An unfortunate alliance: Keynesianism and the Conservatives, 1945–1964' in A. F. Cottrell and M. S. Lawlor, *New perspectives on Keynes*, Durham, NC: Duke University Press.

Tomlinson, Jim (1996a) '"Liberty with order": Conservative economic policy, 1951–1964' in M. Francis and I. Zweiner-Bargielowska, *The Conservatives and British society, 1880–1990*, Cardiff: University of Wales Press.

Tomlinson, Jim (1996b) 'Inventing "decline": the falling behind of the British economy in the post-war years', *Economic History Review*, vol. XLIX, no. 4, pp. 731-57.

Tomlinson, Jim (1996c) 'Jim Tomlinson interviewed by Anthony Seldon', *Contemporary British History*, vol. 10, no. 2 (Summer 1996).

Tomlinson, Jim (1997) 'Conservative modernisation, 1960–64: too little, too late?', *Contemporary British History*, vol. 11, no. 3, pp. 18-38.

Tomlinson, Jim (2000) *The politics of decline: understanding post-war Britain*, Harlow: Longman.

Tomlinson, Jim (2002) 'The British "productivity problem" in the 1960s', *Past and Present*, 175 (May 2002), pp. 188-210.

Tomlinson, Jim (2003), 'Economic growth, economic decline' in K. Burk, *The British Isles since 1945*, Oxford: Oxford University Press.

Tomlinson, Jim and Tiratsoo, Nick (1998) 'An old story, freshly told'? A comment on Broadberry and Crafts' approach to Britain's early post-war economic performance', *Business History*, vol. 40, no. 2 (April 1998), pp. 62-72.

Toonen, Theo A. J. (1998) 'Networks, management and institutions: public administration as "normal science", *Public Administration*, vol. 76 (Summer 1998), pp. 229-52.

TUC Report (1959) *Report of proceedings at the 91st Annual Trades Union Congress, Blackpool, September 6 to11, 1959*, London: Trades Union Congress.

TUC Report (1960) *Report of proceedings at the 92nd Annual Trades Union Congress, Douglas, September 5 to 10, 1960*, London: Trades Union Congress.

TUC Report (1961) *Report of proceedings at the 93rd Annual Trades Union Congress, Portsmouth, September 4 to 8 1961*, London: Trades Union Congress.

TUC Report (1962) *Report of proceedings at the 94th Annual Trades Union Congress, Blackpool, September 3 to 7 1962*, London: Trades Union Congress.

TUC Report (1963) *Report of proceedings at the 95th Annual Trades Union Congress, Brighton, September 2 to 6 1963*, London: Trades Union Congress.

TUC Report (1964) *Report of proceedings at the 96th Annual Trades Union Congress, Blackpool, September 7 to 11 1964*, London: Trades Union Congress.

TUC Report (1965) *Report of proceedings at the 96th Annual Trades Union Congress, Blackpool, September 6 to 10 1965*, London: Trades Union Congress.

TUC Report (1966) *Report of proceedings at the 96th Annual Trades Union Congress, Blackpool, September 5 to 9 1966*, London: Trades Union Congress.

TUC (1969) *Industrial training since the 1964 Act: report of a conference of trade union members of Industrial Training Boards*, London: Trades Union Congress.

Turner, H. A. (1994) *Macmillan*, Harlow: Longman.

Ulman, Lloyd and Flanagan, Robert J. (1971) *Wage restraint: a study of incomes policies in western Europe*, Berkeley, CA: University of California Press.

Vickerstaff, Sarah (1985) 'Industrial training in Britain: the dilemmas of a neo-corporatist policy' in A. Cawson, *Organised interests and the state*, London: Sage.

Walsh, James I. (2000) 'When do ideas matter? Explaining the successes and failures of Thatcherite ideas', *Comparative Political Studies*, vol. 33, no. 4 (May 2000), pp. 483-516.

Walsha, R. (2000) 'The One Nation Group: a Tory approach to backbench politics and organization, 1950–55', *Twentieth Century British History*, vol. 11, no. 2 (2000), pp. 183-214.

Weiner, Martin J. (1985) *English culture and the decline of the industrial spirit, 1850–1980*, Harmondsworth: Penguin.

Weir, M (1989), 'Ideas and politics: the acceptance of Keynesianism in Britain and the United States' in P. A. Hall, *The political power of economic* ideas, Princeton: Princeton University Press.

Wellens, J. (1960) 'The battle is joined' in *Technical Education*, October 1960.

Wellens, J. (1962a) 'Changing patterns of employment – 1', *Technical Education and Industrial Training*, vol. 4, no. 2 (Feb. 1962), pp. 4-9.

Wellens, J. (1962b) 'Changing patters of employment – 2', *Technical Education and Industrial Training*, vol. 4, no. 3 (March 1962), pp. 16-19.

Wellens, J. (1962c) 'The Common Market – 1: Towards a planned manpower policy', *Technical Education and Industrial Training*, vol. 4, no. 4 (April 1962), pp. 8-10.

Wellens, J. (1962d) 'Towards a planned manpower policy – 2', *Technical Education and Industrial Training*, vol. 4, no. 5 (May 1962), pp. 14-19.

Wellens, J. (1963a) 'The government proposals', *Technical Education and Industrial Training*, vol. 5, no. 1 (Jan. 1963), pp. 8-9.

Wellens, J. (1963b) 'The White Paper on Industrial Training: a closer analysis', *Technical Education and Industrial Training*, vol. 5, no. 3 (March 1963), pp. 118-22.

Wellens, J. (1964) 'The Industrial Training Bill, 1963', *Technical Education and Industrial Training*, vol. 6, no. 1 (Jan. 1964).

Weller, Patrick *et al* (1997) (eds.) *The hollow crown: countervailing trends in core executives*, London: Macmillan.

Whiting, R. C. (1998) 'Ideology and reform in Labour's tax strategy, 1964–1970', *The Historical Journal*, vol. 41, no. 4, pp. 1121-40.

Whiting, R. C. (2001) *The Labour Party and taxation*, Cambridge: Cambridge University Press.

Wickham-Jones, Mark (1992) 'Monetarism and its critics: the university economists' protest of 1981', *Political Quarterly*, vol. 63, pp. 171-185.

Wickham-Jones, Mark (2000) *Hopeless dreams, lost opportunities: British social democracy and the Swedish model, 1951–1964*, Bristol University, Department of Politics: unpublished paper.

Wigham, Eric (1961) *What's wrong with the unions?*, Harmondsworth: Penguin.

Wilensky, Harold L. and Turner, Lowell (1987) *Democratic corporatism and policy linkages: the interdependence of industrial, labor-market, incomes and social policies in eight countries*, Berkeley, CA: Institute of International Studies, University of California.

Williams, Gertrude (1957) *Recruitment to skilled trades*, London: Routledge and Keegan Paul.

Williams, Gertrude (1959) *Training for skill*, London: Fabian Society (Research Series, no. 205).

Williams, Gertrude (1963) *Apprenticeship in Europe: the lesson for Britain*, London: Chapman and Hall.

Williamson, Peter J. (1985) *Varieties of corporatism: a conceptual discussion*, Cambridge: Cambridge University Press.

Williamson, Peter J. (1989) *Corporatism in perspective: an introductory guide to corporatist theory*, London: Sage.

Wilson, Harold (1955) 'Let us face the future', *Fabian Journal*, May 1955, pp. 1-5.

Wilson, Harold (1957) *Post-war economic policies in Britain*, London: Fabian Society (Tract no. 309).

Wilson, Harold (1964) (ed.) *The new Britain: Labour's plan*, Harmondsworth: Penguin.

Wilson, Harold (1971) *The Labour government, 1964–1970*, London: Weidenfeld and Nicolson.

Wilson, Harold (1976) *The governance of Britain*, London: Weidenfeld and Nicolson.

Wilson, Harold (1986) *Memoirs: the making of a Prime Minister, 1916–1964*, London: Weidenfeld and Nicolson.

Wood, Stewart (1997) *Capitalist constitutions: supply-side reform in Britain and West Germany, 1960–1990*, Harvard University: unpublished PhD thesis.

Wood, Stewart (2000) 'Why "indicative planning" failed: British industry and the formation of the National Economic Development Council (1960–64)', *Twentieth Century British History*, vol. 11, no. 4 (2000), pp. 431-59.

Work, A. L. (1964) *Industrial training*, London: Association of Technical Institutions.

Worswick, G. D. N. (1971) 'Fiscal policy and stabilization in Britain' in A. Cairncross, *Britain's economic prospects reconsidered*, London: Allen and Unwin.

Worswick, G. D. N. and Ady, P. (1962) *The British economy in the nineteen-fifties*, Oxford: Oxford University Press.

Wright, Maurice (1988) 'Policy community, policy networks and comparative industrial policies', *Political Studies*, vol. 36, no. 4, pp. 593-612.

Yin, Robert K. (1993) *Applications of case study research*, London: Sage.

Yin, Robert K. (1994) *Study research: design and methods*, London: Sage.

Young Conservatives (1961) *The young idea: a report by the Young Conservatives on youth in the 1960s*, London: Conservative Political Centre (pamphlet no. 228).

Young, Hugo (1989) *One of us: a biography of Margaret Thatcher*, London: Pan.

Young, S. C. and Lowe, A. V. (1974) *Intervention in the mixed economy: the evolution of British industrial policy, 1964–72*, London: Croom Helm.

Ziderman, Adrian (1978) *Manpower training: theory and practice*, London: Macmillan.

Ziegler, Philip (1993) *Wilson: the authorised life of Lord Wilson of Rievaulx*, London: Weidenfeld and Nicolson.

Index